THE FACTS ON FILE DICTIONARY OF

Classical and Biblical Allusions

THE FACTS ON FILE DICTIONARY OF

Classical and Biblical Allusions

MARTIN H. MANSER

David H. Pickering, Associate Editor

Checkmark Books®
An imprint of Facts On File, Inc.

The Facts On File Dictionary of Classical and Biblical Allusions

Biblical quotations are from the King James Version of the Bible

Checkmark Books
An imprint of Facts On File, Inc.
132 West 31st Street
New York NY 10001

Library of Congress Cataloging-in-Publication Data
Manser, Martin H.
    The Facts On File dictionary of classical and biblical allusions / [edited by] Martin H. Manser: associate editor, David H. Pickering.
        p.   cm.
    Companion to: Facts On File dictionary of cultural and historical allusions.
    Includes bibliographical references and index.
    ISBN 0-8160-4868-1 (HC)—0-8160-4869-X (PB)
    1. Allusions—Dictionaries. 2. Allusions in literature—Dictionaries. 3. Mythology, Classical, in literature—Dictionaries. 4. Bible—In literature—Dictionaries. I. Title: Dictionary of classical and biblical allusions. II. Manser, Martin H. III. Pickering, David, 1958–IV. Facts On File, Inc.

    PN43 .F16 2003
    809—dc21   2002192752

Checkmarks Books are available at special discounts when purchased in bulk quantities for businesses, associations, institutions, or sales promotions. Please call our Special Sales Department in New York at (212) 967-8800 or (800) 322-8755.

You can find Facts On File on the World Wide Web at http://www.factsonfile.com

Text design by Sandy Watanabe
Cover design by Cathy Rincon

Printed in the United States of America

MP Hermitage 10 9 8 7 6 5 4 3 2 1

This book is printed on acid-free paper.

Contents

Acknowledgments

The Editors wish to thank Rosalind Desmond and Lynda Drury for their very careful checking and typing of the manuscript, and Martin Selman, Stephen Curtis, John Barton, and Angela Gluck Wood for their helpful comments on earlier drafts of the text.

Martin H. Manser
David H. Pickering

Introduction

An allusion is a reference that evokes a certain set of aspects or features of a person or thing. A kind and selfless person, for example, may be referred to as a *Good Samaritan;* harsh or severe action may be described as *draconian;* a place that offers happiness and security may be thought of as a *promised land* or a place that is notorious for its depravity and vice likened to *Sodom and Gomorrah;* one's conscience may be regarded as a *still small voice;* a fatal weakness may be referred to as a person's *Achilles' heel;* something complex may be described as *labyrinthine;* and something that rises anew in the face of defeat may be compared to a *phoenix rising from the ashes.*

The *Facts On File Dictionary of Classical and Biblical Allusions* is a companion volume to the *Facts On File Dictionary of Cultural and Historical Allusions.* This dictionary contains allusions drawn from the Bible and Greek, Roman, and Norse mythology, as well as a few Egyptian and Celtic allusions. None dates after A.D. 1000.

Arrangement of entries

Allusions are listed in their original form and under the source of the original reference. Entries are listed in strict letter-by-letter alphabetical order:

go and do thou likewise

God save the king/queen

Godwin's oath

go from strength to strength

Pronunciation

Pronunciation is given in parentheses for a word or words that include a proper name, are of non-English origin, or are not a common English expression:

> **ex pede Herculem** (eks peday <u>her</u>kyoolem)
>
> **valley of Jehoshaphat** (jǎh<u>ō</u>shǎfat)

Stress is shown by an <u>underscore</u> in the pronunciation. Pronunciation is as in American English and uses the following key:

a (c<u>a</u>b)

ǎ (<u>a</u>bout)

ah (c<u>a</u>r, l<u>a</u>wn, fl<u>au</u>nt)

air (fl<u>air</u>)

ay (d<u>ay</u>, st<u>a</u>te)

b (<u>b</u>ut)

ch (<u>ch</u>ip)

d (<u>d</u>anger)

e (s<u>e</u>ll)

ee (f<u>ee</u>t)

er (robb<u>er</u>, thi<u>r</u>st)

f (<u>f</u>ine)

g (<u>g</u>et)

h (<u>h</u>and)

i (<u>i</u>ll)

ī (w<u>i</u>ne)

j (<u>j</u>olly)

k (<u>k</u>itten, <u>c</u>an)

ks (mi<u>x</u>)

kw (<u>qu</u>ell, <u>qu</u>ake)

l (<u>l</u>ie)

m (<u>m</u>ole)

n (<u>n</u>ine)

ng (lo<u>ng</u>er)

o (f<u>o</u>g)

ō (teleph<u>o</u>ne)

oi (pl<u>oy</u>)

oo (l<u>oo</u>se, gl<u>ue</u>)

or (s<u>or</u>e)

ow (c<u>ow</u>)

p (<u>p</u>ink)

r (<u>r</u>ed)

s (<u>s</u>ilent)

sh (<u>sh</u>ut)

t (<u>t</u>ip)

th (<u>th</u>eater)

u (l<u>u</u>ck)

v (<u>v</u>ery)

w (<u>w</u>et)

y (<u>y</u>oung)

yoo (<u>u</u>nisex)

yoor (<u>Eu</u>ropean)

z (fi<u>zz</u>)

zh (fu<u>s</u>ion)

Definitions

The entry begins with an explanation of the use of the word or phrase in contemporary English.

> **Achilles' heel** (ăkileez) A fatal weakness, a place where an otherwise strong person or thing is vulnerable. . . .

Biblical allusions also include the Bible reference and sometimes the text from which the expression is derived. All quotations are from the King James Version of the Bible.

> **Good Samaritan** (samairĭtăn) A person who kindly and selflessly helps a stranger in distress or difficulty. The expression alludes to the parable that Christ told, recorded in Luke 10:25–37, about a Jew who was brutally attacked while on his way from Jerusalem to Jericho. . . .

Examples

Examples of allusions are given for nearly every entry. They may come from English literature or contemporary citations, or are constructed to show typical usage. In this way the illustrative sentence shows the usage of the allusion.

Additional Information and Derived Forms

Additional information, variants, and phrases derived from the main allusion are included in many entries.

Cross-References

Cross-references are included where users might expect an entry.

> **eye of a needle** *See* CAMEL: GO THROUGH AN EYE OF A NEEDLE.

> **rest on one's laurels** *See* LAURELS.

Entries A to Z

Aaron *See* AARON'S BEARD; AARON'S ROD; AARON'S SERPENT.

Aaron's beard (<u>air</u>unz) Popular name of one of a variety of wild plants, including meadowsweet, Saint-John's-wort *(Hypericum calycinum)*—which is also known as rose of Sharon—and ivy-leaved toadflax. The name comes from Psalm 133:2: "It is like the precious ointment upon the head, that ran down upon the beard, even Aaron's beard: that went down to the skirts of his garments." According to Exodus 4:14, Aaron was the brother of Moses and became the first high priest of the Israelites. His name may come from *haaron* (meaning "ark"). *Among the plants she identified as having magical powers was Aaron's beard.*

Aaron's rod (<u>air</u>unz) Popular name of a widespread plant *(Verbascum thapsus)* with woolly leaves and tall spikes of yellow flowers. The allusion is to the rod used by Aaron to perform various miracles in Egypt prior to the Exodus. According to Numbers 17:1–13, when Aaron's rod was placed among 12 rods representing the tribes of Israel in the tabernacle, it blossomed overnight and produced almonds. It was by this sign that Aaron was recognized as having the strongest claim to the priesthood. Henceforth his rod was, according to the apostle Paul, kept in the ARK OF THE COVENANT itself. Aaron's rod is today a symbol of authority and, in the East, also of travel. *Aaron's rod makes an attractive addition to any garden border. See also* AARON'S SERPENT.

Aaron's serpent (<u>air</u>unz) Something that is so powerful it easily consumes lesser beings or entities. The allusion is to Exodus 7:8–12 and to AARON'S ROD, which turned into a serpent and devoured the rods of his Egyptian enemies after they too had turned into serpents. *Like Aaron's serpent, the new*

1

conglomerate has swallowed up virtually all the smaller companies that were once its rivals.

Abaddon (ăba̱don) Alternative name for the devil, the ruler of hell. He is described at Revelation 9:11 as "the angel of the bottomless pit" who rules over an army of locusts with stings like scorpions. His name means "destruction" in Hebrew, although he is sometimes referred to by his Greek name *Apollyon.* "And my father preached a whole set of sermons on the occasion; one set in the morning, all about David and Goliath, to spirit up the people to fighting with spades or bricks, if need were; and the other set in the afternoons, proving that Napoleon (that was another name for Bony, as we used to call him) was all the same as an Apollyon and Abaddon" (Elizabeth Gaskell, *Cranford,* 1851–53).

Abednego *See* FIERY FURNACE.

Abel *See* CAIN AND ABEL.

abigail (a̱bigayl) A lady's maid; female domestic servant. The reference is to Abigail, the wife of Nabal according to 1 Samuel 25. When Nabal, the wealthy owner of goats and sheep in Carmel, refuses to provide food for David's followers, Abigail apologizes for her husband's ungenerosity and offers sustenance to David, thus forestalling an attack upon their own people. Abigail calls herself "thine handmaid" no less than six times in the space of 17 verses and, after Nabal dies 10 days later, becomes David's wife. Sir Francis Beaumont and John Fletcher subsequently gave the name to a lady's maid in their play *The Scornful Lady* (1610) and thus popularized it as an informal name for any woman engaged in such a post. Its identification with such subservient roles was further cemented by the notoriety of Abigail Hill Masham, a lady-in-waiting to Queen Anne of Great Britain who used her influence over the monarch to advance her own interests. *Her grandmother served as an abigail in one of the great Scottish castles.*

abomination of desolation Something loathsome or disgusting. The expression comes from the Old Testament book of Daniel (9:27; 11:31; 12:11; see also Matthew 24:15–21) and is thought to allude to a pagan altar to Zeus that was erected in the Temple on the orders of Antiochus

Epiphanes. In Daniel, the sacrilege was seen as an abomination, a horror that made the Temple emptied, or desolate, of God. "In truth all that night had been the abomination of desolation to me" (Joseph Conrad, *The Arrow of Gold,* 1919).

Abraham (a̲ybră̆ham) Archetypal patriarch. One of the most important figures of the Old Testament, Abraham is usually considered the father of the Hebrew people and the ancestor of all Jews and is referred to as "the father of many nations" in Genesis 17:5. His name is often invoked as an image of patriarchal values or wisdom or as a symbol of fertility. "In the latter quarter of each year cattle were at once the mainstay and the terror of families about Casterbridge and its neighbourhood, where breeding was carried on with Abrahamic success" (Thomas Hardy, *The Mayor of Caster-bridge,* 1886). *See also* ABRAHAM'S BOSOM; ABRAHAM'S SUPREME TEST.

Abraham's bosom (a̲ybră̆hamz) The Christian paradise; heaven as the restful abode of the blessed dead. The phrase comes from Luke 16:19–31, in which Jesus relates the parable of Lazarus and the rich man: "The beggar Lazarus died, and was carried by the angels into Abraham's bosom." It has been suggested that the image of leaning on the bosom of a friend may relate to the classical custom of reclining on a friend's chest when dining (hence the expression a "bosom friend"). "The sons of Edward sleep in Abraham's bosom" (William Shakespeare, *Richard III,* 1592–93).

Abraham's supreme test (a̲ybră̆hamz) An ultimate challenge or sacrifice. The reference is to God's command to Abraham to sacrifice his only son, Isaac, as a burned offering on Mount Moriah. Abraham readily agreed to comply and was about to kill Isaac with his knife when God, satisfied that Abraham's faith was genuine, intervened by providing a ram caught in a thicket to take Isaac's place (Genesis 22:1–19; see also Romans 4; Hebrews 11:8–19; James 2:20–26). *The president faces his own version of Abraham's supreme test, being forced to choose between instinctive loyalty to his vice president or to his own political principles.*

Absalom (a̲bsă̆lom) Archetype of a rebellious son, especially one who meets a tragic end. Absalom is identified in 2 Samuel 13–18 as the third son of King DAVID, remarkable for his great beauty and adored by both his father and his people. Unfortunately, he sided with Ahithophel in rebellion against David and was consequently slain by Joab after getting his long hair entangled in the branches of a tree while trying to escape. David's grief over his slain son was overwhelming and gave rise to his famous lament "O my son Absalom, my son, my son Absalom! Would God I had died for thee!" (2 Samuel 18:33). "Sometimes, the worthy gentleman would reprove my mother for being over-indulgent to her sons, with a reference to old Eli, or David and Absalom, which was particularly galling to her feelings" (Anne Brontë, *The Tenant of Wildfell Hall,* 1848).

academia (akădeemeeă) The academic world. The word comes from the Greek *Akademeia,* the name of the public garden (with a grove) in Athens where the philosopher Plato instructed his pupils toward the end of the fourth century B.C. The grove in turn was named after the legendary hero Academus. In modern usage students may still be said to toil in the GROVES OF ACADEME. Other words from the same root include *academy, academe*, and *academic*. *The announcement has sent a ripple of concern through academia.*

Aceldama (ăseldămă) A battlefield or any other place where much blood has been spilled. The name means "field of blood" in Hebrew and refers to the field that was reputedly bought by Judas with the THIRTY PIECES OF SILVER he had received in payment for betraying Christ. According to Peter in Acts 1:18–19, once Judas had purchased the field he fell headlong onto it and "burst asunder in the midst, and all his bowels gushed out," hence the field's name. "Is there any haunting of the Bank Parlour, by the remorseful souls of old directors, in the nights of these later days, I wonder, or is it as quiet as this degenerate Aceldama of an Old Bailey?" (Charles Dickens, *The Uncommercial Traveller,* 1860). *See also* POTTER'S FIELD.

Achates (ăkayteez) Archetype of a loyal friend. Achates appears as the devoted friend of the hero Aeneas in Virgil's *Aeneid* (30–19 B.C.), sometimes referred to as *"fidus Achates"* (meaning "faithful Achates"). *He proved a true fidus Achates, sticking by his friend through thick and thin.*

Acheron (ăkăron) The underworld, the abode of the dead. According to Greek mythology, Acheron was one of the four rivers surrounding Hades, although Homer's *Iliad* (c. 700 B.C.) identifies it as the only river flowing through the underworld. The name itself means "river of woe." "Mrs Grantly, as she got into the carriage, smiled slightly, thinking of the battle, and as she sat down she gently pressed her daughter's hand. But Mrs Proudie's face was still dark as Acheron when her enemy withdrew, and with angry tone she sent her daughter to her work" (Anthony Trollope, *Framley Parsonage,* 1861).

Achilles and Patroclus (ăkĭleez, pătrăklăs) Archetypes of devoted friendship. The fondness and loyalty of the Greek heroes Achilles and Patroclus during the Trojan War was legendary, and when Patroclus was killed after Achilles absented himself from the battlefield (*see* SULK IN ONE'S TENT), the latter was inconsolable. He eventually returned to the fray to avenge his friend by killing Patroclus's slayer, Hector. "Or perchance he was some Achilles, who had nourished his wrath apart, and had now come to avenge or rescue his Patroclus" (Henry David Thoreau, *Walden,* 1854).

Achilles' heel (ăkĭleez) A fatal weakness; a place where an otherwise strong person or thing is vulnerable. The allusion is to the legends surrounding the great Greek hero Achilles, who became virtually invulnerable after being dipped by his mother, Thetis, in the waters of the River Styx as a child. But in order to dip him, Thetis had to hold him by his heel, so this one area was not touched by the water and remained the one part of his body in which he could be wounded. Ultimately, Achilles met his death when he was shot in the heel by a poisoned arrow fired by Paris during the Trojan War. On the basis of the same legend, the fibrous cord that connects the heel to the muscles of the calf is known as the *Achilles tendon. Her sense of vanity is her Achilles' heel, and all her enemies know it.*

acropolis (ăkropălis) A citadel within an ancient Greek city, usually housing the headquarters of the city's administrative and legislative institutions. The original Acropolis was a group of temples that surmounted the fortified hill around which the city of ancient Athens was built. Chief among these buildings was the Parthenon, dedicated to the goddess Athena. *The townsfolk retreated to the acropolis, leaving the lower part of the city to be sacked by the invaders.*

Actaeon (ak<u>tee</u>ăn) Archetype of a hunter. According to Greek mythology Actaeon was a hunter who accidentally caught sight of the goddess Artemis bathing and as punishment was transformed by her into a stag. He was then torn apart by his own hounds. A variant of the legend explains that Actaeon was put to death as punishment for boasting that he was more skilled at hunting than Artemis. Because Actaeon was turned into a stag and cuckolds according to ancient tradition had horns, the name Actaeon may also be applied to a man whose wife is unfaithful. "In a minute, a gentleman-farmer, panting with Actaeonic excitement, rode up to the two pedestrians, and Grace being a few steps in advance he asked her if she had seen the fox" (Thomas Hardy, *The Woodlanders,* 1887).

Actium (<u>ak</u>teeăm) A decisive defeat. The promontory of Actium in western Greece overlooks the waters in which the Roman fleet of Octavian destroyed that of Mark Antony and Cleopatra VII in 31 B.C. *The scale of the defeat was such that, as for Mark Antony after Actium, there was no prospect of a recovery.*

Adam (<u>a</u>dăm) The archetypal man, especially one who is completely alone or in a state of innocence. The allusion is to the biblical Adam, who became the first man on earth. The human race as a whole has often been referred to as *sons of Adam*. Christ is sometimes called the *new Adam, second Adam,* or *last Adam* (1 Corinthians 15:45). "But here . . . shut in by the stable hills, among which mere walking had the novelty of pageantry, any man could imagine himself to be Adam without the least difficulty" (Thomas Hardy, *The Return of the Native,* 1880). *See also* ADAM AND EVE; ADAM'S ALE; ADAM'S APPLE; ADAM'S CURSE; ADAM'S PROFESSION; ADAM'S RIB; EVE; GARDEN OF EDEN; KNOW SOMEONE FROM ADAM, NOT TO; WHIP THE OFFENDING ADAM.

Adam and Eve (<u>a</u>dăm, eev) The archetypal man and woman. According to Genesis 2, Adam and Eve were the man and woman created by God to inhabit the GARDEN OF EDEN. Their names may be invoked in a variety of contexts, variously with reference to their state of happy innocence before the FALL, to their nakedness, to their fallibility, to their disobedience, or to their joint guilt for committing the first sin. "'O pooh! He is the fallen

Adam with a soured temper. We are Adam and Eve unfallen—in paradise'" (George Eliot, *The Mill on the Floss,* 1860). *See also* ADAM; EVE.

Adam's ale (ădămz) Water. This humorous epithet refers ironically to the fact that the biblical ADAM had only water to drink. Sometimes called *Adam's wine. He said he owed his longevity to his refusal to drink anything stronger than Adam's ale.*

Adam's apple (ădămz) The visible projection of the thyroid cartilage of the larynx in the throat. According to legend, when ADAM bit from the fruit of the forbidden tree a piece of the fruit lodged in his throat, and ever since men have had this visible projection from their throat in remembrance of this first sin. This incident is not, however, mentioned in the book of Genesis, and nowhere is the forbidden fruit identified as an apple. *She could remember little about her assailant beyond the fact that he had bulging eyes and a prominent Adam's apple.*

Adam's curse (ădămz) Ironic colloquialism for work. After ADAM committed the sin of eating of the fruit of the tree of knowledge, against God's command, he and Eve were expelled from the GARDEN OF EDEN. Ever since, as part of their punishment, they and their descendants have known the toil and onerousness of work: "In the sweat of thy face shalt thou eat bread" (Genesis 3:19). Related terms include the ***penalty of Adam***, which refers to the labors implicit in living a life governed by nature and the turn of the seasons in comparison with the easier life enjoyed by people in urban surroundings. *Too many people's lives today are ruled by Adam's curse than by their life outside work.*

Adam's profession (ădămz) Gardening or agriculture. The allusion is to the one occupation that, according to the book of Genesis, was available to ADAM in the GARDEN OF EDEN prior to the Fall (Genesis 2:15). "There is no ancient gentlemen but gardeners, ditchers, and grave-makers; they hold up Adam's profession" (William Shakespeare, *Hamlet,* 1600–01).

Adam's rib (ădămz) A woman. The phrase alludes to the biblical origin of EVE, who, according to Genesis 2:21–23, was fashioned by God from a rib plucked out of ADAM's body while he slept so that he might have a companion in Eden: "And the LORD God caused a deep sleep to fall upon Adam and he slept: and he took one of his ribs, and closed up the flesh instead thereof; And the rib which the LORD God had taken from the man, made he a woman, and brought her unto the man. And Adam said, This is now bone of my bones, and flesh of my flesh: she shall be called Woman, because she was taken out of Man." As a consequence of the biblical tradition, for many years it was popularly believed that men had one rib less than women. *The minister muttered something beneath his breath about how life would be a lot easier without the problematic legacy of Adam's rib and left shortly after.*

Adam's wine *See* ADAM'S ALE.

add a colophon *See* COLOPHON.

add a cubit to his stature To exceed one's natural limitations. The phrase is biblical in origin, appearing in Matthew 6:27: "Which of you by taking thought can add one cubit unto his stature?" The cubit was a measure of length equivalent to the distance from a person's elbow to his or her fingertips. "For his temperament (not uncommon in a misty climate) had been born seven feet high; and as a man cannot add a cubit to his stature, so neither can he take one off" (John Galsworthy, *The Forsyte Saga,* 1922).

Admah and Zeboiim (a̲d̲mah, zebo̲eem) Places of wickedness and sin. The citizens of Admah and Zeboiim are identified in Deuteronomy 29:23 as having abandoned themselves to lives of sin and debauchery, and in consequence their cities suffer much the same fate as the better-known SODOM AND GOMORRAH, both being destroyed as punishment for offending God. *The two villages were shunned by people living in the surrounding hills, who considered them modern versions of Admah and Zeboiim.*

Admetus *See* ALCESTIS.

adonis (ă̲d̲o̲nis) An exceptionally handsome young man. According to Greek mythology, Adonis was a beautiful youth who attracted the amorous attentions of Aphrodite, the goddess of love. When he was killed while hunting a boar (possibly the jealous god of war, Ares, in disguise), he was brought back to life by Persephone. The flower called the anemone sprang up where his blood had spilled. Spending part of the year in the underworld with Persephone and part on earth with Aphrodite, Adonis was worshiped as a nature god, and his absence in the underworld accounted, in myth, for the dormancy of nature in winter. His name came from the Phoenician *adoni* (meaning "my lord"), a title borne by the god Tammuz. "'I really can't see any resemblance between you, with your rugged strong face and your coal-black hair, and this young Adonis, who looks as if he was made out of ivory and rose-leaves'" (Oscar Wilde, *The Picture of Dorian Gray,* 1891).

adullamite (adulămīt) A refugee or fugitive. Adullam is identified at 1 Samuel 22:1–2 as the name of the cave in which DAVID sought shelter when fleeing from the wrath of King Saul, being joined there by a host of other individuals seeking similar refuge: "And every one that was in distress, and every one that was in debt, and every one that was discontented, gathered themselves unto him." The term is generally reserved today for dissident members of political groups who leave to form their own cliques. It was first employed with reference to members of the British Liberal Party who withdrew to form their own group in 1866. *These latter-day adullamites gathered in the lobby of the House of Commons and joined in noisy discussion of their outrage at the behavior of their cabinet colleagues.*

Aegean (ijeeăn) The sea, part of the Mediterranean, between Greece and Turkey. It was named after Aegeus, king of Athens and father of the hero THESEUS. According to Greek mythology, before Theseus sailed to Crete to bring about an end to the payments Athens had to pay to King Minos, he promised his father that if he was successful, he would hoist white sails on his return to indicate that he was safe. If he perished, then his ship would hoist black sails, and Aegeus would know his son was dead. Unfortunately, on his return Theseus forgot his promise and his ship sailed in with black sails. Seeing this and presuming his son dead, Aegeus threw himself into the sea, which has borne his name ever since. "After an extended cruise in the Aegean and the Black Sea on their steam-yacht *Ibis,* Mr and Mrs Mortimer Hicks and their daughter are established at the Nouveau Luxe in Rome" (Edith Wharton, *Glimpses of the Moon,* 1922).

aegis (<u>ee</u>jis) Auspices; protection. The word is Greek in origin (deriving from a word meaning "goat skin") and has its roots in mythology. It was the name of the shield of Zeus, which was forged for him by Hephaestus, and covered with the skin of the goat Amalthea. By shaking this shield Zeus created storms and thunder. Those who enjoyed his protection were thus *under his aegis,* the context in which the word usually appears today. (Athena was also depicted carrying an aegis with the head of the gorgon Medusa in its center.) "So saying, she turned her fine shoulders twice, once this way and once that, and went out. She had never told even Stanley her ambition that at Becket, under her aegis, should be laid the foundation-stone of the real scheme, whatever it might be, that should regenerate 'the Land'" (John Galsworthy, *The Forsyte Saga,* 1921).

Aeneas (ă<u>nee</u>ăs) Archetypical classical hero and man of destiny: the legendary forefather of the Romans. As described in Virgil's epic poem the *Aeneid* (30–19 B.C.), Aeneas was a Trojan prince, the son of Anchises and Aphrodite, who escaped the fall of Troy and embarked on a long and arduous voyage in search of a new home. In the course of his many adventures he effectively prepared the way for his descendants Romulus and Remus to found the city of Rome. "Thus he proceeded, like Aeneas with his father" (Thomas Hardy, *The Return of the Native,* 1880, referring to Virgil's account of how Aeneas carried his old, frail father on his back out of the burning city of Troy). *See also* DIDO AND AENEAS.

aeolian (ay<u>o</u>leeăn) Of or relating to the wind. Aeolus was identified in Greek mythology as a god of the winds. In modern usage the word Aeolian is usually employed in relation to sounds produced naturally by the wind as it passes over a stretched string, as in the case of an *aeolian harp.* In musical theory, an *Aeolian mode* is a natural diatonic scale from A to A that forms the basis of the modern minor key. Stones that have been deposited or worn by the wind may sometimes be referred to as *aeolian rocks.* "I do love a good tree. . . . How grand its voice is, too, when it talks with the wind: a thousand aeolian harps cannot equal the beauty of the sighing of a great tree in leaf" (H. Rider Haggard, *Allan Quatermain,* 1887).

Aeschylean (eeskă<u>lee</u>ăn) Tragic on a grand or epic scale. The allusion is to the tragedies of the celebrated Greek playwright Aeschylus (525–456

B.C.), whose dramas typically dealt with tragedies resulting from pride or defiance of the gods. Of his 90 or so plays, just seven survive, including the trilogy known as the *Oresteia* (458 B.C.). Aeschylus is said to have been killed when an eagle, mistaking his bald head for a stone, dropped a tortoise on it in order to break its shell. "A few minutes after the hour had struck something moved slowly up the staff, and extended itself upon the breeze. It was a black flag. 'Justice' was done, and the President of the Immortals, in Aeschylean phrase, had ended his sport with Tess" (Thomas Hardy, *Tess of the D'Urbervilles,* 1891).

Aesculapius *See* STAFF OF AESCULAPIUS.

Aesop (<u>ee</u>sop) A teller of simple tales with a moral. The allusion is to the deformed Phrygian slave Aesop (c. 620–560 B.C.), who is traditionally identified as the author of a collection of animal fables illustrating a variety of morals. In reality, many of these tales seem to predate his era by hundreds of years. Nonetheless, several later writers have been dubbed Aesops of their age, including the English writer John Gay (1685–1732), called the Aesop of England, and the French fabulist Jean de la Fontaine (1621–95), known as the Aesop of France. "But how moral you've become all of a sudden, at twelve o'clock at night! Instead of being Mrs Radcliffe, I shall think you're Mr Aesop'" (Anthony Trollope, *Doctor Thorne,* 1858).

Agamemnon *See* BRAVE MEN BEFORE AGAMEMNON, THERE WERE; WRATH OF AGAMEMNON.

Aganippe *See* HELICON.

Aglaia *See* THREE GRACES.

Ahab (<u>ay</u>hab) Archetype of an arrogant, wicked tyrant. Ahab is identified in 1 Kings 16:29–22:40 as a king of ancient Israel and the husband of the evil JEZEBEL: "But there was none like unto Ahab, which did sell himself to work wickedness in the sight of the LORD, whom Jezebel his wife stirred up" (1 Kings 21:25). He colluded in the introduction of pagan worship and, when Naboth refused to hand over his vineyard (see NABOTH'S VINE-YARD), had him stoned to death. Subsequently he was warned by ELIJAH that he faced divine vengeance and the fall of his dynasty, which duly occurred, Ahab himself being killed in battle and his blood being licked up by dogs. *Like the biblical Ahab, he ignored all warnings that he would have to answer for his wicked ways, possibly with his life.*

Ahasuerus *See* ESTHER.

Ajax (ayjaks) Archetype of a brave, strong warrior. The Greek hero Ajax is depicted in Homer's *Iliad* (c. 700 B.C.), which tells the story of the Trojan War, as second only to Achilles in courage and strength but also as arrogant and foolish. Ajax was deeply offended when Achilles' armor was won by Odysseus and in his rage slaughtered a flock of sheep. When he recovered he was overcome with shame and killed himself. "She sat as helpless and despairing among her black locks as Ajax among the slaughtered sheep" (George Eliot, *The Mill on the Floss,* 1860).

Alastor (ălastor) A vengeful god or spirit. The name was one of several titles borne by Zeus, ruler of the gods in Greek mythology. "Their impulse was well-nigh to prostrate themselves in lamentation before untimely rains and tempests, which came as the Alastor of those households whose crime it was to be poor" (Thomas Hardy, *The Mayor of Casterbridge,* 1886).

Alcestis (alsestis) Archetype of a woman who sacrifices herself for others. The allusion is to the Greek legend of Alcestis, the wife of King Admetus of Thessaly, who volunteered to die in her husband's place when Apollo agreed to spare his life if he could find someone to take his place. Persephone (or Hercules) subsequently rescued her from Hades and restored her to her husband, as described in the tragedy *Alcestis* (438 B.C.) by Euripides. *The headmistress appeared ready to play Alcestis for the sake of her secretary, but such a monumental sacrifice on her part was not necessary in the end.*

Alcibiades (alsibīădeez) Archetype of a debauchee. Alcibiades (c. 450–404 B.C.) was an Athenian statesman and general who won notable victories at Abydos (411 B.C.) and Cyzicus (410 B.C.). His many lovers may have included Socrates, who, according to Plato's *Symposium,* demonstrated his tremendous self-control by spending the night with the beautiful Alcibiades without attempting to make love to him. *The field marshal was the Alcibiades of his day, combining undoubted military prowess with scandalous exploits in the casinos and brothels of Paris.*

Alecto *See* FURIES.

Alexander the Great (aleks<u>zan</u>der) Archetype of a great military commander. Alexander the Great (356–323 B.C.) was the son of Philip II of Macedon and studied as a youth in Athens under Aristotle. He became king of Macedon at 20 and soon established a reputation as a brilliant military leader, conquering Greece (336 B.C.), Egypt (331 B.C.), and the Persian Empire (328 B.C.) before his premature death from fever at the age of 32. He was well known for treating any women who became his prisoners with respect, and the *continence of Alexander* acquired proverbial status. *The president appears to think himself Alexander the Great, but his critics prefer to liken him to Donald Duck.*

all flesh is grass *See* FLESH IS GRASS.

all is vanity *See* VANITY OF VANITIES.

all roads lead to Rome All the alternatives will lead to the same result. The allusion is to the road system that was built to connect all parts of the far-flung Roman Empire with Rome. "All roads lead to Rome, and there were times when it might have struck us that almost every branch of study or subject of conversation skirted forbidden ground" (Henry James, *The Turn of the Screw*, 1898).

all the days of one's life *See* DAYS OF ONE'S LIFE, ALL THE.

all things are possible with God Anything can happen, especially if willed by God. The proverb in its current form is biblical in origin, appearing in Matthew 19:26: "With men this is impossible; but with God all things are possible." A similar sentiment had been voiced in earlier times, as in Homer's *Odyssey* (c. 700 B.C.): "With the gods all things can be done." *No one thought he would make it, but all things are possible with God.*

all things in common The shared ownership of property, goods, and possessions. The phrase comes from Acts 2:44–45, which describes how the first Christians gathered in communal groups, sharing their wealth and possessions equally and owning nothing individually. *All those who enter the monastery surrender their right to ownership of property, as the rules demand holding all things in common.*

all things to all men Compromising and flexible adaptation of opinions, actions, etc., regardless of principle, in order to appease a variety of conflicting interests. The expression comes from 1 Corinthians 9:22, in which Paul, explaining how he seeks converts among both Jews and Gentiles, writes, "I am made all things to all men, that I might by all means save some." *The church leader was criticized for not making his own views clear and for attempting to be all things to all men.*

alpha and omega (alfă, ōmaygă) The entirety or most important part of something; the first and last of something. The phrase appears in Revelation 1:8, 21:6, and 22:13 and, according to the *NIV Study Bible,* means, "God is the beginning and the end. . . . He rules sovereignly over all human history. In 22:13 Jesus applies the same title to himself." Alpha and omega are respectively the first and last letters of the Greek alphabet, which was adopted around 1000 B.C. *Engine performance is the alpha and omega of all research done at this facility.*

Alpheus and Arethusa (alfeeăs, arăthooză) Archetypes of lovers who are so close they appear indivisible. According to Greek mythology, Alpheus was a river god who fell in love with the nymph Arethusa. The virginal Arethusa fled from Alpheus and, at her own request, was transformed by the goddess Artemis into a sacred spring on the island of Ortygia, near Sicily. Alpheus, however, transformed himself into a river and flowed under the Peloponnesus to mingle with her. The legend may have been inspired by the fact that the Alpheus River does indeed flow underground in certain places. *They're like Alpheus and Arethusa, more or less joined at the hip!*

Althaea's brand (altheeăz) An event that has fatal consequences. The allusion is to Greek mythology and the legend of Althaea and her son Meleager, who was fated to live as long as a certain log of wood remained unburned. After Meleager murdered her brothers, Althaea threw the log into the fire and brought about her son's death, as related in Ovid's *Metamorphoses* (A.D. 1–8). "As did the fatal brand Althaea burned" (William Shakespeare, *Henry VI*, 1592).

Amalekite (ămalăkīt) Archetype of a wicked, untrustworthy enemy. The Amalekites are described in the Bible as a nomadic warlike tribe descended from Amalek (Esau's grandson) and the perpetual enemies of the Israelites: "The LORD will have war with Amalek from generation to generation" (Exodus 17:16). *The troops regard their opponents as modern-day Amalekites, quick to resort to violence and on no account to be trusted.*

Amalthea *See* CORNUCOPIA.

Amaryllis (amărilis) A shepherdess or country girl. It is the name of a shepherdess featured in the pastorals of Theocritus and (c. 310–250 B.C.) and Virgil (70–19 B.C.). In modern usage it is best known as an alternative title for the belladonna lily or of several other related plants. "Were it not better done as others use, / To sport with Amaryllis in the shade / Or with the tangles of Neaera's hair?" (John Milton, *Lycidas*, 1637).

amazon (amăzon) A large, robust, or aggressive woman. The Amazons were, according to Greek mythology, a race of warrior women who inhabited Scythia, on the shores of the Black Sea. They were called Amazons (meaning "without breast") because of their practice of removing the right breasts in order to facilitate the drawing of a bow. They only consorted with men for the purpose of procreation. Led by their queen, Hippolyta, they were renowned for their fierceness in battle. The Amazon River in South America is said to have been so called by the Spanish explorer Francisco de Orellana, who reported seeing female warriors in the region in 1541. In 1997 the discovery in southern Russia of ancient graves of what appeared to be female warriors suggested a possible source of the legend of the Amazons. In modern usage, anyone with a clean-shaven face may be said to have an ***Amazonian chin.*** *I didn't offer to break down the door, since if the door needed breaking down this amazon looked quite capable of doing the job herself.*

ambrosia (am<u>brä</u>zhǎ) A delicious or sweet-smelling food. The allusion is to Greek mythology and the belief that the gods on Olympus fed on such food, which gave them immortality. "We feasted that evening as on nectar and ambrosia" (Charlotte Brontë, *Jane Eyre,* 1847). *See also* NECTAR.

amillennialism *See* MILLENNIUM.

Am I my brother's keeper? *See* MY BROTHER'S KEEPER.

ammonia (ǎ<u>mō</u>nyǎ) A colorless soluble gas widely used in making fertilizers and other compounds. The word comes from the name of the Egyptian god Ammon (meaning "the hidden one"), as the salt or gum resin that is the source of ammonia was supposedly first obtained from plants growing near a temple dedicated to him in Libya. *This machine measures the amount of ammonia produced in the process.*

Amphitrite (am<u>fi</u><u>trī</u>tee) A woman who loves the sea. Amphitrite was identified in Greek mythology as a goddess of the sea, the wife of Poseidon and mother of Triton. The name itself comes from the Greek for "wearing away on all sides." *She stood in the vessel's prow, staring at the distant horizon, Amphitrite in her element at last.*

Amyclaean silence (ami<u>klee</u>ǎn) A self-imposed silence. According to ancient Greek legend, the inhabitants of Amyclae were so scared by repeated rumors that the Spartans were attacking that they forbade any mention of the subject. Thus, when the Spartans really did attack, no one spread the news, and the town was captured. *The senior members of the government seem to have agreed to answer the questions of the press with an Amyclaean silence.*

Anacreontic (ǎnakree<u>on</u>tik) In praise of love or wine; convivial. Anacreon was a celebrated Greek lyric poet who lived in the sixth century B.C. He was well known for his verses on the glories of love and wine, and his name has subsequently been applied to many poets and artists whose work deals with similar themes. *The following week the magazine published a collection of Anacreontic lyrics by anonymous readers.*

Ananias club (anănīas) A band of liars or deceivers. The allusion is biblical, referring to a rich man called Ananias who, in expectation of Christ's Second Coming, attempted to join the devout community led by the apostle Peter. Ananias and his wife, Sophia, had sold a piece of property. With his wife's full knowledge, Ananias had retained some of the money from the sale for himself and brought the rest and put it at the apostle's feet. Ananias claimed to have given all his money, but Peter knew that the offer was insincere. He accused Ananias of dishonesty, and the latter was immediately struck dead. According to the account in Acts 5:1–12, the same fate also befell Ananias's wife, when she, unaware of her husband's demise, also came to Peter and maintained that they had laid before him all their worldly wealth. Ever since, the name has often been applied to liars, but it was U.S. president Theodore Roosevelt (1858–1919) who coined "Ananias club," directing it specifically at his political enemies and at journalists who betrayed his confidence. *The Ananias club of news reporters and paparazzi was barred from entering the building so that the various leaders could discuss matters without the fear that their words would be publicly distorted.*

anathema (ănathămă) Something or someone deemed detestable or otherwise accursed or intolerable. Originally a Greek word implying "something hung up in a temple and dedicated to a god," it took on a more negative connotation through the Hebrew practice of "dedicating" their defeated enemies to God by sacrificing them. In the New Testament the word thus came to denote anything abhorrent to the Lord and by extension anything evil or accursed. The Book of I Corinthians ends with the apostle Paul writing, "If any man love not the Lord Jesus Christ let him be Anathema Maranatha" (16:22). (*Maranatha* means "the Lord cometh" and is intended merely as a closing benediction to the letter but sometimes is mistakenly treated as an intensification of *anathema*). It also came to be applied to formal denunciations or the curse of excommunication (or curses in general). *The idea of taking a vacation in a country where women were treated as second-class citizens was anathema to her.*

Anchises (ankīseez) Archetype of an aged but respected parent. According to Greek mythology, the goddess of love, Aphrodite, fell in love with Anchises when he was a handsome young Trojan prince and in due course bore him the hero AENEAS. When Aeneas was allowed to go free after the sack of Troy by the Greeks, who greatly respected his prowess, and permitted to take the one thing he most valued with him Aeneas chose the now aged and infirm Anchises, carrying him on his shoulders through the flames. Anchises subsequently accompanied Aeneas on his voyages and died in Sicily aged 80. "Ay, as Aeneas our great ancestor / Did from the flames of Troy upon his shoulder / The old Anchises bear, so from the waves of Tiber / Did I the tired Caesar" (William Shakespeare, *Julius Caesar,* 1599).

Androcles and the lion (ăndrăkleez) Legendary incident illustrating the moral that those who behave kindly to others may reap the benefit of their generosity later. Androcles (or Androclus) was a Roman slave who was sentenced to be killed by wild beasts in the circus. When he was placed in the arena with a fierce lion, however, the lion did not kill him but greeted him with every sign of friendship. It transpired that some time earlier Androcles, having escaped from his master, had befriended the lion in the wilderness by removing a thorn from the animal's paw, thus relieving its agony. Duly impressed, the authorities released Androcles and presented him with the lion. The legend is perhaps best known today through its dramatization as *Androcles and the Lion* (1912) by British writer George Bernard Shaw. *It was like Androcles and the lion: The magistrate descended from his bench and warmly embraced the felon who had been brought in for admonishment.*

Andromeda (andrŏmădă) A constellation in the Northern Hemisphere, located between Cassiopeia and Pegasus. It was named after the legendary Andromeda, daughter of King Cepheus of Ethiopia and Cassiopeia, who was greatly admired for her beauty. When Cassiopeia boasted that her daughter was more beautiful than the sea nymphs known as the Nereids, they persuaded the sea god Poseidon to send a monster to ravage Cepheus's land. In order to appease the monster, Andromeda was chained to a rock and offered as a sacrifice. She was rescued by Perseus, who killed the monster by showing it the severed head of Medusa, who turned all who looked at her into stone. Perseus and Andromeda subsequently married. After her death she was placed among the stars. "With these were to be seen at intervals some of maturer years, full-blown flowers among the opening buds, with that conscious look upon their faces which so many women wear during the period when they never meet a single man without having his monosyllable ready for him,—tied as they are, poor things! on the rock of expectation, each of them an Andromeda waiting for her Perseus" (Oliver Wendell Holmes, *Elsie Venner,* 1861).

angel of death Personification of death. The angel of death is usually assumed to be of biblical origin, being variously identified as Apollyon (*see* ABADDON), Azrael, or Michael. "Some day soon the Angel of Death will sound his trumpet for me" (Bram Stoker, *Dracula,* 1897).

anger of Juno *See* JUNOESQUE.

anointed of the Lord The clergy, or others deemed to have been chosen by God. The phrase comes from 1 Samuel 24:10, in which David protests accusations that he plotted the death of King Saul: "I will not put forth mine hand against my lord; for he is the LORD's anointed." *It was his mother's dearest wish that he would elect to join the church and enjoy the respect deserving the anointed of the Lord.*

Antaeus (an<u>tee</u>ăs) A powerful person who has to renew his or her strength periodically. The allusion is to the giant Antaeus, who, according to Greek mythology, was in the habit of killing any opponent who could not defeat him at wrestling. The son of Poseidon and the earth goddess Gaea, he depended for his strength on being in contact with the earth, so when Hercules held him off the ground, he was powerless to prevent himself being strangled to death. *The big man was uneasy in the abstract realms of thought, needing, like Antaeus, to keep his feet firmly on the ground.*

Antichrist A person who opposes Christ or is the implacable enemy of all that is good. The Antichrist is described in the Bible as the enemy of Christ (1 John 2:18–21), who will inflict great wickedness upon the world prior to being overcome in a final battle by Christ at the Second Coming. The Antichrist denies the fundamental truths about Jesus Christ; instead, Christ coming is seen as a sign of the "last days." Similar biblical figures include the "man of lawlessness" (2 Thessalonians 2:3–12) and the beast

(Revelation 11:7). The title "Antichrist" has been bestowed upon many notorious figures and institutions over the centuries, among them the Roman emperors Caligula and Nero, the Roman Empire in general, Muhammad, the papacy, Napoléon Bonaparte, and Adolf Hitler. *His excesses over the years had turned him into an Antichrist-type figure as far as the rest of his family was concerned.*

anthropophagi (anthrăpofăgī) Cannibals. According to Greek mythology, the Laestrygones were a race of cannibalistic anthropophagi (meaning "eaters of human beings") encountered by the Greek hero Odysseus, who only narrowly escaped them. "And of the Cannibals that each other eat, / The Anthropophagi, and men whose heads / Do grow beneath their shoulders" (William Shakespeare, *Othello,* 1603–04).

Antigone (antĭgănee) Archetype of a woman who sacrifices herself for her family. The allusion is to the Greek myth about Antigone, daughter of Oedipus and his mother, Jocasta. Antigone was condemned to death by being buried alive for having given burial rites to the body of her brother Polyneices against the order of her uncle, King Creon of Thebes. Antigone committed suicide. "As Antigone said, 'I am neither a dweller among men nor ghosts' " (Thomas Hardy, *Jude the Obscure,* 1895).

Antiphates' wife (antifayteez) Epitome of ugliness. According to Greek mythology, the wife of Antiphates, leader of the cannibalistic Laestrygones, was appallingly ugly. *Not since Odysseus laid eyes upon Antiphates' wife had any man been so revolted by the physical form of a woman.*

Antisthenes *See* CYNIC.

Antony and Cleopatra (antănee, kleeōpatră) Archetypes of doomed lovers. The Roman general Mark Antony (82–30 B.C.) became a member of the Second Triumvirate, alongside Octavian and Lepidus, in 43 B.C. and had responsibility for Rome's eastern provinces. He repudiated his wife to join Cleopatra VII (69–30 B.C.), queen of Egypt, but their joint forces were defeated by Octavian at ACTIUM in 31 BC, after which Antony committed suicide having been told (inaccurately) that Cleopatra was dead. Cleopatra killed herself shortly afterward, letting a poisonous asp bite her. "Passion is destructive. It destroyed Antony and Cleopatra, Tristan and Isolde" (William Somerset Maugham, *The Razor's Edge,* 1944).

Anubis (ănoobis) Personification of death. The jackal-headed Anubis was identified in ancient Egyptian mythology as the son of Osiris and as the god of the dead who escorted the deceased to judgment. The Greek equivalent was Hermes. *The gloom that concealed this melancholy spot might have been the shadow of Anubis himself.*

Aphrodite (afrōdītee) A beautiful or sexually desirable woman. The goddess of love in Greek mythology, Aphrodite was variously described as having been born from the foam *(aphros)* of the sea or, according to Homer, as the daughter of Zeus and Dione. She was forced to marry the ugly Hephaestus and was notoriously unfaithful to him, allegedly possessing a magic girdle (also called the **cestus** or, by the Romans, the **girdle of Venus**) supposed to have the power to make her sexually irresistible to any person she might wish to attract. Her name inspired the word **aphrodisiac,** which describes any substance or other influence that is deemed to excite sexual desire. "No, her mood now was that of Aphrodite triumphing. Life—radiant, ecstatic, wonderful—seemed to flow from her and around her" (H. Rider Haggard, *She,* 1887).

Apicius (apishăs) A gourmand. The name belonged to three celebrated Roman epicures, the most famous of whom was Marcus Gavius Apicius, who lived in the first century A.D. and was the author of a book of recipes known as *Of Culinary Matters.* When he was faced through financial difficulty with having to restrict himself to a plain diet, he killed himself rather than suffer such privation. *This Apicius dedicated his life to seeking out new taste sensations in the restaurants and hotels of Manhattan.*

apocalypse (ăpōkalips) A catastrophic or climactic event involving total destruction. The book of Revelation, in which John reveals how the world will end, is sometimes referred to as the Apocalypse. The word itself comes from the Greek *apokalyptein* (meaning "to disclose"). The derivative adjective is **apocalyptic.** "The events of September 11 were so apocalyptic that it seemed in the immediate aftermath that the landscape of travel would be altered forever" (*The Guardian,* September 7, 2002). *See also* FOUR HORSE-MEN OF THE APOCALYPSE.

apocryphal (ăpo̱krăfăl) Of dubious authenticity or authorship; sham. The word refers to the Apocrypha, the books appended to the Old Testament but not forming part of the Hebrew canon and not included in the Protestant Bible. It comes from the Greek *apokryptein* (meaning "to hide away"). *The story that it was here that the conquistadores held their first mass is probably apocryphal.* The apocryphal books are also know as the deuterocanonical (secondarily canonical) books. For many centuries, they were read as part of the Latin (Vulgate) Bible, having been included in the Septuagint, or Greek translation of the Old Testament, but not the Hebrew Bible; despite their inclusion, their value was regarded as somewhat ambiguous. At the Reformation, however, the Roman Catholic Church fixed their number at twelve and included them in their editions of the Bible, whereas the Protestant denominations formally excluded them. They include some additions to the books of Esther, Daniel (including the history of Susanna and the Song of the Three Holy Children), and Jeremiah, as well as a number of historical works (1 and 2 Maccabees and 1 Esdras), an apocalyptic book (2 Esdras), three short stories (Tobit, Judith, and Bel and the Dragon), two wisdom books (Ecclesiasticus, or Sirach, and the Wisdom of Solomon) and three other works of various kinds (the Prayer of Manesses, the Letter of Jeremiah, and Baruch). They have been preserved in Greek but many were probably written originally in Hebrew or Aramaic (Selman and Manser, *The Hearthside Bible Dictionary*).

Apollonian (apălo̱neeăn) Serene, harmonious, ordered. The word alludes to the Greek sun god Apollo, the son of Zeus and Leto, who represented such positive attributes as light, music, poetry, healing, and prophecy. He was conventionally depicted as a handsome youth, and even today a beautiful young man may be termed an *apollo*. *Nietzsche contrasts the Apollonian need for light, order, and harmony with the Dionysian urge for darkness, wild passion, and destruction.*

Apollyon *See* ABADDON.

apostle (ăpŏsăl) A devoted follower of a particular belief, faith, movement, etc. From the Greek *apostolos* (meaning "a messenger"), the word acquired new significance through the work of Christ's apostles—originally the 12 disciples (Matthew 10:2)—who were chosen by Christ to preach the gospel. It is also used to refer to Paul, commissioned to be an apostle by the risen Christ. The apostles' basic qualification was that they had been with Jesus during his earthly ministry and had witnessed his resurrection. The apostles were recognized as the founders of the church. The word *apostle* is also used more generally to refer to a representative or messenger of a particular church. Subsequently the term came to be applied to any individual who sought to spread Christianity around the world and more generally to anyone publicly espousing a particular cause or movement. *Over the last two years he has emerged as a leading apostle of the political Left.*

appeal from Philip drunk to Philip sober To seek a decision or complete some other task at a more favorable time. The allusion is to a legendary incident in which a Macedonian noblewoman sought a legal ruling from Philip II of Macedon (382–336 B.C.), but found her petition refused by the king, who was in a drunken, unsympathetic mood. The woman announced her intention to appeal against the decision. When the outraged king demanded to whom she intended to make her appeal, she replied, undaunted, "To Philip sober." Legend has it that she subsequently won her case. *When her husband returned home late that night, somewhat the worse for wear, he refused to countenance her suggestion and she resolved to wait until the following morning, when she might appeal from Philip drunk to Philip sober.*

appease his manes (mayneez) To observe the wishes of a dead person. According to Roman belief, the spirit, or *manes,* of the deceased would rise up in anger if survivors failed to show due respect to his or her wishes. *In order to appease his manes, they scattered the old man's ashes on the cliff top, as he had instructed.*

apple of discord A cause of argument. The allusion is to Greek mythology and the golden apple that was offered by Eris, the goddess of discord, to the most beautiful of the guests at the wedding of Peleus and Thetis, to which she had not been invited. The resulting contest between the goddesses Hera, Athena, and Aphrodite was settled by Paris (see JUDG-MENT OF PARIS) but resulted in much resentment and bloodshed and ultimately the outbreak of the Trojan War. In modern usage, to **throw the apple of discord** means to provoke conflict. "I suppose he specified sincere because it was no longer sincere: he hurled the offer into Musgrove Cottage by way of an apple of discord—at least so I infer from the memorandum, with which he retired at present from the cash hunt" (Charles Reade, *Hard Cash,* 1863).

apple of knowledge *See* FORBIDDEN FRUIT.

apple of one's eye Someone or something that is very precious to a particular person. The phrase is biblical in origin, appearing in Deuteronomy 32:10, which describes God's love for Israel—"He kept him as the apple of his eye"—and again in Psalm 17:8 and Proverbs 7:2. The apple is understood to be a metaphor for the pupil of the eye, which is not dissimilar in shape. "'He's the only minister I ever had much use for. He's God's own if ever a man was. And he loves you—yes, sir, he loves you like the apple of his eye'" (Lucy Maud Montgomery, *The Chronicles of Avonlea,* 1912).

apples of Sodom *See* DEAD SEA FRUIT.

apples of the Hesperides *See* LABORS OF HERCULES.

arachnid (ăraknid) An anthropod of the class Arachnida, characterized by eight legs and simple eyes. The arachnids, which include spiders, owe their name to Greek mythology, specifically to a girl from Lydia named Arachne who offended the goddess Athena after challenging her to a weaving contest. When Arachne won the contest Athena destroyed Arachne's tapestry, prompting the latter to attempt to hang herself. Instead, Athene turned the rope into a cobweb and Arachne into a spider. The study of arachnids is known as **arachnology.** *Ever since she was a child she had nursed a terror of all arachnids, especially spiders.*

Arcadian (ahrkaydeeăn) Rustic, pastoral, harmonious, idealized. According to Greek mythology, Arcadia was a mountainous area of the Greek Peloponnese whose inhabitants were said to pursue peaceful, harmonious lives in bucolic surroundings. The notion of Arcadia representing an idealized rural setting was taken up with some enthusiasm by English poets of the late 16th century. "I had not forgotten Sebastian. He was with me daily in Julia; or rather it was Julia I had known in him, in those distant Arcadian days" (Evelyn Waugh, *Brideshead Revisited*, 1945).

Archilochian bitterness (arkilōkeeăn) Mocking, personalized satire. The allusion is to the writings of the seventh-century B.C. Greek satirical poet Archilochus, who expressed personal resentments and bitterness in his verse. *It was just as well that the author of such Archilochian bitterness had elected to remain anonymous as he or she would doubtless have been sued for libel.*

Archimedean (ahrkămeedeeăn) Of or relating to the mathematical or physical theories of Archimedes. A Greek mathematician and scientist, Archimedes (c. 287–c. 212 B.C) made many notable and profoundly influential discoveries in such fields as geometry, mechanics, and hydrostatics, such as the *Archimedes principle* and the *Archimedes screw.* "It was at this juncture that Mr. Monck Mason (whose voyage from Dover to Weilburg in the balloon Nassau occasioned so much excitement in 1837) conceived the idea of employing the principle of the Archimedean screw for the purpose of propulsion through the air" (Edgar Allan Poe, "The Balloon-Hoax," 1850). *See also* EUREKA.

Ares (aireez) Personification of war. Ares was identified in Greek mythology as the son of Zeus and Hera and the god of war. In Roman mythology he was called Mars. *The spirit of Ares loomed over the conference table and made any substantial agreement well nigh impossible.*

Arethusa *See* ALPHEUS AND ARETHUSA.

argonaut (ahrgănot) A seafarer, especially one who embarks in a spirit of adventure. In Greek mythology the Argonauts were the heroes who accompanied Jason in his pursuit of the GOLDEN FLEECE. Including such famous names as HERCULES and ORPHEUS among their number, they took their name from their vessel, the *Argo* (meaning "swift"). "This was our second parting, and our capacities were now reversed. It was mine to play the Argonaut, to speed affairs, to plan and to accomplish—if need were, at the price of life; it was his to sit at home, to study the calendar, and to wait" (Robert Louis Stevenson, *The Wrecker,* 1892).

Argus (ahrgăs) An eagle-eyed watchkeeper or guardian. Argus Panoptes appears in Greek mythology as a monster with 100 eyes who was appointed by Hera to guard over the heifer into which Io had been transformed by Zeus. He was, however, lulled to sleep by the music Hermes played on his lyre. Hermes then killed him, and his 100 eyes were placed by Hera in the tail of the peacock, her favorite bird. In his memory, anyone who proves him- or herself vigilant may be described as being *Argus-eyed.* "Now Argus, the poets say, had an hundred eyes, and was set to watch with them all, as she does, with her goggling ones" (Samuel Richardson, *Pamela,* 1741).

Ariadne *See* LABYRINTH.

Arion (ărīon) A musician. According to Greek mythology, Arion was a celebrated poet and player of the kithara who lived in the seventh century B.C. When threatened by the crew of the vessel in which he sailed home victorious from a musical contest, he played his kithara and then hurled himself into the sea, from which he was rescued by music-loving dolphins and carried home. "But then there were some sceptical Greeks and Romans, who, standing out from the orthodox pagans of their times, equally doubted the story of Hercules and the whale, and Arion and the dolphin; and yet their doubting those traditions did not make those traditions one whit the less facts, for all that" (Herman Melville, *Moby-Dick,* 1851).

Aristotelian (aristăteeleeăn) Of or relating to the philosophical ideas of Aristotle. The Greek philosopher Aristotle (384–322 B.C.) studied under Plato and later became tutor to Alexander the Great. Founder of the Peripatetic School in Athens, he wrote influential works on logic, ethics, politics, poetics, rhetoric, biology, zoology, and metaphysics. In modern usage, this adjective is usually used in reference to his work on logic or to philosophical positions that incorporate some of his ideas, notably his recommendation that a philosopher should adopt an objective viewpoint independent of social or moral contexts. "In morals he was a profest

Platonist, and in religion he inclined to be an Aristotelian" (Henry Fielding, *Tom Jones,* 1749).

ark A large boat or other vessel that serves as a means to rescue people, animals, or something else under threat of annihilation. The allusion is to the floating Ark that, according to the book of Genesis (6:14), Noah built on God's orders and in which he preserved his family and two of every species of animal on earth when the world was inundated by the Flood. Related phrases include *out of the ark,* signifying something that is so old or out of date that it may well date back to the Ark itself. "In ancient times some Mr. Bell was sailing this way in his ark with seeds of rocket, saltwort, sandwort, beach-grass, samphire, bayberry, poverty-grass, &c., all nicely labelled with directions, intending to establish a nursery somewhere; and did not a nursery get established, though he thought that he had failed" (Henry David Thoreau, *Cape Cod,* 1865).

Ark of the Covenant Something considered sacrosanct or greatly revered, especially a ruling or opinion widely regarded as irrefutable. According to Exodus 25:10–12, the original Ark of the Covenant was the gold-covered wooden chest in which were kept the two tablets inscribed with the Ten Commandments. The ark was the most sacred symbol of the covenant formed between God and the Israelites and was carried by them into battle against the Philistines, who captured it. It was subsequently returned to Israel and enshrined in the HOLY OF HOLIES in the Temple at Jerusalem on the orders of Solomon but vanished, presumably destroyed, when the city fell to Nebuchadnezzar in 586 B.C. Some claim that it is now located in the church of St. Mary of Zion in Axum (Aksum), northern Ethiopia. Related phrases include to *lay hands on the ark,* meaning to abuse a sacred object, opinion, etc. *The attendant handled the casket with such care it might have been the Ark of the Covenant itself.*

Armageddon (ahrmăgĕdăn) A decisive, cataclysmic confrontation; the end of the world. From the Hebrew *Har Magedon* (meaning "hill of Megiddo"), the term refers to the Palestinian city of Megiddo, which was located between Mount Carmel and the coast. Because of its favorable location, the city was frequently fought over in ancient times and thus became synonymous with bloodshed and war. Armageddon is identified in the book of Revelation 16:14–16 as where the climactic battle between the forces of good and evil will be fought. In modern usage, the term is widely employed in referring to any catastrophic conflict that threatens universal disaster, often specifically to nuclear war. "'Armageddon Now,' declared *Kommersant*, the Russian business daily" (*Daily Telegraph*, September 13, 2001). *See also* JUDGMENT DAY.

Artemis (ahrtămis) Personification of youthful female vigor and athleticism. Artemis, or Diana in Roman mythology, was the ancient Greek goddess of the hunt and the moon, a virgin armed with bow and arrow, twin sister of Apollo. She appeared in numerous legends, including the stories of ACTAEON and THESEUS. "Ah! here is the duchess, looking like Artemis in a tailor-made gown" (Oscar Wilde, *The Picture of Dorian Gray*, 1891). *See also* DIANA OF THE EPHESIANS; EIGHTH WONDER OF THE WORLD.

as a tree falls, so shall it lie A person's end corresponds to the life that he or she has led, and any last-minute changes of opinion or belief will not change this. This proverb is of biblical origin, appearing in Ecclesiastes 11:3: "In the place where the tree falleth, there it shall be." It was first recorded in its present form in 1678. "She sent a message . . . to the old father to come and see her before she died . . . His answer was, 'As a tree falls so shall it lie'" (W. H. Hudson, *Traveller in Little Things*, 1921).

Ascalaphus (askălayfăs) According to Greek mythology, when Persephone was rescued from the underworld, it was Ascalaphus who revealed the fact that she had eaten some pomegranate seeds while in Hades, thus breaking the condition that she must not eat anything during her abduction. As a result, Persephone was condemned to spend six months in the underworld and six months on earth for the rest of her life. In revenge for this betrayal, Persephone transformed Ascalaphus into an owl. *The pair resolved to have their revenge upon their former colleague who, like Ascalaphus betraying Persephone, had brought about their utter ruin when they were within sight of victory.*

Asgard *See* VALHALLA.

ashes *See* SACKCLOTH AND ASHES.

ashes to ashes *See* UNTO DUST SHALT THOU RETURN.

Ashtoreth (<u>ash</u>tăreth) Symbol of fertility or sexuality. Ashtoreth (Ashtorath) is identified in the Bible as the Phoenician fertility goddess Astarte, equivalent to the Greek Aphrodite, whom the Israelites briefly adopted as an idol, to the great offense of God: "And the children of Israel did evil again in the sight of the LORD, and served Baalim, and Ashtaroth" (Judges 10:6). "The bailiff was pointed out to Gabriel, who, checking the palpitation within his breast at discovering that this Ashtoreth of strange report was only a modification of Venus the well-known and admired, retired with him to talk over the necessary preliminaries of hiring" (Thomas Hardy, *Far from the Madding Crowd,* 1874).

ask and it shall be given you If you want something, you must take positive action to get it, rather than do nothing at all. The proverb is of biblical origin, appearing in Matthew 7:7, and is sometimes encountered in its fuller form: "Ask, and it shall be given you; seek, and ye shall find; knock, and it shall be opened unto you." Variants include *ask and thou shall receive* and the more colloquial *them as asks, gits; them as don't ask, don't git. The old woman handed over the envelope of money with a smile and whispered, "Ask and it shall be given you."*

as old as Methuselah (me<u>thoo</u>zălă) Very old, ancient. Methuselah is the oldest man mentioned in the Bible who, according to Genesis 5:27, died at the advanced age of 969. "Now, you are my witness, Miss Summerson, I say I don't care—but if he was to come to our house with his great, shining, lumpy forehead night after night till he was as old as Methuselah, I wouldn't have anything to say to him'" (Charles Dickens, *Bleak House,* 1852–53). A *methuselah* is also an oversized wine bottle with a capacity of eight standard wine bottles.

Aspasia (as<u>pay</u>zhă) A prostitute. Aspasia was a celebrated Athenian courtesan of the fifth century B.C. whose devoted admirers included Pericles, who made her his mistress. "The man who acts, decides, and achieves; the woman who encourages, applauds, and—from a distance—inspires: the combination is common enough; but Miss Nightingale was neither an Aspasia nor an Egeria" (Lytton Strachey, *Eminent Victorians,* 1918).

as rich as Croesus (<u>kree</u>săs) Immensely wealthy. Croesus (d. 546 B.C.) was the last king of Lydia and, through his conquests, the possessor of seemingly unlimited wealth. He was overthrown by Cyrus of Persia. "'And as for Lizzie—she's your cousin, and all that. And she's ever so pretty, and all that. And she's as rich as Croesus, and all that'" (Anthony Trollope, *The Eustace Diamonds,* 1873).

assume the mantle of Elijah *See* MANTLE OF ELIJAH.

as you sow, so shall you reap *See* REAP WHAT YOU SOW.

Atalanta's race (atălantăz) A contest that is won through trickery. The allusion is to Greek mythology and the race that was run between the fleet-footed huntress Atalanta and her suitor Hippomenes (sometimes identified as Melanion). If Hippomenes won the race, according to the agreement, Atalanta would become his wife, but if he lost he would be put to death, like all her previous suitors. Before the race, Aphrodite gave Hippomenes the three golden apples of the Hesperides, which Hippomenes dropped along the route so that Atalanta would pause to pick them up. By this ruse Hippomenes won the race, and they were married. "Laurie reached the goal first and was quite satisfied with the success of his treatment, for his Atalanta came panting up with flying hair, bright eyes, ruddy cheeks, and no signs of dissatisfaction in her face" (Louisa M. Alcott, *Little Women,* 1868).

Ate (<u>ay</u>tee) Personification of mischief. According to Greek mythology, Zeus was so incensed at the goddess Ate's mischief making that he hurled her from Olympus. Ever since she has busied herself making trouble among inhabitants of the mortal world. "Caesar's spirit, ranging for revenge, / With Ate by his side, come hot from hell, / Shall, in these confines with a monarch's voice, / Cry 'havoc' and let slip the dogs of war" (William Shakespeare, *Julius Caesar,* 1599).

at ease in Zion (<u>zi</u>on) Living a life of comfort and luxury. The phrase comes from Amos 6:1, in which the prophet Amos criticizes the complacency of those who live indolent, comfortable existences: "woe to them that are at ease in Zion." *It was a long time since the regiment had seen* *action. The general accused them of having grown soft, living at ease in Zion. See also* ZION.

Athena (ăthēenă) Personification of female wisdom and civilization. Known as Minerva by the Romans, Athena was depicted in Greek mythology as a virgin goddess who embodied practical skills and prudence in warfare. She was identified as the patron goddess of Athens (the city being named after her) and sided with the Greeks in the Trojan War. Legend had it that she was not born but sprang fully armed from the head of Zeus. *She held court at her mansion like some Athena presiding over the doings of lesser mortals. See also* PALLADIUM.

Atlantis (atlăntis) A fabled lost city or land. The name was first applied to a lost continent described by Plato (c. 427–c. 347 B.C.) in *Timaeus* and *Critias* that was home to a great civilization existing some 9,000 years before the emergence of ancient Greece. According to legend, Atlantis sank beneath the waters of the east Atlantic, destroyed by earthquakes and floods as punishment for the wickedness of its citizens. It has been suggested that this lost land of fable may have been inspired by the Canary Islands or the Azores. "As for Owen Ford, the 'Margaret' of his book, although she had the soft brown hair and elfin face of the real girl who had vanished so long ago, 'pillowed where lost Atlantis sleeps,' had the personality of Leslie Moore, as it was revealed to him in those halcyon days at Four Winds Harbor" (Lucy Maud Montgomery, *Anne's House of Dreams,* 1917).

atlas (atlăs) A book of maps. The word refers to Greek mythology, specifically to Atlas, one of the Titans who attempted to overthrow Zeus. When the rebellion was defeated, Atlas was condemned to support the heavens upon his shoulders as punishment. One legend had it that he was transformed into the Atlas Mountains in northern Africa after Perseus, offended at Atlas's refusal to offer him hospitality, showed him the head of Medusa and turned him to stone. Any person who has to bear a heavy burden may be dubbed an Atlas or said to have **Atlantean shoulders.** The association with cartography dates from 1595, when maps compiled by Rumold Mercator included a depiction of Atlas supporting the earth on the title page. "Maple White Land it became, and so it is named in that chart which has become my special task. So it will, I trust, appear in the atlas of the future" (Sir Arthur Conan Doyle, *The Lost World,* 1912).

Atreus *See* HOUSE OF ATREUS.

Atropos *See* FATES.

at the eleventh hour At the last moment; in the nick of time. The expression is biblical in origin, appearing in Matthew 20:1–16, which relates the parable of the laborers in the vineyard and describes how workers who started work at the 11th hour received the same payment as those who had begun much earlier. "I am not easily shocked; and I can be implicitly trusted.' I hesitated even now, at the eleventh hour, sitting alone with him in his own room" (Wilkie Collins, *Armadale,* 1866).

at the Greek calends (ka̲lendz) Never. The CALENDS marked the first day of the month in the Roman calendar. (They were unknown to the Greeks.) *He promised to repay the loan "at the Greek calends" and disappeared before anyone could ask when that might be.*

attic The space beneath the roof of a building. The word has its origins in the Attic style of architecture developed in ancient Athens (Attica) in the classical era. It acquired its modern meaning in the 18th century when Attic-style pilasters were widely used to decorate the outer walls of upper stories of classical facades. *Attic salt* describes a refined, biting wit, alluding to the reputation for sophisticated wit possessed by the inhabitants of ancient Attica. *Attic faith* is synonymous with trustworthiness or dependability, a reflection of how ancient Athenians believed themselves honorable and civilized. "'I see well enough you're going to get that old dress suit out of the cedar chest in the attic, and try to make me put it on me'" (Booth Tarkington, *Alice Adams,* 1921).

Attila the Hun (ă̲tĭlă) Nickname for someone who behaves in a barbaric, cruel, and destructive manner. The historical Attila the Hun (A.D. c. 406–453) was the leader of the Huns, a nomadic people from central Asia who ravaged swaths of the Roman Empire in the fifth century, causing great destruction and loss of life. He was eventually defeated by the

Romans and Visigoths at Châlons-sur-Marne. *The heart of the city became a wasteland, as if the contract for redeveloping it had been given by mistake to Attila the Hun.*

Augean stables *See* LABORS OF HERCULES.

August The eighth month of the year. The name comes from the Roman emperor Octavian (63 B.C.–A.D. 14), who was granted the title Augustus (meaning "venerable") by the senate in recognition of his life's work. He named August after himself in imitation of his predecessor Julius Caesar, who had renamed July in his own honor. In order that Augustus's month should have no fewer days than Caesar's, he transferred one day from February to August so that both July and August would have 31 days. *By noon the day was as sultry as August, but she still felt a chill in her heart.*

Augustan Age (ogăstăn) A time of great prosperity and cultural achievement. The allusion is to the reign of the first Roman emperor, Augustus Caesar (63 B.C.–A.D. 14), which witnessed a great flowering of the arts and commerce in the peace following lengthy civil war. Notable products of this golden era included the building of many roads and aqueducts, the rebuilding of Rome, and the creation of many fine sculptures and literary masterpieces, among them the works of Horace, Ovid, and Virgil. In modern usage, the term is often employed in reference to literature (for instance, that of early 18th-century England). "You will perceive that I demand something which no Augustan nor Elizabethan age, which no culture, in short, can give" (Henry David Thoreau, *Walking,* 1851).

aurora (orŏră) Atmospheric phenomenon in which bands or curtains of light move across the sky in polar regions (called the *aurora australis* over the South Pole and the *aurora borealis* over the North Pole). The phenomenon was named after Aurora, the Roman goddess of the dawn, equivalent to Eos in Greek mythology. The term is also used as a poetic description of the dawn. "It was morning; and the beautiful Aurora, of whom so much hath been written, said, and sung, did, with her rosy fingers, nip and tweak Miss Pecksniff's nose" (Charles Dickens, *Martin Chuzzlewit,* 1843).

Autolycus (o<u>to</u>likăs) Archetype of a cunning thief. Autolycus was identified in Greek mythology as the son of Hermes and grandfather of Odysseus and had a reputation as a crafty robber, being able to change the appearance of the property he stole. He attempted to refute charges that he had stolen the cattle of Sisyphus by changing their color but was undone by the fact that Sisyphus had marked his cattle under their feet. A pickpocket named Autolycus is a character in William Shakespeare's *The Winter's Tale* (1609). This Autolycus was well known by the local police, who had arrested him on countless occasions in the past for petty larceny of one form or another.

avenging angel Person bent on exacting retribution. According to Judeo-Christian tradition, the avenging angels, whose task it was to punish those who broke the laws of God, were among the first angels created by God. Twelve in number, they included Gabriel, Michael, Nathanael, Raphael, Satanel, and Uriel. "Harry smiled blandly till they were well on the pavement, saying some nothing, and keeping the victim's face averted from the avenging angel; and then, when the raised hand was sufficiently nigh, he withdrew two steps towards the nearest lamp-post" (Anthony Trollope, *Doctor Thorne*, 1858).

Avernus (ăv<u>er</u>năs) Hell; the underworld. In Roman mythology, a cave beside the volcanic lake of Avernus in Campania, central Italy, was identified as the entrance to the underworld and thus the name of the lake became synonymous with hell itself. The name itself means "without birds," a reference to the ancient belief that the sulphurous exhalations of the lake killed any birds flying in the area. Avernus is often referred to in the context of a line from Virgil's *Aeneid* (30–19 B.C.), *"Facilis descensus Averno"* (easy is the descent to Avernus). "Little boys at school are taught in their earliest Latin book that the path of Avernus is very easy of descent" (William Makepeace Thackeray, *Vanity Fair*, 1847–48).

Baal (bahl) A false god; an idol. The name, from the Hebrew *ba'al* (meaning "lord"), was originally applied to various ancient Semitic fertility gods and also appeared in Phoenician mythology as the name of the supreme sun god and god of fertility. Baal is identified in the Bible as the false pagan idol to which the Israelites briefly devoted themselves at the prompting of JEZEBEL (1 Kings 16–21). "What had he now brought down upon himself by sojourning thus in the tents of the heathen? He had consorted with idolaters round the altars of Baal, and therefore a sore punishment had come upon him" (Anthony Trollope, *Barchester Towers,* 1857).

Babel *See* TOWER OF BABEL.

babes and sucklings, out of the mouths of *See* OUT OF THE MOUTHS OF BABES AND SUCKLINGS.

Babylon (babilon) A city, place, society, etc., notorious for corruption or depravity. The reference is to the biblical city of Babylon, the wealthy capital of ancient Babylonia on the Euphrates River. In the New Testament, Babylon is a symbol for a prosperous human society that has no time for God. Its fall is described in Revelation 18. Many cities have since been identified as modern Babylons. "There is iron-dust on everything; and the smoke is seen through the windows rolling heavily out of the tall chimneys to mingle with the smoke from a vaporous Babylon of other chimneys" (Charles Dickens, *Bleak House,* 1852–53). *See also* BABYLONIAN CAPTIVITY; BABYLONIAN NUMBERS; WHORE OF BABYLON.

Babylonian captivity (babilōneeǎn) A lengthy period of exile or subjugation. The original Babylonian captivity was the time the Jews spent in exile in Babylon in the years 587–538 B.C. (2 Kings 25). The term was subsequently revived to describe the period of exile of the popes to Avignon in the years 1309–77, during which time they were dominated by the French monarchy and presided over a corrupt, materialist court. *He spent the next five years in a kind of willing Babylonian captivity, submitting himself to her every whim.*

Babylonian numbers (babilōneeăn) The involved and unreliable forecasts of astrologers and fortune-tellers. The phrase comes from a quotation from Horace's *Odes* (24–13 B.C.), which in translation reads, "Do not make trial of Babylonian calculations." In classical times Babylonian astrologers were considered among the most sophisticated of their kind. *Her interest in what are sometimes termed Babylonian numbers quickly exasperated her entourage.*

Baca, Valley of *See* VALE OF TEARS.

Bacchae *See* BACCHANTE.

bacchanalia (bakănaylyă) A drunken orgy; any outburst of dissolute, riotous behavior. The word alludes to the orgiastic celebrations that took place in ancient Rome in honor of BACCHUS, the god of wine (himself the equivalent of the Greek god Dionysus). Celebrants abandoned themselves to all manner of licentious excess, including singing, dancing, drinking, and unrestrained sexual indulgence. The festival, which was imported to Rome around 200 B.C., was banned by the Senate in 186 B.C. "The learned profession of the law was certainly not behind any other learned profession in its Bacchanalian propensities" (Charles Dickens, *A Tale of Two Cities,* 1859). *See also* BACCHANTE.

bacchante (băkantee) A drunken female reveler. In ancient Rome the bacchantes, also known as *bacchae* or *maenads,* were women who followed BACCHUS, the god of wine, and were notorious for their indulgence, sexual immorality, and drunkenness—central features of the celebrations known as the BACCHANALIA. (The male form of the word is *bacchant,* but the female form is far more common.) "The praise of folly, as he went on, soared into a philosophy, and Philosophy herself became young, and catching the mad music of Pleasure, wearing, one might fancy, her wine-stained robe and wreath of ivy, danced like a Bacchante over the hills of life, and mocked the slow Silenus for being sober" (Oscar Wilde, *The Picture of Dorian Gray,* 1891).

Bacchus (bak̆ăs) The god of wine and thus, by extension, of any alcoholic drink. Bacchus was the son of Zeus and Semele and the Roman equivalent of Dionysus, the Greek god of wine. He was variously depicted as a bearded, merry man or as a beautiful youth crowned with vines and ivy. Those who imbibe too enthusiastically may be termed *sons of Bacchus* or *priests of Bacchus.* "Raphael's face was found boldly executed on the underside of the moulding board, and Bacchus on the head of a beer barrel" (Louisa May Alcott, *Little Women,* 1868). *See also* BACCHA-NALIA; BACCHANTE.

Balaam's ass (baylamz) Someone or something that serves to remind a person of the correct way to act. The allusion is to the biblical story of Balaam, a Mesopotamian prophet who was commanded by Balak, king of Moab, to curse the Israelites. Balaam set out to do the king's bidding, but on the prompting of his talking donkey prophesied instead future glory for them (as related at Numbers 22–23). People who follow a religion for reasons of profit or gain are sometimes dubbed *Balaamites.* "'By my hilt!' cried the archer, 'I though I be not Balaam, yet I hold converse with the very creature that spake to him'" (Sir Arthur Conan Doyle, *The White Company,* 1891).

balm in Gilead (gileead) A remedy or consolation in times of trouble. The allusion is to Jeremiah 8:22, in which God laments that his people are not yet healed of their sins: "Is there no balm in Gilead; is there no physician there?" There is another reference to Gilead in Genesis 37:25 that runs, "Behold, a company of Ishmeelites came from Gilead with their camels bearing spicery and balm and myrrh, going to carry it down to Egypt." Gilead is the name of a desolate region east of the Jordan, which was well known for the production of aromatic herbs and balm, a resin extracted from the mastic tree *Pistacia lentiscus* and noted for its medicinal properties. "'My garden was all smashed flat,' he continued mournfully, 'but so was Dora's,' he added in a tone which indicated that there was yet balm in Gilead" (Lucy Maud Montgomery, *Anne of Avonlea,* 1908).

balthazar (<u>bal</u>thăzahr) A large wine bottle equivalent to 16 standard bottles. The allusion is to King BELSHAZZAR, who provided huge quantities of wine for guests at a great banquet (*see* BELSHAZZAR'S FEAST). *It is many years since balthazars of fine wine were supplied to the restaurant on a regular basis in advance of royal visits.* See also MAGI.

baptism of fire An arduous initiation or introduction to something. The phrase was coined by early Christians in referring to the spiritual purification given by the presence of the Holy Spirit at the time of Pentecost (Acts 2:1–4). "New Environment Secretary, Mr Tom King, faces a baptism of fire over his decision to withdraw and re-draft the latest rules on council spending" (*Guardian,* January 14, 1983).

Barabbas (Băr<u>ab</u>ăas) A criminal who evades punishment for his crimes. According to Matthew 27:16 and John 18:40, Barabbas was a thief condemned to be crucified at Passover time. At the public crucifixion, the mob was, by long-established custom, offered the choice of one of the men to be pardoned; the group chose Barabbas. He is variously described in the books of Luke and Mark as a seditionist or murderer. Jocularly he is sometimes thought of as a publisher, an identification attributed to the English poet Lord Byron. The story goes that Byron was presented with a beautiful edition of the Bible by his publisher John Murray, but the poet returned the gift after having changed the word *robber* ("Now Barabbas was a robber," John 18:40) to *publisher. Like some latter-day Barabbas, he had successfully hoodwinked the courts and spent much of his adult life enjoying moneyed freedom in the Seychelles.*

Barathron (băr<u>ath</u>răn) A place where garbage is dumped. The original Barathron, or **Barathrum,** was a deep ditch behind the Acropolis in Athens into which criminals were thrown to their death. *The alley was a veritable Barathron, full of all description of trash.*

barbarian A brutish, uncivilized person. The term was coined by the ancient Greeks, who called anyone who could not speak Greek *barbaros* (because the unintelligible Germanic dialects of many such people sounded like "bar-bar-bar" to the Greek ear). In due course the term came to be applied to the cultures of such foreign peoples in general. ". . . a silly, painful, and disgusting ceremony, which can only be considered as a relic of barbarian darkness, which tears the knees and shins to pieces, let alone the pantaloons" (William Makepeace Thackeray, *Adventures of Major Gahagan,* 1839).

Bashan, bull of   *See* BULL OF BASHAN.

basilisk stare   (ba̅sălisk; ba̱zălisk)   A cold stare; a glance that exerts a profound, even deadly influence over the person at whom it is directed. The basilisk (virtually synonymous with the COCKATRICE) was a serpent of mythological origin, hatched by a reptile from the egg of a cock and reputed to be able to kill its victim with a mere glance or with the exhalation of its breath. In modern usage, the word *basilisk* may refer to any example of the genus *Basiliscus* of tropical America, which includes a variety of small arboreal semiaquatic lizards (the males of which often have an inflatable head crest used in display). "Without softening very much the basiliks nature of his stare, he said, impassively: 'We are coming to that part of my investigation, sir'" (Joseph Conrad, *The Secret Agent,* 1907).

Bathsheba   *See* DAVID AND BATHSHEBA.

batrachomyomachia   (bătrako̅mi̅o̅makeeă)   A great deal of fuss about something trivial; much ado about nothing. The word, which means "the battle of the frogs and mice," originated as the title of a mock heroic epic formerly attributed to Homer (eighth century B.C.) but more probably is the work of Pigres of Caria (c. fourth century B.C.). *Billed as an epic struggle, the contest turned out to be more of a batrachomyomachia.*

Baucis   *See* PHILEMON AND BAUCIS.

beam in one's own eye, the   *See* MOTE AND BEAM.

bear/carry/take one's cross   To suffer a trial or affliction patiently. The expression alludes to Christ's words to his disciples: "If any man will come after me, let him deny himself, and take up his cross, and follow me" (Matthew 16:24). "You must try and be strong and bear it bravely. We all have our cross to bear" (Aldous Huxley, *Limbo,* 1920). "'Still, this isn't the time really, is it?' And she smiled, and was carrying her cross ever so bravely really" (G. W. Target, *The Teachers,* 1960).

bear the burden and heat of the day To assume the most laborious or exacting part of a task, particularly in comparison to the lesser efforts of others. The phrase is a quotation from the parable of the vineyard in which Christ compares the differing contributions of the workers, some of whom have worked all day long, while others have arrived much later when the bulk of the work has been done (Matthew 20:1–16). "We do not wish to tax your energies too much. We will bear some of the burden and heat of the day ourselves" (Mark Twain, *The Innocents Abroad,* 1869).

beast with ten horns *See* WHORE OF BABYLON.

beatitude (beeatitood) A blessing, especially one of a formulaic nature. The original Beatitudes were the eight sayings spoken by Christ in the Sermon on the Mount, as recorded at Matthew 5:1–12. In these, Christ promises that the poor in spirit, those who mourn, the meek, those who thirst for righteousness, the merciful, the pure in heart, the peacemakers, and those who are persecuted for righteousness's sake will receive the blessing of heaven. "Indeed, throughout all the great soft-coal country, people who consider themselves comparatively poor may find this consolation: cleanliness has been added to the virtues and beatitudes that money can not buy" (Booth Tarkington, *Alice Adams,* 1921). *See also* MEEK SHALL INHERIT THE EARTH, THE.

beat swords into plowshares To make peace; to adapt the weapons of war for peaceful purposes. The phrase is biblical in origin, appearing in Isaiah 2:4 (and also Micah 4:3), as follows: "And he shall judge among the nations, and shall rebuke many people: and they shall beat their swords into plowshares, and their spears into pruninghooks: nation shall not lift up sword against nation, neither shall they learn war any more." The same imagery recurs at Joel 3:10, but with the reverse meaning: "Beat your plowshares into swords." *On the surface, this latest nuclear disarmament treaty amounts to the most determined attempt in recent years to beat the swords of the two superpowers into plowshares.*

bed of Procrustes *See* PROCRUSTEAN.

Beelzebub (bee<u>e</u>lzebăb) A devil, demon, or very wicked person. Beelzebub is identified in 2 Kings 1:2 as a god of the Philistines and is listed in the Bible as one of the devil's closest allies—sometimes his name is even used as a synonym for SATAN. The word comes from the Hebrew *ba'al zebub* (originally meaning "lord of the heavenly habitation" but later reinterpreted as meaning "lord of the flies"). "Had this history been writ in the days of superstition, I should have had too much compassion for the reader to have left him so long in suspense, whether Beelzebub or Satan was about actually to appear in person, with all his hellish retinue; but as these doctrines are at present very unfortunate, and have but few, if any believers, I have not been much aware of conveying any such terrors" (Henry Fielding, *Tom Jones,* 1749).

before the Flood *See* FLOOD.

be fruitful and multiply To prosper, usually as measured by the production of offspring. The phrase is a quotation from Genesis 1:28, in which God commands Adam to "be fruitful, and multiply, and replenish the earth." It appears once again in Genesis 9:1, in which God repeats the instruction to Noah. The phrase is sometimes cited in defense of arguments against contraception or clerical celibacy. The expression is also found as *go forth and multiply,* in allusion to God's words to Noah: "Go forth of the ark, thou, and thy wife, and thy sons, and thy sons' wives with thee. Bring forth with thee every living thing that *is* with thee, of all flesh both of fowl, and of cattle, and of every creeping thing that creepeth upon the earth; that they may breed abundantly in the earth, and be fruitful, and multiply upon the earth" (Genesis 8:16–17). *The settlers took their duty to be fruitful and multiply very seriously and within five years their small community had doubled in number.*

beginning was the Word, in the *See* IN THE BEGINNING WAS THE WORD.

behemoth (bihee măth) A huge beast or thing. The name appears in Job 40:15–24, where it probably refers to a hippopotamus (although when John Milton described the behemoth in *Paradise Lost* he clearly had an elephant in mind). The word itself comes from the plural form of the Hebrew *behemah* (meaning "beast"). "Adolph tripped gracefully forward, and Tom, with lumbering tread, went after. 'He's a perfect behemoth!' said Marie" (Harriet Beecher Stowe, *Uncle Tom's Cabin,* 1852). *See also* LEVIATHAN.

behold the man *See* ECCE HOMO.

Belial (beeleeăl) Archetypal demon; a personification of wickedness or lawlessness. The word is mentioned several times in the Old Testament, where it is synonymous with "worthlessness" (1 Samuel 1:16 and 2 Samuel 25:17), and is also used in the New Testament as another name for SATAN (2 Corinthians 6:15). John Milton identified Belial in *Paradise Lost* as one of the fallen angels: "Belial came last, than whom a spirit more lewd / Fell not from heaven." The word itself comes from the Hebrew *beliy* (meaning "without") and *ya'al* (meaning "worth"). Rebellious, lawbreaking people are sometimes referred to as *sons of Belial.* "The Presbyterian sternly raised his eyes. 'After the world, and according to the flesh, she is my daughter; but when she became a child of Belial, and a company-keeper, and a trader in guilt and iniquity, she ceased to be a bairn of mine'" (Sir Walter, Scott, *The Heart of Midlothian,* 1818).

Bellerophon *See* LETTER OF BELLEROPHON.

bell the cat To undertake a dangerous mission. The allusion is to the fable attributed to the Greek writer AESOP (c. 620–564 B.C.) that relates how some mice agreed that it would be a good idea to hang a bell around a cat's neck so that they would know when it was approaching but were then faced with the daunting question of who should attempt to attach the bell in the first place. ". . . as he was made of sterner stuff than they, so would it be more difficult to reconcile him to the alterations which were now proposed in the family arrangements. Who was to bell the cat?" (Anthony Trollope, *Ayala's Angel,* 1881).

Belphegor (belfegor) Archetype of a misanthropic lecher. He is identified in Numbers 25:3 as the Assyrian version of BAAL, the pagan god whose veneration took the form of licentious orgies. In later medieval legend

Belphegor was identified as a demon who was sent to earth to investigate the realities of marital bliss. Having probed the truths behind married life, Belphegor fled earth to escape the horrors of female companionship. *After his divorce, he assumed the mantle of Belphegor, muttering darkly about the vagaries of woman and avoiding all contact with the fairer sex.*

Belshazzar (belshazăr) A corrupt or decadent ruler, especially one who is threatened by imminent disaster. The reference is to the biblical Belshazzar, who was the last Chaldean king of Babylon (Daniel 5). His name literally means "Bel protect the king." "To have been Belshazzar, King of Babylon; and to have been Belshazzar, not haughtily but courteously, therein certainly must have been some touch of mundane grandeur" (Herman Melville, *Moby-Dick,* 1851). *See also* BALTHAZAR; BELSHAZZAR'S FEAST; BELSHAZZAR'S PALSY; WRITING ON THE WALL.

Belshazzar's feast (belshazărz) An example of decadent indulgence. The allusion is to the banquet hosted by Belshazzar, who was the last Chaldean king of Babylon, as described in Daniel 5. The feast, attended by a thousand nobles, was remarkable for the magnificence of the gold and silver utensils, which had been seized from the Temple in Jerusalem. "'I always like this room,' said Spandrell as they entered. 'It's like a scene for Belshazzar's feast'" (Aldous Huxley, *Point Counter Point,* 1928). *See also* BELSHAZZAR'S PALSY; WRITING ON THE WALL.

Belshazzar's palsy (belshazărz) A fever, especially one caused by fear. The allusion is to the episode of BELSHAZZAR'S FEAST, a magnificent banquet hosted by BELSHAZZAR, king of Babylon, at which the WRITING ON THE WALL appeared. The shock caused Belshazzar to be seized by a shaking fever, as described at Daniel 5:6: ". . . his thoughts troubled him, so that the joints of his loins were loosed, and his knees smote one against another." *The effect of this news upon the general was startling. His face went deathly pale and his hands shook uncontrollably. Though no doctor, the priest was inclined to diagnose a severe case of Belshazzar's palsy.*

Benjamin (benjămin) The youngest, favorite son in a family. The allusion is to the biblical Benjamin, who is identified in Genesis as the youngest and most loved son of Jacob and Rachel and the brother of Joseph. When

Joseph provides a feast for Jacob's sons, Benjamin is offered five times as much as his other brothers; hence, the largest share of something may be called **Benjamin's mess.** "He got up, put the cage on the table, and paused for a moment to count the mice in it. 'One, two, three, four—Ha!' he cried, with a look of horror, 'where, in the name of Heaven, is the fifth—the youngest, the whitest, the most amiable of all—my Benjamin of mice!'" (Wilkie Collins, *The Woman in White,* 1860).

Beowulf (ba̯yăwălf) Archetypal warrior hero. Beowulf is the central character in an Old English epic poem of unknown authorship dating from the early eighth century. Set in Denmark or Sweden, the Germanic tale relates how the warrior Beowulf volunteers to kill the dreadful monster Grendel, who has been making nightly raids upon the court of King Hrothgar. After a ferocious struggle Grendel is killed, but the following night Beowulf has to do battle with Grendel's equally formidable mother, who seeks revenge for her son's death. Beowulf triumphs and in due course becomes king. Ultimately, many years later, he dies in combat with a dragon. *To his followers he seemed like a warrior from a long past age, a Jason or a Beowulf perhaps.*

berserk (bă̱zerk) Frenzied; uncontrollably violent or destructive. The term was first applied to certain ferocious Norse warriors, who customarily worked themselves up into a wild frenzy before going into battle, often without armor. They were sometimes identified as the descendants of Berserk. The word itself comes from the Icelandic *björn* (bear) and *serkr* (shirt), a reference to the fact that the berserks were often clad in bearskins. "The Professor, with his face flushed, his nostrils dilated, and his beard bristling, was now in a proper berserk mood" (Sir Arthur Conan Doyle, *The Lost World,* 1912).

bethel (bethăl) A Nonconformist chapel. The word comes from the Hebrew *beth El,* meaning "house of God," and appears in Genesis 28:19 as the name of the town on the west bank of the Jordan River where Jacob had his dream about God and heaven. "His family was a little Bethel, for the Worship of God constantly and exactly maintained in it" (Cotton Mather, "The Life of John Eliot," 1702).

Bethesda, pool of *See* RISE, TAKE UP THY BED, AND WALK.

better a dinner of herbs than a stalled ox where hate is It is better to be poor or to eat modest fare among friends than to be rich or to eat well in hostile surroundings. The saying comes from the Bible, appearing in Proverbs 15:17: "Better is a dinner of herbs where love is, than a stalled ox and hatred therewith." "Well has Solomon said—'Better is a dinner of herbs where love is, than a stalled ox and hatred therewith.' I would not now have exchanged Lowood with all its privations for Gateshead and its daily luxuries" (Charlotte Brontë, *Jane Eyre*, 1847).

better to give than to receive *See* IT IS BETTER TO GIVE THAN TO RECEIVE.

better to marry than to burn It is preferable to enjoy the satisfactions of marriage than to be tortured by inappropriate passions as an unmarried person. This proverbial advice is of biblical origin, a quotation of Paul (himself a bachelor), as recorded in 1 Corinthians 7:8–9: "I say therefore to the unmarried and widows, It is good for them if they abide even as I. But if they cannot contain, let them marry: for it is better to marry than to burn." "'It is better to marry than to burn,' says St Paul, where we may see what it is that chiefly drives men into the enjoyments of a conjugal life" (John Locke, *Essay Concerning Human Understanding*, 1690).

between Scylla and Charybdis (silǎ, kǎribdis) Having to confront one or the other of two equally dangerous hazards. The allusion is to Greek mythology and the Strait of Messina. Scylla aroused the jealousy of the goddess Amphitrite by attracting the amorous attentions of Amphitrite's husband, Poseidon. Transformed by Amphitrite into a monster with six dogs' heads, each with three rows of teeth, Scylla made her home in a cave in the Strait of Messina directly opposite the abode of the equally horrific Charybdis, who was the daughter of Poseidon and Gaea and had been turned into a monster by Zeus. Any vessel that passed between the two was likely to be attacked and the sailors devoured; the more they tried to evade one threat, the more likely they were to fall prey to the other. In more prosaic terms, Scylla was identified as a vast promontory of rock, while Charybdis was described as a whirlpool. *Louis considered which woman to choose, feeling himself caught like a hapless seaman between Scylla and Charybdis.*

Beulah *See* LAND OF BEULAH.

beware of Greeks bearing gifts Do not trust gifts or favors if they come from an enemy. This advice has its roots in the story of the TROJAN HORSE, the treacherous subterfuge by which the Greeks finally overcame their Trojan adversaries at the end of the Trojan War. It is occasionally encountered in its Latin form *timeo Danaos et dona ferentes* (meaning "I fear the Greeks, even when they offer gifts"). *This offer of the Democrats looks suspicious to their opponents, a case of "beware of Greeks bearing gifts."*

bible An authoritative book or other source of information. The word is most familiar as the name for the collected sacred writings of Christianity, consisting of the Old and New Testaments and in certain versions the Apocrypha. The word itself comes from the Greek *biblion* (meaning "book"), which in turn derives from *biblos* (meanings "papyrus"), named after Bublos, the Phoenician port where the Greeks obtained Egyptian papyrus. *This pamphlet is a bible for everyone in the motivational seminar industry.*

Bibulus (<u>bi</u>byoolǎs) An idler; an office holder who does no actual work. The allusion is to Bibulus, an ally of Julius Caesar who held high office but acted merely as a cipher for his friend. *The deputy president of the company is widely regarded as a yes-man for the board, a real Bibulus.*

birthright, sell one's *See* SELL ONE'S BIRTHRIGHT FOR A MESS OF POTTAGE.

blessed are the meek *See* MEEK SHALL INHERIT THE EARTH, THE.

blind leading the blind A situation in which those who show the way are as misguided or ignorant as those they lead. The phrase appears in Matthew 15:14, in which Christ responds to the suggestion that he has offended the Pharisees: "Let them alone: they be blind leaders of the blind. And if the blind lead the blind, both shall fall into the ditch." It is also used in Luke 6:39. "The staff of the Archaeological Department are insufficiently trained by precept and experience—indeed as regards the students and junior members it is a case of the blind leading the blind, and the quality of the department is likely to deteriorate progressively" (Mortimer Wheeler, *Still Digging,* 1955). "Neil Hannon's 20s coincided with the 1990s when the bland led the bland" (*The Guardian,* October 22, 2001).

blood crieth from the ground The guilt of those who have committed murder or other acts of violence cannot be concealed. The expression is a quotation from Genesis 4:10, in which God confronts Cain after the latter has put his brother Able to death: "What hast thou done? the voice of thy brother's blood crieth unto me from the ground." "In the book that our teachers worship I have heard it read, that the voice of blood crieth from the ground! This is the voice—Hermanric, this is the voice that I have heard! I have dreamed that I walked on a shore of corpses, by a sea of blood!" (Wilkie Collins, *Antonina,* 1850). *See also* BLOOD WILL HAVE BLOOD.

blood for blood *See* BLOOD WILL HAVE BLOOD.

blood of the lamb *See* WASHED IN THE BLOOD OF THE LAMB.

blood will have blood Violence breeds violence. In this form the proverb dates from the 16th century, but it is of biblical origin, appearing in Genesis 9:6: "Whoso sheddeth man's blood, by man shall his blood be shed." A variant form is *blood for blood.* "It will have blood; they say blood will have blood" (William Shakespeare, *Macbeth,* 1606).

Boadicea *See* BOUDICCA.

Boanerges (boănerjeez) A fiery preacher or orator; any man with a tempestuous nature. The allusion is to the apostles James and John, the sons of Zebedee, who in Mark 3:17 were dubbed Boanerges—meaning "sons of thunder"—by Christ in acknowledgment of either their impassioned calls for retribution against the Samaritans after they rejected Christ or their generally turbulent temperaments. "At first she resisted, and told him she was not used to be taken to task by her confessors. But he overpowered her, and so threatened her with the Church's curse here and hereafter, and so tore the scales off her eyes, and thundered at her, and crushed her, that she sank down and grovelled with remorse and terror at the feet of the gigantic Boanerges" (Charles Reade, *The Cloister and the Hearth,* 1861).

Boeotian (beeōshăn) Dimwitted, stupid, uneducated. The allusion is to Boeotia, a rural region of ancient Greece whose inhabitants were reputed to be very slow witted (supposedly caused by the cloyingly damp climate of their homeland). By the same token any person suspected of lacking any sensitivity toward music was accused of having **Boeotian ears.** Contrary to their reputation, however, the Boeotians included among their number such intellectual luminaries as Hesiod, Pindar, and Plutarch. "At the same time, who can avoid smiling at the earnestness and Boeotian simplicity (if indeed there be not an underhand satire in it), with which that 'Incident' is here brought forward . . .'" (Thomas Carlyle, *Sartor Resartus,* 1833–34).

bone of my bones *See* FLESH OF MY FLESH.

bones, dry *See* VALLEY OF DRY BONES.

book of life Life itself, the experience of living, or a record of how a life has been spent. The original Book of Life, in which the names and deeds of those who will be saved on JUDGMENT DAY are listed, is described in Revelation 3:5, 20:12–15, and 21:27. It is also sometimes called the **book of fate.** "Now, Mr Copperfield, I hope that you will not render it necessary for me to open, even for a quarter of an hour, that closed page in the book of life, and unsettle, even for a quarter of an hour, grave affairs long since composed" (Charles Dickens, *David Copperfield,* 1849–50).

books, of making many *See* OF MAKING MANY BOOKS.

boreal (<u>bor</u>eeăl) Pertaining to the north; cold, bleak. The word has its origins in Boreas, who was identified in Greek mythology as the god of the north wind. He was the son of Astraeus (one of the Titans) and Eos (the goddess of the dawn) and the brother of Zephyrus (the west wind), Notus (the south wind), and Eurus (the east wind). He was said to live in a cave on Mount Haemus in Thrace. "He knew, and she knew, that, though the fascination which each had exercised over the other—on her part independently of accomplishments—would probably in the first days of their separation be even more potent than ever, time must attenuate that effect; the practical arguments against accepting her as a housemate might pronounce themselves more strongly in the boreal light of a remoter view" (Thomas Hardy, *Tess of the D'Urbervilles,* 1891).

born-again Of or relating to conversion to a particular cause, often specifically referring to a renewed zeal for the Christian faith. The term has biblical origins, appearing in John 3:3 in Christ's explanation to Nicodemus that only by being reborn spiritually could he reach heaven: "Verily, verily, I say unto thee, Except a man be born again, he cannot see the kingdom of God." "They take the risk of financial insecurity in order to be born again workers" (*The Guardian,* December 7, 1984).

bottomless pit A person, project, or other entity that consumes an apparently endless supply of money or other resources; a pit or hole that seems to have no end. In its original biblical context the phrase refers to the pit of hell (Revelation 9:1–2, 11), variously identified elsewhere by such epithets as the Abyss or the pit of the dragon. "Now, what is Costaguana? It is the bottomless pit of 10 per cent loans and other fool investments. European capital has been flung into it with both hands for years" (Joseph Conrad, *Nostromo,* 1904).

Boudicca (boodikă) Archetype of a formidable woman. Boudicca (sometimes less accurately called **Boadicea**) was a queen of the Iceni tribe of eastern England, who rose up in revolt against the Roman occupation. She sacked Colchester. London, and St. Albans before being defeated by the Roman legions under Suetonius Paulinus. She committed suicide by taking poison in A.D. 62. *She stormed into the party like some Boudicca on a chariot.*

bowels of compassion The source of a person's sympathy or pity. In biblical times the bowels were commonly believed to be the seat of a person's emotions, as illustrated by 1 John 3:17: "Whose hath this world's good, and seeth his brother have need, and shutteth up his bowels of compassion from him, how dwelleth the love of God in him?" Other examples include 2 Corinthians 6:12; Colossians 3:12. Jeremiah in his sorrows laments, "My bowels! My bowels!" (4:19), and Job in his mental suffering similarly complains, "My bowels boiled" (30:27). Thus, to **shut up the bowels of compassion** is to behave without compassion or mercy. "It is the proper language—working upon her father's bowels of compassion. Fathers always have bowels of compassion at last" (Anthony Trollope, *Ayala's Angel,* 1881).

brand of Cain *See* MARK OF CAIN.

brave men before Agamemnon, there were (agămemnon) No person, place, or era has a monopoly on achievement or glory. The saying is a quotation from the *Odes* of the Roman poet Horace (65–8 B.C.), whose original Latin version ran *"Vixere fortes ante Agamemnona."* In Greek mythology, Agamemnon was the king of Mycenae who led the Greeks during the Trojan War. *The current national squad are being hailed as the best ever to represent the country, but there were brave men before Agamemnon.*

bread alone, by *See* MAN CANNOT LIVE BY BREAD ALONE.

bread and circuses Food and entertainment as means to keep the masses content. The cynical notion that a populace provided with plenty of free food and entertainment *(panem et circenses)* would never rise up in revolt was familiar to the ancient Romans, as evidenced by the writing of the satirist Juvenal (A.D. c. 55/60–127): "People long eagerly for two things . . . bread and circuses." Successive emperors sponsored spectacles in the circuses of Rome in the belief that these superficial palliatives would preserve them from the anger of the mob over more serious issues. *TV dinners and Monday night football, it has been cynically suggested by observers, are the bread and circuses with which the masses are kept in their place in modern society.*

bread cast upon the waters *See* CAST THY BREAD UPON THE WATERS.

bread of affliction Suffering or trouble. This metaphor is biblical in origin, appearing in 1 Kings 22:27 and in 2 Chronicles 18:26: "Feed him with bread of affliction and with water of affliction." "When I reflect, Brother Toby, upon Man; and take a view of that dark side of him which represents his life as open to so many causes of trouble—when I consider, brother Toby, how oft we eat the bread of affliction, and that we are born to it, as to the portion of our inheritance—I was born to nothing, quoth my uncle Toby, interrupting my father—but my commission" (Laurence Sterne, *Tristram Shandy,* 1759–67).

break Priscian's head (prishănz) To break the rules of grammar. The allusion is to Priscianus Caesariensis, a Roman grammarian of the sixth century

A.D. "Some free from rhyme or reason, rule or check, / Break Priscian's head and Pegasus's neck" (Alexander Pope, *The Dunciad,* 1728).

breath of life Life or something considered as essential as life itself. According to the book of Genesis, God brought Adam to life literally by breathing life into him: "And the LORD God formed man of the dust of the ground, and breathed into his nostrils the breath of life; and man became a living soul" (Genesis 2:7). "Ah, but she won't abandon you. Poetry and art are the breath of life to her. It is poetry you write, Mr Winsett?" (Edith Wharton, *The Age of Innocence,* 1920).

bricks without straw Work that is expected to be done under difficult conditions or without the necessary tools or materials. The phrase refers to the biblical incident in which Pharaoh refused to provide the Hebrews with the straw they needed to make bricks, insisting that they find it themselves: "And Pharaoh commanded the same day the taskmasters of the people . . . saying, Ye shall no more give the people straw to make brick, as heretofore: let them go and gather straw for themselves" (Exodus 5:6–7). Bricks made with mud from the Nile had to include straw to prevent them from cracking as they dried. *The union complained that as a result of the cutbacks, their members were effectively being asked to make bricks without straw.*

brimstone and fire *See* FIRE AND BRIMSTONE.

broad is the way *See* STRAIGHT AND NARROW.

broken reed A weak or damaged person or thing. The phrase is biblical in origin. In Isaiah 36:6 King Hezekiah is advised not to trust the Egyptians: "Lo, thou trustest in the staff of this broken reed, on Egypt; whereon if a man lean, it will go into his hand, and pierce it." In Matthew 12:20 Christ echoes this passage in his words "A bruised reed shall he not break." "'God help thee, my son! He can help when worldly trust is a broken reed.'— Such was the welcome of the matron to her unfortunate grandson" (Sir Walter Scott, *The Black Dwarf,* 1816).

brother's keeper *See* MY BROTHER'S KEEPER.

bruised reed *See* BROKEN REED.

Brute *See* ET TU, BRUTE?

Bucephalus (byoo<u>se</u>fălăs) Archetype of a noble, courageous horse. Bucephalus was the name of the horse that Alexander the Great rode in the course of his celebrated military campaigns. Legend has it that only Alexander proved capable of breaking the horse, whose name—from *bous,* meaning "ox," and *kephale,* meaning "head"—referred to its resemblance to a bull. "Close-reefing top-sails in a gale, there he was, astride the weather yard-arm-end, foot in the Flemish horse as 'stirrup,' both hands tugging at the 'earring' as at a bridle, in very much the attitude of young Alexander curbing the fiery Bucephalus" (Herman Melville, *Billy Budd,* 1924).

bull of Bashan (<u>bash</u>ăn) A very strong or ferocious man; a cruel tyrant. Og was a brutish giant who ruled Bashan, an area east of the Sea of Galilee and famous for its cattle (Deuteronomy 32:14; Psalm 22:12; and Ezekiel 39:18). Og and all his followers were killed in battle against Moses and the Israelites (Deuteronomy 3:1–11). Among the trophies taken by the Israelites after the battle was Og's huge iron bedstead, which measured nine by four cubits (around 13 by 16 feet). To *roar like a bull of Bashan* means to make an excessive noise. ". . . man and steed rushing on each other like wild bulls of Bashan!" (Sir Walter Scott, *Ivanhoe,* 1819).

burden of Isaiah (<u>iza</u>yă) A prophecy of disaster; a complaint against hardships imposed by others. The reference is to ISAIAH's prophecy against Babylon, as described, for example, in 13:1. *He seemed weighed down, as if with the burden of Isaiah, by this realization of the inevitable catastrophe to come.*

burden of Sisyphus *See* SISYPHEAN.

burning bush A source of revelation, especially one of a miraculous nature. The allusion is to the biblical episode concerning the burning bush from which God addressed Moses, as related in Exodus 3:2: "And the angel of the LORD appeared unto him in a flame of fire out of the midst of a bush; and he looked, and behold, the bush burned with fire, and the bush was not consumed." The passage goes on to detail God's instructions to Moses to lead the Israelites out of Egypt and guide them to the Promised Land. The bush has been tentatively identified as a bramble or blackberry bush. The name is now applied to several shrubs or trees with bright red fruits or seeds, as well as to a number of plants with bright red foliage. In medieval times a burning bush was commonly adopted as a symbol of the Virgin Mary. "I think, sir, when God makes His presence felt through us, we are like the burning bush: Moses never took any heed what sort of bush it was—he only saw the brightness of the Lord" (George Eliot, *Adam Bede,* 1859).

burnt offering A jocular reference to an overcooked meal. The allusion is to the various offerings of animals killed and ritually burned, as described in the Old Testament. These included the offering made to God by Noah in Genesis 8:20: "And Noah builded an altar unto the LORD; and took every clean beast, and of every clean fowl, and offered burnt offerings on the altar." "The sleep-walker had wakened to bitter knowledge of love and life, finding himself a failure in both. He had made a burnt offering of his dreams, and the sacrifice had been an unforgivable hurt to Mary" (Booth Tarkington, *The Turmoil,* 1915).

bury the dead *See* LET THE DEAD BURY THE DEAD.

bushel, hide one's light under a *See* HIDE ONE'S LIGHT UNDER A BUSHEL.

buskin Symbol of tragic drama. The buskin, or *cothurnus,* was originally a style of boot with a thick sole that was conventionally worn by performers of tragic roles in the Greek and Roman theater to give actors a few inches of extra height and thus contribute to the grandeur of their performance. "But in that bitter tirade upon Chantilly, which appeared in yesterday's 'Musee,' the satirist, making some disgraceful allusions to the cobbler's change of name upon assuming the buskin, quoted a Latin line about which we have often conversed" (Edgar Allan Poe, "The Murders in the Rue Morgue," 1841). *See also* SOCK.

by bread alone *See* MAN CANNOT LIVE BY BREAD ALONE.

by Jove (jōv) Exclamation of surprise or admiration. The allusion is to the chief Roman god Jupiter, whose Latin name was Jovis. Jupiter was traditionally regarded as a source of good humor, hence the related term *jovial,* meaning "jolly" or "good-humored." "'Oh, by Jove!' said Captain Donnithorne, laughing. 'Why, she looks as quiet as a mouse. There's something rather striking about her, though'" (George Eliot, *Adam Bede,* 1859).

by their fruits ye shall know them *See* FALSE PROPHET.

by the rivers of Babylon (babilon) In exile from a cherished but far-distant place or time. The phrase comes from Psalm 137:1, in which the Israelites in exile in Babylon lamented their lost homeland of ZION: "By the rivers of Babylon, there we sat down, yea, we wept, when we remembered Zion." *The refugees, like the Israelites who wept by the rivers of Babylon, were inconsolable in their lamentations for their lost homeland.*

by the skin of one's teeth *See* SKIN OF ONE'S TEETH, BY THE.

Byzantine (bizănteen; bizăntīn) Labyrinthine, intricate, convoluted, complicated. The allusion is to the intrigue and deviousness that characterized political and bureaucratic dealings in the Byzantine Empire between the time of its foundation in the fourth century A.D. and its dissolution upon invasion by the Turks in 1453. *It took the detectives some considerable time to unravel the Byzantine convolutions of the case, but in due course they conceded reluctantly that they had been pursuing the wrong man.*

C

Cadmean letters (kadmeeăn) The 16 letters of the Greek alphabet. They were named after the legendary Cadmus, king of Phoenicia and Telephassa in Greek mythology, who founded the city of Thebes and was credited with introducing the alphabet to Greece from Phoenicia. *By the end of the term all these young scholars are expected to be familiar with the Cadmean letters and other basics of rhetoric.*

Cadmean victory *See* PYRRHIC VICTORY.

caduceus (kădooseeăs) Emblem of the medical profession: a staff entwined with two serpents. In classical mythology the caduceus was carried by Hermes (or Mercury) as a symbol of his role as messenger of the gods. Such staffs were also traditionally carried by Greek heralds and ambassadors on peace missions. According to legend, the mere touch of this staff could put a person to sleep or revive a corpse. Its adoption as a symbol of medicine relates to its similarity to the STAFF OF AESCULAPIUS. "I had not hopped far before I perceived a tall young gentleman in a silk waistcoat, with a wing on his left heel, a garland on his head, and a caduceus in his right hand" (Henry Fielding, *A Journey from this World to the Next,* 1743).

Caesar (seezer) An emperor, dictator, or other powerful ruler or military commander. The allusion is to the Roman general and statesman Gaius Julius Caesar (100–44 B.C.), who conquered Gaul and Britain before returning to Rome and becoming the effective sole ruler of the Roman state from 49 until his death. He made many important reforms before being assassinated by a group of senators who feared he had become too powerful. After his death, his adopted son and heir Gaius Octavius (later

55

called Augustus) took the name Caesar to help legitimize his reign, and subsequently all Roman emperors up to Hadrian adopted Caesar as a title. The title was revived by rulers of the Holy Roman Empire in the 10th century and became transformed into *kaiser* by the German monarchy. It was also adopted by the Russian royal family, in the form *czar,* and by the Arabs, as *qaysar. The fanfare played, the crowd cheered, and Caesar stepped up to the microphone to address the victorious faithful.* See also CAESAR IS NOT ABOVE THE GRAMMARIANS; CAESAR'S WIFE MUST BE ABOVE SUSPICION; CESAREAN SECTION; I CAME, I SAW, I CONQUERED.

caesarean section *See* CESAREAN SECTION.

Caesar is not above the grammarians (<u>see</u>zer) No one, however exalted his or her rank, can be excused for bad grammar. The reference harks back to the legend of the Roman emperor Tiberius, who was once corrected in his grammar. A courtier purportedly stated that as the emperor had said the mistake, the slip would henceforth be considered good Latin. A grammarian present, however, immediately objected, reminding the emperor, *"Tu enim Caesar civitatem dare potes hominibus, verbis non potes"* ("Caesar, you can grant citizenship to men, but not to words"). *The chief editor sighed and with a rueful smile crossed out what he had written. Even Caesar is not above the grammarians.*

Caesar's wife must be above suspicion (<u>see</u>zerz) People who occupy prominent social positions need to maintain unsullied reputations. The expression alludes to the story of Julius Caesar's second wife, Pompeia, who around 62 B.C. became embroiled in rumors that she was involved in an adulterous affair with the notorious philanderer Publius Clodius. Disguised as a woman, Publius Clodius had apparently infiltrated the all-female rites held at Caesar's house in honor of the goddess Bona Dea and there attempted to seduce the emperor's wife before being discovered. Although the accusations remained unsubstantiated and there was no reason to believe Pompeia had responded to the advances of Publius Clodius, Caesar still insisted on divorcing her on the grounds that even the suggestion that she might be guilty was damaging to him. Thus, any person in such an elevated position may be reminded that they must be *like Caesar's wife*—free of all taint of misdeed. "I am as free as the air. I feel myself as far above suspicion as Caesar's wife" (Charles Dickens, *Bleak House,* 1852–53).

Caiaphas (ka̲yăfas) Archetype of a ruthless, hypocritical politician. Caiaphas appears in the Bible as a Jewish high priest who tries Jesus (John 18:14–28) on the grounds that it is "expedient for us, that one man should die for the people, and that the whole nation perish not" (John 11:50). "Leaving Kennetbridge for this place is like coming from Caiaphas to Pilate!" (Thomas Hardy, *Jude the Obscure,* 1895).

Cain and Abel (kayn, a̲ybăl) Archetype of two brothers whose relationship ends in violent disagreement. The allusion is to the story of Cain and Abel, related in Genesis 4:1–16, which details how Cain, the first son of Adam and Eve and described as a "tiller of the ground," came to murder his brother Abel, a shepherd, through envy: "And Cain talked with Abel his brother: and it came to pass, when they were in the field, that Cain rose up against Abel his brother, and slew him" (Genes is 4:8). "Cain's envy was the more vile and malignant towards his brother, Abel, because when his sacrifice was better accepted there was nobody to look on" (Francis Bacon, "On Envy," 1601). *See also* CAIN'S CITY; MARK OF CAIN; MY BROTHER'S KEEPER; RAISE CAIN.

Cain's city (kayns) A city with a reputation for corruption and evil. The allusion is to the city supposedly founded by Cain after he was banished by God for the murder of his brother Abel. According to Genesis 4:17, Cain "builded a city, and called the name of the city, after the name of his son, Enoch." *The settlement was founded with the best of motives but like Cain's city soon became a notorious den of iniquity.*

Calchas (ka̲lkas) Archetype of a wise prophet. In Greek mythology, Calchas was a soothsayer who advised the Greeks during the Trojan War. It was Calchas who recommended the sacrifice of Iphigenia to appease Artemis before the Greek fleet set sail, persuaded Agamemnon to surrender his prize Chryseis to her father in order to halt a plague sent by Apollo, and advised the Greeks to build the TROJAN HORSE. He died of a broken heart after Mopsus proved himself superior in his skills as a prophet of future events. *The president will miss his closest aide, who has acted as Calchas to the party for over a decade.*

Caleb (kayleb) A faithful servant. According to Numbers 13:6 and 32:12, Caleb was one of those chosen by Moses to spy out the land of Canaan. Of the 12 men sent, only Caleb and Joshua returned with a favorable report. For his loyal service Caleb was eventually granted Hebron as his inheritance. "It is for you to say, with the faith of a Caleb, 'Give me this mountain'" (F. B. Meyer, *Joshua*, 1893).

calends (kalendz) The first day of the month. The calends, or *kalends,* (meaning "proclamation day") had particular significance for the ancient Romans and was so called because it was originally marked by high priests calling the people together to hail the new month and announcing the festivals and sacred days to be observed in the coming weeks. *She celebrates the calends each month by clearing everything off her desk and concentrating on new projects.* See also AT THE GREEK CALENDS.

calf, fatted *See* KILL THE FATTED CALF.

calf, golden *See* GOLDEN CALF.

Caligula (kăligyoolă) Archetype of a cruel and eccentric ruler. Gaius Caesar (A.D. 12–41), nicknamed Caligula, ruled as emperor of Rome for a relatively short time (37–41) and quickly became notorious for his unpredictable and vicious nature. Among his excesses, he declared himself a god, made his horse Incitatus a consul, and ordered his army to collect seashells. His reign ended prematurely when he was murdered. *This fledgling Caligula of the new Asia is full of surprises, even renaming the days of the week according to personal whim.*

Calliope *See* MUSES.

Calpurnia (kalperneeă) Archetype of a devoted wife, who is concerned for her husband's welfare. The wife of the Roman emperor Julius Caesar, Calpurnia was greatly troubled by various portents of death that appeared to threaten her husband. Caesar, however, ignored her warnings and was duly murdered by members of the senate in 44 B.C. *Like Caesar's Calpurnia, she seemed to realize the danger her husband was in but could find no way to make him change his plans.*

calvary (kalvăree) A place or experience that causes intense suffering, especially mental anguish. In the Bible, Calvary is identified as the hill in Jerusalem upon which Christ was crucified (Luke 23:32). The name comes from the Latin *calvaria,* itself a translation of the Greek *kranion* (meaning "skull"). Its other names include **Golgotha** (from the Aramaic *gulguta,* or "skull") and **place of skulls** (Matthew 27:33; Mark 15:22; John 19:17). The actual site of Calvary is disputed, with some identifying it with a vaguely skull-shaped hill near the Garden of Gethsemane and others indicating the site of the Church of the Holy Sepulchre. Legend has it that the skull of Adam was kept at the church. "The horse, a dangerous animal . . . whose martyrdom, and man's shame therein, he has told most powerfully in his Calvary, a tale with an edge that will cut the soft cruel hearts and strike fire from the hard kind ones" (George Bernard Shaw, *Captain Brassbound's Conversion,* 1900).

Calydonian boar hunt (kalădōneeăn) An epic pursuit of a ferocious prey. The original Calydonian boar hunt was a chase in which Meleager, the ruler of ancient Calydon, and various other heroes, including Jason and Theseus, set off in pursuit of a massive boar that had been sent by Artemis to ravage the land. Meleager himself finally succeeded in killing the beast and presented its head to Atalanta, who had inflicted the first wound. *The three operatives privately agreed never to let up on their pursuit of the gangsters, viewing the investigation as a type of modern Calydonian boar hunt.*

calypso (kălipsō) Popular style of West Indian ballad, characterized by syncopated percussion and topical lyrics. It is thought to have been named after Calypso, a sea nymph of Greek mythology who fell in love with Odysseus and detained him for seven years on the island of Ogygia. There, Odysseus spent his nights as Calypso's lover but passed his days in longing for his wife, Penelope. Ultimately, Odysseus refused Calypso's offer of immortality if he would remain with her on the island forever, and on the command of Zeus, Calypso allowed him to continue his journey home to his wife. The island Ogygia is sometimes tentatively identified as Gozo, near Malta. *Tonight the strains of the calypso seemed to lack their usual cheerfulness, reminiscent even of the original Calypso pining for the absent Odysseus.*

camel: go through an eye of a needle A feat that is considered very difficult, if not impossible to achieve. The reference is to the words of Christ related in Matthew 19:23–24, Mark 10:23–25, and Luke 18:24–25, describing the challenge faced by the rich man who wished to enter heaven: "Then said Jesus unto his disciples, Verily I say unto you, That a rich man shall hardly enter into the kingdom of heaven. And again I say unto you, It is easier for a camel to go through the eye of a needle, than for a rich man to enter into the kingdom of God" (Matthew 19:23–24). One theory suggests the imagery used by Christ was intended as a reference to a gate called the "needle's eye" that was so narrow a camel—the largest animal in ancient Palestine—could not pass through it. "It is as hard to come as for a camel / To thread the postern of a small needle's eye" (William Shakespeare, *King Richard II,* 1595). "It is easier for a cannibal to enter the Kingdom of Heaven through the eye of a rich man's needle than it is for any other foreigner to read the terrible German script" (Mark Twain, *Notebook,* 1898).

Camilla (kămĭlă) Personification of a fast runner. Camilla was identified in classical mythology as a Voscian princess and a servant of Diana. She was described as being so fleet of foot that she could run over a field of corn without bending the stalks and could cross the sea without getting her feet wet. "Margaret ran, swift as Camilla, down to the window" (Elizabeth Gaskell, *North and South,* 1854–55).

Cana, marriage in *See* WATER INTO WINE.

Canaan, land of *See* PROMISED LAND.

Can any good thing come out of Nazareth? *See* GOOD THING COME OUT OF NAZARETH.

candle under a bushel *See* HIDE ONE'S LIGHT UNDER A BUSHEL.

Cannae (kanee) A disastrous defeat that brings to an end a run of previous successes. The allusion is to the battle of Cannae that took place in 216 B.C. during the Second Punic War between Rome and Carthage. The Roman army had won the First Punic War, but after the Carthaginian general Hannibal invaded Italy, Rome was soundly defeated and suffered heavy losses at the village of Cannae in southeastern Italy. The Roman generals

Lucius Aemilius Paulus and Gaius Terentius Varro, who had made the reckless decision to attack the center of the Carthaginian force (thus allowing their enemy to encircle them), spent the rest of their lives in disgrace, and the name of the battle became forever associated with catastrophic defeat. *After so many years in undisputed power, this electoral disappointment is already being described as the party's Cannae.*

Capua corrupted Hannibal (kapyooă, hanibăl) Decadence will ruin anyone. The reference is to the winter the Carthaginian leader Hannibal spent in the Italian city of Capua, which was renowned as a center of idleness and luxury, during his campaign on the Italian mainland. Until then he had been victorious everywhere; afterward he failed to reach anew the same degree of success. *As heavyweight champion it seemed for a time that he would never be defeated, but just as Capua corrupted Hannibal, soft living fatally undermined his stamina in the ring.*

carpe diem (kahrpay deeăm) Make the most of one's opportunities, as they may not come again; seize the moment. The slogan comes from the *Odes* of the Roman poet Horace (65–8 B.C.), in which he wrote: *"carpe diem, quam minimum credula postero"* ("enjoy today, trusting little in tomorrow"). It is also rendered as **seize the day** and **take time by the forelock.** "When a man had nothing left in life except his dinner, his bottle, his cigar, and the dreams they gave him—these doctors forsooth must want to cut them off! No, no! Carpe diem! while you lived, get something out of it" (John Galsworthy, *The Forsyte Saga,* 1922).

carry one's cross *See* BEAR/CARRY/TAKE ONE'S CROSS.

Carthaginian peace (kahrthăjineeăn) A peace treaty or other agreement that is extremely harsh and punitive for the loser. The allusion is to the state of affairs that existed following the Punic wars fought between Carthage and Rome. Having suffered defeat in the First and Second Punic Wars, Carthage lost various colonial territories, but the North African state was still substantially intact. The third war, however, ended with the Romans invading the African mainland and setting siege to Carthage itself. The city fell after two years and was utterly devastated, never to regain its past glory. *The Carthaginian peace imposed on Germany* after the First World War sowed the seed for the growth of nationalism in that country. See also PUNIC FAITH.

caryatid (kareeatid) An architectural column in the shape of a female figure. Such columns were a feature of many ancient Greek temples. They were named after the women of Caryae in Laconia, which had unwisely sided with the Persians against the Greeks at the battle of Thermopylae. The victorious Greeks subsequently ravaged Caryae and carried off the women as slaves. To emphasize their subservience to Greece, the sculptor Praxiteles used these women as models for pillars in the place of conventional columns. "As they stepped out into the darkness, a sheet of rain was driven in upon their faces, and the hall lamp, which dangled from the arm of a marble caryatid, went out with a fluff" (Sir Arthur Conan Doyle, *Round the Red Lamp,* 1894).

Caspar *See* MAGI.

Cassandra (kăsandră) A prophet of doom, specifically one whose prophecies are ignored but who is later proved correct. The allusion is to Cassandra, the daughter of King Priam of Troy, who was granted prophetic powers by Apollo but later fated never to be believed as punishment for her having refused his advances. Consequently, when she foretold the fall of Troy no one heeded her warnings. After the fall of Troy, Cassandra was taken by Agamemnon to Greece, where she prophesied Agamemnon's death but was again ignored. Ultimately, she and Agamemnon were murdered by Clytemnestra. "But Cassandra was not believed, and even the wisdom of *The Jupiter* sometimes falls on deaf ears" (Anthony Trollope, *Barchester Towers,* 1857).

Castalian spring (kastayleeăn) A source of inspiration. The allusion is to a sacred spring on Mount Parnassus that was believed by the ancient Greeks to bestow the gift of poetry upon anyone who drank from its waters. "The Aeneid, you know, begins just as he says an epic ought not to begin; and the Aeneid is the greatest Latin epic. In the next place the use of Modesty is to keep a man from writing an epic poem at all but, if he will have that impudence, why then he had better have the courage to plunge into the Castalian stream, like Virgil and Lucan, not crawl in funking and holding on by the Muse's apron-string" (Charles Reade, *Hard Cash,* 1863). *See also* PARNASSIAN.

cast in one's teeth To insult; to revile; to throw a reproof at someone. The idiom comes from Matthew 27:44: "The thieves also, which were crucified with him, cast the same in his teeth." "All his faults observed, / Set in a notebook, learn'd and conn'd by rote, / To cast in my teeth" (William Shakespeare, *Julius Caesar,* 1599).

cast into outer darkness *See* OUTER DARKNESS.

cast money changers out of the temple To criticize or take action against inappropriate commercialism. The allusion is to the biblical episode in which Christ ejected the money changers from the Temple, which had become a place of business, as related at Matthew 21:12–13: "And Jesus went into the temple of God, and cast out all them that sold and bought in the temple, and overthrew the tables of the moneychangers, and the seats of them that sold doves, and said unto them, It is written, My house shall be called the house of prayer; but ye have made it a den of thieves." The money changers had originally been allowed into the Temple to facilitate the selling of doves for ritual sacrifices and the payment of Temple taxes by exchanging Roman currency for Hebrew coinage. *The accountants rule Hollywood, and there is little likelihood that anyone will succeed in casting these money changers out of the temple. See also* DEN OF THIEVES.

Castor and Pollux (kastor, polăks) Archetypes of devoted brothers. Castor and Pollux were identified in Greek mythology as twin brothers, sometimes called the *Dioscuri.* As the son of the god Zeus and the mortal Leda, Pollux enjoyed the gift of immortality, but Castor, being the son of Leda and the mortal Tyndareus, was mortal. When Castor died, Pollux asked to be allowed to die with him so that they might not be parted. Zeus granted his wish and placed the two brothers in the sky as stars (in the constellation of Gemini). *Like Castor and Pollux, the brothers were inseparable as teenagers and maintained this closeness well into adulthood.*

cast pearls before swine *See* PEARLS BEFORE SWINE.

cast the first stone *See* LET HIM WHO IS WITHOUT SIN CAST THE FIRST STONE.

cast thy bread upon the waters To give generously, as acts of generosity or kindness will be rewarded eventually. The sentiment comes from Ecclesiastes 11:1: "Cast thy bread upon the waters: for thou shalt find it after many days." *He little expected that he would ever benefit from this casting of bread upon the waters, but many years later he was pleasantly surprised to find his generosity was paying dividends.*

Catherine wheel (<u>kath</u>rin) A small circular firework that spins rapidly on a pin, shooting out bright sparks. The firework refers to the death of Saint Catherine of Alexandria, who was executed in Alexandria around A.D. 310. Born into a wealthy Egyptian family, she converted to Christianity and was put on trial for her faith. Her eloquence at her trial resulted in the conversion of 50 pagan philosophers, all of whom were subsequently put to death on the orders of the emperor Maxentius. Catherine refused to renounce her faith and was sentenced to be tortured to death on a spiked wheel (hence the name of the modern firework). When this wheel broke she was beheaded. *The Catherine wheel spun several times then flew off the fence at high speed, making the guests scatter in all directions.*

Cato (<u>kay</u>tō) Archetype of an austere moralist and critic. Marcus Porcius Cato (234–149 B.C.) was a Roman statesman and writer who was well known for his contempt for decadence and his implacable hatred of Carthage, which he believed should be destroyed because of the threat it posed to Rome's future prosperity (*see* DELENDA EST CARTHAGO). His grandson, Marcus Porcius Cato (95–46 B.C.), was also a statesman, who in his turn became well known for his opposition to Catiline and Caesar. In modern usage, any person who becomes known for strictness of habits or bluntness of speech may be dubbed a Cato. *For years the paper has acted Cato, calling for an end to the contemporary obsession with celebrity culture.*

cattle of the sun Something forbidden that if enjoyed will bring disaster upon the guilty party. The allusion is to Greek mythology and the cattle on the Island of the Sun, upon which Odysseus and his crew landed in the course of their long voyage home. Odysseus was told that on no account should the cattle be harmed, but when Odysseus temporarily left his hungry

men in order to pray to the gods, they killed and ate some of the cows. The
sun god vented his rage by killing them all but Odysseus and destroying their
ship. *Like the ancient Greeks who were all slaughtered for eating the cattle of the sun,
those who were tempted to help themselves during the power failure have paid heavily
for their crimes.*

cave of Trophonius (trăf̄oneeăs) A cause of depression or fear. According
to Greek mythology, Trophonius was an architect who was deified after his
death and worshiped at a cave near Lebadeia in Boeotia. Those who
entered the cave to consult his oracle were said to be so overawed by the
place that they never smiled again. Thus, any person who seems unusually
gloomy or scared may be said to have *visited the cave of Trophonius.*
"The gardens were arranged to emulate those of Versailles. . . . There is the
Trophonius' cave in which, by some artifice, the leaden Tritons are made
not only to spout water, but to play the most dreadful groans out of their
lead conches" (William Makepeace Thackeray, *Vanity Fair,* 1847–48).

centaur (sentor) One of a race of mythical creatures having the head,
arms, and torso of a man and the lower body and legs of a horse. Centaurs
belonged to Greek mythology and were deemed to represent the bestial
aspects of human nature, although later tradition generally depicts them as
benevolent, gentle creatures. They may have been inspired by the appearance of the ancient Thessalians who were the first to tame horses and learn
how to ride. According to legend, the centaurs were defeated in battle by
the human Lapiths, an epic encounter depicted in the celebrated friezes
that decorated the Parthenon. "He was dressed in a Newmarket coat and
tight-fitting trousers; wore a shawl round his neck; smelt of lamp-oil,
straw, orange-peel, horses' provender, and sawdust; and looked a most
remarkable sort of Centaur, compounded of the stable and the play-house"
(Charles Dickens, *Hard Times,* 1854). *See also* CHIRON.

Cephalus *See* UNERRING AS THE DART OF PROCRIS.

Cerberus (serbărăs) A guardian; a watchkeeper. The allusion is to the
fierce three-headed dog that, according to Greek mythology, guarded the
entrance to the underworld. It has been suggested that the legend of Cerberus may have been inspired by the ancient Egyptian practice of guarding

graves with dogs. "When a woman knows that she is guarded by a watchdog, she is bound to deceive her Cerberus, if it be possible, and is usually not ill-disposed to deceive also the owner of Cerberus. Lady Glencora felt that Mrs Marsham was her Cerberus" (Anthony Trollope, *Can You Forgive Her?* 1864). *See also* LABORS OF HERCULES; SOP TO CERBERUS.

cesarean section (săzaireeăn) A surgical incision through the abdominal and uterine walls to allow for the delivery of a baby. This procedure (also spelled *caesarean section* and often referred to simply as a *cesarean*) traces its name back to the Roman emperor Julius Caesar (100–44 B.C.), who was reputed to have been born in this way. Medical experts however, have questioned whether Caesar's mother could possibly have survived such an operation given the limited knowledge of medical practitioners of the day, and the word, instead, may come simply from *caesus,* past participle of the Latin *caedere* (meaning "to cut"). *The cesarean section left a long vivid scar that did not fade with time.*

cestus *See* APHRODITE.

chaos (kayos) A state of disorder or confusion. The word is Greek; in Greek mythology it described the state of the universe prior to the birth of the gods. Chaos itself was personified as the parent of Night and of Erebus (representing darkness). ". . . order began to emerge from chaos and the vision of a home made happy and comfortable by her skill and care came to repay and sustain her" (Louisa May Alcott, *An Old Fashioned Girl,* 1870).

chariot of fire An apparently miraculous mean of overcoming a natural obstacle or other difficulty. The allusion is to the "fiery chariot" that transported ELIJAH to heaven, as recorded in 2 Kings 2:11: "Behold, there appeared a chariot of fire, and horses of fire, and parted them both asunder; and Elijah went up by a whirlwind into heaven." *With a last wave to the admiring crowd she leapt onto the bike, gunned the engine, and moments later was roaring off toward the horizon on this veritable chariot of fire.*

charity covers a multitude of sins Those who are of a kind and loving disposition will forgive the wrongdoing of others; sometimes used to state that such charity may also be a cloak for bad behavior or a sign of a guilty conscience. The proverb comes from 1 Peter 4:8: "And above all things have fervent charity among yourselves: for charity shall cover the multitude of sins." Sometimes the phrase is encountered with other words replacing *charity,* such as *beauty covers a multitude of sins.* "'John is so sensible, I'm afraid he will think I'm stupid if I ask questions about politics and things.' 'I don't believe he would. Love covers a multitude of sins, and of whom could you ask more freely than of him?'" (Louisa May Alcott, *Little Women,* 1868).

Charlemagne (shahrlămayn) Archetype of a wise, chivalrous ruler. Charlemagne (742–814), otherwise called Charles the Great, became the first Holy Roman emperor in 800, and he and the adventures shared by the paladins who joined his court inspired many legends (*see* ROLAND). Charlemagne himself was said to be at least eight feet tall and immensely strong, being able to bend three horseshoes at once with his bare hands. ". . . at all events Steelkilt was a tall and noble animal with a head like a Roman, and a flowing golden beard like the tasseled housings of your last viceroy's snorting charger; and a brain, and a heart, and a soul in him, gentlemen, which had made Steelkilt Charlemagne, had he been born son to Charlemagne's father" (Herman Melville, *Moby-Dick,* 1851).

Charon (karăn) Personification of death; a ferryman. According to Greek mythology, Charon was the name of the ferryman who rowed the dead across the rivers Styx or Acheron to Hades, the abode of the dead. He was conventionally depicted as a hideous old man dressed in rags. In ancient times a coin, known as *Charon's toll,* was often placed in the mouth of a corpse prior to burial as payment to Charon, to ensure the deceased was seen safely into the underworld. "There stands a gig in the gray morning, in the mist, the impatient traveller pacing the wet shore with whip in hand, and shouting through the fog after the regardless Charon and his retreating ark, as if he might throw that passenger overboard and return forthwith for himself; he will compensate him" (Henry David Thoreau, *A Week on the Concord and Merrimack Rivers,* 1849).

Charybdis *See* BETWEEN SCYLLA AND CHARYBDIS.

cherub (cherăb) A sweet, angelic child. The word was used in the Bible to refer to a class of angels attending upon the throne of God in heaven (for example, Ezekiel 10:2–7). They are generally represented in art as plump, winged babies. "To think o' that dear cherub! And we found her wi' her little shoes stuck i' the mud an' crying fit to break her heart by the far horse-pit" (George Eliot, *Adam Bede,* 1859).

children of light Those who are enlightened or otherwise alive to virtue, culture, faith, etc. The phrase is biblical in origin, appearing in Luke 16:8 and John 12:35–36 when Christ addresses those attending the feast of the Passover: "Yet a little while is the light with you. Walk while ye have the light, lest darkness come upon you . . . While ye have light, believe in the light, that ye may be the children of light" (John 12:35–36). "But the heart of man is the same everywhere, and there are the children of this world and the children of light there as well as elsewhere. But we've many more Methodists there than in this country" (George Eliot, *Adam Bede,* 1859).

children's teeth set on edge How a person behaves reflects on the rest of his or her family or associates. The image appears in Jeremiah 31:29–30, in which this piece of proverbial wisdom is refuted in favor of each person being responsible for his or her own behavior: "In those days they shall say no more, The fathers have eaten a sour grape, and the children's teeth are set on edge. But everyone shall die for his own iniquity." It is also included in Ezekiel 18:2–3. *When, as a young man, he was faced with having to answer for his progenitor's controversial policy, it was a case of the father having eaten a sour grape and the children's teeth being set on edge.*

chimera (kīmĭrǎ) An idle fancy; a fantastic, wild, or implausible product of the imagination. The allusion is to a fire-breathing monster of Greek mythology, described as having the head of a lion, the body of a goat, and the tail of a serpent. She was killed by the arrows of Bellerophon, mounted on the winged horse Pegasus. The creature's name may have been borrowed from that of a volcano similarly named in Lycia; flames shot forth from its summit, while lions prowled its upper slopes and goats and snakes lurked lower down. The name subsequently came to be used to describe any fabulous creature comprising the body parts of several different animals. By extension, anything unlikely or fantastical may be described as *chimerical.* ". . . her spontaneous appeal to that sacred name dissolved his chimera; and let him see with his eyes, and hear with his ears" (Charles Reade, *The Cloister and the Hearth,* 1861).

Chiron (kīron) Archetype of a wise teacher. According to Greek mythology Chiron was unique among the CENTAURs in being wise and kind in nature. He was skilled at hunting and in various arts and in his turn served as tutor to many heroes, including Achilles and Jason. When accidentally hit by a poisoned arrow fired by his friend Hercules while in battle with the other centaurs, Chiron chose to die and passed his immortality on to Prometheus. His name is preserved today as that of a minor planet between Saturn and Uranus discovered in 1977. "Something less unpleasingly oracular he tried to extract; but the old sea Chiron, thinking perhaps that for the nonce he had sufficiently instructed his young Achilles, pursed his lips, gathered all his wrinkles together, and would commit himself to nothing further" (Herman Melville, *Billy Budd,* 1924).

Chloe (klōee) A rustic maiden; a shepherdess. A character of the same name appears in the Greek pastoral romance *Daphnis and Chloe* by the Greek writer Longus, who lived in the third century A.D. *Asleep on the haystack, her flock idly grazing all around, she seemed a true Chloe, as though she had lived in the country all her life. See also* DAPHNIS AND CHLOE.

chosen few A select group of people who enjoy particular favor. The expression comes from Matthew 22:14: "For many are called, but few are chosen." "He considered the years to come when Kim would have been entered and made to the Great Game that never ceases day and night, throughout India. He foresaw honour and credit in the mouths of a chosen few, coming to him from his pupil" (Rudyard Kipling, *Kim,* 1901). *See also* CHOSEN PEOPLE.

chosen instrument A person entrusted with a particular responsibility. The phrase appears in Acts 9:15, in which God tells Ananias that he has selected Paul to represent him among men: "Go thy way: for he is a chosen vessel unto me, to bear my name before the Gentiles, and kings, and the children of Israel." "I was wondering, in my own mind, whether the day of his downfall had come at last, and whether you were the chosen instrument for working it" (Wilkie Collins, *The Woman in White,* 1860).

chosen people A group of people considered select or particularly marked out. In the Bible the phrase is associated with Israel, and in the New Testament the church: "But ye are a chosen generation, a royal priesthood, an holy nation, a peculiar people" (1 Peter 2:9). "The folk here are civil, and, like the barbarians unto the holy apostle, hae shown me much kindness; and there are a sort of chosen people in the land, for they hae some kirks without organs that are like ours, and are called meetinghouses, where the minister preaches without a gown" (Sir Walter Scott, *The Heart of Midlothian,* 1818). *See also* CHOSEN FEW.

Ciceronian (sisărōneeăn) Eloquent; erudite. The word alludes to Marcus Tullius Cicero (106–43 B.C.), the Roman consul, orator, and writer who was widely admired for his eloquence and the purity of his Latin prose style. According to Plutarch, he was given the name Cicero—from *cicer* (meaning "wart")—because of the lump on the end of his nose. By extension, a person who guides sightseers around museums or similar places may be called a *cicerone. Epitaphs for the great man in the national newspapers emphasized his power as a speaker and included extracts from some of his more Ciceronian pronouncements.*

Cimmerian (simireeăn) Very dark or gloomy. According to Greek mythology, as recorded by Homer (eighth century B.C.) the Cimmerians were a tribe who inhabited a land of perpetual gloom situated at the remotest edge of the world and neighboring Hades itself. "A kind of landscape and weather which leads travellers from the South to describe our island as Homer's Cimmerian land, was not, on the face of it, friendly to women" (Thomas Hardy, *The Return of the Native,* 1880).

Cincinnatus (sinsinatăs) Archetype of a great man in retirement. Lucius Quinctius Cincinnatus (c. 519–438 B.C.) was a Roman general and statesman who was widely admired for his frugality and integrity. Assuming dictatorial powers, he saved Rome when it was threatened by invading armies on two occasions (in 458 and 439 B.C.) but each time surrendered his powers as soon as the danger had passed and returned to live quietly on his farm. Many celebrated public figures, including George Washington and Napoléon Bonaparte, have been dubbed a Cincinnatus for their time after giving up their powers and going into retirement. The city of Cincinnati in Ohio was named after the Society of the Cincinnati, made up of retired officers who had served in the Continental army in the American Revolution, that offered help to the dependents of fallen comrades. The name was transferred to the two-year-old city of Losantiville in 1790 by General Arthur St. Clair, president of the Cincinnati society and first governor of the Northwest Territory. "How rude you look, pushing and frowning, as if you wanted to conquer with your elbows! Cincinnatus, I am sure, would have been sorry to see his daughter behave so" (George Eliot, *Middlemarch*, 1871–72).

Circe (sersee) A dangerous temptress. According to Homer's *Odyssey* (c. 700 B.C.), Circe was a beautiful enchantress of the island of Aeaea who was in the habit of transforming men who approached her palace into swine. Several of Odysseus's companions suffered such a fate but Odysseus remained immune to Circe's power with the help of Hermes, who advised him to protect himself by eating some of a mysterious herb called "moly," and obliged her to restore his men to their original form. Odysseus subsequently remained with the enchantress for a year, during which time he visited the underworld with her assistance, before continuing on his voyage. "Wolf Larsen it was, always Wolf Larsen, enslaver and tormentor of men, a male Circe and these his swine, suffering brutes that grovelled before him and revolted only in drunkenness and in secrecy" (Jack London, *The Sea-Wolf*, 1904).

cities of the plain *See* SODOM AND GOMORRAH.

city of refuge A place of safety from one's enemies. The allusion is to Exodus 21:13 and Joshua 20:3, which describe how Moses and Joshua named six cities of refuge "that the slayer that killeth any person unawares and unwittingly may flee thither: and they shall be your refuge from the avenger of blood" (Joshua 20:3). People who had committed accidental homicide were admitted to one of these walled cities (Ramoth, Kedesh, Bezer, Shechem, Hebron, and Golam) in order to evade those who might seek vengeance. "He has been deprived of his city of refuge, and, in my humble opinion, has suffered infinite wrong!" (Nathaniel Hawthorne, *The House of the Seven Gables*, 1851).

city on a hill Utopia; a utopian community or shining example of some kind. The phrase comes from Christ's Sermon on the Mount: "Ye are the light of the world. A city that is set on an hill cannot be hid. Neither do men light a candle, and put it under a bushel, but on a candlestick; and it giveth light unto all that are in the house. Let your light so shine before men, that they may see your good works, and glorify your Father which is in heaven" (Matthew 5:14–16). *Most of her followers eagerly accepted her vision of a city on a hill where all might live in harmony together.*

clay in the potter's hand Easily led; malleable; pliable. The phrase is biblical in origin, appearing at Jeremiah 18:6, in which God's influence on earth is likened to a potter shaping clay: "As the clay is in the potter's hand, so are ye in mine hand." *The soldier easily roused the mob to fury, working them like clay in the potter's hand.*

clean the Augean stables *See* LABORS OF HERCULES.

Cleopatra *See* ANTONY AND CLEOPATRA; CLEOPATRA'S NOSE.

Cleopatra's nose (kleeōp_atrăz) An apparently insignificant thing that is actually of extreme importance and has major consequences. The phrase was popularized by the French philosopher Blaise Pascal (1623–62), who speculated how history would have been different if Cleopatra VII (69–30 B.C.) had not been so beautiful, reflecting in his *Pensées:* "If the nose of Cleopatra had been shorter, the whole face of the earth would have been changed." It was the beauty and charm of the queen of Egypt that beguiled both Julius Caesar and Mark Antony and thus exerted a profound influence on the history of the ancient world. As it was, both Caesar and Mark Antony offered Cleopatra military assistance and thus preserved her throne from the rival claim of her brother. Some historians have, however, questioned the accuracy of modern assumptions about Cleopatra's beauty, pointing out that the few surviving contemporary portraits of her suggest she was somewhat plain, with prominent cheekbones. *It seems strange, looking back, how that one detail, like Cleopatra's nose, decided everything that was to follow later.*

climb Parnassus *See* PARNASSIAN.

Clio *See* MUSES.

clothed and in one's right mind Fully aware and ready to perform any undertaking. The phrase alludes to an exorcism carried out by Christ on a man possessed by demons, as related at Luke 8:35: "Then they went out to see what was done; and came to Jesus, and found the man, out of whom the devils were departed, sitting at the feet of Jesus, clothed, and in his right mind: and they were afraid." *The rest of the family was surprised to find this matriarch, despite her years, clothed and very much in her right mind.*

Clotho *See* FATES.

cloud by day, pillar of fire by night Unfailing guidance or advice. The phrase comes from Exodus 13:21–22, which relates how the Israelites were guided on their journey from Egypt to Canaan by a pillar of cloud by day and a pillar of fire by night. "When I was a boy, I always thought a pillar of cloud by day and a pillar of fire by night was a pit, with its steam, and its lights, and the burning bank,—and I thought the Lord was always at the pit-top" (D. H. Lawrence, *Sons and Lovers*, 1913). *See also* PILLAR OF FIRE.

cloud cuckoo land A realm of fantasy or foolishness; something that exists only in the imagination. The phrase has its origins in the comedy *The Birds*, by the Greek playwright Aristophanes (445-c. 388 B.C.): It is the name of an imaginary city built by the birds where two Athenians hope they will be able escape the attentions of the legal authorities who are pursuing them. *If they think I'm going all that way just to be bored to death then they're living in cloud cuckoo land.*

cloud no bigger than a man's hand A relatively insignificant portent of something much greater about to happen. The phrase alludes to 1 Kings 18:44–45, which describes how, having defeated the prophets of Baal, Elijah eagerly awaits the coming of rain in response to his prayers. The rain duly arrives after Elijah has dispatched his servant to keep watch from Mount Carmel a seventh time: "And it came to pass at the seventh time, that he said, Behold, there ariseth a little cloud out of the sea, like a man's hand . . . And it came to pass . . . that the heaven was black with clouds and wind, and there was a great rain." "The prospect was bright, and the air sunny. In the midst of all which there rose in the horizon a cloud, like that seen by Elijah's servant, a cloud no bigger than a man's hand" (Charles Reade, *Put Yourself in His Place,* 1870).

cloven hoof An evil nature; some physical indicator of such a nature. According to the law as laid down by Moses, only animals with cloven hoofs were suitable as food or as sacrificial offerings (Deuteronomy 14:3–8). The devil was conventionally depicted by medieval artists as having cloven hoofs, a detail probably borrowed from pagan gods, hence the modern significance of the term. According to popular belief, the devil, no matter his disguise is unable to hide his cloven hoofs and can always be detected in this way. To *show the cloven foot* means to reveal a base motive or innate wickedness. *Several people who witnessed the great man's actions that evening privately agreed that they might have caught a first glimpse of his cloven hoof.*

Clytemnestra (klītemnestră) Archetype of a vengeful mother or faithless wife. In Greek mythology Clytemnestra was the daughter of Leda and King Tyndareus of Sparta and became the wife of Agamemnon, leader of the Greeks during the Trojan War. With the help of her lover Aegisthus, she murdered Agamemnon in his bath upon his return from the war in revenge for the sacrifice of her daughter Iphigenia, who had been put to death to appease the goddess Artemis after the Greek fleet was becalmed at Aulis. She, in her turn, was murdered by her son Orestes. *The Duchess turned out to be a Clytemnestra in disguise, plotting a bloody revenge upon her husband.*

coals of fire *See* HEAP COALS OF FIRE.

coat of many colors A multicolored garment. The original coat of many colors was the coat presented by Jacob to his favorite son, Joseph, as a sign of his special love for him, as related in Genesis 37:3: "Now Israel loved Joseph more than all his children, because he was the son of his old age: and he made him a coat of many colours." The gift made Joseph's brothers so jealous that they stole the coat, stained it with blood, and told their father that Joseph had been killed by wild animals, while selling Joseph into slavery. In some translations the coat is perhaps more accurately described as being a long robe with sleeves or a richly ornamented robe.

His mother's latest acquisition was a truly hideous coat of many colors, guaranteed to cause alarm wherever she dared to wear it.

cockatrice (<u>ko</u>kătris) A monster who can kill with a single glance; by extension, a dangerous, treacherous person. The cockatrice was a legendary serpent hatched by a serpent from a cock's egg. It could kill any enemy with a single glance or with its breath. The creature appears in Isaiah 11:8, 14:29, and 59:5 and also in Jeremiah 8:17. "This will so fright them both that they will kill one another by the look, like cockatrices" (William Shakespeare, *Twelfth Night,* 1601). *See also* BASILISK STARE.

coliseum (kolă<u>see</u>ăm) A large theater or other building used for entertainment, sports, and other events. The original Colosseum was the vast amphitheater in Rome that was begun by the emperor Vespasian and completed by Titus in A.D. 80. The venue for a wide variety of entertainments, ranging from gladiatorial combats and naval battles to executions, the Colosseum was so named in reference to a huge statue (colossus) of Nero that once stood nearby. *In this utopia every town was well furnished with facilities for public entertainment, including at least one major coliseum for the performance of spectacles on a large scale.*

colophon (<u>ko</u>lăfon) A publisher's emblem, traditionally placed at the end of a book. The allusion is to the ancient Ionian city of Colophon, whose horsemen were renowned for turning the tide of battle with last-minute charges. By the same token, to ***add a colophon*** means to add the finishing stroke. "Master Gridley took out a great volume from the lower shelf,—a folio in massive oaken covers with clasps like prison hinges, bearing the stately colophon, white on a ground of vermilion, of Nicholas Jenson and his associates" (Oliver Wendell Holmes, *The Guardian Angel,* 1887).

colossus (kă<u>lo</u>săs) Something that is very large in size. The reference is ultimately to a huge statue of ancient Egypt, described by the Greek historian Herodotus (c. 484–c. 430/420 B.C.) but is more usually associated with the Colossus of Rhodes, a massive bronze statue of Apollo that formerly stood at the entrance to the harbor of Rhodes. Erected around 292–280 B.C., it was destroyed by an earthquake in 225 B.C. The modern conception that the statue actually bestrode the harbor entrance is thought to be erroneous. In due course the word came to be applied to any large statue and may now be used to refer to any person or thing of impressive size, reputation, power, etc. "I found the wall—it was only a foot or two beyond my reach. With a heave I had my foot on the spike, and turning, I had both hands on the opposite wall. There I stood, straddling like a Colossus over a waste of white waters, with the cave floor far below me in the gloom" (John Buchan, *Prester John,* 1910). *See also* EIGHTH WONDER OF THE WORLD.

come, let us reason together An appeal to someone to come to terms, especially someone who might otherwise be considered beyond salvation. The phrase is a quotation from Isaiah 1:18: "Come now, and let us reason together, saith the LORD: though your sins be as scarlet, they shall be as white as snow; though they be red like crimson, they shall be as wool." *Management has made friendly overtures to the union, clearly believing that a "come, let us reason together" approach will do them more good in the long run than being belligerent.*

comforter, Job's *See* JOB'S COMFORTER.

Concordia (kon<u>kor</u>deeă) Personification of peace. Concordia was identified in Roman mythology as the goddess of peace and harmony. *The warring parties quickly reached a compromise and for a time Concordia reigned over the entire scene.*

consider the lilies *See* LILIES OF THE FIELD.

continence of Alexander *See* ALEXANDER THE GREAT.

continence of a Scipio (<u>si</u>peeō) Self-restraint or moral integrity; the ability to refuse temptation. According to Roman legend, the Roman general Publius Cornelius Scipio Africanus (237–183 B.C.), who led the Roman army against the Carthaginians during the Second Punic War, was once offered the chance to meet a beautiful princess whom his men had taken prisoner but declined the opportunity on the grounds that he might be tempted to forget his principles. *To work in such company and not* *be tempted to try one's luck with one of the ladies would require the continence of a Scipio.*

Corinth, it is not for every man to go to (korinth) Some things, such as great wealth, are fated to be enjoyed by only a few. This is a quotation from the *Epistles* of Horace (65–8 B.C.). Corinth, which was famed for its great wealth, was deemed difficult to get to either because of the expense required to travel there or because it was awkwardly situated between two seas. *As a young man he had dreamed of making his million, but it is not for every man to go to Corinth. See also* CORINTHIAN.

Corinthian (kărintheeăn) Licentious, dissolute. The lax morals of the inhabitants of Corinth were widely known throughout the ancient world. The word *Corinthian* also denotes the most richly decorated of the five orders of Greek architecture. "He never passed the line which divides the spruce vices from the ugly; and hence, though his morals had hardly been applauded, disapproval of them had frequently been tempered with a smile. This treatment had led to his becoming a sort of regrater of other men's gallantries, to his own aggrandizement as a Corinthian, rather than to the moral profit of his hearers" (Thomas Hardy, *Far from the Madding Crowd,* 1874). *See also* DORIC; IONIC; TUSCAN.

Coriolanus (koreeōlaynăs) Archetype of an arrogant politician. According to Roman legend, Gaius Marcus Coriolanus was a Roman general who threatened to lead his army against Rome in the fifth century B.C. until dissuaded from so doing by his mother and wife. His contempt for the public in general was memorably depicted in William Shakespeare's play *Corialanus* (1608), in which he was portrayed lamenting the fact that he was obliged to recruit popular support for his cause. *The press was unforgiving in its accounts of the minister's arrogance, calling him a Coriolanus for his time.*

corners of the earth The remotest, most distant parts of the globe. The notion that the earth has corners comes from Isaiah 11:12, which describes how God will "assemble the outcasts of Israel, and gather together the dispersed of Judah from the four corners of the earth." "'I can run out of the house,' cried her ladyship, wildly. 'I can fly to the uttermost corners of the earth; but I can not hear that person's name mentioned!'" (Wilkie Collins, *Man and Wife,* 1870).

cornucopia (kornăkōpeeă) A great abundance of something; a plentiful supply, especially of food and drink. The reference is to Greek mythology and one of the horns of Amalthea, the goat that suckled Zeus. Zeus presented the horn to the daughters of Melisseus, king of Crete, and it overflowed immediately with whatever food or drink its owners desired. Also known as the *horn of plenty,* the cornucopia subsequently became a symbol of plenty widely used in art and literature. "The last time they had had a big basket with them and all their Christmas marketing to do—a roast of pork and a cabbage and some rye bread, and a pair of mittens for Ona, and a rubber doll that squeaked, and a little green cornucopia full of candy to be hung from the gas jet and gazed at by half a dozen pairs of longing eyes" (Upton Sinclair, *The Jungle,* 1906).

corruptible and incorruptible That which is flawed may yet prove perfect. The expression comes from 1 Corinthians 15:42–44, 52–54, in which Paul discusses the resurrection, through which the weak and perishable body is made strong and imperishable: "It is sown in corruption, it is raised in incorruption: it is sown in dishonour, it is raised in glory" (1 Corinthian 15:42–43). "Now that the incorruption of this most fragrant ambergris should be found in the heart of such decay; is this nothing? Bethink thee of that saying of St. Paul in Corinthians, about corruption and incorruption; how we are sown in dishonour, but raised in glory" (Herman Melville, *Moby-Dick,* 1851).

Corybantian (koreebanteeăn) Wild, ecstatic, noisy, or unrestrained in manner. The allusion is to the Corybantes of Greek mythology, who were attendants of the goddess Cybele and were well known for their frenzied rituals, which featured the repeated crashing of cymbals and wild dancing. Legend had it that the infant Zeus escaped death at the hands of his father when his crying was drowned out by the noise made by the Corybantes. "Again, at Eleusis, home of Ceres, I see the modern Greeks dancing, I hear them clapping their hands as they bend their bodies, I hear the metrical shuffling of their feet. I see again the wild old Corybantian dance, the performers wounding each other" (Walt Whitman, *Leaves of Grass,* 1855).

Corydon (<u>kor</u>idăn) A rustic or shepherd. A lovesick shepherd of this name appears in Virgil's *Eclogues* (42–37 B.C.). "'Gad, what a debauched Corydon!' said my lord—what a mouth for a pipe!'" (William Makepeace Thackeray, *Vanity Fair,* 1847–48).

Coryphaeus (kori<u>fee</u>ăs) A leader, especially the most active member of a board, expedition, etc. The term was originally reserved in ancient Greek theater for the leader of the chorus. By extension, the leading dancer of a ballet troupe may sometimes be termed a ***Coryphée.*** *This Coryphaeus dominated the meeting, and by the end of the evening few of the directors had any doubts about which way they should vote.*

cothurnus *See* BUSKIN.

counsel of perfection A commendation of something beyond a minimum; an unattainable ideal. The phrase alludes to the biblical episode in which Christ told a rich young man what he needed to do in order to reach heaven: "Jesus said unto him, If thou wilt be perfect, go *and* sell that thou hast, and give to the poor . . . But when the young man heard that saying, he went away sorrowful, for he had great possessions" (Matthew 19:21–22). *Advocating better manners among sports fans smacks of a counsel of perfection.*

count the cost To consider the advantages, disadvantages, or risks before deciding to do something; consider the possible effects or results of something. The expression comes from Jesus' words as recorded in Luke 14:28: "For which of you, intending to build a tower, sitteth not down first, and counteth the cost, whether he have sufficient to finish it?" *You must count the cost before you make up your mind to take off a year from school to travel around Europe.*

court of the Gentiles Those people who are not Jews, not one of God's chosen. The court of the Gentiles was a feature of Herod's Temple and is described in Josephus and the Mishnah; it is alluded to in Revelation 11:2, and since it was where the money changers carried on their business, it is also referred to indirectly in Matthew 21:12. In biblical times Jews were tried by their own court in the Jewish Temple, while others appeared before court of the Gentiles. *Such a superior attitude was unlikely to be welcome in the court of the Gentiles.* See also CHOSEN PEOPLE.

cover a multitude of sins *See* CHARITY COVERS A MULTITUDE OF SINS.

Cressida *See* TROILUS AND CRESSIDA.

Cretan bull *See* LABORS OF HERCULES.

Croesus *See* AS RICH AS CROESUS.

Cronos (krōnus) Personification of time. Cronos (also rendered as *Cronus* or *Kronos*) was identified in Greek mythology as the youngest of the Titans, a son of Uranus and Gaea and the equivalent of the Roman Saturn. Entrusted with the government of earth, he presided over a GOLDEN AGE. He devoured his own children by Rhea because of a prophecy that one of them would overthrow him but failed to kill his son Zeus, who tricked him into disgorging his siblings. He was defeated in battle by his offspring and imprisoned in Tartarus. *They hoped to get to the ancient ruins in time to see the dawn, but it seemed that Cronos had decreed against them as the sky was already growing pink to the east.*

crooked shall be made straight Things will be made right in the end. The phrase appears in Isaiah 40:4, which foretells how all will be made well at the coming of the Messiah: "The crooked shall be made straight, and the rough places plain." It is also quoted in the New Testament in Luke 3:5. *It is hoped that through the introduction of these new standards the crooked shall be made straight and performance will be improved across the board.*

crossing of the Red Sea A miraculous escape, especially one made with divine assistance. The allusion is to the crossing of the Red Sea by the Israelites from Egypt to Sinai, under the guidance of Moses. According to the biblical narrative, the waters of the Red Sea parted at Moses' command but closed behind them, blocking the Egyptians who followed in pursuit (Exodus 14:21–30). *A path through the rain suddenly opened up for them and they dashed for it, like the Hebrews at the crossing of the Red Sea.*

cross over Jordan To die and enter heaven. The reference is to the biblical episode in Joshua 3 describing how the Israelites invaded Canaan under the leadership of Joshua. When they came to the Jordan River the water parted as promised by God (verse 7) to allow the Israelites to cross into Canaan, the PROMISED LAND. *The old lady crossed over the Jordan last night, and the family is therefore in mourning.*

cross the Rubicon (roobăkon) To take an irrevocable step, especially a decision from which there is no going back. Under the laws of ancient Rome it was illegal for a military commander to lead troops over the Rubicon River, which divided Cisalpine Gaul from Italy. (Such a measure was intended to prevent any wayward general seizing power by force.) In 49 B.C. Julius Caesar defied the prohibition by leading his army over the Rubicon, went on to defeat Pompey in the ensuing civil war, and became the effective head of state. If he had failed, he would have faced the death penalty. *With this act the state legislature has crossed the Rubicon. There is no going back now.* See also DIE IS CAST, THE.

crown of thorns A symbol of great suffering and humiliation. According to the biblical account of Christ's crucifixion, Jesus was forced to wear a crown of thorns in mockery of his claim to be king of the Jews, as related in Matthew 27:29: "And when they had platted a crown of thorns, they put it upon his head . . . and they bowed the knee before him, and mocked him, saying, Hail, King of the Jews!" (See also Mark 15:17 and John 19:2–5.) *He wore his injured pride like a crown of thorns, appealing for sympathy from anyone who would hear his story.*

crumbs that fall from the rich man's table The meager benefits that are left to the poor after the rich have taken their fill of something. The expression is biblical in origin, appearing in the Gospels. It features, for example, in the story of the Gentile woman who professes her faith in Christ with the words, "Truth, Lord: yet the dogs eat of the crumbs which fall from their masters' table" (Matthew 15:27). (See also Mark 7:24–30.) In Luke 16:20–21, it appears in the story of the beggar Lazarus: "And there was a certain beggar named Lazarus, which was laid at his gate, full of sores. And desiring to be fed with the crumbs which fell from the rich man's table: moreover the dogs came and licked his sores."

'I mean that I am content to give what I have given and must always give, and take in payment those crumbs that fall from my mistress's table, the memory of a few kind words, the hope one day in the far undreamed future of a sweet smile or two of recognition, a little gentle friendship" (H. Rider Haggard, *She,* 1887).

crying in the wilderness *See* VOICE CRYING IN THE WILDERNESS.

cry of blood *See* BLOOD CRIETH FROM THE GROUND.

Cui bono? (kwee bōnō) For what purpose? For whose benefit? This legal phrase is of Roman origin, being attributed ultimately to the Roman judge Lucius Cassius Longinus Ravilla (fl. second century B.C.), who was in the habit of posing this question in cases brought before him. "'And may I not paint one like it for you?' 'Cui bono? No'" (Charlotte Brontë, *Jane Eyre,* 1847).

Cumaean sibyl *See* SIBYL.

cunctator (kănktaytor) Delayer; someone who employs delay as a tactic. The title is most closely associated with Quintus Fabius Maximus (d. 203 B.C.), the Roman general who cunningly adopted delaying tactics against the invading Carthaginian armies of Hannibal, avoiding any direct confrontation. Initially held in contempt for his apparent cowardice, Fabius eventually won hero status after the wisdom of his policy was realized. *The managing director's colleagues privately dubbed him cunctator because of his reputation for putting things off time and time again. See also* FABIAN.

Cupid (kyoopid) Personification of love. The son of Aphrodite, Cupid was the god of love in Roman mythology and the equivalent of the Greek god Eros. He was usually depicted as a winged naked boy, sometimes blindfolded, carrying a bow from which he fired arrows of desire. To *play Cupid* means to act as matchmaker, while *Cupid's bow* describes the shape of the upper lip in humans. "And off I started, cursorily glancing sideways as I passed the toilet-table, surmounted by a looking-glass: a thin irregular face I saw, with sunk, dark eyes under a large, square forehead, complexion destitute of bloom or attraction; something young, but not youthful, no object to win a lady's love, no butt for the shafts of Cupid" (Charlotte Brontë, *The Professor,* 1857).

cup is full *See* MY CUP RUNNETH OVER.

cup runneth over, my *See* MY CUP RUNNETH OVER.

curse God and die *See* JOB'S WIFE.

curse of Cain *See* MARK OF CAIN.

curse the day I was born An expression of despair at the situation one finds oneself in. The expression comes from Job 3:1–11, in which Job laments the pain he suffers from the boils with which he is afflicted: "After this opened Job his mouth, and cursed his day . . . Let the day perish wherein I was born, and the night *in which* it was said, There is a man child conceived . . . Why died I not from the womb? *Why* did I *not* give up the ghost when I came out of the belly?" *At this latest blow the general loudly cursed the day he was born and retired to his room, where he remained for the next three days, sulking.*

cut the Gordian knot (gordeeăn) To take a direct route in solving a complex problem. The allusion is to the story of the intricate knot with which Gordius, a peasant who became king of Phrygia, attached his wagon to the yoke. It was said that any person who could untie the knot would become ruler of all Asia. When Alexander the Great was presented with the challenge of unloosing the knot he simply cut through it with his sword. "When he became prime minister last April, Koizumi was supposed to be the clean-up kid who would cut through Japan's Gordian knot of bureaucratic inertia and political torpor to bring about reform" (*Guardian Weekly,* February 14, 2002). " 'Is not such the doom of all speculative men of talent?' said she. 'Do they not all sit wrapt as you now are, cutting imaginary silken cords with their fine edges, while those not so highly tempered sever the everyday Gordian knots of the world's struggle and win wealth and renown?' " (Anthony Trollope, *Barchester Towers,* 1857).

Cyanean rocks *See* SYMPLEGADES.

Cybele (<u>si</u>bilee) Personification of the Earth or of nature. Cybele was identified as the Phrygian goddess of nature, equivalent to the Greek Rhea or Demeter. Her worshipers were noted for their orgiastic rites, which included much spilling of blood. "He had scarce finished his story, when a most violent noise shook the whole house . . . The priests of Cybele do not so rattle their sounding brass" (Henry Fielding, *Tom Jones,* 1749).

cyclopean (sīklō<u>pee</u>ăn) Anything one-eyed or limited in vision; a building style characterized by the use of large undressed blocks of stone. The allusion is to the Cyclops of Greek mythology, one of a breed of giants (Cyclopes) with only one eye, located in the middle of the forehead. The poet Hesiod (c. 800 B.C.) said there were just three Cyclopes, who were cannibals and lived in Sicily and the western coast of Italy. Others claimed they lived on volcanoes, forging thunderbolts for Zeus, and that Mount Etna was their chief abode. To them were attributed various massive edifices erected by otherwise unknown hands in prehistoric times. The word itself comes from the Greek *kuklos* (meaning "circle") and *ops* (meaning "eye"). "He had forgotten that the dead seldom plan their own houses, and with a pang he discovered the name he sought on the cyclopean base of a granite shaft rearing its aggressive height at the angle of two avenues" (Edith Wharton, *The Touchstone,* 1900). *See also* POLYPHEMUS.

cynic (<u>si</u>nik) A person who is inclined automatically to think the worst of people or things. The word was originally applied, for obscure reasons, to the followers of the Greek philosopher Antisthenes (c. 445–c. 360 B.C.), whose number included Diogenes (411–322 B.C.). One suggestion is that the group acquired the name from *kunikos* (meaning "doglike"), a reference to their coarse manners, while another has it that they used to meet in a school called the Kunosarges (meaning "white dog"). The Cynics rejected the conventions and standards of society and instead emphasized self-discipline of the individual. "There is very little intelligent design in the majority of marriages; but they are none the worse for that. Intelligence leads people astray as far as passion sometimes. I know you are not a cynic" (Joseph Conrad, *Chance,* 1914).

Cynthia (<u>sin</u>theeă) Personification of the Moon. As a surname of Artemis and Diana in classical mythology, Cynthia was so called after Mount Cynthius in Delos, where she was reputed to have been born. In Elizabethan times the name became one of the epithets by which several leading poets addressed Elizabeth I (1533–1603). *The pale orb of Cynthia dominated the scene, casting a wan glow over the lawns leading down to the river.*

Daedalian (di<u>day</u>leeăn) Skillful, ingenious, or labyrinthine. The adjective, also encountered in the variant forms **Daedalean** or **Daedelic,** refers to the legendary Athenian craftsman Daedalus, who was renowned for his skill as an inventor and engineer. Having fled his native Athens after murdering his pupil Talos in a fit of professional jealousy, he was employed by King Minos of Crete and built the wooden cow with which Queen Pasiphae coupled and consequently gave birth to the monstrous Minotaur. Daedalus also designed the LABYRINTH at Knossos in which the Minotaur was imprisoned until its eventual destruction at the hands of Theseus. The outraged King Minos, realizing that Theseus could never have escaped from the Labyrinth without the help of its creator, had Daedalus and his son Icarus confined there, knowing that not even they could find the way out without aid. Daedalus, however, overcame the problem by designing two pairs of wings with which he and his son were able to soar into the air and escape from Crete. Unfortunately, Icarus ignored his father's warning not to fly too high as the heat of the sun's rays would melt the wax holding the wings together, and the lad plummeted into the Aegean Sea and was drowned. Daedalus completed his flight safely and found refuge at the court of the king of Sicily. As further proof of his ingenuity, Daedalus was also credited with the invention of the saw, the ax, and the gimlet, among other devices. *The engineers were confronted by a problem of such Daedalian complexity that for a time it seemed a solution would be beyond any of them.*

Dagon (<u>day</u>gon) A sea monster or whale. In the Bible, Dagon is a Philistine god, possibly with a human upper half and fishlike lower half (Judges 16:23–24 and 1 Samuel 5:1–5). Other authorities do not consider him to be a fish god but rather a storm or grain god, since *Dagon* is related to a Hebrew word for "grain." Samson destroyed the temple to Dagon at Gaza, and Dagon himself died when the ark of God was brought to his house, his body being found next morning with severed head and hands. John Milton, meanwhile, in *Paradise Lost* (1667) identifies Dagon as one of the fallen angels. "In fact, placed before the strict and piercing truth, this whole story will fare like that fish, flesh, and fowl idol of the Philistines, Dagon by name; who being planted before the ark of Israel, his horse's head and both the palms of his hands fell off from him, and only the stump or fishy part of him remained" (Herman Melville, *Moby-Dick,* 1851).

daily bread The income or sustenance necessary in order to live. The phrase has its origins in the Lord's Prayer, where it appears in the form of the petition "Give us this day our daily bread" (Matthew 6:11). ". . . these true gentlefolk showed Polly their respect and regard, put many pleasures in her way, and when they paid her for her work, gave her also the hearty thanks that takes away all sense of degradation even from the humblest service, for money so earned and paid sweetens the daily bread it buys, and makes the mutual obligation a mutual benefit and pleasure" (Louisa May Alcott, *An Old Fashioned Girl,* 1870).

Damascus, road to *See* ROAD TO DAMASCUS.

Damocles, sword of *See* SWORD OF DAMOCLES.

Damon and Pythias (<u>day</u>măn, <u>pith</u>eeas) The archetype of perfect friendship. Damon and Pythias (or ***Phintias***) were two close friends who lived in Sicily under the tyrannical rule of Dionysius of Syracuse in the fifth century B.C. Pythias was a philosopher and follower of Pythagoras who found himself under a death sentence on charges of treason. Dionysius agreed to the condemned man's request to be allowed to go home to settle his affairs on condition that he find someone willing to take his place if he did not return by the due date. Damon immediately volunteered to take his friend's place, and Pythias set off for home. When Pythias was delayed on his return, it seemed Damon would have to be executed in his stead, but at the last moment Pythias rushed back to save his friend's life. Dionysius was deeply moved by the pair's willingness to sacrifice themselves for each other and, having pardoned Pythias, asked to be allowed to participate in their friendship. "Papa, I am really longing to see the

Pythias to your Damon. You know, I never saw him but once, and then we were so puzzled to know what to say to each other that we did not get on particularly well" (Elizabeth Gaskell, *North and South,* 1854–55). *See also* DAVID AND JONATHAN.

danegeld (dayngeld) Payment made to ward off a threat of some kind. The word was coined in the 10th century to describe the payments made by the English on the orders of their king, Ethelred II (978–1016), to appease the Danes, who otherwise threatened to extend their settlements in England. In the event, the policy failed to work, and Ethelred was forced to flee the country in 1013. Danegeld continued to be collected under Canute and subsequent kings even though the threat from the Danes no longer existed. *The shopkeepers carried on paying danegeld to the mafia for decades before plucking up the courage to put up some resistance.*

Daniel come to judgment, a (danyăl) A person who reaches a wise conclusion about something that has left others bewildered, especially one who displays wisdom beyond his or her years. The allusion is to the biblical Daniel, as described in Daniel 5 (where he explained the meaning of the WRITING ON THE WALL). The phrase in its modern form comes from William Shakespeare's *The Merchant of Venice* (c. 1596), in which Shylock hails Portia with the following words: "A Daniel come to judgment! yea a Daniel! / O wise young judge, how I do honour thee!" In a story related in the apocryphal book of Susanna the youthful Daniel successfully defends Susanna against the accusation of being found committing adultery in the shade of a tree by asking her two accusers what kind of tree it was. The two men give different answers and Susanna's innocence is proved. By much the same token any judge who earns respect for his great wisdom might be referred to simply as a *Daniel. It was in this moment of crisis that this young prodigy really proved himself a Daniel come to judgment.*

Daniel in the lions' den (danyăl) A person who is in a position of great danger. The phrase alludes to the biblical story of Daniel in which the Hebrew prophet is accused of defying the rulers of Babylon and is thrown into a cage full of hungry lions: "Then the king commanded, and they brought Daniel, and cast him into the den of lions" (Daniel 6:16). Daniel's courage and faith is rewarded when God saves his life by sealing the lions' mouths so they cannot eat him. By the same token, a ***den of lions*** signifies any situation in which a person finds himself or herself surrounded by others who mean the person harm. *Finding himself suddenly surrounded by rogues and bandits of all description, the journalist quickly appreciated that he was like Daniel in the lions' den.*

Dan to Beersheba, from (dan, beer<u>shee</u>bă) Everywhere; from one end of a kingdom to the other. The biblical town of Dan was located in the north of Canaan and marked the northern limit of ancient Israel, while Beersheba was situated on the southern limit of the kingdom. The phrase appears in Judges 20:1, in which the Israelites are described as being "gathered together as one man, from Dan even to Beer-sheba." *News of his downfall spread quickly, and soon everyone from Dan to Beersheba knew that his star had been eclipsed.*

Daphne (<u>daf</u>nee) The archetype of a woman who seeks to defend her chastity. Daphne was a NYMPH who attracted the amorous attentions of the god Apollo. He pursued her until she called on the other gods to help her and was transformed by them into a laurel, or bay, tree. Apollo swore that from thenceforth he would wear bay leaves in tribute to her. "A spasm passed through Grace. A Daphnean instinct, exceptionally strong in her as a girl, had been revived by her widowed seclusion" (Thomas Hardy, *The Woodlanders,* 1887).

Daphnis and Chloe (<u>daf</u>nis, <u>klō</u>ee) An archetypal pair of young lovers. A celebrated ancient Greek pastoral romance relates how Daphnis and Chloe fell in love and eventually married. Their story was subsequently retold in Allan Ramsay's *Gentle Shepherd* (1725) and Jacques-Henri Bernardin de Saint-Pierre's *Paul et Virginie* (1787), as well as the ballet *Daphnis et Chloe* (1912), with music by Maurice Ravel and choreography by Michel Fokine. *A couple sauntered among the trees and flowers, for all the world like a latter-day Daphnis and Chloe. See also* CHLOE.

darkness *See* EGYPTIAN DARKNESS.

darkness, outer *See* OUTER DARKNESS.

Daughter of Zion *See* ZION.

daughters of Eve *See* EVE.

daughters of men Women. The phrase is biblical in origin, appearing in Genesis 6:1–4 in the course of a passage describing how men or possibly angels began to couple with any woman they chose: "When men began to multiply on the face of the earth . . . the sons of God saw the daughters of men that they were fair; and they took them wives of all which they chose . . . and they bare children to them, the same became mighty men which were of old, men of renown." "She might have been—except for that something radiant in her that marked her apart from all the other daughters of men" (Joseph Conrad, *The Arrow of Gold,* 1919).

David (dayvid) A person noted for his wisdom, courage, chastity, or skill as a musician. In the Bible David was a hero, born the son of Jesse, who slew the giant Goliath and eventually became king of Judah and Israel. According to the Gospel of Luke, he was also an ancestor of Christ. His skill as a harpist brought him the favor of Saul, who found solace in his musicianship, as related in 1 Samuel 16:23: " . . . when the evil spirit from God was upon Saul, that David took an harp and played with his hand: so Saul was refreshed, and was well, and the evil spirit departed from him." The link between David and chastity alludes to the story of the aged David sharing his bed with a young woman named Abishag so that she might chastely warm his body with hers: "The damsel was very fair and cherished the king, and ministered to him: but the king knew her not" (1 Kings 1:4). "You make me feel as I have not felt these twelve months. If Saul could have had you for his David, the evil spirit would have been exorcised without the aid of the harp" (Charlotte Brontë, *Jane Eyre,* 1847). *See also* DAVID AND BATHSHEBA; DAVID AND GOLIATH; DAVID AND JONATHAN; EWE LAMB.

David and Bathsheba (dayvid, bathsheebă) A guilty or treacherous love affair. The allusion is to the biblical episode of 2 Samuel 11, 12, in which King David falls in love with the beautiful Bathsheba and arranges to have her husband, Uriah, sent into the heat of battle to be killed, leaving David free to claim Bathsheba as his wife. The couple later have a child who dies. Psalm 51 records David's repentance. *They looked as guilty as David and Bathsheba, and it was not difficult to guess what had been going on.*

David and Goliath (da̱yvid, goli̱ăth) A contest in which the two sides are unequally matched. The allusion is to the biblical story of David, a humble but devout shepherd boy, who alone faces and defeats the Philistine giant GOLIATH by killing him with a slingshot: "[David] smote the Philistine in his forehead, that the stone sunk into his forehead; and he fell upon his face to the earth" (1 Samuel 17:49). "It is David and Goliath; the man in overalls against the suits in Brussels; UK sovereignty versus burgeoning European power" (*The Guardian,* April 10, 2001).

David and Jonathan (da̱yvid, jo̱năthăn) The epitome of close friendship between two members of the same sex. The biblical hero David, Saul's heir, and Jonathan, the son of Saul, are described as inseparable companions: "It came to pass . . . that the soul of Jonathan was knit with the soul of David, and Jonathan loved him as his own soul" (1 Samuel 18:1). When Saul subsequently became jealous of David, Jonathan attempted to mend relations between his father and his friend, and when Jonathan was ultimately killed in battle, David uttered a sincere lamentation for him. *The pair were inseparable, like David and Jonathan.*

David and Nathan *See* EWE LAMB.

day of judgment *See* JUDGMENT DAY.

day of small things Apparently insignificant details may in time prove to be the beginning of much greater things. The expression appears in the Bible in Zechariah 4:10, in which God reassures Zechariah after some of his people scoff at the relatively unimpressive beginnings of his rebuilding of the Temple: "For who hath despised the day of small things? for they shall rejoice." "I am but the incumbent of a poor country parish: my aid must be of the humblest sort. And if you are inclined to despise the day of small things, seek some more efficient succour than such as I can offer" (Charlotte Brontë, *Jane Eyre,* 1847).

days of one's life, all the For as long as a person lives. The expression comes from Psalm 23:6, in which it appears in the form: "Surely goodness and mercy shall follow me all the days of my life: and I will dwell in the house of the LORD for ever." *That is something to remember all the days of one's life.*

days of our years A person's lifetime, emphasizing the relatively brief time that mortals have on earth. The phrase comes from Psalm 90:10, where it appears in the passage: "The days of our years are threescore years and ten." *Modern science threatens to prolong the days of our years beyond anything our forebears would have believed possible.*

dead bury their dead, let the *See* LET THE DEAD BURY THE DEAD.

dead lion *See* LIVING DOG IS BETTER THAN A DEAD LION, A.

Dead Sea fruit A bitter disappointment or disillusion. The allusion is biblical in origin, referring to the fruit trees grown on the shores of the Dead Sea by the morally degenerate Sodomites. The fruit of these trees was said to be beautiful to look at but bitter to the taste and "within full of ashes," in the words of the French traveler Jean de Thevenot (1633–67). It is also known by the name *apples of Sodom*. "Like to the apples on the Dead Sea shore, / It is all ashes to the taste" (Lord Byron, *Childe Harold,* 1817).

Death, where is thy sting? Death is nothing to fear. The expression comes from 1 Corinthians 15:55, which questions the significance of mortal death when compared with everlasting life in heaven: "O death, where is thy sting? O grave, where is thy victory?" In modern usage, the phrase is best known for its inclusion in funeral services. *He died with a smile on his face, as if to say, "Death, where is thy sting?"*

death's door, at At the point of death; very ill. The phrase derives from Miles Coverdale's translation of Psalm 107:18, as found in the *Book of Common Prayer*: "Their soul abhorred all manner of meat: and they were even hard at death's door." "He had had more than one attack of delirium tremens after his father's death, and had almost been at death's door" (Anthony Trollope, *Doctor Thorne,* 1858).

Deborah (debrǎ) A courageous woman, especially one noted for her virtue or devotion to God. The original Deborah was a biblical prophet and judge who urged Barak to lead an army against the invading Canaanites, spurring him on to victory at the Kishon River, a triumph she celebrated in a memorable victory ode dubbed the "Song of Deborah" (Judges

5:1–31). "Stay, stay thy hands! Thou art an Amazon / And fightest with the sword of Deborah" (William Shakespeare, *Henry VI, Part I*, 1589).

deep calleth unto deep A metaphor evoking a profound spiritual or philosophical understanding between two individuals, parties, etc. The phrase comes from Psalm 42:7, which interprets waterfalls or cataracts as representing the soul's restless yearning for God: "Deep calleth unto deep at the noise of thy waterspouts: all thy waves and thy billows are gone over me." *There existed an immediate bond of mutual understanding between the two great men, a vivid illustration of deep calleth unto deep.*

Deimos (dāymăs) A personification of fear. In Greek mythology, Deimos was identified as the god of fear, son of Ares and Aphrodite. *The spirit of Deimos had possessed them and they charged as one for the exit.*

Deirdre (deerdră, deerdree) The archetype of a woman whose beauty causes only tragedy. According to Irish legend, Deirdre was the daughter of a storyteller whose beauty, it was predicted, would bring about the ruin of Ulster. King Conchobar's plans to marry her were disrupted when she eloped with Naoise, one of the three sons of Usnech, and fled with him to Scotland. Conchobar lured them back with promises of forgiveness, but when they returned, he had the three brothers killed. Deirdre is variously said to have committed suicide or to have died of grief a year later. Her story was dramatized by both William Butler Yeats (*Deirdre*, 1907) and John Millington Synge (*Deirdre of the Sorrows*, 1910). *What with all her moaning and grieving she's a regular Deirdre and no mistake.*

delenda est Carthago (delendă est kahrthahgō) Any obstacle that stands in the way must be removed at all costs. This proverbial phrase is a quotation from Cato the Elder (234–149 B.C.), who took to ending every speech he made in the Roman senate with these words after visiting Carthage in 157 B.C. and realizing that it was becoming a serious rival to Rome. *The president will not be moved on this issue. It's a case of delenda est Carthago.*

Delilah (dălīlă) A seductive, treacherous woman; a temptress. The biblical Delilah, whose name means "dainty one," was a Philistine whore who at the command of the Philistine leaders used her seductives wiles to trick

SAMSON into revealing the secret of his great strength (his long hair) and then used this knowledge to bring about his ruin, having his hair cut short as he slept in her lap, as related at Judges 16:4–20. "What is the good of the love of woman when her name must needs be Delilah?" (H. G. Wells, *The Invisible Man,* 1897).

deliver us from evil A prayer for protection against harm. The expression comes from the Lord's Prayer: "And lead us not into temptation, but deliver us from evil" (Matthew 6:13). In modern usage it is sometimes quoted ironically in the form of a plea for relief from some minor irritation. "'Lead us not into temptation but deliver us from evil. But what is temptation? What is evil?'" (Anthony Trollope, *Barchester Towers,* 1857).

Delphic (delfik) Obscure in meaning; enigmatic; ambiguous. The Delphic oracle was a shrine situated at Delphi on the slopes of Mount Parnassus, thought by ancient Greeks to be the center of the world. Here a priestess known as the Pythia, seated upon a tripod, communicated messages from the god Apollo on a wide range of topics, from domestic matters to international affairs, often at the request of rulers or other powerful political figures. Many of these pieces of advice were obscure in meaning and open to a variety of interpretations, hence the use of the term *Delphic* to describe anything that sounds important but is in fact unclear in meaning. At one point in the fifth century B.C. the pronouncements of the oracle at Delphi became noticeably more specific, recommending that the Greeks give up their hopeless resistance against the Persians. When the Persians were subsequently defeated, the oracle was heavily criticized, and future pronouncements were wisely delivered with more of their former ambiguity. The temple at Delphi was finally closed down in A.D. 390 on the command of the emperor Theodosius. ". . . it was his wont to relapse into grim silence when interrogated in sceptical sort as to any of his sententious oracles, not always very clear ones, rather partaking of that obscurity which invests most Delphic deliverances from any quarter" (Herman Melville, *Billy Budd,* 1924).

Demeter (dămeeter) A personification of fertility. In Greek mythology, Demeter was a corn goddess equivalent to the Roman Ceres. She was the goddess of fruit, crops, and vegetation and the mother of Persephone.

When Persephone was carried off to the underworld by Hades, Demeter threatened that the earth would remain barren until Persephone was returned to her. It was eventually agreed that Persephone would spend nine months of the year with her mother, when crops would grow and plants would bear fruit, and three months with Hades, when the earth would remain barren. *There was real warmth in the spring sunshine, suggesting that Demeter had at long last been released from the underworld and returned to the light.*

Demosthenic (demosthǎenik) Eloquent; persuasive; possessing or showing great powers of oratory or eloquence. The Athenian statesman Demosthenes (384–322 B.C.) was greatly admired as an orator, although as a youth he struggled with a weak voice and stammer. He improved his speaking technique by such devices as learning to talk clearly with his mouth stuffed with pebbles and competing in volume with the sound of the waves crashing on the shore. Ultimately, his skill as an orator proved his undoing after his criticisms of Philip of Macedonia incurred the latter's wrath and he was obliged to kill himself by taking poison when the Macedonians invaded. "Those are distinctions which we hardly understand on this thick-headed side of the water. But demagogues, democrats, demonstrations, and Demosthenic oratory are all equally odious to John Eustace" (Anthony Trollope, *The Eustace Diamonds,* 1873). *See also* PHILIPPIC.

denarius (denahreeǎs) Ready money; cash. The denarius was the basic silver coin in ancient Rome. *I bet that car cost a pretty denarius.*

den of lions *See* DANIEL IN THE LIONS' DEN.

den of thieves A place where thieves or other dishonest characters are likely to be found. According to Matthew 21:13 Christ entered the Temple only to find that it had been taken over as a place of business by money changers, causing him to lament, "It is written, My house shall be called the house of prayer; but ye have made it a den of thieves." Christ then overturned their tables and threw the money changers out of the Temple. In modern usage the phrase is often applied to any financial institution or business suspected of using unscrupulous methods. "The ordinary of Newgate preached to women who were to swing at Tyburn for a petty theft as if they were worse than other people,—just as though he would not have been a pickpocket or shoplifter, himself, if he had been born in a den of thieves and bred up to steal or starve!" (Oliver Wendell Holmes, *Elsie Venner,* 1861). *See also* CAST MONEY CHANGERS OUT OF THE TEMPLE.

depart in peace *See* NUNC DIMITTIS.

desert shall blossom, the The land will be returned to its rightful owners one day. The phrase comes from Isaiah 35:1–2, which consists of the prophecy that the Israelites shall one day reclaim their homeland in Zion: "The desert shall rejoice, and blossom as the rose. It shall blossom abundantly, and rejoice even with joy and singing." This was originally a promise that the Babylonian exiles would return to their homeland in Palestine, but in modern times the prophecy has been quoted many times by those defending the controversial extension of Israeli settlements into areas formerly populated by Palestinians. *The Israeli government has promised that the desert shall bloom, but without detailing the cost they are prepared to pay in lives.*

deus ex machina (dayǎs eks makǐnǎ) An unexpected or contrived solution to an apparently insoluble difficulty. Literally translated from Latin as "a god from a machine," the expression referred originally to the practice of Euripides (c. 484–406 B.C.) and other classical Greek dramatists of bringing their plots to an artificial resolution in the final act through the sudden appearance on stage of a god, who used his powers to make everything right. It is thought that such characters were lowered from above the stage using some kind of mechanical device, hence "from a machine." "Dr Gwynne was the Deus ex machina who was to come down upon the Barchester stage and bring about deliverance from these terrible evils" (Anthony Trollope, *Barchester Towers,* 1857).

devil *See* SATAN.

devil chained A potentially harmful individual, creature, organization, etc., that has been placed under restraint. The expression alludes to the image given to John of Satan being put in chains: "And he laid hold on the dragon, that old serpent which is the Devil, and Satan, and bound him a thousand years" (Revelation 20:2). *The vicious old man thrashed and strained in the arms that held him back, like a devil chained.*

devils believe and tremble Even the most wicked people have a conscience or lingering belief in good that may trouble them. The sentiment appears in the Bible: "Thou believest that there is one God; thou doest well: the devils also believe, and tremble" (James 2:19). *Fear convulsed the murderer's face when he was shown photographs of his victim, proving that even devils believe and tremble, as the saying goes.*

Diana of the Ephesians (dīanǎ, e̲f̲e̲e̲zhǎnz) Someone or thing that serves to distract attention from the truth. According to Acts 19:24–28, Diana of the Ephesians was a fertility goddess with many breasts. Paul urged Diana's worshipers to give her up but met with objections from the local silversmiths, who were earning a great deal of money selling trinkets at the temple of Diana. The followers of Diana shouted "Great is Diana of the Ephesians," and ever since then the phrase has been quoted in circumstances when a person stands accused of being blinded by his or her own self-interest. "Then he wad rather claver wi' a daft quean they ca' Diana Vernon (weel I wet they might ca' her Diana of the Ephesians, for she's little better than a heathen—better? she's waur—a Roman, a mere Roman)" (Sir Walter Scott, *Rob Roy,* 1817). *See also* ARTEMIS.

diaspora (dīa̲spǎrǎ) The dispersion of people through migration or forced removal. The word was originally applied to the scattering of the Jews after the Babylonian exile. In modern usage the word has been applied much more generally, though it is still often understood to refer specifically to Jewish communities scattered throughout the world. *The extent of the Scottish diaspora means that a Scotsman abroad can be confident of finding sympathetic hosts in any major city in the developed world.*

Dido and Aeneas (dīdō, ǎne̲e̲as) An archetype of tragic love. The love affair between the Trojan adventurer Aeneas and Dido, queen of Carthage, was told in Virgil's *Aeneid* (29–19 B.C.). Dido fell in love with Aeneas after the latter was shipwrecked off Carthage but was ultimately unable to dissuade him from sailing on to Italy on the command of Jupiter. After he left she committed suicide by throwing herself onto a pyre. *One had the feeling that their love was doomed from the start, like Dido and Aeneas. See also* AENEAS.

die is cast, the An irrevocable step has been taken; there is no going back now. This common expression, in its Latin form *alea jacta est,* originated in a saying by Julius Caesar as he ordered his army across the Rubicon River toward Rome in 49 B.C., a step tantamount to an act of war. The reference is to gambling with dice (from the obvious truth that once a die is thrown, the cast cannot be taken back). "'But I have no purpose of debating these points with you, my lord,' waving his hand, as if to avoid farther discussion; 'the die is cast with you; allow me only to express my sorrow for the disastrous fate to which Angus M'Aulay's natural rashness, and your lordship's influence, are dragging my gallant friend Allan here, with his father's clan, and many a brave man besides'" (Sir Walter Scott, *A Legend of Montrose,* 1819). *See also* CROSS THE RUBICON.

die like roland *See* ROLAND.

dies irae (<u>dee</u>ayz <u>ee</u>ray) A day of reckoning. Latin for "day of wrath," the phrase appears at Zephaniah 1:15, in which Zephaniah foresees a "day of wrath, a day of trouble and distress," generally interpreted as a reference to the Day of Judgment. Subsequently it became widely familiar as the opening words of a medieval Latin hymn used in funeral and requiem masses. "One thing is certain,—that there is a mustering among the masses, the world over; and there is a dies irae coming on, sooner or later" (Harriet Beecher Stowe, *Uncle Tom's Cabin,* 1852). *See also* JUDGMENT DAY.

dii penates *See* LARES AND PENATES.

dilemma, horns of a *See* HORNS OF A DILEMMA.

dinner of herbs *See* BETTER A DINNER OF HERBS THAN A STALLED OX WHERE HATE IS.

Diogenes (dīojăneez) A seeker of truth and honesty, especially one who is cynical about his or her chances of finding it. The original Diogenes (c. 412–320 B.C.) was a Greek philosopher who founded the Cynics, a school of philosophers whose ideals included the pursuit of asceticism and independence. According to tradition, he lived in an earthenware tub and carried a lantern in broad daylight to further his search for an honest man. His name may also be encountered in that of the *Diogenes crab,* which is a West Indian hermit crab that inhabits the abandoned shells of other creatures (reminiscent of the philosopher in his tub), and also in that of the *Diogenes cup,* the hollow formed in the palm of the hand when the fingers are unstraightened (a reference to the simple lifestyle associated with the Cynics). "The magistrate took the light out of the servant-maid's hand, and advanced to his scrutiny, like Diogenes in the street of Athens, lantern-in-hand, and probably with as little expectation as that of the cynic, that he was likely to encounter any especial treasure in the course of his researches" (Sir Walter Scott, *Rob Roy,* 1817).

Diomedean exchange (dīō<u>mee</u>deeăn) A bargain in which one side gets all the benefit. The phrase alludes to an episode in Homer's *Iliad* (c. 700 B.C.) in which Glaucus and Diomedes exchange suits of armor. Glaucus hands over a fine suit of armor "of gold divinely wrought," whereas all Diomedes has to offer is an almost worthless suit of brass armor "of mean device." Also known as a *Glaucus swap. With the benefit of hindsight it seems clear that this was a Diomedean exchange, with the government getting nothing out of it.*

Diomedes *See* LABORS OF HERCULES.

Dionysian (dīō<u>nee</u>zheeăn, dīō<u>nee</u>shăn) Wild, frenzied, uninhibited, abandoned, orgiastic. In Greek mythology Dionysus was the son of Zeus and Semele and the god of wine, fruitfulness, and vegetation, equivalent to the Roman Bacchus. It was Dionysus who, according to myth, invented wine and developed the cultivation of grapes. The five festivals held in Athens each year in his honor were notorious for the frenzied and licentious behavior of the celebrants, who indulged freely in drink and sex. These festivals gave birth to the Greek theater. *As a student he had pursued a Dionysian lifestyle, holding riotous parties and rarely spending an evening at home.*

Dioscorea (dios<u>kor</u>eeă) A genus of plants belonging to the yam family. It was named in honor of the Greek physician Dioscorides Pedanius

(c. A.D. 40–c. 90), who studied a wide variety of plants in order to gather information about their medicinal properties while serving as a surgeon in the Roman army. He was later recognized as one of the fathers of modern botany. *There are probably many more secrets to learn about* Dioscorea.

Dioscuri *See* CASTOR AND POLLUX.

disciple A follower or pupil of a religious teacher or other leader. The word is most familiar from its application in the Bible to the 12 apostles and to followers of Christ more generally. ". . . the doctrine it contain'd was by degrees universally adopted by the philosophers of Europe, in preference to that of the abbé; so that he lived to see himself the last of his sect, except Monsieur B——, of Paris, his élève and immediate disciple" (Benjamin Franklin, *Autobiography,* 1793).

discord, apple of *See* APPLE OF DISCORD.

Dives (dīveez) A very rich man, especially one who is obsessed with material concerns and ignores the interests of others. In the Bible, Christ tells the story of a rich man named Dives who ignores the plight of the beggar Lazarus at his gate and is consequently condemned to an eternity in hell while Lazarus goes to heaven (Luke 16:19–31). The rich man is not actually named in the original text but acquired the name in the Latin version of the New Testament, apparently from the Latin *dives,* meaning "rich." "Remember, we are bid to work while it is day—warned that 'the night cometh when no man shall work.' Remember the fate of Dives, who had his good things in this life" (Charlotte Brontë, *Jane Eyre,* 1847).

divided against itself *See* HOUSE DIVIDED AGAINST ITSELF, A.

divide the sheep from the goats *See* SEPARATE THE SHEEP FROM THE GOATS.

dog days The hottest days of summer. The concept is of ancient Roman origin, having its roots in early astronomy and the fact that the star SIRIUS, the brightest star in the night sky and commonly called the dog star, rose with the Sun at this time of year. Romans believed that the dog star, so-named because it was placed at the head of the constellation Canis Major (meaning "greater dog"), added its heat to that of the Sun and exerted a baleful influence upon human affairs, making mortals drowsy and listless and bringing forth droughts and disease. Changes in the movements of the stars over the centuries mean that Sirius today rises some time later in the year in the Northern Hemisphere. *The long-standing difference of opinion ignited once more during the dog days of summer, when the heat made everybody irritable and argumentative.*

dog has his day, every *See* EVERY DOG HAS HIS DAY.

dog in the manger, a A person who selfishly prevents others from enjoying what he or she cannot enjoy him or herself. The expression comes from a fable by the Greek writer Aesop (620–560 B.C.) in which a surly dog sits on a pile of hay in a manger, preventing some cows from eating it, even though he cannot eat it himself. "'I suppose it is wrong and selfish,' he said. 'I suppose I am a dog in a manger. But I do own that there is a consolation to me in the assurance that she will never be the wife of that scoundrel'" (Anthony Trollope, *The Last Chronicle of Barset,* 1867).

dog must be bad indeed that is not worth a bone, the *See* LABORER IS WORTHY OF HIS HIRE, THE.

dog returneth to his vomit, a Fools and criminals tend to be drawn irresistibly back to their follies or crimes. This proverb is biblical in origin, appearing in Proverbs 26:11, "As a dog returneth to his vomit, so a fool returneth to his folly," and in 2 Peter 2:22. In modern usage the proverb is usually quoted with reference to criminals who cannot resist returning to the scene of their crimes. *The gang came back to the scene of the murder that very evening, drawn like dogs to their vomit.*

do not let your left hand know what your right hand is doing *See* LEFT HAND KNOW WHAT YOUR RIGHT HAND IS DOING, DO NOT LET YOUR.

don't go to bed angry *See* SUN GO DOWN ON ONE'S ANGER, DON'T LET THE.

doomsday (doomzday) A final, terrible day of reckoning, especially one marking the end of the world. In Anglo-Saxon England the word *doom* signified a "legal ruling," but in modern usage the word evokes images of the destruction accompanying the end of the world as described in the Book of Revelation. "'I was all riled up, Anne, and I said she might stay till doomsday if she waited for that; and I stuck to it'" (Lucy Maud Montgomery, *Anne of Avonlea,* 1909). *See also* JUDGMENT DAY.

Dorcas Society (dorkăs) A women's group that makes clothing for charity. These Anglican church groups take their name from the biblical Dorcas (also called Tabitha), a Christian woman of Joppa who, according to Acts 9:39, was noted for her good works, which included making "coats and garments" for needy widows. When she died and was laid out for burial, Peter brought her back to life through his prayers. "'Do any of you wish to take articles home, to do at odd times?' said Fan, who was president of this energetic Dorcas Society" (Louisa May Alcott, *An Old-Fashioned Girl,* 1870).

Doric (dorik) Simple, rustic, or uncouth. The inhabitants of the mountainous region of Doris in ancient Greece and their way of life (especially the dialect of Greek that they spoke) were considered simple and unrefined in comparison with other Greek peoples and their more sophisticated lifestyles (*see* ATTIC). The term *Doric* is still used today to imply a rustic, pastoral character, especially in relation to rural dialects and the arts: Pastoral poetry is occasionally called the **Doric reed,** for example. The **Doric order** in ancient Greek architecture was similarly denoted by its strong and relatively plain, unsophisticated character. "When, early in a summer afternoon, we have been shaking the dust of the village from the skirts of our garments, making haste past those houses with purely Doric or Gothic fronts, which have such an air of repose about them, my companion whispers that probably about these times their occupants are all gone to bed" (Henry David Thoreau, "Walking," 1851). *See also* CORINTHIAN; IONIC; TUSCAN.

do thou likewise *See* GO AND DO THOU LIKEWISE.

doubting Thomas (tomăs) A person who remains unconvinced about something until firm proof is proffered. The allusion is to the biblical Thomas, the apostle who declined to believe in Christ's resurrection until allowed to see and touch Christ's wounds for himself: "But he said unto them, Except I shall see in his hands the print of the nails, and put my finger into the print of the nails, and thrust my hand into his side, I will not believe" (John 20:25). Christ eventually showed himself so that Thomas might satisfy his doubts but rebuked him for his lack of faith. *His uncle remained stubbornly unconvinced and it seemed nothing would persuade this doubting Thomas.*

do unto others *See* GOLDEN RULE.

dove of peace A symbol of peace and reconciliation. The association between doves and peace is biblical in origin, arising from the story of the dove that was sent out by Noah to see if the Flood was receding (Genesis 8:8–12). When the dove returned with an olive branch in its beak, Noah interpreted this as a sign that God was reconciled with humankind once more and that the waters were retreating. Because the Holy Spirit descended to Christ in the form of a dove at his baptism, the bird may also be treated as a symbol of the Holy Spirit, purity, or divine inspiration. *The dove of peace has settled on this land today and the sound of gunfire is heard no more. See also* OLIVE BRANCH.

draconian (drăkōneeăn, draykōneeăn) Excessively harsh or severe. The word alludes to Draco, the lawyer who in 621 B.C. drew up the first written code of justice for his fellow Athenians. The laws imposed in Draco's name, supposedly written in blood rather than ink, were notorious for their severity, with the death sentence being imposed for even relatively petty offenses, hence the modern use of the term *draconian*. In reality, Draco's code did not last very long, and in 590 B.C. a less exacting code of laws was devised by the Athenian statesman Solon. Although popular in his own time for putting the law in some kind of order, albeit harsh, Draco himself came to a premature end when he was smothered under the heaps of garments and flowers that admiring Athenians showered on him during a visit to the theater. "Such an attitude should hearten China's draconian womb police, who have spent two decades trying to control the nation's burgeoning population through any means possible" (*Time*, July 30, 2001).

dragon's teeth *See* SOW DRAGON'S TEETH.

drink hemlock To voluntarily sacrifice oneself by resigning, committing suicide, etc. The phrase alludes to the death of the Athenian philosopher Socrates (469–399 B.C.), who was obliged to kill himself by drinking hemlock after speaking out against the ruling elite in Athens and being sentenced to death at the subsequent trial. *The head of the party took the honorable way out, drinking hemlock by giving up his post and throwing himself on the mercy of the press.*

drop in the ocean A tiny or insignificant amount; something that makes little real difference. The phrase is biblical in origin, having its roots in Isaiah 40:15, which compares the relatively minor importance of nations with the immense grandeur of God: "Behold, the nations are as a drop of a bucket, and are counted as the small dust of the balance: behold, he taketh up the isles as a very little thing." "And what is our life? One line in the great story of the Church, whose son and daughter we are; one handful in the sand of time, one drop in the ocean of 'For ever'" (Charles Reade, *The Cloister and the Hearth,* 1861).

dryad *See* NYMPH.

dry bones, valley of *See* VALLEY OF DRY BONES.

dulce et decorum est pro patria mori (<u>doo</u>lkay et de<u>kor</u>ăm est prō <u>p</u>atreeă <u>mo</u>ree) It is sweet and becoming to die for one's country. This patriotic sentiment is a quotation from the *Odes* of Horace (65–8 B.C.). "My breast heaved—my form dilated—my eye flashed as I spoke these words. 'Tyrants!' said I, 'dulce et decorum est pro patria mori.' Having thus clinched the argument, I was silent" (William Makepeace Thackeray, *The Adventures of Major Gahagan,* 1839).

dust, unto *See* UNTO DUST SHALT THOU RETURN.

dust to dust *See* UNTO DUST SHALT THOU RETURN.

dybbuk (<u>di</u>băk) A demonic spirit or machine that has the power to take over a person. The dybbuk appeared early in the annals of Jewish folklore, being described originally as a type of malevolent wandering soul that could possess a living person until formally exorcised. The term became more widely familiar through the classic Yiddish play *The Dybbuk* (1920) by Solomon Ansky. *His grandmother decided that his behavior was so untypical the only explanation was that he had been taken over by a dybbuk.*

e

ears to hear The ability to hear or understand. The phrase is biblical in origin, coming from Matthew 13:43, and on certain other occasions at the conclusion of Jesus' parables: "Who hath ears to hear, let him hear." A misprint in an 1810 version of the Bible that read "Who hath ears to ear, let him hear" led to that version being known as the "Ears to Ear Bible." "One of those wretches whose hearts the Lord had hardened, who, having ears, heard not, having eyes, saw not, and who should find no place for repentance though they sought it even with their tears" (Samuel Butler, *The Way of All Flesh,* 1903). *The headmaster said, "If any student has ears to hear, then will he please note the school rule that smoking is strictly forbidden on all school premises at all times."*

earthshaking Momentous; of fundamental importance. The notion that some events and ideas are so important they make the earth shake has its roots in Greek mythology. The sea god Poseidon was often referred to as "Earthshaker" because he could raise storms and tidal waves. Homer also identified Poseidon as the god of earthquakes. *This discovery could have earthshaking consequences for everyone involved in deep space research.*

ease in Zion *See* AT EASE IN ZION.

east of Eden (<u>ee</u>dăn) A featureless, desolate place or situation; a place of wandering or exile. According to Genesis 4:16, it was to an area "on the east of Eden" that Cain was exiled after he murdered his brother Abel. The phrase is best known today as the title of a 1952 novel by John Steinbeck that relates the events that unfold after Adam Trask moves to California with his warring sons Caleb and Aaron. *He lives somewhere east of Eden, out beyond the bounds of civilized society. See also* LAND OF NOD.

eat, drink, and be merry Enjoy yourself while you have the chance. The expression comes from the parable of the rich fool related at Luke 12:16–21, in which Christ describes a rich farmer who stores up his wealth for future indulgence and dies before ever enjoying the benefits of it. The parable serves as a warning to those who see the enjoyment of material wealth rather than devotion to God as the ultimate ambition of their lives. The phrase also appears at Ecclesiastes 8:15 in the form "a man hath no better thing under the sun, than to eat, and to drink, and to be merry." In modern usage the phrase is equally likely to be quoted as a criticism of those who indulge in worldly pleasures without thought for the future and, paradoxically, as a justification by those making the most of an immediate opportunity to indulge themselves in the knowledge that the chance may not be there for long. The sentiment is often extended to *eat, drink, and be merry, for tomorrow we die*, as found in Isaiah 22:13 and 1 Corinthians 15:32. "Such a man, nevertheless, was the Reverend Samuel Pentecost, and such a woman was the Reverend Samuel's mother; and in the dearth of any other producible guests, there they were, engaged to eat, drink, and be merry for the day at Mr Armadale's pleasure party to the Norfolk Broads" (Wilkie Collins, *Armadale*, 1866).

eater, out of the *See* OUT OF THE STRONG CAME FORTH SWEETNESS.

eat from the tree of knowledge *See* TREE OF KNOWLEDGE.

Ebenezer chapel (ebăneezer) A Nonconformist chapel. This informal title alludes to the biblical episode related in 1 Samuel 7:12 in the course of which Samuel sets up a memorial stone in thanks to God for his victory over the Philistines, giving it the name Ebenezer (meaning "stone of help") and explaining, "Thus far has the LORD helped us." *The family attended the local Ebenezer chapel and took their religion very seriously.*

ecce homo (ekay hōmō) A depiction of Christ wearing a crown of thorns. A Latin phrase usually translated as "behold the man," it appears in John 19:5 as the words spoken by Pontius Pilate when he presented Christ to the people. In modern usage, the phrase is sometimes applied in both its Latin and English forms more widely to any person who is presently a subject of attention. *"Ecce homo!" exclaimed the bishop as the inspector entered the room.*

echo A repetition of a sound or other radiation when reflected by some solid medium; any repetition or imitation of an idea, event, etc. In Greek mythology, Echo was a mountain nymph who fell in love with the beautiful youth Narcissus but wasted away when he ignored her until all that was left of her was her voice. *The echo of breaking glass reverberated through the empty house.*

Eden, Garden of *See* GARDEN OF EDEN.

Egeria (ăjeereeă) A woman counselor or adviser. According to Roman mythology, the original Egeria was a nymph who gave valuable advice to Numa Pompilius (753–673 B.C.), the second king of Rome; thus, her name is sometimes cited in describing any female source of inspiration. "Thus, false to his nation, yet true to the new Egeria of his thoughts and actions—traitor to the requirements of vengeance and war, yet faithful to the interests of tranquillity and love—did he seek, night after night, Antonina's presence" (Wilkie Collins, *Antonina,* 1850).

Egyptian darkness (ăjipshăn) Impenetrable darkness. The phrase alludes to the all-enveloping darkness that fell upon Egypt at God's command, constituting the ninth of the 10 plagues with which the Egyptians were afflicted, according to Exodus 7–12. The phrase may sometimes also describe deep melancholy or some other mental state making a person's thoughts inaccessible to others. "And one, more grave, lost in a man's hat and feather, walked in Egyptian darkness, handed by a girl; another had the great saucepan on his back, and a tremendous three-footed clay-pot sat on his head and shoulders, swallowing him so as he too went darkling led by his sweetheart three foot high" (Charles Reade, *The Cloister and the Hearth,* 1861). *See also* NINTH PLAGUE OF EGYPT; PLAGUES OF EGYPT.

Egyptian gold (ăjipshăn) Something of value whose theft or borrowing from its former owners is felt to be justified on the grounds that it may now be put to better use. The phrase alludes to the theft of jewels and vessels of gold and silver from the Egyptians on the flight of the Israelites from the country, as described in Exodus 12:35. Some Christian theologians interpreted the episode as justification for borrowing from pagan tradition anything that could be put to a better Christian purpose. *This Egyptian gold* *was now put to much better use, funding the establishment of various small enterprises throughout the region that otherwise might never have found backing.*

Egypt's firstborn *See* PLAGUES OF EGYPT.

eighth wonder of the world An outstanding edifice or achievement of some kind; alternatively and ironically, a remarkable failure. The ancient world boasted just seven wonders, as recorded by the Greek historian Herodotus in the fifth century B.C. Although his was not the only list and there was some debate about what should be included prior to medieval times, the list is now generally accepted as including the Pyramids at Giza, the Hanging Gardens of Babylon, the Statue of Zeus at Olympia, the Temple of Artemis at Ephesus, the Mausoleum of Halicarnassus, the Colossus of Rhodes, and the Pharos of Alexandria. Many lists of remarkable buildings or other feats have since been compiled following much the same pattern. "A handsome man was an eighth wonder of the world, at Miss Wigger's school" (Wilkie Collins, *Evil Genius,* 1886).

Electra complex (ălektră) The subconscious sexual attraction of a daughter to her father or a father figure, often to the exclusion of the mother. This Freudian concept takes its name from the Greek myth about Electra, which was brought to life in great dramas by Aeschylus, Euripides, and Sophocles. Electra was the daughter of Agamemnon, king of Mycenae, and Clytemnestra. Electra helped her brother Orestes kill their mother and her lover after Clytemnestra had murdered their father. *She gave up on her psychoanalyst and stormed off in a high temper after he had the temerity to suggest she might be suffering from some kind of an Electra complex. See also* OEDIPUS COMPLEX.

Eleusinian mystery (elyoosineeăn) Any obscure ritual or process. The original Eleusinian mysteries were the rituals observed in strict secrecy in honor of the corn goddess Demeter and her daughter Persephone at Eleusis, near Athens. Only the participants knew what took place at the rituals. The purpose of the rites was to ensure divine protection of crops in the year ahead. The rituals, which also had significance for devotees of Dionysus, were eventually abolished by the emperor Theodosius toward the end of the fourth century A.D. "They were, and felt themselves to be, the only true depositaries left of certain Eleusinian mysteries, of certain deep and wondrous services of worship by which alone the gods could be rightly approached" (Anthony Trollope, *Barchester Towers,* 1857).

eleventh hour, at the *See* AT THE ELEVENTH HOUR.

Elijah (ălījă) A prophet, especially one who foresees coming disaster. The biblical prophet Elijah warned King Ahab of a forthcoming drought (1 Kings 17:1) and mocked the king's false prophets (1 Kings 18:27) and their god Baal before fleeing the country. *This Elijah on the loose stormed through the Capital, haranguing any member of Congress who ventured out of his or her office to see what the commotion was. See also* CHARIOT OF FIRE; MANTLE OF ELIJAH.

Elijah's fiery chariot *See* CHARIOT OF FIRE.

Elijah's mantle *See* MANTLE OF ELIJAH.

Elisha (ălīshă) A devoted follower; a disciple. According to 2 Kings 2:13, Elisha was the son of a prosperous farmer who was made the heir of Elijah when the latter rose to heaven in a fiery chariot. His name may also be invoked when a person is taunted of the grounds of baldness, Elisha being himself bald headed. *He was surprised to find that in the intervening years his cousin had lost all his hair and was now as bald as Elisha.*

elysian fields (ălĭzhăn) Heaven, paradise, or some other idyllic place. *Elysium* (meaning "happy, delightful") was the name of paradise in Greek and Roman mythology, a pastoral place situated "at the world's end" and ruled by Rhadamanthus, judge of the dead. At Elysium heroes could take their ease after death. It is described as a place of perpetual springtime and sunlight, where there are no storms, rain, or snow. The name has since been featured in a number of addresses in the real world, among them the Champs-Elysées in Paris and the Elysian Fields district of New Orleans. "To the eyes of the frequenters of these Elysian fields, where so many men and shadows daily steal recreation, to the eyes of all drinking in those green gardens their honeyed draught of peace, this husband and wife appeared merely a distinguished-looking couple, animated by a leisured harmony" (John Galsworthy, *The Forsyte Saga,* 1922).

empiric A person who pretends to be something he or she is not; a quack. The word was applied originally to the school of medicine founded by Serapion of Alexandria (c.200-150 B.C.), who placed particular emphasis on observation and experiment in treatment rather than on the opinions of conventional medical authorities. This led to the practitioners of this school acquiring reputations as quacks. "He once more endeavored to pass the supposed empiric, scorning even the parade of threatening to use the knife, or tomahawk, that was pendent from his belt" (James Fenimore Cooper, *The Last of the Mohicans,* 1826).

empty the vials of one's wrath *See* VIALS OF WRATH.

empyrean (empīreeăn) Alternative name for heaven or the heavens. The Greek astronomer, mathematician, and geographer Ptolemy (second century A.D.) developed the theory that there are five heavens, the fifth of which (the Empyrean) is the abode of God himself. This ultimate heaven is supposedly composed of elemental fire, hence its name, derived from the Greek *empuros* (meaning "fiery"). In modern usage the word is often employed in references to the sky. "She would be able to arrange her life as she pleased, to soar into that empyrean of security where creditors cannot penetrate" (Edith Wharton, *The House of Mirth,* 1905).

encomium (enkōmeeăm) A hymn of praise; a eulogy. The word is Greek in origin, being derived from *komos* (meaning "revel"). In ancient Greece encomiums were usually delivered in praise of victors of the Olympic Games as they were carried home in triumph. "He said the alliance was such as he sincerely wished; then launched forth into a very just encomium on the young lady's merit" (Henry Fielding, *Tom Jones,* 1749).

end is not yet, the There is more yet to happen before something is finished. The expression is biblical in origin, appearing in Matthew 24:6: "And ye shall hear of wars and rumours of wars: see that ye be not troubled: for all these things must come to pass, but the end is not yet." "'I joke very seldom,' Blunt protested earnestly. 'That's why I haven't mentioned His Majesty—whom God preserve. That would have been an exaggeration. . . . However, the end is not yet. We were talking about the beginning'" (Joseph Conrad, *The Arrow of Gold,* 1919).

Endor, Witch of *See* WITCH OF ENDOR.

Endymion (en<u>di</u>meeăn) The archetype of a beautiful young man. In Greek mythology, Endymion was a handsome young shepherd who attracted the attention of the moon goddess Selene while sleeping on Mount Latmus. Having fallen passionately in love with Endymion, Selene begged Zeus to grant the youth a wish. Wishing to remain perpetually youthful, Endymion asked for the gift of eternal sleep. Selene was thus able to embrace him each night without him knowing. Today his name is most familiar from the celebrated poem *Endymion* (1818) by John Keats. *Washed and restored, he looked like some young Endymion, so it was doubly unfortunate when he turned out to have the table manners of a satyr.*

Ennius (<u>en</u>eeăs) Epithet sometimes applied to a poet or writer considered to be the founder of, or first outstanding figure in, a nation's literature. The original Ennius (239–169 B.C.) was a Roman writer who was dubbed the Father of Roman Poetry by his admirers. Later writers considered to share such a founding role included England's Layamon (fl. 1200) and Geoffrey Chaucer (c.1340–1400), France's Guillaume de Lorris (fl. 1230) and Jean de Meun (c. 1240–c. 1305), and Spain's Juan de Mena (1411–56). *Who is the German Ennius? Wagner presumably thought it was Hans Sachs.*

Enoch (<u>ee</u>nok) An upright, virtuous man. According to Genesis 5:21–24, Enoch was the father of Methuselah; he is described as one who "walked with God." Enoch and Elijah were both taken away into the presence of God without experiencing death (2 Kings 2:11; Hebrews 11:5). ". . . I, in whose daily life you discern the sanctity of Enoch—I, whose footsteps, as you suppose, leave a gleam along my earthly track, whereby the Pilgrims that shall come after me may be guided to the regions of the blest" (Nathaniel Hawthorne, *The Scarlet Letter,* 1850).

enter into one's closet To retire to a private place, especially for prayer or contemplation. The phrase comes from Christ's Sermon on the Mount, as related in Matthew 6:6, in which Christ urges the faithful to pray in private rather than in public, where they may be tempted to do so only to impress others: ". . . when thou prayest, enter into thy closet, and when thou hast shut thy door, pray to thy Father which is in secret; and thy Father which seeth in secret shall reward thee openly." *At the bishop's invitation the two men entered into his closet so that their conversation might not be overheard.*

Eos *See* AURORA.

epicurean (epikyooreeăn) Having a refined taste in food and wine. The word alludes to the Greek philosopher Epicurus (341–270 B.C.), who encouraged his followers to indulge in simple pleasures with moderation and self-control, although his suggestion that the pursuit of pleasure is the primary goal of life means that *epicurean* today is often interpreted as signifying unrestricted hedonistic indulgence in physical pleasure. By the same token, any person who is believed to have discrimination in food matters may be described as an ***epicure.*** "Rose knew very well that the Epicurean philosophy was not the true one to begin life upon, but it was difficult to reason with Charlie because he always dodged sober subjects and was so full of cheery spirits, one hated to lessen the sort of sunshine which certainly is a public benefactor" (Louisa May Alcott, *Rose in Bloom,* 1876).

epiphany (epifănee) A revelatory appearance, manifestation, or realization. In the Bible the word is applied to the presentation of the infant Christ to the Three Wise Men (Matthew 2:11), as commemorated by the Feast of Epiphany (commonly called Twelfth Night) on January 6. The word itself comes from the Greek *epiphaneia* (meaning "manifestation"). *This epiphany was followed by the most extraordinary and unexpected series of events.*

epithalamium (epithălaymeeăm) A wedding song. In ancient Greece such songs were sung by young boys and girls outside the bridal chamber. The genre was developed by such classical poets as Pindar and Sappho circa the sixth century B.C. and was adopted many centuries later by such notable writers as Edmund Spenser, whose wedding poem *Epithalamion* (1595) is counted among his finest works. "And then, with one of those extraordinary transitions of which I have already spoken, she again threw off her veil, and broke out, after the ancient and poetic fashion of the dwellers in Arabia, into a paean of triumph, or epithalamium, which, wild and beautiful as it was, is exceedingly difficult to render into English, and ought by rights to be sung to the music of a cantata, rather than written and read" (H. Rider Haggard, *She,* 1887).

e pluribus unum (ee plooribăs oonăm) Out of many (made) one. This line from "Moretum," a Latin poem attributed to the Roman poet Virgil (70–19 B.C.), is best known today as the motto on the seal of the United States of America. "The more you examine the structure of the organs and the laws of life, the more you will find how resolutely each of the cell-republics which make up the E pluribus unum of the body maintains its independence" (Oliver Wendell Holmes, *Medical Essays,* 1883).

Erato *See* MUSES.

Erebus (erebăs) Darkness. In Greek mythololgy Erebus was the personification of dark, the brother of Nyx (night) and son of Chaos. His name was later applied to the gloomy caverns through which the souls of the dead had to pass on their way to Hades and eventually became more or less synonymous with hell. "Walking to the taffrail, I was in time to make out, on the very edge of a darkness thrown by a towering black mass like the very gateway of Erebus" (Joseph Conrad, *The Secret Sharer,* 1912).

Erinyes *See* FURIES.

Eris *See* APPLE OF DISCORD.

erotic Provoking sexual desire. The word comes from the name of the Greek god Eros, who personified sexual love and whose name now represents the sexual instinct, or libido. Conventionally depicted as a blindfolded youth with wings and carrying a bow and arrows, Eros was the son of Ares, the god of war, and Aphrodite, goddess of love, and combined elements of both their characters. Equivalent to the Roman CUPID, he fired arrows at both gods and men, thus causing them to fall in love. The term *erotic* appears to have entered the English language around the middle of the 17th century. Related words include *erotica,* sexually provocative topics and material. *The erotic content of the book caused a sensation at the time but seems fairly mild by today's standards.*

Erymanthean boar *See* LABORS OF HERCULES.

Esau (<u>ee</u>sah) A person who allows himself to be parted with something of value without receiving much in return. According to Genesis 25:24–34, Esau foolishly sold his birthright to his treacherous twin brother, Jacob, in exchange for a dish of soup or stew (*see* SELL ONE'S BIRTHRIGHT FOR A MESS OF POTTAGE). His name may also be applied to people who are unusually hairy or red haired, Esau himself being described in the Bible as "an hairy man" with red hair, while Jacob was smooth shaven. " 'He's of a rash, warm-hearted nature, like Esau, for whom I have always felt great pity,' said Dinah" (George Eliot, *Adam Bede,* 1859).

escape by the skin of one's teeth To make a narrow escape from something. The expression is biblical in origin, appearing in Job 19:20 in the following form: "I am escaped with the skin of my teeth." *The stuntman only escaped serious injury by the skin of his teeth, rolling aside as the tower came crashing down on top of the place where he had been sitting.*

Esther (<u>es</u>ter) The archetype of a beautiful, virtuous heroine. The biblical Esther was chosen to become the queen of King Ahasuerus (Xerxes) of Persia on account of her beauty (Esther 2:17). As queen she protected the captive Israelites from persecution by her husband, thereby becoming a heroine to the Jews. The name itself means "star" and was probably originally derived from that of Ishtar, the Babylonian goddess of love. "Mrs. van der Luyden beamed on her with the smile of Esther interceding with Ahasuerus; but her husband raised a protesting hand" (Edith Wharton, *The Age of Innocence,* 1920). *See also* FOR SUCH A TIME AS THIS.

Eternal City The city of Rome. This commonly heard nickname for Rome is of ancient origin, having been used by Ovid (43 B.C.–A.D. 17) and Tibullus (c. 55–c. 19 B.C.), among other writers. "Then ensued an eager description, by the two women, of what had been done, and what should be done, to penetrate the thick wall of fees, commissions, and chicanery, which stood between the patrons of art and an unknown artist in the Eternal City" (Charles Reade, *The Cloister and the Hearth,* 1861).

Ethiopian change his skin *See* LEOPARD CANNOT CHANGE ITS SPOTS, A.

Et tu, Brute? (et too <u>broo</u>tay) Expression of reproachful surprise at a betrayal (usually a relatively minor act of disloyalty) by a friend or colleague. The words, meaning "You too, Brutus?" were allegedly spoken by Julius Caesar when he discovered his close friend Marcus Junius Brutus (85–42 B.C.) among his murderers on the Ides of March in 44 B.C. According to Suetonius (A.D. c. 69–c. 122), Caesar actually spoke the line in Greek, but the Latin form is more familiar today from its use in William Shakespeare's tragedy *Julius Caesar* (1599–1600). "Some months afterwards, when the much-belaboured head of affairs was in very truth made to retire, when unkind shells were thrown against him in great numbers, when he exclaimed, 'Et tu, Brute!' till the words were stereotyped upon his lips, all men in all places talked much about the great Gatherum Castle confederation" (Anthony Trollope, *Framley Parsonage,* 1861).

Eucharist *See* LAST SUPPER.

Euclidean (yoo<u>kli</u>deeăn) Of or relating to a system of geometry based on the discoveries of the Greek mathematician Euclid, who lived in Alexandria in the third century B.C. Euclid's teachings dominated geometry for some 2,000 years. Such was his dominance that for many years geometry itself was informally known as *Euclid.* The term *Euclidean* may also be interpreted more generally as meaning "clearly presented" or "well ordered." "Quoin is not a Euclidean term. It belongs to the pure nautical mathematics. I know not that it has been defined before" (Herman Melville, *Moby-Dick,* 1851).

euhemerism (yoo<u>hee</u>mărizăm) The belief that the gods of mythology were derived from real historical characters. The word comes from the name of the Sicilian Greek philosopher Euhemerus, who lived in the fourth century B.C. and first suggested the theory in his book *Sacred History.* According to Euhemerus, the idea came to him after he read an inscription supporting the theory on a gold pillar on an island in the Indian Ocean. *The discovery of the temple did little to discourage those scholars who were passionately attached to the theory of euhemerism, the idea that the heroes of myth were based on real characters.*

Eumaeus (yoo<u>may</u>ăs) A swineherd. Going back to Greek legend, the original Eumaeus was a slave and swineherd under Ulysses. *The pigs are* *kept in a state-of-the-art piggery and tended by scientists, a far cry from the Eumaeus of legend.*

Eumenides *See* FURIES.

Euphorbia (yoo<u>for</u>beeă) A genus of plants of the spurge family. This popular ornamental plant takes its name from Euphorbus, a Greek physician who flourished in the first century A.D. Tradition claims that the plant was named in honor of Euphorbus by one of his patients, King Juba II of Mauritania. *She planted some* Euphorbia *around the front gate.*

Euphrosyne *See* THREE GRACES.

Eureka! (yoo<u>ree</u>kă) Expression of delightful triumph at making a discovery of some kind or in reaching a solution to a problem. According to tradition, the Sicilian mathematician Archimedes (287–212 B.C.) uttered "Eureka!" (meaning "I have found it!") after solving the problem of how to assess the amount of gold in a supposedly solid-gold crown. The crown, made on the orders of Heiron II of Syracuse, was suspected of having been adulterated with cheaper alloys, the presence of which could not be detected by visual examination or by weight. The king called on the mathematician to find a way to verify its content without damaging the crown. As he lay in his bath, Archimedes noticed how his body displaced some of the water and realized that the answer lay in comparing the volume of water displaced by the crown and that displaced by the equivalent amount of pure gold when both were immersed, as the density of gold was known to be different to that of any other metal. If there was a difference between the two, the king had been cheated—as proved the case. "Eureka!" is also the motto of California, recalling the gold rush that took place there. "In one place I suddenly found myself near the model of a tin-mine, and then by the merest accident I discovered, in an air-tight case, two dynamite cartridges! I shouted 'Eureka!' and smashed the case with joy" (H. G. Wells, *The Time Machine,* 1895).

Euryalus *See* NISUS AND EURYALUS.

Eurydice *See* ORPHEUS.

Euterpe *See* MUSES.

Eve (eev) The archetypal woman. According to the Book of Genesis, Eve was the first woman, created by God as a companion for ADAM and named by Adam himself: "And Adam called his wife's name Eve; because she was the mother of all living" (Genesis 3:20). The name Eve itself comes from the Hebrew *hawwah* (meaning "life"). It was Eve who succumbed to the persuasion of the serpent to eat the forbidden fruit of the tree of knowledge and thus brought about the expulsion of Adam and Eve from the GARDEN OF EDEN. The Virgin Mary is sometimes referred to as "the new Eve." Woman in general are sometimes referred to as *daughters of Eve.* "Joanna the faithless, the betrayer: Joanna who mocked him, whispered about him behind his back, trapped and tortured him. Joanna Eve" (Fay Weldon, *The Cloning of Joanna May,* 1989). *See also* ADAM AND EVE; ADAM'S RIB.

even Homer nods *See* HOMER SOMETIMES NODS.

every dog has his day Even the most lowly and humble will eventually get their opportunity for glory or success. This proverb has its roots in a Roman saying and was popularly attributed to a legend concerning the death (in 406 B.C.) of the Greek playwright Euripides, who was reputedly torn to pieces by dogs set upon him by his rivals Arrhidaeus and Crateuas. "Let Hercules himself do what he may, the cat will mew, and dog will have his day" (William Shakespeare, *Hamlet,* c. 1600).

ewe lamb A greatly prized possession. The phrase alludes to 2 Samuel 12:1–14, in which Nathan tells King David a parable about a rich man who seizes a poor man's "little ewe lamb" that he has nurtured as though it was his own daughter. When David expresses his rage at this injustice, Nathan accuses David of similar wickedness in having Bathsheba's husband killed so that he can marry her. Later, the child born to Bathsheba and David dies. "'Jane, I never meant to wound you thus. If the man who had but one little ewe lamb that was dear to him as a daughter, that ate of his bread and drank of his cup, and lay in his bosom, had by some mistake slaughtered it at the shambles, he would not have rued his bloody blunder more than I now rue mine'" (Charlotte Brontë, *Jane Eyre,* 1847).

exile *See* BABYLONIAN CAPTIVITY.

exodus A mass migration or departure. The word comes from the Greek *exodos* (meaning "marching out") and in the Old Testament describes the departure of the Israelites from Egypt (Exodus 12:31) under Moses and their subsequent 40-year wanderings in the wilderness before coming to the PROMISED LAND. "Away streamed the Members, but still the noble lord went on speaking, struggling hard to keep up his fire as though no such exodus were in process" (Anthony Trollope, *Can You Forgive Her?*, 1864).

ex pede Herculem (eks p̱eday ẖerkyoolem) By examining a small sample of something, much may be learned about the whole. The phrase literally means "from the foot of Hercules" and alludes to a calculation supposedly made by the Greek mathematician Pythagoras (c. 580–c. 500 B.C.). In order to work out the height of the great hero Hercules, Pythagoras began by comparing the length of the average Greek stadium (600 feet) with that of the stadium of Hercules at Olympia and from this calculated the size of Hercules' foot, with which he would have paced out the distance. Having gleaned this information, it was relatively simple to calculate his height as there is a certain ratio between foot size and height. An alternative phrase with much the same meaning is *ex ungue leonem* (meaning "from the claw of the lion"). ". . . and as for Testacio, one of the highest hills in modern Rome, it is but an ancient dust heap; the women of old Rome flung their broken pots and pans there, and lo—a mountain. 'Ex pede Herculem; ex ungue leonem'" (Charles Reade, *The Cloister and the Hearth*, 1861).

extra mile *See* GO THE EXTRA/SECOND MILE.

eye for an eye, an Retribution by extracting like for like. The phrase comes from Exodus 21:24: "Eye for eye, tooth for tooth, hand for hand, foot for foot." *He was an old-fashioned judge who believed in an eye for an eye when it came to crimes against the person.*

eye hath not seen Something invisible to ordinary sight or not readily perceived by the senses. Paul uses the phrase in 1 Corinthians 2:9 in describing the wondrous rewards that God has prepared in heaven for those who are faithful to him: "But as it is written, Eye hath not seen, nor ear heard, neither have entered into the heart of man, the things which God hath prepared for them that love him." "Vast chain of being, which from God began, / Natures aethereal, human, angel, man, / Beast, bird, fish, insect! what no eye can see, / No glass can reach!" (Alexander Pope, *Essay on Man,* 1733–34).

eyeless in Gaza (gah̲ză) Reduced to a state of wretched helplessness in hostile surroundings. The phrase alludes to the ill treatment suffered by SAMSON at the hands of the Philistines, who, according to Judges 16:1–3 and 21, captured him and put out his eyes before imprisoning him "with fetters of brass" at Gaza. The image of the mighty Samson thus pitifully reduced has since been variously adopted by writers over the centuries, from John Milton, who depicted Samson as "eyeless in Gaza at the mill with slaves" in *Samson Agonistes* (1671), to Aldous Huxley, who wrote an autobiographical novel entitled *Eyeless in Gaza* (1936). "Ask for this great deliverer now, and find him Eyeless in Gaza, at the mill with slaves. It is the same story. Great power reduced to impotence, great glory to misery, by the hand of Fate . . ." (Anthony Trollope, *The Last Chronicle of Barset,* 1867).

eye of a needle *See* CAMEL: GO THROUGH AN EYE OF A NEEDLE.

Fabian (<u>fay</u>beeăn) Cautious; avoiding direct confrontation. The word alludes to the Roman general Quintus Fabius Maximus (d. 203 B.C.), nicknamed CUNCTATOR (delayer), who adopted the tactic of harassment instead of making a direct challenge against the invading Carthaginian armies of Hannibal during the Second Punic War. This policy of avoiding pitched battles provoked accusations of cowardice in Rome but ultimately proved successful. During the American War of Independence, George Washington adopted a similar approach against the British and was consequently known as the American Fabius. In 1884 a group of British Socialists who preferred to achieve their aims through democratic methods rather than through violent revolution opted to call themselves the Fabian Society to emphasize their nonconfrontational *Fabian tactics.* *The government would appear to have adopted Fabian tactics in dealing with the threat posed by the unions.*

Fabricius (fă<u>brish</u>ăs) Archetype of incorruptibility and honesty. Gaius Fabricius Luscinus (d. c. 270 B.C.) was a Roman consul who became famous for his refusal to accept bribes or in any other way compromise his principles. He lived a frugal life and left nothing to his daughters when he died, but the Senate decided to provide for their future. *He is widely regarded as the Fabricius of the White House, the one person who can be relied on to give an honest appraisal of the situation.*

face that launched a thousand ships *See* HELEN OF TROY.

faction A minority group within a large body, especially one that holds dissenting views. The original factions were the chariot-racing teams, or *factiones,* of ancient Rome. Identified by a particular color, the *factiones* were well-organized sporting enterprises, and each had a committed following, who in time came to wield considerable political influence. The most famous were the Blues, who enjoyed the support of the aristocracy, and the Greens, who were the most popular team among the general populace. On occasion, clashes between the *factiones* could lead to wider unrest, culminating in a full-scale riot in 509 A.D. "All these things tended to make us excessively obnoxious to the great sacerdotal clan, the most powerful because the most united faction in the kingdom" (H. Rider Haggard, *Allan Quatermain,* 1887).

faith, hope, and charity The three theological virtues (in contrast to the cardinal virtues of prudence, temperance, fortitude, and justice). Paul identifies the virtues in 1 Corinthians 13:13, using "charity" as a synonym for "love" and singling out charity as the most important of the three: "And now abideth faith, hope, charity, these three; but the greatest of these is charity." "Still—if I have read religious history aright—faith, hope, and charity have not always been found in a direct ratio with a sensibility to the three concords, and it is possible—thank Heaven!—to have very erroneous theories" (George Eliot, *Adam Bede,* 1859).

faith will move mountains With faith anything is possible. This saying comes from Matthew 17:20: "If ye have faith as a grain of mustard seed, ye shall say unto this mountain, Remove hence to yonder place; and it shall remove; and nothing shall be impossible unto you." A variant form is *faith can move mountains. She firmly believes that she can make him change his ways, and faith will move mountains, so she may yet succeed.*

faith without works A person's good intentions are meaningless unless supported by good actions. The phrase comes from the Book of James 2:14–26: "Yea, a man may say, Thou hast faith, and I have works: show me thy faith without thy works, and I will show thee my faith by my works. . . . But wilt thou know, O vain man, that faith without works is dead? Was not Abraham our father justified by works, when he had offered Isaac his son upon the altar?" (James 2:14–21). *The government has expressed good intentions but failed to do much about them, and critics have observed that it is a case of faith without works.*

Falernian (fălerneeăn) Of or having to do with a wine of a superior quality. The term refers to a particularly fine wine that was made in the Falernian region of Campania in Roman times. Its qualities were praised by Horace and Virgil among others. "Sand-banks, marshes, forests, savages,— precious little to eat fit for a civilized man, nothing but Thames water to drink. No Falernian wine here, no going ashore" (Joseph Conrad, *Heart of Darkness,* 1902).

Fall, the A lapse from a previously happier state. The allusion is to the Fall of the human race as described in the Book of Genesis, when ADAM and EVE disobeyed God's command not to eat the fruit of the tree of knowledge of good and evil (Genesis 3:6), so committing the first sin. As a punishment for their disobedience they were expelled from the Garden of Eden. "What Eve, what serpent hath suggested thee / To make a second fall of cursed man?" (William Shakespeare, *Richard II,* 1595). *See also* ORIGINAL SIN.

fall among thieves To find oneself among bad company or at the mercy of wicked people. The phrase comes from the parable of the GOOD SAMARITAN, in which a man on his way from Jerusalem to Jericho "fell among thieves, which stripped him of his raiment, and wounded him, and departed, leaving him half dead" (Luke 10:30). *Her son was a harmless enough kid, but he fell among thieves and by the time he was out of his teenage years was well known to the local police.*

fall by the wayside To give up or fail at something; to become useless. The phrase is biblical in origin, appearing in the parable of the sower and the seed related in Matthew 13:4, which describes how some seeds inevitably fall by the wayside and fail to germinate. "While other internet bosses have fallen by the wayside, he remains in charge after overseeing his company's flotation and sale" (*The Guardian,* April 23, 2001). *See also* PARABLE OF THE SOWER.

fallen angel A person who has suffered a lapse in fortune or reputation. The original fallen angels were Lucifer and other rebels, who according to Christian tradition tried unsuccessfully to overthrow God and were consequently consigned to hell, as related in Isaiah 14:12 and Revelation 12:7–9. The term entered common currency after the publication of Milton's *Paradise Lost* (1667), which retold the story. "'Mr Finn knows,' said

Lady Laura, 'that since he first came into Parliament I have always believed in his success, and I have been very proud to see it.' 'We shall weep over him, as over a fallen angel, if he leaves us,' said Lady Cantrip" (Anthony Trollope, *Phineas Finn,* 1869).

fall from grace To fall in status; to lose a privileged position or favor. The expression comes from Galatians 5:4, in which the Galatians are reprimanded for relying on their own efforts to observe the law rather than depending on God's help: "Christ is become of no effect unto you, whosoever of you are justified by the law; ye are fallen from grace." *Few remember now how he dominated the world of business prior to his sensational fall from grace.*

fall of a sparrow Even the most insignificant events are not outside the care and knowledge of God (or others in authority), who governs everything. The phrase comes from Matthew 10:29–31: "Are not two sparrows sold for a farthing? and one of them shall not fall on the ground without your Father. . . . Fear ye not therefore, ye are of more value than many sparrows." *He ran the estate with a gimlet eye, to the extent that not even the fall of a sparrow took place without his knowledge.*

fall of Jericho *See* WALLS OF JERICHO.

fall on stony ground To receive an unfavorable reception; to be ignored or fail to prosper. The phrase appears in Mark 4:5–6, which relates the PARABLE OF THE SOWER and the seed: "And some fell on stony ground, where it had not much earth; and immediately it sprang up, because it had no depth of earth: But when the sun was up, it was scorched; and because it had no root, it withered away." *The young woman made several suggestions at her first board meeting, but most of her ideas fell on stony ground.*

false prophet A person who purports to speak the truth, but whose words are not in fact to be trusted. The phrase appears several times in the Bible, for example, in Matthew 7:15–17: "Beware of false prophets, which come to you in sheep's clothing, but inwardly they are ravening wolves. Ye shall know them by their fruits. Do men gather grapes of thorns, or figs of thistles? Even so every good tree bringeth forth good fruit; but a corrupt tree bringeth forth evil fruit." "The clergyman had not, it would seem, forgot the observation which ranked him with the false prophets of Dunbar, for he addressed Mr. Maxwell upon the first opportunity" (Sir Walter Scott, *Waverley,* 1814). *See also* WOLF IN SHEEP'S CLOTHING.

fascism (fashizăm) Right-wing authoritarianism. The Fascist movement founded by Benito Mussolini in 1919 took its name from the *fasces* that were carried before the senior magistrates of ancient Rome as a symbol of their authority. These comprised a bundle of rods tied with a red thong, from which an ax projected. The *fasces* were subsequently adopted as a symbol by Mussolini's Fascists, who sought to make links between their movement and the glories of ancient Rome, and the term soon came to be applied more widely to other right-wing totalitarian organizations, political parties, policies, and regimes, including Nazi Germany. *The rise of fascism and communism in the 20th century was the greatest disfiguring phenomenon in international affairs.*

Fates (fayts) The implacable divinities who are commonly believed to control the lives of mortal men and women. The Fates (also called the *Moirae* by the Greeks or the *Parcae* by the Romans) were depicted in Greek and Roman mythology as three sisters—identified as daughters of Night—who handled the *thread of destiny* (a length of thread representing each individual life). Clotho spun the thread at birth, Lachesis measured its length and determined the amount of luck the person would enjoy, and Atropos cut it with her shears at the moment of death. "'Ah!' He shivered as one shivers at the thought of disaster narrowly averted. 'The fates were good that I only came near it!'" (Booth Tarkington, *His Own People,* 1907).

Father, forgive them Expression of exasperation at the nonsensical actions of others. The allusion is to the seven last sentences of Christ on the Cross, often referred to as the *Seven Last Words*. The second of these, in which Christ requests forgiveness for those who have brought about his death, runs: "Father, forgive them; for they know not what they do" (Luke 23:34). "Lo! where the crucified Christ from his Cross is gazing upon you! See! in those sorrowful eyes what meekness and holy compassion! Hark! how those lips still repeat the prayer. 'O Father, forgive them!'

Let us repeat it now, and say, 'O Father, forgive them'" (H. W. Longfellow, *Evangeline,* 1847). *See also* KNOW NOT WHAT THEY DO, THEY.

fat of the land A life of luxury. The expression comes from Genesis 45:18, in which Pharaoh offered the brethren of Joseph the best treatment: "I will give you the good of the land of Egypt, and ye shall eat the fat of the land." A person who is said to *live off the fat of the land* is one who enjoys the best of everything. "By—, those fellows, who haven't got a pound belonging to them, think that they're to live on the fat of the land out of the sweat of the brow of such men as me" (Anthony Trollope, *Ayala's Angel,* 1881).

fatted calf, kill the *See* KILL THE FATTED CALF.

fat years and lean years Periods of prosperity and misfortune, which tend to alternate. The phrase comes from Genesis 41:25–27, in which Joseph interprets Pharaoh's dream about seven lean cows consuming seven fat cows as meaning that seven years of plenty would be followed by seven years of famine. *The family has known both fat years and lean years but has always held together until now.*

faun (fahn) A species of minor rural deity having the body of a man and the legs, tail, ears, and horns of a goat. Fauns (similar to the SATYRs of Greek tradition) were a feature of Roman mythology and were apparently derived from Faunus, the god of nature and fertility and the Roman equivalent of the Greek god Pan. They are generally depicted in art and literature as sprightly and mischievous. "As he stood there in the lamp-light, with dead leaves and bits of bramble clinging to his mud-spattered clothes, the scent of the night about him and its chill on his pale bright face, he really had the look of a young faun strayed in from the forest" (Edith Wharton, *The Reef,* 1912).

fauna (fahnă) The native or indigenous animal life of a particular place or period of time. The word comes from Fauna, the name of the sister of Faunus, the Roman god of nature and fertility. It was first used in its modern sense by the Swedish botanist Linneaus in 1746. "'You've never been to Kew?' Denham remarked. But it appeared that she had come once as a small child, when the geography of the place was entirely different, and the fauna included certainly flamingoes and, possibly, camels" (Virginia Woolf, *Night and Day,* 1919). *See also* FAUN; FLORA.

favonian (făvōneeăn) Of or relating to the west wind. Favonius (or Favonianus) was the Roman name for the west wind, which for its relatively gentle nature was considered favorable to living things. *A warm, favonian breeze ruffled the grasses on the hilltop and filled the sails of the ships in the bay.*

fear and trembling, in *See* IN FEAR AND TREMBLING.

fed with Saint Stephen's bread *See* SAINT STEPHEN'S LOAVES.

feeding the five thousand The providing of food or something else for a large number of people. The reference is to the miracle of the loaves and fishes related in Matthew 14:13–21, in which Christ miraculously fed a crowd of 5,000 people with just five loaves and two fish—and had several baskets of food left over after all had eaten. *It was like feeding the five thousand, trying to make sure every child had roughly the same amount and choice of food.*

feet of clay A fundamental character flaw, especially one that is not immediately obvious in someone or something that is otherwise greatly admired. The allusion is to Daniel 2:31–33, which relates a dream in which the Babylonian king Nebuchadnezzar dreamed of a huge figure with a head of gold, breast and arms of silver, belly and thighs of brass, legs of iron, and feet of iron and clay. When the feet are smashed by a stone, the whole statue falls. Daniel explained the image as a symbol of Nebuchadnezzar's empire and the feet of clay as a representation of the inherent weakness that would lead to its collapse. *For as long as anyone could remember the old man had been considered the ultimate authority on such matters, but now he was revealed to have feet of clay.*

fell among thieves *See* FALL AMONG THIEVES.

few are chosen *See* MANY ARE CALLED, BUT FEW ARE CHOSEN.

fiddle while Rome burns To occupy oneself with trivialities while ignoring a much more serious problem. The allusion is to the tradition that in the year A.D. 64 the emperor Nero (who considered himself a fine musician) played his fiddle rather than take action to prevent the city of Rome from being destroyed in a disastrous fire. Rumors that Nero had started the fire himself to clear a large area for his own ambitious building plans added to the resentment felt against him for this callousness (even though he was not apparently in the city at the time the fire broke out), and his reign only lasted another four years, despite his attempts to transfer the blame for the conflagration to the city's Christian population. "[Prime Minister Tony] Blair fiddles while Cumbria burns" (*Guardian,* April 2, 2001).

field of blood *See* ACELDAMA.

fiery furnace A punishment that rebounds on the persons inflicting it while leaving its intended victims unscathed. The allusion is to the biblical story of Shadrach, Meshach, and Abednego, who were hurled into a fiery furnace on the orders of King Nebuchadnezzar after they refused to worship a golden idol set up by him. According to the account given in Daniel 3, the three remained miraculously unharmed by the flames, although the people who threw them in were all scorched to death. "Tom stood silent; at length he said, 'Him that saved Daniel in the den of lions,—that saves the children in the fiery furnace,—Him that walked on the sea, and bade the winds be still,—He's alive yet; and I've faith to believe he can deliver you'" (Harriet Beecher Stowe, *Uncle Tom's Cabin,* 1852).

fight the good fight To pursue a goal (especially a religious one) with determination and courage. The expression comes from 1 Timothy 6:12: "Fight the good fight of faith, lay hold on eternal life, whereunto thou art also called, and hast professed a good profession before many witnesses." The phrase is commonly applied to the struggle of life itself, and Paul, foreseeing his own death, wrote, "I have fought the good fight, I have finished my course" (2 Timothy 4:7). "He did become member for East Barsetshire, but he was such a member—so lukewarm, so indifferent, so prone to associate with the enemies of the good cause, so little willing to fight the good fight, that he soon disgusted those who most dearly loved the memory of the old squire" (Anthony Trollope, *Doctor Thorne,* 1858).

fig leaf Something that serves, usually inadequately, to conceal a person's weaknesses or innermost feelings. The allusion is to the fig leaves with which Adam and Eve sought to conceal their nakedness after tasting the fruit of the tree of knowledge of good and evil and losing their innocence: "And the eyes of them both were opened, and they knew that they were naked; and they sewed fig leaves together, and made themselves aprons" (Genesis 3:7). *This gesture was not well received and was generally considered a very inadequate fig leaf to cover up for past indiscretions.*

filthy lucre Money; material wealth. The phrase appears in 1 Timothy 3:3, in which Timothy warns that leaders of the church should be "not greedy of filthy lucre." "Mrs Dean was a very good woman, but she had aspirations in the direction of filthy lucre on behalf of her children, or at least on behalf of this special child, and she did think it would be very nice if Frank would marry an heiress" (Anthony Trollope, *The Eustace Diamonds,* 1873).

finger of God Divine guidance, power, or authority. The phrase appears in Exodus 8:19 and elsewhere in the Old Testament. The image of God's pointing finger has been variously employed as a symbol of divine creativity, guidance, and punishment. The similar expression *hand of God* points to "God's sovereign power in creation and in his actions on his people's behalf, especially in redemption. Also used as a symbol of authority and in taking oaths" (*NIV Thematic Reference Bible,* p. 1,385), as in "Shall we receive good at the hand of God, and shall we not receive evil?" (Job 2:10). *Surely, if nowhere else, the finger of God may be detected in the great paintings of the Renaissance masters.*

fire and brimstone Zealotry threatening eternal damnation or other punishment by God. The phrase is biblical in origin, appearing in the Book of Revelation, where a *lake of fire and brimstone* represents the agonies that guilty souls will suffer in hell. In Genesis 19:24 the sinful cities of SODOM AND GOMORRAH are similarly punished with fire and brimstone (*brimstone* is an alternative name for sulfur). In modern usage the phrase is sometimes applied to the sermons of those preachers who threaten their congregations with eternal condemnation if they do not turn back to God. "'Deceit is, indeed, a sad fault in a child,' said Mr Brocklehurst; 'it is akin to falsehood, and all liars will have their portion in the lake burning with fire and brimstone; she shall, however, be watched, Mrs Reed'" (Charlotte Brontë, *Jane Eyre,* 1847).

fire that is not quenched *See* WORM THAT DIETH NOT.

first shall be last, the Those who are apparently least deserving shall not necessarily be the last to be rewarded. The expression is of biblical origin, coming from Matthew 20:16, in which Christ is questioned about who most deserves everlasting life and is quoted as replying, "So the last shall be first, and the first last." *The old rogue winked at me as he took his payment ahead of the captain, as if to remind the world that sometimes the last shall be first.*

fisher of men An evangelist. The phrase appears in Matthew 4:18–20 in references to Christ's recruitment of the disciples: "Jesus, walking by the sea of Galilee, saw two brethren, Simon called Peter, and Andrew his brother, casting a net into the sea: for they were fishers. And he saith unto them, Follow me, and I will make you fishers of men. And they straightway left their nets, and followed him." The pope, considered the heir of Peter as the chief fisher of men, wears a fisherman's ring at his investiture. This ring is used for sealing papal briefs and is destroyed at the pope's death. *The local populace soon tired of being berated by this offensive fisher of men and returned to their homes, grumbling at his insolence.*

five thousand, feeding the *See* FEEDING THE FIVE THOUSAND.

flaming sword A highly effective weapon of some kind, especially one used to keep a person at bay. The allusion is to the flaming sword wielded by God as he drove Adam and Eve out of the Garden of Eden and prevented their approaching the Tree of Life, as related at Genesis 3:24: "So he drove out the man; and he placed at the east of the garden of Eden Cherubims, and a flaming sword which turned every way, to keep the way of the tree of life." Some swords with a wavy edge are traditionally called flaming swords. "She had felt lonely enough when the flaming sword of Nick's indignation had shut her out from their Paradise; but there had been a cruel bliss in the pain" (Edith Wharton, *Glimpses of the Moon,* 1922).

flesh is grass All living things soon perish, just as grass is mowed down as hay. The phrase appears in Isaiah 40:6–7: "And he said, What shall I cry? All flesh is grass, and all the goodliness thereof is as the flower of the field: The grass withereth, the flower fadeth: because the spirit of the LORD bloweth upon it: surely the people is grass." These verses are referred to in the New Testament in 1 Peter 1:24. "All flesh is grass—an' tesn't no bad thing—grass" (John Galsworthy, *The Forsyte Saga,* 1922).

flesh is weak, the Humans are physically frail and find temptations of the flesh hard to resist. The phrase comes from Matthew 26:40–41 and Mark 14:38, in which the disciples fall asleep in the Garden of Gethsemane despite Christ's entreaties that they remain awake with him: "What, could ye not watch with me one hour? Watch and pray, that ye enter not into temptation: the spirit indeed is willing, but the flesh is weak" (Matthew 26:40–41). "You must not mark me. I feel called to leave my kindred for a while; but it is a trial—the flesh is weak" (George Eliot, *Adam Bede,* 1859). *See also* SPIRIT IS WILLING, BUT THE FLESH IS WEAK, THE.

flesh of my flesh Offspring; children; one's own creation. The phrase comes from Genesis 2:23, where God presented Adam with his companion Eve, fashioned from one of his own ribs. Adam responds with the words: "This is now bone of my bones, and flesh of my flesh." "No woman was ever nearer to her mate than I am: ever more absolutely bone of his bone, flesh of his flesh" (Charlotte Brontë, *Jane Eyre,* 1847).

fleshpot Place where a person may indulge in sinful luxury or self-indulgence. The term appears in Exodus 16:3, in which the Israelites protest against Moses at the conditions they have to endure in the wilderness: "Would to God we had died by the hand of the LORD in the land of Egypt, when we sat by the fleshpots, and when we did eat bread to the full: for ye have brought us forth into the wilderness, to kill this whole assembly with hunger." *She did not like him to go on business trips abroad, fearing he might be lured to the fleshpots she had read about in magazines.*

Flood An overwhelming, extraordinary inundation of water. The original Flood was sent by God to punish the human race for the sinful ways it had fallen into. For 40 days and 40 nights the waters covered the entire face of the world, but God allowed Noah and his family to survive by building an ark, in which they preserved every species on earth (see Genesis 6–9). The Flood is recorded early in the Bible, and thus any reference to times **before the Flood** is understood to allude to the very earliest historical periods. *It was a phenomenon the like of which the world had not seen since before the Flood.*

flora (flŏrǎ) The native or indigenous plant life of a particular place or period of time. The word comes from Flora, the Roman goddess of flowers, youth, and spring, as depicted in Sandro Botticelli's famous painting *Primavera.* Her name derived from the Latin *flos,* meaning "flower." "Nor less the place of curious plant he knows; / He both his Flora and his Fauna shows" (George Crabbe, *The Borough,* 1810). *See also* FAUNA.

fly in the ointment A difficulty or flaw that constitutes a significant drawback in an otherwise ideal situation. The expression is biblical in origin, coming from Ecclesiastes 10:1: "Dead flies cause the ointment of the apothecary to send forth a stinking savour: so doth a little folly him that is in reputation for wisdom and honour." *The fete went very well. The only fly in the ointment was the poor weather.*

food of the gods *See* AMBROSIA; NECTAR.

foolish virgins *See* PARABLE OF THE WISE AND FOOLISH VIRGINS.

forbidden fruit Something that is especially desirable but prohibited. The phrase is commonly applied to the fruit of the Tree of Knowledge of Good and Evil described in Genesis 3:1–16, which Adam and Eve are forbidden to eat on God's command. When on the prompting of the serpent Adam and Eve disobey God's order and eat the fruit (commonly depicted as an apple or, in Islamic tradition, as a banyan, or Indian fig), they are expelled from the Garden of Eden. (See also Proverbs 9:17.) In the fuller proverbial form *forbidden fruit tastes sweetest,* the implication is that something becomes infinitely more desirable simply because it is prohibited. "Then this spring, three more newspapers—the *Independent,* the *Daily News* and the *Standard*—nibbled the forbidden fruit, and got a heavy legal case for their pains" (*Guardian,* July 13, 1987).

for such a time as this At such a favorable opportunity, referring to the choice of a person who will have a widespread, significant influence. This phrase alludes to an episode recorded in the book of Esther. Mordecai, a Jewish captive from Judah, held a post at the palace of King Ahasuerus (Xerxes) of Persia at Shushan. When Queen Vashti disobeyed the king and was to be replaced, many young girls from all over the kingdom were brought to the palace to see whom the king would choose. Mordecai put forward his adopted daughter Esther (also known as Hadassah) for the honor. She was beautiful and was chosen by King Ahasuerus to become queen; the king did not know that she was a Jew. Haman, one of the king's high officials, was an anti-Semite and instigator of one of the first pogroms against the Jews. Mordecai heard about Haman's plot to have all the Jews killed and sent word to Esther, asking her to plead with the king to save the Jews: "For if thou altogether holdest thy peace at this time, then shall there enlargement and deliverance arise to the Jews from another place; but thou and thy father's house shall be destroyed: and who knoweth whether thou art come to the kingdom for such a time as this?" (Esther 4:14). This was a life-threatening petition, however, for one could only come into the king's presence at his request, and unless the king held out his golden scepter to Esther she would die in the undertaking. Esther asked that all the Jews fast for three days, and she went to the king, who spared her life. She invited him to several banquets at her palace and included Haman in the invitation. During these she exposed Haman's treachery, he was hanged, and the Jews were saved. *The young man was unexpectedly chosen out of all his peers to become leader. His background equipped him perfectly for the task: He had become a leader for such a time as this.*

Fortuna (for<u>too</u>nă) Personification of luck. Fortuna was identified as the goddess of fortune and good luck in Roman mythology, the equivalent of the Greek Tyche. *It seemed that Fortuna herself smiled on the party the next day, and they made better progress than they had done for many weeks past.*

Fortunate Islands/Isles *See* ISLANDS OF THE BLEST.

forum (<u>fo</u>răm) A place or opportunity for discussion of a particular issue or issues. The word alludes to the forum (meaning "public place") of ancient Roman society, a large open space in the center of a town or city that served as the marketplace. It was here that much financial and legal business was transacted, and meetings would also be held on matters of public interest or concern. The word itself comes ultimately from the Latin *foris,* meaning "outside." The ruins of the most famous forum of all, that of Rome, are preserved within the heart of the modern city. In modern usage the word may be applied much more widely, referring to any medium for discussion, such as a magazine or television program, or in computing to "virtual" meeting places on the World Wide Web, where people interested in a particular subject may air their views. "What is called eloquence in the forum is commonly found to be rhetoric in the study" (Henry David Thoreau, *Walden, or Life in the Woods,* 1854).

forty days and forty nights *See* FLOOD.

found wanting *See* WRITING ON THE WALL.

fountain of youth A source of perpetual youth. The notion of a fountain of youth dates back to classical times. Legend had it that Alexander the Great located the whereabouts of a fountain of youth and that both he and his soldiers enjoyed its benefits after bathing in its waters. Subsequently such fountains were a subject of great fascination to medieval scholars and explorers, and many expeditions were mounted in search of such a marvel (including, most notably, the exploration of the Florida Keys area by the Spanish explorer Juan Ponce de León in the early 16th century). In modern usage the phrase tends to be used metaphorically. "You'll never grow old, Teacher,' said Paul. 'You are one of the fortunate mortals who have found and drunk from the Fountain of Youth,—you and Mother Lavendar" (Lucy Maud Montgomery, *Anne's House of Dreams,* 1917).

Four Horsemen of the Apocalypse Personifications of war, famine, pestilence, and death. The Four Horsemen of the Apocalypse are described in the book of Revelation 6:1–8, in which John foresees the end of the world. According to this account, War rides a white horse, Pestilence (or strife) a red horse, Famine a black horse, and Death a pale horse. "Malnutrition, malaria, infant mortality, an AIDS epidemic, with more than half a million people HIV positive; some 3 million people driven out of their homes in a decades-long civil war with the country's large ethnic minorities; rampant corruption, drug abuse and the drugs trade, sexual exploitation, forced labour (you see the road gangs as you travel round the country), banditry; and most recently, allegations of the systematic use of rape by army units, as a weapon of war: every curse and plague of the world, every horseman of the Apocalypse, seems to be marching through Burma's jungles" (*Guardian,* July 11, 2002).

frankincense, gold, and myrrh *See* MAGI.

Freyja (frayă) Personification of fertility. Freyja was identified in Norse mythology as the goddess of prosperity and peace as well as love and fertility. She was the wife of Odin and the Norse equivalent of Venus. *It was a valley ruled by Freyja, the trees heavy with fruit and everything blooming in profusion.*

Friday The sixth day of the week. It was called Frigedaeg in Old English, having been named originally in honor of the Norse goddess Frig (or Frigga), who was identified as the wife of Woden (after whom Wednesday was named) and the mother of Thor (after whom Thursday was named). Venerated as the goddess of married love, she in turn was linked with FREYJA, the Norse goddess of love and fertility. *Some people fear Friday the 13th.*

from Dan to Beersheba *See* DAN TO BEERSHEBA, FROM.

from the mouths of babes come words of wisdom *See* OUT OF THE MOUTHS OF BABES AND SUCKLINGS.

fruit of one's labors The product of hard work. The expression comes from Philippians 1:22: "But if I live in the flesh, this is the fruit of my labour: yet what I shall choose I wot not." *It is a bitter thing to see the fruit of one's labors ignored in such a manner.*

fruits, know them by their *See* KNOW THEM BY THEIR FRUITS.

Furies Avenging spirits. The Furies, also known as the *Erinyes,* were depicted in Greek mythology as three winged, snake-haired goddesses named Tisiphone, Alecto, and Megaera, who were merciless in their pursuit of unpunished criminals, especially those who had committed offenses against their own kin, blasphemed against the gods, or betrayed a guest or host. They were variously said to be the daughters of Gaea or to have sprung up from the blood of Uranus. Because it was thought unlucky to allude to the Furies by name, they were sometimes referred to euphemistically as the *Eumenides,* meaning "Kindly Ones." The story of how they pursued Orestes for having killed his mother Clytemnestra is related in the play *Eumenides* by Aeschylus (525–456 B.C.). "The Vengeance, uttering terrific shrieks, and flinging her arms about her head like the forty Furies at once, was tearing from house to house, rousing the women" (Charles Dickens, *A Tale of Two Cities,* 1859).

Gabriel (g<u>ay</u>breeăl) A messenger of God. The archangel Gabriel appears four times in the Bible, each time bringing a message from God, such as that to Zechariah in Luke 1:19: "I am Gabriel, that stand in the presence of God; and am sent to speak unto thee, and to shew thee these glad tidings." His most notable appearance is in Luke 1:26–38, when he announces to Mary the forthcoming birth of Jesus: "The angel Gabriel was sent from God . . . Fear not, Mary: for thou hast found favour with God. And, behold, thou shalt conceive in thy womb, and bring forth a son, and shalt call his name JESUS" (Luke 1:26, 30–31). In Islamic tradition, it is Gabriel who reveals the Qur'an to Muhammad. "Alida Fischer calls him Archangel Gabriel, because his true self came out of its shell when her son was arrested" (Alan Paton, *Ah, but Your Land Is Beautiful,* 1981).

Gabriel's trumpet *See* LAST TRUMP.

Gadarene (g<u>a</u>dăreen) Headlong; reckless; hasteful. The adjective alludes to the biblical story of the Gadarene swine to which, according to the account given in Mark 5:1–17 and Luke 8:26–37, Christ transferred demons that had possessed two men and made them mad. Under the influence of the demons the swine rushed madly down a steep slope into the Sea of Galilee and was drowned. *In his dream he was hurtling with Gadarene haste into a fire-brimmed pit, unable and even unwilling to stop. See also* MY NAME IS LEGION.

Gaea (j<u>ī</u>ă) Personification of the Earth, especially with reference to its ecology. In Greek mythology Gaea (also called *Gaia* or *Ge*) gave birth to the sky, mountains, and sea and became the mother of Uranus, who united with him to create the Titans, the Cyclops, and the giants. *The term*

Gaea *has now acquired a much wider meaning, signifying a worldview of environmental issues.*

Galatea (galăteeă) The archetype of a beautiful woman. In Greek myth Galatea was the stone statue of a perfect woman as created by the sculptor Pygmalion, who had been repulsed by the imperfections of mortal women. Aphrodite made Pygmalion fall in love with his creation but finally took pity on his misery and brought the statue to life. The concept of the artist constructing his ideal woman is familiar in modern times from the play *Pygmalion* (1913) by George Bernard Shaw, which provided the basis for the popular stage and motion-picture musicals *My Fair Lady* (1956 and 1964, respectively). ". . . with a sudden motion she shook her gauzy covering from her, and stood forth in her low kirtle and her snaky zone, in her glorious, radiant beauty and her imperial grace, rising from her wrappings, as it were, like Venus from the wave, or Galatea from her marble, or a beatified spirit from the tomb" (H. Rider Haggard, *She,* 1887).

galenical A medicine derived from plant or animal tissue. The word comes from the name of the Greek physician Galen (A.D. 129–199), whose ideas exerted a profound influence on the development of medicine for more than 1,000 years. Galen's name also appears alongside that of the equally renowned physician Hippocrates (c. 460–c. 377 B.C.) in the saying ***Galen says "Nay" and Hippocrates "Yea,"*** which patients have been known to quote wearily when their doctors disagree. *Some of the most interesting new medicines of recent years have been of galenical origin.*

gall and wormwood Spite; bitterness; feelings of mortification. The phrase is biblical in origin: "And I said, My strength and my hope is perished from the LORD: Remembering mine affliction and my misery, the wormwood and the gall" (Lamentations 3:18–19). "It was gall and wormwood to his soul to see that splendid, highly-accomplished woman, once so courted and admired, transformed into an active managing housewife, with hands and head continually occupied with household labours and household economy" (Anne Brontë, *Agnes Grey,* 1847).

Gallio (galeeō) A person who seems completely indifferent to something, especially a petty official who refuses to concern himself with matters outside his immediate province. The historical Gallio (c. 5 B.C.–A.D. 65) was the elder brother of the philosopher Seneca and was proconsul of the Roman province of Achaia in 51–52. While serving in this capacity he refused to listen to accusations made against the preaching of the apostle Paul because the charges against him related to Jewish, not Roman law (as related in Acts 18:12–13). "And ne'er was there mair need of poorfu' preachers than e'en now in these cauld Gallio days, when men's hearts are hardened like the nether mill-stone, till they come to regard none of these things" (Sir Walter Scott, *The Heart of Midlothian,* 1818).

Gamaliel (gămayleeăl) A teacher, especially a religious teacher. The biblical Gamaliel was a Pharisee rabbi, or doctor of law, and a mentor of Paul, who claimed to have studied sitting "at the feet of Gamaliel" (Acts 22:3). Gamaliel spoke up in defense of Paul and his companions when they were put on trial and is traditionally supposed to have subsequently converted to Christianity. "No man—that is, no gentleman—could possibly be attracted to Mr. Slope, or consent to sit at the feet of so abhorrent a Gamaliel" (Anthony Trollope, *Barchester Towers,* 1857).

Ganymede (ganimeed) An exceptionally beautiful youth. In Greek myth, Ganymede was a young man from Phrygia who was selected by Zeus as the most beautiful of mortals and on his command carried off by an eagle to serve as his cupbearer in heaven. Ganymede is also the name of one of the Galilean moons of Jupiter and is the largest satellite in the solar system. "I don't believe Ganymede cried when the eagle carried him away, and perhaps deposited him on Jove's shoulder at the end" (George Eliot, *Adam Bede,* 1859).

Garden of Eden (eedăn) Paradise or some other unspoiled, idyllic place, or a state of perfect bliss or innocence. The biblical Garden of Eden, from which ADAM and EVE were expelled after disobeying God's command not to eat from the Tree of the Knowledge of Good and Evil, is described briefly in Genesis: "And the LORD God planted a garden eastward in Eden; and there he put the man whom he had formed. And out of the ground made the LORD God to grow every tree that is pleasant to the sight, and good for food; the tree of life also in the midst of the garden, and the tree of knowledge of good and evil. And a river went out of Eden to water the garden" (Genesis 2:8–10). The Hebrew word *eden,* incidentally, is usually translated as "pleasure" or "delight." Tradition variously places the historical site of the Garden of Eden as being in Mesopotamia, Armenia, or somewhere at the head of the Persian Gulf, possibly at Eridu, where clay tablets have been found telling of a garden with a sacred palm tree. "Versailles! It is wonderfully beautiful! You gaze, and stare, and try to understand that it is real, that it is on the earth, that it is not the Garden of Eden" (Mark Twain, *The Innocents Abroad,* 1869).

gasp, at the last *See* LAST GASP, AT THE.

Gath, tell it not in *See* TELL IT NOT IN GATH.

Gaza, eyeless in *See* EYELESS IN GAZA.

Ge *See* GAEA.

geese that saved the Capitol The bearers of a timely warning that prevents disaster. The allusion is to the story of the sacred geese that warned of a Gaulish attack on the Capitoline Hill in 390 B.C. The Gauls had climbed unnoticed to the top of the hill before the cackling of the geese alerted Marcus Manlius, who roused the garrison just in time to drive off the attack. In gratitude, the Romans commemorated the event each year by carrying a golden goose in procession to the Capitol. *The two journalists were praised for their courage in pursuing the story, and their revelations were considered vital in staving off disaster. One paper even dubbed them the geese that saved the Capitol.*

Gehenna (gehenă) Hell or any wicked or unpleasant place. The name comes from the Hebrew *ge-hinnom,* meaning "valley of the son of Hinnom," which is identified in the Bible in Jeremiah 7:31–32 as the place where the followers of the god Molech sacrificed their children in fires at a "high place" called Tophet (or Topheth). This valley was located to the southwest of Jerusalem. It became associated with burning, especially as a site for the burning of the corpses of outcasts, which made it an effective analogy for the fires of hell and of everlasting judgment. *Go to Gehenna* is accordingly an alternative to *go to hell.* "Down to Gehenna or up to the

Throne, / He travels fastest who travels alone" (Rudyard Kipling, *The Story of the Gadsbys,* 1890).

generation of vipers A band of evil, untrustworthy people. The phrase appears in Matthew 3:7 ("O generation of vipers, who hath warned you to flee from the wrath to come?" and Luke 3:7, attributed to John the Baptist, and in Matthew 12:34 and 23:33, where it is credited to Christ in his condemnation of the Pharisees and Sadducees. *Eyeing the gun with growing unease, the young man began to suspect he had fallen in with a generation of vipers.*

genesis A beginning; the origin of something. The word comes from the Greek for "to be born" and is best known as the name of the first book of the Old Testament, which relates God's creation of the world. *The genesis of the project goes back to Duckworth's work in the late 1990s.*

genie (jeenee) A supernatural or magical being who will grant a person's wishes or carry out his or her commands and, by extension, a person who performs apparently impossible feats. The word comes from the Arabic *jinni,* a species of demon in Muslim mythology that inhabits the mountains since long before the birth of Adam. The jinn are credited with the power to change their appearance and assume the form of animals or humans; they play a leading role in numerous folktales. Some are good natured and beautiful, but others are hideously ugly and not to be trusted. "His closing exclamation is jerked out of the venerable gentleman by the suddenness with which Mr Squod, like a genie, catches him up, chair and all, and deposits him on the hearth-stone" (Charles Dickens, *Bleak House,* 1852–53).

genius loci (jeenyăs lōsī, jeeneeăs lōkee) The presiding spirit or deity of a particular place. The notion that there are supernatural entities that watch over specific locations and need to be honored and appeased was very familiar to the ancient Romans, who named them so. The modern notion of genius signifying intellectual brilliance is derived from the related belief that each individual has his or her personal guardian spirit who guides them through life. Another facet of the belief system suggests that each person has both a good genius and an evil genius who contend to influence the individual's thought and behavior. "His sudden appearance was to darkness what the sound of a trumpet is to silence. Gloom, the genius loci at all times hitherto, was now totally overthrown, less by the lantern-light than by what the lantern lighted" (Thomas Hardy, *Far from the Madding Crowd*, 1874).

gentian (jenshăn) A plant of the genus *Gentiana*, with attractive blue (but also sometimes yellow, white, or red) flowers. The name is thought to have come from the Illyrian king Gentius, who lived in the second century B.C. and is traditionally supposed to have been the first person to employ gentian flowers medicinally. The color of gentian flowers has also inspired the naming of a particular shade of purple-blue as *gentian blue*. "'Bother the woman!' she thought. 'I do want that gentian dress got ready, but now I simply can't give it to her to do'" (John Galsworthy, *The Forsyte Saga*, 1922).

Gethsemane (gethsemănee) A painful ordeal; a place of anguish or suffering. The Garden of Gethsemane, at the foot of the Mount of Olives outside Jerusalem, was the place where Christ prayed after the Last Supper on the night of his betrayal and arrest: "Then cometh Jesus with them unto a place called Gethsemane, and saith unto the disciples, Sit ye here, while I go and pray yonder" (Matthew 26:36). According to one tradition, it was in Gethsemane that Mary was buried. The word itself means "oil press" in Greek. *That afternoon the stadium became the team's Gethsemane, their ultimate humiliation and yet the foundation of famous triumphs to come in the years ahead.*

get thee behind me, Satan (saytăn) Do not try to tempt me; I refuse to be tempted. This is a quotation from the Bible, appearing in Matthew 4:10 and Luke 4:1–8, which both recount Christ's reply to the devil in the wilderness when the latter tries to lure him with promises of power over all the kingdoms of the world in exchange for his allegiance: "Get thee behind me, Satan: for it is written, Thou shalt worship the Lord thy God, and him only shalt thou serve" (Luke 4:8). The phrase also appears in Matthew 16:23 as Christ's reply when Peter tries to persuade him against willingly going to crucifixion. *"Get thee behind me, Satan," said the colonel as he hurried past the beckoning open door of the saloon bar.*

giant A person or thing of exceptional size, importance, etc. The huge ogres of European folklore are descended from a supernatural race in

Greek myth, identified as the offspring of GAEA (representing the earth) and URANUS (representing the sky). According to legend, the giants, who had terrifying faces and serpents' tails for legs, rebelled against the gods on Olympus and waged war with them for 10 years before being defeated and killed or consigned by Zeus to Tartarus. One suggestion is that the story of the epic struggle between the gods and the giants was inspired by volcanic eruptions. *Stories about human-eating giants are common to many cultural traditions, and many are apparently of great antiquity.*

giants in the earth The heroes of a bygone age, when humans were far more glorious beings than they are today. The phrase is biblical, appearing in Genesis 6:4: "There were giants in the earth in those days." It is sometimes believed that after the time of Adam and Eve's expulsion from the Garden of Eden the world was populated by a race of magnificent giants called the Nephilim, who were produced by the union of various heavenly beings with human women. The terms *Nephilim* and *giants* are also applied to some of the pre-Israelite inhabitants of Canaan (Numbers 13:33), who were also referred to as the Rephaim/Rephaites and Anakim/Anakites (Deuteronomy 2:11; 3:11), and Goliath was one of their descendants, but they are not heard of after the time of David. The biblical references in Genesis 6:4 and Numbers 13:33 have also led to the expression *land of giants*, "sometimes used figuratively to refer to areas of great opportunity that contain apparently formidable difficulties" (Manser, *King James Bible Word Book,* p. 253). *But things were different then, and there were giants in the earth.*

Gideons (gideeănz) An interdenominational Christian organization that works to make the Bible available to as many people as possible throughout the world. Founded in the United States in 1899 by three traveling businessmen—Samuel E. Hill, William J. Knights, and John H. Nicholson—the Gideon Society takes its name from Gideon, the great Israelite soldier and judge who led his people to victory over the Midianites, as recounted in Judges 6–7. *The room was sparsely furnished, the only extras being a jug of water and a Gideon Bible in the bedside cabinet.*

gift of tongues The ability to speak in many languages without having previously learned them. This ability, technically termed *glossolalia,* was a feature of early Christian worship and alludes to the biblical account of the apostles, who miraculously acquired the power to communicate in a variety of languages during the Feast of Pentecost (as related in Acts 2:4–12); the apostle Paul also refers to its use, with interpretation of tongues, in 1 Corinthians 12 and 14. "Ane wad hae needed the gift of tongues to ken preceesely what they said—but I pelieve the best end of it was, 'Long live MacCallummore and Knockdunder!'" (Sir Walter Scott, *The Heart of Midlothian,* 1818).

Gilead, balm in *See* BALM IN GILEAD.

Ginnungagap (ginăngăgap) A great void or abyss. In Norse mythology, Ginnungagap is the name given to the endless void that is said to separate NIFLHEIM, a region of intense cold, and Muspelheim, a region of intense heat. Having no beginning or end and no day or night, it was said to have existed long before the appearance of heaven and earth. *Into this purgatory, this spiritual Ginnungagap, vanished all his ideals and hopes for the future.*

girdle of Venus *See* APHRODITE.

gird up thy loins To get ready for action; to prepare to apply oneself to a difficult task or to make a journey. The phrase appears several times in the Bible, such as in 1 Kings 18:46, where Elijah gathers up his long flowing robes and fastens ("girds") them with his belt ("girdle") in order to run freely: "And the hand of the LORD was on Elijah; and he girded up his loins, and ran before Ahab to the entrance of Jezreel." "'Yet,' said the Rabbi, 'take courage, for this grief availeth nothing. Gird up thy loins, and seek out this Wilfred, the son of Cedric'" (Sir Walter Scott, *Ivanhoe,* 1819).

give up the ghost To die; to give in; to cease working. The phrase appears in various forms at several places in the Bible, as in Genesis 25:8, which describes how "Abraham gave up the ghost, and died in a good old age." "Why died I not from the womb? Why did I not give up the ghost when I came out of the belly?" (Thomas Hardy, *Jude the Obscure,* 1895).

give us this day our daily bread *See* DAILY BREAD.

gladiator A person who fights for or supports a particular cause or campaign. Derived from the Latin *gladius* (meaning "sword"), the term was applied to the combatants who fought to the death with a range of weapons as a form of public entertainment in the arenas of ancient Rome. Gladiatorial contests were eventually suppressed in the Eastern Empire in A.D. 325 and in the West in A.D. 500. *The two fighters squared up to each other like gladiators on the sands of the Colosseum.*

glad tidings of great joy *See* GOOD TIDINGS OF GREAT JOY.

glass darkly, through a *See* SEE THROUGH A GLASS DARKLY.

Glaucus (glahkăs) A person who is destroyed by his passion for something. In Greek mythology, Glaucus was a son of Sisyphus. Glaucus was devoted to his horses but could not be persuaded to breed them. This provoked the anger of Venus, who made the horses tear their owner to pieces. *Like Glaucus, his passion for the turf proved his undoing.*

Glaucus swap *See* DIOMEDEAN EXCHANGE.

glory, in all one's *See* IN ALL ONE'S GLORY.

glory is departed, the The times are not what they were; the golden age has passed. The expression is biblical, appearing in 1 Samuel 4:21, where Phineas's wife names her new baby **Ichabod** (meaning "inglorious" or "no glory") after hearing that the Philistines have captured the Ark of the Covenant and that both the child's father and grandfather are dead. By the same token, the name Ichabod has in times past been used as an exclamation. "That pulpit would indeed be his own. Precentors, vicars, and choristers might hang up their harps on the willows. Ichabod! Ichabod! The glory of their house was departing from them" (Anthony Trollope, *Barchester Towers,* 1857). "And then, Ichabod! Ichabod! the glory will be departed from us" (T. H. Huxley, "A Liberal Education," 1899).

glory to God in the highest *See* GOODWILL TO ALL MEN.

gnashing of teeth *See* WEEPING AND GNASHING OF TEETH.

147

gnome (nōm) A diminutive creature resembling an old, deformed man: A familiar character of fairy tale and legend, conventionally described as living underground in mines or quarries, the gnome has obscure ancient roots and was probably named from the Greek *genomos* (meaning "earth dweller"). "Hitherto he had been treated very much as if he had been a useful gnome or brownie—a queer and unaccountable creature, who must necessarily be looked at with wondering curiosity and repulsion, and with whom one would be glad to make all greetings and bargains as brief as possible, but who must be dealt with in a propitiatory way" (George Eliot, *Silas Marner,* 1861).

go and do thou likewise Do the same thing; act in a similar fashion. The expression is biblical, appearing in Luke 10:37 in the parable of the Good Samaritan, where it is spoken by Christ and intended as encouragement to behave with the same charity. In modern usage it often appears in a rather more discouraging context in the form of an euphemistic admonition to someone to go away or otherwise refrain from interfering or some other action. *I told that jerk to get lost, and if you're sensible you'll go and do thou likewise before I get really angry.*

go and sin no more You will not be punished for what you have done but do not do wrong again. The expression comes from the biblical account of the **woman taken in adultery** in John 8:5–12, in which Christ forgives a woman who is faced with death by stoning on charges of adultery. When Christ challenges any member of the mob who is not guilty of sin himself to cast the first stone, no one comes forward. *The headmaster admonished them both for about an hour, then considered they had been punished enough and told them to go and sin no more. See also* LET HIM WHO IS WITHOUT SIN CAST THE FIRST STONE.

God and mammon *See* MAMMON.

God forbid May it never happen (used as a strong exclamation of dissent). The phrase appears in the Bible in Genesis 44:7 and in many subsequent passages, usually as a translation of the Hebrew *halilah,* from the verb *halal,* meaning "to defile or pollute." It was William Tyndale in his English translation of the Bible, begun in 1525, who settled on "God forbid" as his preferred English translation (in spite of the fact that God is not mentioned in corresponding Hebrew and Greek idioms). "If this cleaving distrust from which I cannot free myself should be in very truth the mute prophecy of evil to come—to come, I know not when—if it be so (which God forbid!), how soon she may want a friend, a protector near at hand, a ready refuge in the time of her trouble!" (Wilkie Collins, *After Dark,* 1856).

god from a machine *See* DEUS EX MACHINA.

go down to the sea in ships To journey across the sea by boat. The expression is biblical in origin, appearing in Psalm 107:23: "They that go down to the sea in ships, that do business in great waters; These see the works of the LORD, and his wonders in the deep." The phrase has become a cliché for the business of seafaring and was probably the inspiration for the famous opening lines of John Masefield's poem "Sea Fever" (1902): "I must go down to the seas again, to the lonely sea and sky."

God save the king/queen Long live the king, or queen. This expression of loyalty to a reigning monarch is biblical in origin, appearing in 1 Samuel 10:24 as a shout of acclamation in honor of Saul. Elsewhere in the Bible it appears with reference to Absalom, Adonijah, Solomon, and Joash in such forms as "may the king live"—the word *God* being too sacred to use. Today it is perhaps best known as the title of the British national anthem. *With a shout of "God save the king!" the sergeant leapt into the throng of struggling bodies and was seen no more.*

Godwin's oath (godwinz) A protestation of innocence that is immediately shown to be false. The expression alludes to an oath made by Godwin, Earl of Wessex (d. 1053), who at the end of a long career of political double-dealing and treachery stood accused of murdering Edward the Confessor's brother Alfred. He swore he was innocent of the crime and added that heaven should strike him down at once if this was not so. Without further ado he choked to death on a piece of bread. *This promise proved to be like Godwin's oath, quickly revealed to be as hollow as a drum and the exact opposite of what was really intended.*

go forth and multiply *See* BE FRUITFUL AND MULTIPLY.

go from strength to strength To become more and more successful. The phrase comes from the Bible, where it appears in Psalm 84:7: "They go from strength to strength, every one of them in Zion appeareth before God." *Under their new captain and coach the team is going from strength to strength.*

Gog and Magog (gog, <u>may</u>gog) Godless forces that threaten the end of the world through war. Gog and Magog are identified in Revelation 20:8 as the personification of nations at the farthest ends of the earth in the final apocalyptic conflict between good and evil. (See also Ezekiel 38–39.) Statues of Gog and Magog, depicted as giant warriors, stood for many years outside the Guildhall in London; these were destroyed by the Great Fire of 1666 but replaced in 1709 and once more in 1953 after their destruction during the bombing of London in 1940. ". . . it was shown that likeness in sound made them impossible: it was a method of interpretation which was not tested by the necessity of forming anything which had sharper collisions than an elaborate notion of Gog and Magog: it was as free from interruption as a plan for threading the stars together" (George Eliot, *Middlemarch,* 1871–72).

golden age A period of history considered to have been notably prosperous or creative. The golden age of myth was a legendary era that marked the beginnings of human history on earth, when humans lived in idyllic harmony with nature and one another. (It was followed by the legendary SILVER AGE and the historical Iron Age). Historical periods commonly referred to as golden ages include that of Egypt (c. 1312–1235 BC), of Assyria (c. 700–600 BC), of Athens (443–429 BC), and of Persia (c. AD 531–628). "'I have brought you a book for evening solace,' and he laid on the table a new publication—a poem: one of those genuine productions so often vouchsafed to the fortunate public of those days—the golden age of modern literature" (Charlotte Brontë, *Jane Eyre,* 1847).

golden apple *See* APPLE OF DISCORD.

golden bowl Life, youth, or anything else that is fragile or once lost cannot be regained. The image of life as a golden bowl comes from the Bible, where it appears in Ecclesiastes 12:1, 6–7: "Remember now thy Creator in the days of thy youth, while the evil days come not . . . or ever the silver cord be loosed, or the golden bowl be broken, or the pitcher be broken at the fountain, or the wheel broken at the cistern. Then shall the dust return to the earth as it was: and the spirit shall return unto God who gave it." The image of a broken bowl has long been a symbol of death: Its association here with a cord may suggest that the bowl in question is part of a lamp, which goes out when the cord breaks and the bowl falls. The phrase is perhaps best known today as the title of the Henry James novel *The Golden Bowl* (1904). *But the golden bowl had been broken, and there was no rousing the girl's lifeless body.*

golden calf Money, riches, or material values. The description of the golden calf comes from the biblical episode related in Exodus 32:1–14 in which the Israelites worshiped such an idol, made by Aaron from golden earrings, in the absence of Aaron's brother Moses. In modern usage people who place undue emphasis on the pursuit of material values may be accused of *worshiping the golden calf.* "The golden calf they worship at Boston is a pigmy compared with the giant effigies set up in other parts of that vast counting-house which lies beyond the Atlantic; and the almighty dollar sinks into something comparatively insignificant, amidst a whole Pantheon of better gods" (Charles Dickens, *American Notes,* 1842).

Golden Fleece Something of great value that is much sought after but very hard to obtain. In the Greek myth of Jason and the Argonauts, the Golden Fleece was a ram's fleece of pure gold that hung on an oak tree in a sacred grove in Colchis until Jason managed to carry it off. Australia is sometimes referred to as the "Land of the Golden Fleece" because of its extensive production of wool. ". . . a worn-out royal gun-brig condemned to sale, to be had dog-cheap: this he proposed that they two, or in fact Boyd with his five thousand pounds, should buy; that they should refit and arm and man it;— and sail a-privateering 'to the Eastern Archipelago,' Philippine Isles, or I know not where; and so conquer the golden fleece" (Thomas Carlyle, *The Life of John Sterling,* 1851).

golden rule The one principle or guideline that should be followed at all times. The original Golden Rule was the advice given by Christ during the Sermon on the Mount, as related in Matthew 7:12: "Therefore all things whatsoever ye would that men should do to you, do ye even so to them: for this is the law and the prophets." Christ's Golden Rule may be rendered in a variety of ways, among them "treat others as you would like to be treated yourself" and the succinct "do as you would be done by." "The golden rule is that there are no golden rules" (George Bernard Shaw, "Maxims for Revolutionists," *Man and Superman,* 1905).

golden shower Money, especially in the form of a bribe. The expression alludes to the Greek legend of Zeus and Danaë, in the course of which Zeus gained access to Danaë, the beautiful daughter of King Acrisius of Argos, by disguising himself as a shower of gold and subsequently foiled the king's attempts to protect his daughter's chastity. As a result of this union Danaë gave birth to Perseus. ". . . he folds his arms about him, and sits in expectation of some revolution in the state that shall raise him to greatness, or some golden shower that shall load him with wealth" (Samuel Johnson, "Idle Hope," *Essays,* 1753).

gold of Ophir (ōfer) Something of the finest quality. In the Bible Ophir is the country from which fine gold is imported to decorate the Temple (1 Chronicles 29:4); thus, gold of Ophir was of the finest quality. *His opinions are like the gold of Ophir, and many admirers hang on his every word.*

gold of Tolosa *See* HE HAS GOT GOLD OF TOLOSA.

Golgotha *See* CALVARY.

Goliath (gǎliǎth) A formidable opponent or obstacle. The allusion is to the Philistine giant Goliath, "six cubits and a span high," in the biblical tale of DAVID AND GOLIATH, as related in 1 Samuel 17. Such was Goliath's strength that the youthful David was the only Israelite prepared to answer his challenge to single combat. "Violent crime and AIDS are probably each of them individually bigger Goliaths than ever apartheid was" (*Christianity and Renewal,* September 2001).

Gomorrah *See* SODOM AND GOMORRAH.

good fight, fight the *See* FIGHT THE GOOD FIGHT.

good for nothing *See* SALT OF THE EARTH.

Good Samaritan (sămairĭtăn) A person who kindly and selflessly helps a stranger in distress or difficulty. The expression alludes to the parable that Christ told, recorded in Luke 10:25–37, about a Jew who was brutally attacked while on his way from Jerusalem to Jericho and left for dead. His plight was ignored by a priest and a Levite who *passed by on the other side* without giving him any help at all. But later a Samaritan who happened by took compassion on the man, and in spite of the fact that the Samaritans were open enemies of the Jews, the Samaritan looked after him, paying an innkeeper to take care of him. The phrase Good Samaritan does not, incidentally, appear in the actual text of the King James Bible (1611) and appears not to have become an accepted translation until at least 1640. "No one would remember the Good Samaritan if he'd only had good intentions. He had money as well" (Margaret Thatcher, television interview, January 6, 1986). *See also* FALL AMONG THIEVES.

Good Shepherd Jesus Christ. Of many epithets by which Jesus is referred to in the Bible, this one appears in John 10:11 and alludes to the image of Christ as a shepherd tending his flock. It evokes the parable of the lost sheep related in Matthew 18:12–14, in which a shepherd goes to the aid of the single sheep that is lost, despite the fact that the other 99 sheep in his flock are all safely accounted for. The title is on occasion applied to anyone who assumes responsibility for the welfare of others. *I will put my faith in the Good Shepherd to see us safely home.*

good thing come out of Nazareth (nazărăth) Something good that comes from an unexpected source. The expression alludes to Christ, who spent his childhood in Nazareth. The phrase appears in John 1:46, where Nathanael expresses surprise upon learning that Jesus came from the insignificant town of Nazareth: "And Nathanael said unto him, Can there any good thing come out of Nazareth? Philip said unto him, Come and see." "She had almost fancied that a good thing could come out of Nazareth—a charming woman out of Tablothay's Dairy" (Thomas Hardy, *Tess of the D'Urbervilles,* 1891).

good tidings of great joy Good news. The phrase alludes to Luke 2:10, in which the angel of the Lord brings the good news of Christ's birth to shepherds tending their flocks in the field: "And the angel said unto them, Fear not: for, behold, I bring you good tidings of great joy, which shall be to all people." Sometimes this phrase is rendered as *glad tidings of great joy,* ". . . and though of the same religious sentiments as Mr Treat, yet his attention was turned to those glad tidings of great joy, which a Savior came to publish" (Henry David Thoreau, *Cape Cod,* 1865).

goodwill to all men Charitable feeling to all of humanity. This exhortation to the faithful to behave with generosity toward their fellow humans (especially during the Christmas season) has its origins in Luke 2:14, in which the birth of Christ at Bethlehem is a cause of much rejoicing: "suddenly there was with the angel a multitude of the heavenly host praising God, and saying, Glory to God in the highest, and on earth peace, good will toward men." *After all, it's Christmas, the season of goodwill to all men.*

good works Charitable acts; actions carried out to help others. The phrase appears several times in the Bible, as in Acts 9:36: "Now there was at Joppa a certain disciple named Tabitha, which by interpretation is called Dorcas: this woman was full of good works and almsdeeds which she did." "'I like to hear your adventures and good works so much,' said Polly, ready to be amused by anything that made her forget herself" (Louisa May Alcott, *An Old Fashioned Girl,* 1870).

Gordian knot *See* CUT THE GORDIAN KNOT.

gorgon A monstrously ugly or frightening woman. In Greek mythology, the Gorgons were three loathsome sisters, with wings, sharp tusklike teeth, brazen claws, and snakes for hair. The most famous of them was Medusa, whose ugliness was so extreme that anyone who saw her was immediately turned to stone. Medusa was beheaded by Perseus; her sisters were immortal. "Her mother is perfectly unbearable. Never met such a Gorgon . . . I don't really know what a Gorgon is like, but I am quite sure that Lady Bracknell is one" (Oscar Wilde, *The Importance of Being Earnest,* 1895).

gospel Something undeniably true or accepted as true; something strongly believed. The word derives from an Anglo-Saxon translation of the Latin *evangelium* as *godspell,* signifying "good tidings." The biblical Gospels are the New Testament books of the life of Christ, as written by

Matthew, Mark, Luke, and John. The word is often used as a synonym for the actual teachings of Christ or, more specifically, the message of God's salvation of humanity through the life, death, and resurrection of Christ (as in Romans 1:16). In modern usage a *gospel truth* is something that is generally regarded as irrefutable, while any source or authority described as *gospel* is considered essential or reliable. ". . . the mere opportunity of venting a little ill-nature against the offending Miss Price, and affecting to compassionate her weaknesses and foibles, though only in the presence of a solitary dependant, was almost as great a relief to her spleen as if the whole had been gospel truth" (Charles Dickens, *Nicholas Nickleby,* 1838–39).

go the extra/second mile   To make a special effort to do something beyond the norm; to go beyond the call of duty. The allusion is to Christ's saying in the Sermon on the Mount: "And whosoever shall compel thee to go a mile, go with him twain" (Matthew 5:41). "I was sort of lukewarm about the British before, but I'm more positive now they're willing to go the extra mile" (*The New York Observer,* October 12, 2001).

go the way of all flesh   To die or disappear finally. The expression alludes to the biblical phrase "go the way of all the earth" in Joshua 23:14 and 1 Kings 2:2. "And yet—what could one do? Buy them and stick them in a lumber-room? No; they had to go the way of all flesh and furniture, and be worn out" (John Galsworthy, *The Forsyte Saga,* 1906–21).

Gothic   An essentially medieval style of art and architecture whose characteristics include pointed arches, rich detail, and flamboyant decoration. The Gothic style was condemned by Renaissance artists and architects as primitive to the point of barbarism, hence the link with the warlike Goths, the Germanic people who destroyed many fine works of art as they laid waste to much of the Roman Empire between the third and fifth centuries A.D. The style nonetheless became popular again during the Gothic Revival of the late 18th and 19th centuries. The term *gothic* also came to be applied to a genre of literature characterized by gloom and the grotesque that enjoyed a considerable vogue during the Gothic Revival. It is still used today in discussing novels, films, and like that have a similarly brooding, melodramatic atmosphere. "Its whole visible exterior was ornamented with quaint figures, conceived in the grotesqueness of a Gothic fancy, and drawn or stamped in the glittering plaster, composed of lime, pebbles, and bits of glass, with which the woodwork of the walls was overspread" (Nathaniel Hawthorne, *The House of the Seven Gables,* 1851).

go to Gehenna *See* GEHENNA.

go to the ant, thou sluggard Don't be lazy; stir yourself to action. This expression appears in Proverbs 6:6–9 as follows: "Go to the ant, thou sluggard; consider her ways, and be wise: Which having no guide, overseer, or ruler, Provideth her meat in the summer, and gathereth her food in the harvest. How long wilt thou sleep, O sluggard? when wilt thou arise out of thy sleep?" *The foreman tipped the boy out of his hammock. "Go to the ant, thou sluggard," he said. "There's work to be done."*

Götterdämmerung (gerter<u>de</u>mărung, gerter<u>da</u>mărung) The end of the world; any titanic clash resulting in a universal cataclysm or collapse. From the German for "twilight of the gods," Götterdämmerung is described in detail in Norse mythology, which suggests that the world will come to an end after a dreadful battle between the good and evil gods in which all the good gods will die heroic deaths. A new world will then arise from the ashes of the old. Today the term is most familiar from *Götterdämmerung* (1876), the last of Richard Wagner's four operas in the Ring cycle. *If his life had been an opera he would have considered this last blow a prelude to his own personal Götterdämmerung. See also* RAGNAROK.

gourmand's prayer The wish of diners that they could savor the taste of good food for longer. It is rendered by Aristotle (384–322 B.C.) in his *Ethics* in the form "O Philoxenos, Philoxenos, why were you not Prometheus?" Philoxenos was an epicure who wished to have the neck of a crane so that he might enjoy longer the taste of his food as he swallowed it; Prometheus was the creator of humans, who sadly did not include a cranelike neck in his final design. *The meal that night was so good that I was not the only diner to close his eyes in ecstasy and mutter to himself the gourmand's prayer that it would never come to an end.*

Graces *See* THREE GRACES.

grail *See* HOLY GRAIL.

grain of mustard seed Anything that has small beginnings but grows into something much larger. This striking image is biblical in origin, being ascribed to Christ in Matthew 13:31–32, Mark 4:30–32, and Luke 13:18–19 and used as a metaphor for the kingdom of heaven, which like a mustard seed starts from the tiniest beginnings and blossoms into a huge tree, with birds nesting on its branches. "It is compared also to leaven, to sowing of seed, and to the multiplication of a grain of mustard-seed; by all which compulsion is excluded; and consequently there can in that time be no actual reigning" (Thomas Hobbes, *Leviathan,* 1651).

graven image A statue or other object that is worshiped as a god or idol. The phrase appears several times in the Bible but is best known from the second of the Ten Commandments: "Thou shalt not make unto thee any graven image, or any likeness of any thing that is in heaven above, or that is in the earth beneath, or that is in the water under the earth" (Exodus 20:4). "'Still, he who would do justice,' she proceeded, 'will not forget that the cunning of our hands was bound by the prohibition, "Thou shalt not make unto thee any graven image, or any likeness of anything"; which the Sopherim wickedly extended beyond its purpose and time'" (Lew Wallace, *Ben Hur,* 1880).

Grave, where is thy victory? *See* DEATH, WHERE IS THY STING?

greater love hath no man The sacrifice of one's own life or interests for the good of others is the supreme virtue. The expression appears in the Bible in John 15:13, where Christ, in his last address to his disciples, teaches that "Greater love hath no man than this, that a man lay down his life for his friends." *"Greater love hath no man," quipped their friend as he stood up to accept the blame on their behalf.*

greatest of these is charity *See* FAITH, HOPE, AND CHARITY.

Greek calends *See* AT THE GREEK CALENDS.

Greek chorus A group of singers or speakers who comment on the action taking place. In early Greek drama such a body of performers took a leading role as there were only one, two, or at most three individual actors on stage at any one time. The same device has been used by dramatists through the centuries, although since Shakespeare's time the role has often been fulfilled by one performer alone. ". . . it is always a source of pleasure and awe to me to remember that the ultimate survival of the Greek chorus, lost elsewhere to art, is to be found in the servitor answering the priest at Mass" (Oscar Wilde, *De Profundis,* 1905).

Greeks bearing gifts *See* BEWARE OF GREEKS BEARING GIFTS.

green pastures A place of ease and plenty, offering respite from the world. The image comes from Psalm 23:1–3, in which David writes of God: "The LORD is my shepherd; I shall not want. He maketh me to lie down in green pastures: he leadeth me beside the still waters; he restoreth my soul." In modern usage the phrase is most familiar from its inclusion in funeral services, in which it may be interpreted as representing heaven. Shakespeare's character Falstaff in *Henry V* (1598/1599) is reported to have "babbled of green fields" as he lay dying, and deathbed visions of pleasant fields have long been one of the subjects of popular novels and films. "But I've noticed that in these villages where the people lead a quiet life among the green pastures and the still waters, tilling the ground and tending the cattle, there's a strange deadness to the Word, as different as can be from the great towns, like Leeds, where I once went to visit a holy woman who preaches there" (George Eliot, *Adam Bede,* 1859).

Gregorian chant (grăgoreeăn) A style of vocal unaccompanied chant, best known as the official liturgical plainsong of the Roman Catholic Church. It was named after Pope Gregory I (c. 540–604), who promoted the use of plainsong in liturgical services during his papacy. *Recordings of Gregorian chant have been a surprising best-seller in the past year or two.*

Grendel (grendăl) A ferocious monster. In the epic Anglo-Saxon poem *Beowulf* (c. 700) Grendel is a fearsome underwater monster descended from Cain who repeatedly emerges from his lake at night to devour Danish warriors as they sleep in the banqueting hall of their king, Hrothgar. After 12 years of these ravages the hero Beowulf of the Geats arrives to fight Grendel, and after a long struggle Beowulf manages to kill him by tearing off his arm, to general rejoicing. Grendel's equally fearsome mother seeks to avenge her son, but Beowulf follows her into the lake and kills her, too. *Like some latterday Grendel he hauled himself out of the water and bore down upon his opponent, growling menacingly.*

groves of academe (<u>a</u>kădeem, akă<u>deem</u>) Academic circles in general or a college, university, or other place of study or research. Academe was the name of a public garden (with a grove) in Athens, in which the Greek philosopher Plato gave lessons. The garden itself had formerly been owned by a citizen of the city called Academus. *It seemed unlikely that the inspector, a diamond of the roughest kind, would be familiar with the rules of etiquette that governed this particular grove of academe.*

Gyges' ring (g<u>ī</u>jeez) The power of invisibility. According to Plato (c. 428–348/347 B.C.), Gyges was a Lydian shepherd of the seventh century B.C. who descended into a chasm in the earth, where he found a brazen horse. Inside the horse was the body of a giant, with a brazen ring on his finger. When Gyges slipped the ring on to his own finger he found it made him invisible. He went on to use the ring to make his fortune; usurp the reigning king; marry his wife, Candaules; and with her found a new dynasty. *As if he possessed some electronic Gyges' ring, he found he could roam wherever he liked on the Net without the slightest chance of his presence being detected.*

Hades (<u>hay</u>deez) The underworld or abode of the dead, according to Greek mythology. It took its name from Hades, the brother of Zeus who became the lord of the dead and was the equivalent of the Roman Pluto. Hades was said to be a sunless void separated from the mortal world by the waters of five rivers, the chief of these being the Styx. The most guilty souls were consigned to Tartarus, while those who were less guilty resided in the asphodel meadows. The entrance to Hades was guarded by the three-headed dog Cerberus. *"I'll see you in Hades first," quoth Sir Archibald defiantly.* See also ELYSIAN FIELDS.

Hagar *See* ISHMAEL.

halcyon days (<u>hal</u>seeăn) Happy, prosperous times of peace and harmony. The word *halcyon* was the Greek name for the kingfisher (from *hals,* "the sea," and *kuo,* "to breed on"), a bird whose habits were shrouded in mystery in the classical era. It was believed that kingfishers nested far out to sea at the time of the winter solstice, when the seas remained calm for 14 days so that the birds could incubate their eggs on the waves. This notion harked back to the legend of Halcyon, the daughter of Aeolus, god of the winds, who married the mortal Ceyx and threw herself into the sea after her husband died in a shipwreck. Both were transformed into kingfishers. "He knew the world too well to risk the comfort of such halcyon moments, by prolonging them till they were disagreeable" (Anthony Trollope, *The Warden,* 1855). *Life in today's universities seems a far cry from the halcyon days of the 1970s and 1980s when money seemed no object.*

half is more than the whole It is better sometimes to settle for a share of something rather than spend a great deal in trying to gain more. This proverbial expression is supposed to have been first uttered by the ninth-century B.C. Greek poet Hesiod as advice to his brother Perseus when the latter was considering fighting a legal battle over an estate, thereby risking most of it being frittered away on lawyers' fees. *The lawyers conferred, then decided to settle on the grounds that half is sometimes more than the whole.*

Halicarnassus *See* EIGHTH WONDER OF THE WORLD.

halt and the blind *See* MAIMED, THE HALT, THE BLIND, THE.

hamadryad *See* NYMPH.

Haman, hang as high as *See* HANG AS HIGH AS HAMAN.

hand, left *See* LEFT HAND KNOW WHAT YOUR RIGHT HAND IS DOING, DO NOT LET YOUR.

hand, right *See* IF THY RIGHT EYE OFFEND THEE; LEFT HAND KNOW WHAT YOUR RIGHT HAND IS DOING, DO NOT LET YOUR.

hand against every man *See* ISHMAEL.

hand findeth to do, whatsoever thy *See* WHATSOEVER THY HAND FINDETH TO DO.

hand offend thee, if thy right *See* IF THY RIGHT EYE OFFEND THEE.

hand of God *See* FINGER OF GOD.

hands, wash one's *See* WASH ONE'S HANDS OF.

handwriting on the wall *See* WRITING ON THE WALL.

hang as high as Haman (haymăn) To suffer the fate that one has prepared for someone else. The phrase alludes to the biblical story of Haman, the favorite minister of King Ahasuerus (Xerxes) of Persia who was outmaneuvered by Esther and hanged on the very gallows he had built for the execution of his enemy Mordecai, Esther's father (Esther 7:9–10). Esther's triumph is commemorated by the Jewish festival of Purim, when celebrants eat triangular pastries called hamantaschen (meaning "Haman's purses" in Yiddish). "And they hanged Private Simmons—hanged him as high as Haman in hollow square of the regiment; and the Colonel said it was Drink; and the Chaplain was sure it was the Devil; and Simmons fancied it was both, but he didn't know, and only hoped his fate would be a warning to his companions" (Rudyard Kipling, "In the Matter of a Private," 1890).

Hanging Gardens of Babylon *See* EIGHTH WONDER OF THE WORLD.

Hannibal (ha̲nibăl) A great military leader. Hannibal (247–182 B.C.) was a Carthaginian general who in 218 took the Romans by surprise, leading his army over the Alps and ravaging Italy, although he failed to take Rome itself. Ultimately he was defeated by Scipio Africanus at Zama in 202. *The general was revered by his troops and was ready to lead them, Hannibal-like, over the mountains.*

Happy Islands *See* ISLANDS OF THE BLEST.

hare and the tortoise A patient, methodical approach may succeed better than a more hurried one. The allusion is to the fable of the hare and the tortoise attributed to the Greek writer AESOP (c. 620–560 B.C.). The tale relates how the hare lost a running race to the much slower tortoise because he was so confident of victory that he decided to take a short rest before completing the course. *When it comes to investment policies it is often a case of the hare and the tortoise as the more glamorous options often underperform compared to less exciting choices.*

harmless as doves *See* WISE AS SERPENTS AND HARMLESS AS DOVES.

Harmonia's necklace (hahrmō̲neeăz) A possession that brings bad luck to its owner. The allusion is to the necklace that King Cadmus gave to his bride, Harmonia, the daughter of Ares and Aphrodite. The necklace, which had been given to Cadmus by Hephaestus (Aphrodite's former husband), brought evil to all who owned it. After suffering many misfortunes

Cadmus and Harmonia were changed into serpents by the gods, all of whom had attended the wedding. *Like Harmonia's necklace the property seemed to work like a curse on all who had possession of it.*

harpy (<u>hahr</u>pee) A predatory, grasping, shrewish woman. In Greek mythology, Harpies (meaning "snatchers" or "robbers") were loathsome monsters with the bodies of birds, the heads of women, and the claws of vultures. Variously given as one, two, or three in number, they were sometimes identified as personifications of the winds that could carry people off or as the souls of the dead who looked for opportunities to snatch the souls of the living. They are best known from the adventures of Jason and the Argonauts, in which they are depicted perpetually seizing food prepared for the blind king Phineus. "Nothing short of the twelve dollars and a half will satisfy this harpy, I perceive; and surely my reputation as judge is worth that trifle" (James Fenimore Cooper, *The Pioneers,* 1823).

hath shall be given, to him that *See* WHOSOEVER HATH, TO HIM SHALL BE GIVEN.

haughty spirit before a fall *See* PRIDE GOETH BEFORE A FALL.

heap coals of fire To act with generosity or kindness to someone who has behaved badly, thereby causing the person to realize the wrongdoing and experience pangs of remorse. The expression appears in the Bible in Proverbs 25:22 in the form: "If thine enemy be hungry, give him bread to eat; and if be thirsty, give him water to drink: For thou shalt heap coals of fire upon his head, and the LORD shall reward thee." The same illustration is referred to in Romans 12:20: ". . . for in so doing thou shalt heap coals of fire on his head. Be not overcome of evil, but overcome evil with good." *These generous compliments were almost more than she could bear, each new expression of admiration heaping further coals of fire upon her head.*

heaven The Christian paradise; any ideal place or situation. The biblical heaven is depicted as the throne of God, accompanied by hosts of angels (as in Isaiah 6:1 and Revelation 4:1–11). The term is also used more widely to refer to the sky above or to the night sky with its stars and planets. "The Brahmin legends assert that this city is built on the site of the ancient Casi, which, like Mahomet's tomb, was once suspended between heaven and earth" (Jules Verne, *Eighty Days Around the World,* 1873).

heaven's gate A place or situation in which a person faces the possibility of imminent death. The phrase alludes to the story of Jacob, who on waking from his dream about a ladder ascending to heaven exclaims, "Surely the LORD is in this place; and I knew it not. And he was afraid, and said, How dreadful is this place! this is none other but the house of God, and this is the gate of heaven" (Genesis 28:16–17). *The enemy brought up some cannon, and the general's confidence faltered as he realized, somewhat tardily, that they were trapped before heaven's gate.*

Hebe (heebee) Personification of youth. In Greek mythology she is identified as the daughter of Zeus and Hera and the cupbearer to the gods before being replaced by Ganymede. Another tradition has it that she lost her position after stumbling and falling while serving NECTAR to the gods. "Olivia, now about eighteen, had that luxuriancy of beauty with which painters generally draw Hebe; open, sprightly, and commanding" (Oliver Goldsmith, *The Vicar of Wakefield,* 1766).

Hecate (hekătee) Personification of witchcraft and sorcery. In Greek mythology Hecate was a moon goddess who ruled the underworld and by association the witches, ghosts, and world of magic. She is often depicted with three heads as she was identified with Selene in heaven, Artemis on earth, and Persephone in the underworld. *Drunken and screaming foul oaths, she erupted out of the shadows like Hecate from the underworld.*

hecatomb (hekătōm) A great sacrifice. The word comes from the Greek *hekaton,* meaning "a hundred," and *bous,* meaning "an ox," and referred originally to the sacrifice of 100 head of oxen in religious rituals. "Thirteen years later the Mahdi's empire was abolished forever in the gigantic hecatomb of Omdurman; after which it was thought proper that a religious ceremony in honour of General Gordon should be held at the palace at Khartoum" (Lytton Strachey, *Eminent Victorians,* 1918).

hector To badger, bully, or intimidate others. The word is an allusion to Hector, the hero of Homer's *Iliad* (c. eighth century B.C.), who led the

Trojans against the besieging Greeks. The son of King Priam and Hecuba, he was a courageous warrior and the personification of every virtue. He died a hero's death in battle against Achilles, but the latter dishonored his corpse, dragging it behind his chariot and refusing it proper burial until the gods intervened. His name was invoked to describe brave and virtuous knights in medieval times, and it was only toward the end of the 17th century that it came to be applied in a negative sense, initially to gangs of wealthy young men who called themselves "Hectors" and terrorized the streets of London, frightening innocent passersby. ". . . several personages, who would otherwise have been admitted into the parlour and enlarged the opportunity of hectoring and condescension for their betters, being content this evening to vary their enjoyment by taking their spirits-and-water where they could themselves hector and condescend in company that called for beer" (George Eliot, *Silas Marner,* 1861).

Hecuba (hekyăbă) Personification of grief and misfortune. In Greek legend, Hecuba was the second wife of King Priam of Troy and saw many of her sons (who included Hector and Paris) slain one by one in the course of the Trojan War, as related by Homer in the *Iliad* (c. eighth century B.C.). After the fall of Troy Hecuba was claimed as a slave by the victorious Odysseus. Her grief was further intensified by the death of her daughter Polyxena (sacrificed on the demand of the ghost of Achilles) and of her grandson Astyanax (murdered at the hands of the Greeks). Ultimately she was turned into a dog and threw herself into the sea. *Grandmother took up her Hecuba pose of the mortally aggrieved innocent bystander.*

hedonism The belief that the pursuit of pleasure or happiness is the aim of life. The word comes from the Greek *hedone,* meaning "pleasure," and the concept was first developed by the Greek philosopher Aristippus (c. 435–c. 356 B.C.). "Yes: there was to be, as Lord Henry had prophesied, a new Hedonism that was to recreate life and to save it from that harsh uncomely puritanism that is having, in our own day, its curious revival" (Oscar Wilde, *The Picture of Dorian Gray,* 1891).

hegira (hijīeră, hejără) An exodus or any flight to safety from oppression, especially from religious persecution, and by extension a change of policy or other move designed to put a person in a more favorable position. The term (meaning "departure") originally denoted the flight of Muhammad from Mecca to Medina in A.D. 622, the date marking the foundation of the Islamic faith. *The revolution prompted a hegira of Muslims from the country under the threat of punitive action by the new regime.*

he has got gold of Tolosa (tolōsă) A person who obtains something by dubious means will not benefit from it. The allusion is to the sacking and looting of the Temple of Apollo at Tolosa (Toulouse) by the Roman consul Caepio. The gold and silver he looted was stolen from him in turn, and he and his men were defeated in battle in 106 B.C. with heavy losses. *It was truly said of Dobbs as he faced death at the hands of bandits that he had got gold of Tolosa.*

Helen of Troy (helăn, troi) Archetype of a beautiful woman, especially one whose beauty influences the course of events. The daughter of Zeus by Leda, Helen was the sister of Clytemnestra, Castor, and Pollux and won admiration as the most beautiful woman in the world. Many men competed for her hand, and it was agreed that whoever was successful would win the right to be defended by all the others. Menelaus of Sparta was the lucky suitor, but after a few years of marriage, she was abducted and carried off by Paris to Troy. The Greeks banded together to reclaim her and laid siege to Troy. After 10 years Troy fell, and Helen was restored to Menelaus in Sparta. Her beauty is legendary, and hers is often said to be *"the face that launched a thousand ships,"* a quotation from the play *Doctor Faustus* (1604) by Christopher Marlowe. *She may have looked like a real Helen of Troy, but she was the loneliest woman I ever met.*

Helicon (helikon) A source of artistic inspiration. According to Greek mythology, Mount Helicon in Boeotia was the home of the MUSES. Its features included the spring of Aganippe and the fountain of Hippocrene, whose waters are supposed to give poetic inspiration to those who drink from them. "O for a beaker full of the warm South, / Full of the true, the blushful Hippocrene" (John Keats, "Ode to a Nightingale," 1819).

Helios (heeleeăs, heeleeōs) Personification of the Sun. Helios was the sun god of Greek mythology, equivalent to the Roman Sol, and was conventionally depicted driving his chariot from east to west across the sky, pulled by four white horses. *Helios was directly overhead, and there was little shade from his blazing heat to be had anywhere.*

hell A place of suffering or other unpleasantness. According to Christian tradition, hell is the place of eternal punishment intended for Satan, his demons, and human beings who choose to reject God. It is conventionally depicted as a vast burning pit; in Revelation 19:20 it is described as "a lake of fire burning with brimstone." "For them Methodisses make folks believe as if they take a mug o' drink extry, an' make theirselves a bit comfortable, they'll have to go to hell for't as sure as they're born" (George Eliot, *Adam Bede*, 1859).

Hellespont (he̱lăspont) The strait (presently called the Dardanelles) that separates Europe from Asia in Turkey and connects the Sea of Marmora with the Aegean Sea. Its name (meaning "sea of Helle") is an allusion to an episode in the story of the Golden Fleece, in which a girl named Helle falls into this body of water from the back of an airborne golden ram as she flees from her mother-in-law, Ino, and is drowned. *I believe he would have swum the Hellespont to be with her, if only he had known what had happened.* See also HERO AND LEANDER.

hemlock *See* DRINK HEMLOCK.

hem of his garment, touch the To show great reverence for someone; to demonstrate one's faith in another's abilities or gifts. The image of touching or kissing the hem of a person's garment is biblical in origin, alluding to the story related in Matthew 9:20–22, Mark 5:25–34, and Luke 8:43–48 of the sick woman who dared to touch the hem of Christ's robe in the belief that he could perform miraculous cures by mere touch. "Considered from the point of view of a creator of character he ranks next to him who made Hamlet. Had he been articulate, he might have sat beside him. The only man who can touch the hem of his garment is George Meredith. Meredith is a prose Browning, and so is Browning" (Oscar Wilde, *Intentions*, 1891).

Hephaestus (he̱fĕstăs, he̱fēstăs) Personification of skilled craftsmanship. In Greek mythology Hephaestus was the god of fire who served as blacksmith of the gods and made the armor of Achilles. He was the equivalent of the Roman god Vulcan. *The wrought ironwork of the gates marked their maker as a veritable Hephaestus.*

Hera (<u>heer</u>ă) Archetype of a quarrelsome, vindictive, jealous wife. In Greek mythology, Hera was the wife and sister of Zeus and the equivalent of the Roman Juno. She was identified as the daughter of Cronos and Rhea and by Zeus gave birth to Ares, Hebe, Hephaestus, and Eileithyia. Several legends concern her revenge for the various love affairs of her husband. *Hera herself would have been proud of the way she nagged her husband about his indiscretions. See also* APPLE OF DISCORD.

Hercules (<u>herk</u>yooleez) A man who possesses great physical strength and courage. Hercules, or *Heracles*, was one of the most celebrated figures in Greek mythology, a demigod who was the son of Zeus and the mortal Alcmena. He gave early notice of his remarkable powers when as a babe in arms he strangled two snakes placed in his crib by Zeus's jealous wife Hera, and went on to complete the formidable series of challenges now dubbed the LABORS OF HERCULES. When finally he died (*see* SHIRT OF NESSUS), his soul was taken to join the gods in heaven, where he was reconciled with Hera and married her daughter Hebe. The adjective *Herculean* denotes a task demanding a prodigious effort or great strength. *This Hercules of wrestling has captured a second world championship title in indefatigable style.*

hermaphrodite A plant or animal that possesses both male and female reproductive organs. The word alludes to the Greek god Hermaphroditus, who was the son of Hermes and Aphrodite. According to legend, Hermaphroditus rejected the suit of the nymph Salmacis when bathing in her pool. She embraced him nonetheless and petitioned the gods to keep them united permanently. The gods granted her request, and the couple became one entity incorporating both their genders. "Oh, it is pitiable to see him making of himself a thing that is neither male nor female, neither fish, flesh, nor fowl—a poor, miserable, hermaphrodite Frenchman!" (Mark Twain, *The Innocents Abroad,* 1869).

Hermes *See* HERMETIC; MERCURY.

hermetic Airtight, usually referring to a seal. The word has its origin in Hermes Trismegistus (meaning "Hermes, thrice-greatest"), which was the name by which Greeks knew Thoth, the Egyptian god of learning. It was also the name bestowed upon a celebrated third-century B.C. alchemist who was credited with using magic to invent the first airtight containers. *On inspection it was found that the hermetic seal on the canister had been broken and the contents contaminated.*

Hero and Leander (<u>hee</u>rō, lee<u>an</u>der,) Archetypal young lovers of Greek legend. Hero was a beautiful young priestess of Aphrodite who became the lover of Leander, a young man who lived on the opposite side of the HELLE-SPONT. Each night Leander swam across the strait to see Hero, guided by the lantern she held for him. Unfortunately, one night the light was extinguished by a storm, and Leander was drowned. Hero found his body on the shore and in her grief threw herself into the sea, faithful to her lover even in death. Lord Byron was among those subsequently inspired by the myth and famously re-created Hero's swim across the Dardanelles in 1810. *Their tragic story gave the two lovers the status of a modern Hero and Leander.*

Herod *See* OUT-HEROD HEROD.

Herodotus (he<u>ro</u>dătăs) Herodotus (480–425 B.C.) was a Greek historian who wrote some of the earliest chronicles and is remembered today for his systematic collection and arrangement of material and his testing of their accuracy. *He was the Herodotus of Napoleonic history, with scores of books and articles to his name.*

Hestia *See* VESTA.

he that hath, to him shall be given *See* WHOSOEVER HATH, TO HIM SHALL BE GIVEN.

he that is without sin *See* LET HIM WHO IS WITHOUT SIN CAST THE FIRST STONE.

he that runs may read The meaning is so clear that it may be taken in at once. The expression alludes to the Old Testament book of Habakkuk 2:2, in which God addresses the prophet Habakkuk as follows: "Write the vision, and make it plain upon tables, that he may run that readeth it." "But thieves from o'er the wall / Stole the seed by night. / Sow'd it far and wide / By every town and tower, / Till all the people cried / "Splendid is the flower." / Read my little fable: / He that runs may read" (Alfred, Lord Tennyson, *Enoch Arden,* 1864).

he that watereth Those who make the necessary effort are more likely to be rewarded. One of many parallel expressions of the same moral, it appears in the Bible in Proverbs 11:25: "The liberal soul shall be made fat: and he that watereth shall be watered also himself." "We have seen that the duties of bishop and pastor are to see and feed; and, of all who do so it is said, 'He that watereth, shall be also watered himself.' But the reverse is truth also. He that watereth not, shall be withered himself" (John Ruskin, *Sesame and Lilies*, 1865, 1871).

hewers of wood and drawers of water Those who do hard, menial jobs. The phrase is biblical in origin, appearing in a curse delivered by Joshua against the Gibeonites, who had attempted to deceive him into making terms with them by disguising themselves as strangers from a distant country: "Now therefore ye are cursed, and there shall none of you be freed from being bondmen, and hewers of wood and drawers of water for the house of my God . . . And Joshua made them that day hewers of wood and drawers of water for the congregation" (Joshua 9:23–27). ". . . what Roy Hattersley calls 'the modern hewers of wood and drawers of water'" (*Guardian,* June 30, 2001).

he who is not with me is against me Unless one supports a given person, cause, etc., one will be considered to be opposing the person, cause, etc. The phrase comes from the words of Jesus: "He that is not with me is against me" (Matthew 12:30). *Speaking at the election rally, the party leader tried to rally his supporters with the words, "He who is not with me is against me."*

hide one's light under a bushel To be modest about one's talents, abilities, virtues, etc. The phrase comes from Christ's Sermon on the Mount, in the course of which he compares the faithful to a lit candle: "Ye are the light of the world. A city that is set on a hill cannot be hid. Neither do men light a candle, and put it under a bushel, but on a candlestick; and it giveth light unto all that are in the house" (Matthew 5:14–15). A bushel is a unit of measurement traditionally gauged by using a wooden or earthenware container, thus, to be **under a bushel** signified being hidden from view. "Now did the Reverend Samuel Pentecost, whose light had hitherto been hidden under a bushel, prove at last that he could do something by proving that he could eat" (Wilkie Collins, *Armadale*, 1866).

hind of Arcadia *See* LABORS OF HERCULES.

hip and thigh, smite them *See* SMITE THEM HIP AND THIGH.

Hippocrates *See* GALENICAL; HIPPOCRATIC OATH.

Hippocratic oath (hipōkratik) The ritual promise traditionally made by doctors on qualifying for medical practice to the effect that they will observe the highest ethical standards and observe the confidentiality of their patients. Hippocrates (c. 460–c. 370 B.C.) was a Greek physician who for his 87 treatises on medical practice is remembered today as the father of medicine. Students under Hippocrates were believed to take such an oath. The name of Hippocrates is also preserved in *Hippocrates' sleeve*, a square piece of flannel folded into a triangle and used to strain liquids. *Many doctors practicing today have only a hazy notion of what the Hippocratic oath really says, although they are aware of the seriousness that it has for patients.*

Hippocrene *See* HELICON.

hippogriff (hipōgrif) Symbol of love. In Greek mythology, the hippogriff was a winged horse, the offspring of a griffin and a filly. *Her head swam with emotion: The winged hippogriff of love had planted its hooves in her heart.*

Hippolyta *See* AMAZON; LABORS OF HERCULES.

holier than thou Self-righteous; inclined to look down on others. The phrase appears in the Bible in Isaiah 65:5, where "a rebellious people" are condemned for their arrogance toward others: "Which say, Stand by thyself, come not near to me; for I am holier than thou. These are a smoke in my nose, a fire that burneth all the day." *His holier-than-thou attitude did not go down well with the troops, who began to murmur resentfully among themselves.*

holy grail A final goal or destination achieved only with much difficulty; the object of a quest, especially one of a mystical or mythical character. The original Holy Grail was the cup or dish supposedly used at the Last Supper and also by Joseph of Arimathea to catch the blood dripping from the crucified Christ. Traditionally it is thought to have been brought in the first century A.D. to Glastonbury, England, by Joseph of Arimathea. The Grail became an object of great veneration in medieval times and remains best known today as a central icon of Arthurian legend, in pursuit of which many brave knights roamed far and wide. *A cure for cancer is the holy grail of modern medical research.*

holy of holies A very special or private place; an inner sanctum to which few are admitted. The allusion is to the sacred inner chamber of the Tabernacle in the wilderness and the Temple of Jerusalem, in which the ARK OF THE COVENANT was kept, according to Exodus 26:31–34 and 1 Kings 6:16–19. Only the high priest was permitted to enter the room, once a year, to make an animal sacrifice on behalf of the people. *It was only after much checking of credentials and letters of recommendation that he was finally admitted to the holy of holies, the Oval Office, in order to discuss his concerns with the president. See also* VEIL OF THE TEMPLE RENT.

Homeric (hōmerik) Heroic, epic, mythic. The reference is to the celebrated eighth-century B.C. blind Greek poet Homer, traditionally credited with authorship of the *Iliad*, which recounts the latter stages of the Trojan War, and of the *Odyssey,* which describes the wanderings of Odysseus as he sails home after that war. ***Homeric laughter*** denotes unrestrained mirth of epic proportions, as heard at the feast of the gods according to the *Iliad.* "With a boy, trouble must be of Homeric dimensions to last overnight" (Booth Tarkington, *Penrod,* 1914).

Homer sometimes nods (hōmer) Even the wisest or most capable person can make a mistake. The reference is to the celebrated eighth-century B.C. blind Greek poet Homer, author of the *Iliad* and the *Odyssey*. The expression, also found in the form *even Homer sometimes nods,* is thought to have made its first appearance in *Ars Poetica* (359) by the Roman poet Horace, in which the author laments that Homer occasionally lapses from the highest standards in his writing, but quickly adds that such flaws are readily forgivable in one so great. *The final chapter of the book is a disappointment, as though the master had lost his concentration at the vital moment, but as they say "even Homer sometimes nods."*

hope deferred makes the heart sick Delay or disappointment in realizing one's hopes can be the cause of great unhappiness. The saying has biblical origins: "Hope deferred maketh the heart sick: but when the desire cometh, it is a tree of life" (Proverbs 13:12). "She had not suffered so much from a want of food, however, as from a want of air and exercise; from unremitting, wasting toil at a sedentary occupation, from hope deferred and from sleepless nights" (James Fenimore Cooper, *Autobiography of a Pocket-Handkerchief,* 1843).

Horatian (hǎrayshǎn) Of or relating to a balanced viewpoint, especially one that is satirical and respectful by turns. The adjective refers to the celebrated Roman lyric poet and satirist Horace (65–8 B.C.), who wrote relatively gentle satires during the reign of the emperor Augustus. He was renowned both for his wisdom and his sincerity. *The editorial comprised a subtly Horatian analysis of the situation that offered neither side much comfort.*

Horatius at the bridge (hǎrayshǎs, hǎraysheeǎs) A person who behaves heroically in the face of vastly superior odds. The allusion is to the Roman legend of Horatius Cocles (530–500 B.C.), the heroic warrior who with two companions (Herminius and Lartius) kept the entire Etruscan army of Lars Porsena at bay by blocking their passage over a bridge on the Tiber River leading directly to Rome. By thus delaying the enemy the three heroes secured enough time to demolish the bridge behind them, thereby saving the city. Their task complete, Horatius sent his two companions back before following them to safety by swimming the Tiber in full armor. It has been suggested that the legend of Horatius and his companions may have been invented as propaganda to counter criticism of Roman aggression toward the Etruscans. The phrase *Horatius at the bridge* became widely familiar after the publication of Thomas

Babington Macaulay's *Lays of Ancient Rome* (1842). *The secretary of state mounted a staunch defense of the government, but he looked increasingly like Horatius at the bridge, and few were convinced that he would manage to stem the tide of criticism for long.*

Horeb *See* MOUNT SINAI.

Horeb, rock in *See* SMITE THE ROCK.

horn of plenty *See* CORNUCOPIA.

horns of a dilemma A difficult choice between two alternatives, neither of which is ideal. The phrase is Greek in origin, referring to a "double lemma" (an ambiguous proposition) and coming ultimately from *lambanein* (meaning "to take"), in the sense of "something taken for granted." "Each had repeatedly hung the other on the horns of a dilemma, but neither seemed to be a whit the worse for the hanging; and so the war went on merrily" (Anthony Trollope, *Barchester Towers,* 1857).

horns of the altar, to the A loyal friend through thick and thin. This expression of devoted friendship alludes to the sacred horns that adorned altars in biblical times. According to Exodus 29:12 the altar at the Tabernacle had a projecting horn at each of its four corners, and these were ceremonially smeared with the blood of animal sacrifices (they may also have been used to tether the animals before sacrifice). These horns are referred to again in 1 Kings 1:50: "And Adonijah feared because of Solomon, and arose, and went, and caught hold on the horns of the altar." Ancient Romans similarly laid hold of the horns of the altar when swearing loyalty to their friends. "Thinkest thou, Waldemar, that the wily Archbishop will not suffer thee to be taken from the very horns of the altar, would it make his peace with King Richard?" (Sir Walter Scott, *Ivanhoe,* 1819).

horse, wooden *See* TROJAN HORSE.

houri (<u>hoo</u>ree) A beautiful dark-eyed woman. In Muslim mythology, the houris are the perpetually young and beautiful maidens who tend the faithful in paradise, renewing their virginity at will. "That houri, appearing, shakes him up in the usual manner and is charged by the old gentleman to remain near him" (Charles Dickens, *Bleak House,* 1852–53).

house divided against itself, a Those who cannot agree among themselves cannot expect to succeed. The expression comes from Matthew 12:25, in which Christ responds to the accusations of the Pharisees that he had drawn on the powers of the Devil to achieve the miraculous healing of a deaf and mute man, pointing out that evil would hardly seek to destroy evil: "Every kingdom divided against itself is brought to desolation; and every city or house divided against itself shall not stand." Similar sentiments are expressed in Mark 3:25: "If a house be divided against itself, that house cannot stand." *The board of the company is at loggerheads over the issue, and you know what they say, a house divided against itself cannot stand.*

household gods *See* LARES AND PENATES.

house not made with hands Heaven; God's heavenly abode. The phrase comes from 2 Corinthians 5:1, in which Paul contrasts the physicality of the human body occupied by the soul on earth with the heavenly house that it may one day attain, "a building of God, an house not made with hands, eternal in the heavens." *His mother died last night at her huge old mansion in the hills and resides now in a house not made with hands.*

house of Atreus (aytreeăs) A family or other group who seem to be doomed to misfortune or under a dreadful curse. The allusion is to the cursed family of Atreus, king of Mycenae and father of Agamemnon and Menelaus. According to Greek mythology, the curse originated with Atreus's father, Pelops, who was slaughtered and served up by his own father, Tantalus, at a banquet to which all the gods had been invited (*see* IVORY SHOULDER OF PELOPS). *The company has become a house of Atreus, rocked by one misfortune after another.*

house of God A church or other place of worship. The phrase appears in the Bible in Genesis 28:17, in which Jacob awakes from his dream of a ladder reaching to heaven and exclaims, "How dreadful is this place! this is none other but the house of God, and this is the gate of heaven." "None of them, not even Dr Grantly, could close his ears, nor leave the house of

God during the hours of service. They were under an obligation of listening, and that too without any immediate power of reply" (Anthony Trollope, *Barchester Towers,* 1857).

house of many mansions A spacious building or other place; any organization or other entity offering a wide range of aspects, possibilities, or opportunities. The phrase comes from Christ's farewell sermon to his disciples, in which it signifies heaven: "Let not your heart be troubled: ye believe in God, believe also in me. In my Father's house are many mansions: if it were not so, I would have told you. I go to prepare a place for you" (John 14:2). "There was, of course, a better world. 'In my Father's house are many mansions' was one of Aunt Juley's favourite sayings—it always comforted her, with its suggestion of house property, which had made the fortune of dear Roger" (John Galsworthy, *The Forsyte Saga,* 1922).

How are the mighty fallen! An exclamation of amazement at how those who were once rich, successful, or otherwise considered superior to their fellows have been brought down to a much more humble level. The phrase is a quotation from 2 Samuel 1:19, in which David laments the deaths of Saul and Jonathan: "The beauty of Israel is slain upon thy high places: how are the mighty fallen!" "Once it took the head of my family a day's hard riding to make the circuit of his estates, but the mighty are fallen. Fast women and slow horses" (William Somerset Maugham, *Of Human Bondage,* 1915).

howling wilderness A wild, desolate place; a situation complete devoid of potential, style, or interest. The phrase comes from Deuteronomy 32:10, in which Moses recalls God finding the Israelites "in a desert land, and in the waste howling wilderness." Several 19th-century writers, including William Makepeace Thackeray, used the phrase to describe locations where unfashionable people lived. "In the old war, when I was out under Sir William, I travelled seventy miles alone in the howling wilderness, with a rifle bullet in my thigh, then cut it out with my own jack-knife" (James Fenimore Cooper, *The Pioneers,* 1823).

How long, O Lord? A rhetorical question expressing dismay at how long something is taking. The phrase has its origins in the Bible, as in Psalm 13:1, where it is a cry for deliverance from a life-threatening illness, and in Revelation 6:9–10, in which it is a cry for the martyrs who have died for their faith. "Now and then, as if to show the thoughts which were most poignant, he muttered—'Lepers, lepers! They—my mother and Tirzath—they lepers! How long, how long, O Lord!'" (Lew Wallace, *Ben Hur,* 1880).

hubris (hyoobris) Arrogant self-confidence or pride. The term is of Greek origin, referring to the refusal of characters to accept the authority of the gods in ancient Greek tragedy. This arrogance is invariably followed by the character concerned being punished by the gods for his impudence (usually at the hands of NEMESIS). *Hubris drove him to strike back at those who had sought to belittle him in the eyes of the public.*

hyacinth A lily of the genus *Hyacinthus* with usually blue, pink, or white flowers. The name of the plant alludes to Hyacinthus, a youth whose beauty, according to Greek mythology, attracted the attention of the sun god Apollo and of Zephyrus, the god of the west wind. Hyacinthus favored Apollo, thus incurring the wrath of Zephyrus, who took his revenge by bringing about the accidental death of Hyacinthus as he and Apollo tossed an iron discus to each other in play. A sudden gust of wind blew the discus off course, and it hit Hyacinthus on the head, killing him instantly. The flower that the grieving Apollo caused to spring up from the young man's spilled blood has borne his name ever since. *The pool was fringed with hyacinths and rhododendron bushes.*

hydra-headed Many headed. In Greek mythology the Hydra was a fearsome monster faced by HERCULES in the course of the LABORS OF HERCULES. The Hydra had nine heads, each of which when severed was replaced by two more. Hercules overcame the Hydra by cutting off the heads and having his companion Iolaus scorch the wounds before they could grow back. In modern usage the term *hydra-headed* is usually applied to a troublesome, multifaceted problem or one that keeps recurring despite everything being done to solve it. *The club faces a hydra-headed conundrum: how to attract new supporters without offending long-standing members who are more than happy to keep things as they are.*

hygiene The science concerned with the safeguarding of health, especially through observing clean or healthy practices. The word comes from the name of the Greek goddess of health Hygeia, who was sometimes identified as the wife or daughter of Aesculapius, the god of medicine. *The link between hygiene and the outbreak of disease has been known for centuries.*

hymen A fold of membrane that partially covers the entrance to the vagina and is usually broken when sexual intercourse takes place for the first time. The word comes from Hymenaeus, the name of the Greek god of marriage. He was the son of Dionysus and Aphrodite and was traditionally depicted leading the revels at wedding feasts, often carrying a burning torch and crowned with a garland of flowers. *On inspection the girl's hymen was found to be unruptured and she was declared "virgo intacta."*

hyperborean Frigid; arctic; from the far north. According to Greek mythology, the Hyperboreans were a race of people who lived in a remote sunny land in the extreme north (*hyper* meaning "beyond" and *Boreas* meaning "North Wind"). This faraway country was said to be protected by Apollo, and its inhabitants lived in a state of perpetual happiness. "It's the unnatural combat of the four primal elements.—It's a blasted health.—It's a Hyperborean winter scene" (Herman Melville, *Moby-Dick,* 1851).

Hyperion to a satyr (hĭpeereeăn, sayter) A contrast between two opposites. In Greek mythology, Hyperion was one of the Titans and the father of Helios (the Sun), Selene (the Moon), and Eos (the dawn). His name is sometimes employed as a synonym for the Sun itself. In contrast to the Titan satyrs were much more humble, sylvan gods, who were half human and half goat. This expression was popularized by William Shakespeare, who used it in *Hamlet* (1601), in the course of Hamlet's first soliloquy: "So excellent a king; that was, to this, Hyperion to a satyr."

hypnosis An artificially induced state of relaxation revealing the subconscious self. The word was derived from the name of Hypnos, the Greek god of sleep and the equivalent of the Roman Somnus. *A course of hypnosis was suggested, but the doctors were inclined to dismiss such an approach as mere quackery.*

i

I am that I am I am as I appear to be, no more, no less. The expression is biblical in origin, appearing in Exodus 3:14 as God's reply to Moses when Moses asks his name during the episode of the burning bush. "I am" is one translation of God's Old Testament name Yahweh or Jehovah. This phrase has appeared in many guises throughout world literature, perhaps most notably in William Shakespeare's tragedy *Othello* (c. 1604), in which Iago misquotes it in the form "I am not what I am."

I came, I saw, I conquered I have achieved what I set out to do. These were the words (in Latin *veni, vidi, vici*) uttered by Julius Caesar (100–44 B.C.) as he looked back on his conquest in the Black Sea campaign of 47, according to Suetonius (c. A.D. 69–c. 140) in *Lives of the Caesars. "I came, I saw, I conquered," said the victor as he lay down his racket and reached for his jacket.*

Icarus (ĭkărăs) A person who brings about his or her downfall through carelessness or recklessness. The allusion is to the Greek myth of Daedalus and his son Icarus who effected their escape from King Minos of Crete by constructing wings of wax and feathers and using them to fly off the island and over the ocean. Unfortunately, Icarus ignored his father's instructions not to fly too high as the heat of the sun would melt the wax; consequently, Icarus fell to his death in the sea. The waters of the Aegean are still sometimes called the ***Icarian Sea.*** "He, like Icarus, had flown up towards the sun, hoping that his wings of wax would bear him steadily aloft among the gods" (Anthony Trollope, *Phineas Finn,* 1869). *See also* DAEDALIAN.

Ichabod *See* GLORY IS DEPARTED, THE.

ichor (ī́kor) A watery, foul-smelling discharge from a wound or ulcer. In Greek mythology, *ichor* (meaning "juice") is the name given to the colorless blood of the gods. "The first indication of revival was afforded by a partial descent of the iris. It was observed, as especially remarkable, that this lowering of the pupil was accompanied by the profuse out-flowing of a yellowish ichor (from beneath the lids) of a pungent and highly offensive odor" (Edgar Allan Poe, *The Facts in the Case of M.Valdemar,* 1845).

Ida, Mount (ī́dǎ) A place from which one can observe events without getting personally involved. In Greek mythology, Mount Ida was a "many-fountained" mountain or ridge in Asia Minor identified as the vantage point from which the gods followed the course of events during the Trojan War. This mountain (or one of the same name in Crete) was also said to be the birthplace of Zeus, the place where Ganymede was abducted, and the location for the JUDGMENT OF PARIS. "As Juno may have looked at Paris on Mount Ida, so did Mrs Proudie look on Ethelbert Stanhope when he pushed the leg of the sofa into her lace train" (Anthony Trollope, *Barchester Towers,* 1857).

Ides of March (ī́dz) A day of reckoning, especially one that has been foretold. In ancient Rome, the Ides (from the verb *iduo,* meaning "to divide") marked the halfway point of a month. It was on the Idea of March (March 15) that Julius Caesar was murdered in the Capitol, as previously prophesied by a soothsayer with the doom-laden words "Beware the Ides of March." *On considering the alternatives left after this unexpected turn of events, the only conclusion one can reach is that the Ides of March would appear to have arrived for the Republican Party.*

if any would not work, neither should he eat Those who are not prepared to work do not deserve any reward. This saying comes from 2 Thessalonians 3:10, in which Paul advises the Thessalonians that only those who work for their bread actually deserve to have any. *The manager shrugged his shoulders and repeated the biblical injunction that if any would not work, neither should he eat.*

if the blind lead the blind, both shall fall into the ditch *See* BLIND LEADING THE BLIND.

if thy right eye offend thee If part of you tempts you to do wrong, then you need to take radical action to deal with it. This piece of proverbial advice comes from Christ's Sermon on the Mount, as recounted in Matthew 5:29: "And if thy right eye offend thee, pluck it out, and cast it from thee: for it is profitable for thee that one of thy members should perish, and not that thy whole body should be cast into hell." The line is sometimes quoted with reference to the expulsion of rebellious members of organizations or institutions. It is also found in the variant form *if thy right hand offend thee.* "If it chance your eye offend you, / Pluck it out, lad, and be sound" (A. E. Housman, *A Shropshire Lad,* 1896).

Iliad (i̱leeăd, i̱leead) A written work or other tale of epic proportions, especially one dealing with acts of heroism. The original *Iliad* was a celebrated epic poem of great length supposedly composed by the Greek poet Homer around 700 B.C. Its title comes from the Greek *Iliados* (meaning "of Ilium," Ilium being an alternative name for Troy), and it relates the events that took place toward the end of the Trojan War, which culminated in the death of Hector at the hands of Achilles. Only a very select number of great literary works have since been considered good enough to be ranked alongside Homer's *Iliad,* including the medieval *Romance of the Rose* (13th century), which came to be dubbed the French Iliad, and the *Nibelungenlied* (early 13th century), sometimes called the German Iliad. The series of disasters suffered by both sides during the war gave rise to the phrase *an Iliad of woes* to describe any series of setbacks or misfortunes. *This third film brings this Iliad of modern warfare and trilogy of Vietnam movies to a tragic and dispiriting close.*

immaculate conception Something that comes about in an unconventional or apparently inexplicable manner. The reference is to the conception of the Virgin Mary as defined in the dogma ("Ineffabilis Deus" of Pope Pius IX, December 8, 1854): "from the first moment of her conception the Blessed Virgin Mary was, by the singular grace and privilege of Almighty God, and in view of the merits of Jesus Christ, Saviour of mankind, kept free from all stain of original sin." Biblical allusions to this doctrine are held to be Genesis 3:15 and Luke 1:28, but this teaching is rejected by Protestants. The term is sometimes employed in modern usage in a somewhat sarcastic tone. *People tend to forget that such structures have been designed* *in detail by teams of engineers, preferring to believe they came about through some process of immaculate conception.*

in all one's glory In all one's beauty; having a beautiful appearance. The phrase comes from Matthew 6:29, which celebrates the beauty of the LILIES OF THE FIELD: "And yet I say unto you, That even Solomon in all his glory was not arrayed like one of these." In modern usage the phrase may sometimes appear in laconic references to a person who is entirely naked. *The girls squealed as the man emerged grinning from the pool in all his glory.*

in fear and trembling In an anxious, frightened way. The origin of the expression is Philippians 2:12: "Wherefore, my beloved, as ye have always obeyed, not as in my presence only, but now much more in my absence, work out your own salvation with fear and trembling." *The pupils waited outside the principal's office in fear and trembling.*

inherit the wind To provoke trouble, especially to bring trouble down on one's own head. The phrase is a quotation from Proverbs 11:29: "He that troubleth his own house shall inherit the wind." *They had known prosperous times but had laid up little for the future and feared that in their old age they would find they had inherited the wind.*

in my father's house *See* HOUSE OF MANY MANSIONS.

inner man A person's soul or spiritual being, or more jocularly, his or her appetite. The phrase comes from Ephesians 3:16: "That he would grant you, according to the riches of his glory, to be strengthened with might by his Spirit in the inner man." "It is on the inner man, on his nature and disposition, that the happiness of a wife must depend." (Anthony Trollope, *Ayala's Angel,* 1881).

innocent as doves *See* WISE AS SERPENTS AND HARMLESS AS DOVES.

in the beginning was the Word Underlying everything else is the concept of divine order and reason. The phrase comes from John 1:1: "In the beginning was the Word, and the Word was with God, and the Word was God."

The concept of the Word predated John but as used by him came to refer to Jesus Christ himself. These words reflect the opening words of the Bible "In the beginning" (Genesis 1:1). *"In the beginning was the Word," murmured the bishop, when his charges ventured to voice doubts.* See also WORD, THE.

in the sweat of thy face *See* ADAM'S CURSE.

in vain the net is spread in the sight of the bird Setting a trap is futile if the proposed victim of it is allowed to see the trap being prepared. This advice comes from Proverbs 1:17: "Surely in vain the net is spread in the sight of any bird." "'If they come, we shall be ready,' said Bessas. 'In vain the net is spread in the sight of the bird.'" (L. Sprague De Camp, *The Dragon of the Ishtar Gate,* 1961).

invita Minerva (inveetă minervă, inweetah minerwah) Uninspired, lackluster. Meaning in Latin "against the will of Minerva," the phrase, which first appeared in *Ars Poetica* by Horace (65–8 B.C.), has generally been reserved for literary or artistic works that do not meet expectations. Minerva was the goddess of wisdom and patroness of the arts and trades in Roman mythology, thus to proceed without her support doomed any artistic enterprise to failure. *Contemporaries were inclined to view her final book of poetry as misjudged and invita Minerva.*

in word and deed *See* WORD AND DEED, IN.

Io (īō) Archetype of a person who changes his or her shape or appearance. In Roman mythology Io was identified as a priestess of Juno who attracted the attentions of Jupiter. In order to prevent any liaison Juno transformed Io into a heifer, and in this form she wandered far and wide over the earth until finally restored to human form in Egypt. *Like some bewitched Io, once in costume, she instinctively assumed all the characteristics of the creature she portrayed.*

Ionic (īonik) Belonging to an order of architecture typified by capitals decorated with volutes. The order was named after Ionia, an ancient region of west central Asia Minor that was colonized by the Greeks around 1100 B.C. and where the style was first developed. "The State Bank, stucco masking wood. The Farmers' National Bank. An Ionic temple of marble. Pure, exquisite, solitary" (Sinclair Lewis, *Main Street*, 1920). *See also* CORINTHIAN; DORIC; TUSCAN.

I only am escaped I am the sole survivor. This expression is biblical in origin, coming from Job 1:15, in which Job's faith is tested by God by a series of catastrophes, news of which is brought to him by a series of single survivors who end their reports with more or less the same words. Herman Melville incorporates the line as the opening refrain in the epilogue of his novel *Moby-Dick* (1851), in which the reader learns that the narrator, Ishmael, was the only survivor of the sinking of the ship *Pequod*.

I only am left I am the only one remaining. The expression is biblical in origin: It reflects Elijah's self-pity after he flees to Horeb when Jezebel threatens his life following his success in defeating the prophets of Baal on Mount Carmel: "And he said, I have been very jealous for the LORD God of hosts: because the children of Israel have forsaken thy covenant, thrown down thine altars, and slain thy prophets with the sword; and I, *even* I only, am left; and they seek my life, to take it away" (1 Kings 19:14). In contemporary usage the expression *only I am left* is sometimes used. *"Only I am left," murmured the administrative assistant after all her colleagues had left early that afternoon.*

Irene (īreen, īreenee) Personification of peace and reconciliation. In Greek mythology, Irene was the goddess of peace and prosperity. She is conventionally depicted carrying PLUTUS (representing wealth) in her arms and sometimes with an OLIVE BRANCH or CORNUCOPIA. *The spirit of Irene reigned in the negotiating chamber that afternoon, though in the event this period of perfect harmony was to prove but short-lived.*

iris The colored part of the eye surrounding the pupil and, by extension, the area surrounding a source of illumination. The name comes from Iris, the Greek goddess of the rainbow who is reputed to have traveled between heaven and earth by means of a rainbow in order to fulfill her role as messenger of the gods. She was conventionally depicted with wings on her shoulders and a herald's staff in her left hand. The name has also been applied to a genus of plants notable for their showy, brightly colored blooms and, poetically, to the rainbow itself. "Filled with these thoughts—so filled that he had an unwholesome sense of growing larger, of being placed in some new and diseased relation towards the objects among which he passed, of seeing the iris round every misty light turn red—he went home for shelter" (Charles Dickens, *Hard Times*, 1854).

Isaac *See* ABRAHAM'S SUPREME TEST.

Isaiah (īzayă) Archetypal prophet. The prophecies of the biblical Isaiah are detailed in the Old Testament book that bears his name. It describes the threat of the Assyrian conquest and offers promise to the exiles in Babylon and later a message of hope to the Jews after they return from exile. *The old man stood at the doors of the theater like some Isaiah, exhorting the crowd not to go in to witness such a degrading spectacle.*

Ishmael (ishmayăl) A social outcast. Ishmael appears in the Bible as the son of Abraham and Hagar, who was the Egyptian maidservant of Sarah. According to Genesis 16–25, Sarah allowed Hagar to become pregnant by Abraham as she believed herself barren, but the two women quarrelled, and after Sarah gave birth to Isaac, Hagar and her son were thrown out of the house and sent into the desert, hence the adoption of Ishmael's name (or the term *Ishmaelite*) for anyone who is expelled from society. God saved the pair from death from thirst by providing them with a well of water. Ishmael in his turn had 12 sons. The Ishmaelites were a tribal people who lived in Edom (Psalm 83:6); God's promise that Ishmael's descendants would become a great nation (Genesis 17:20; 21:17–18) has traditionally been thought to be fulfilled through the Arab peoples. If a person is described as having *a hand against every man,* this is a reference to a prophecy given by an angel at the time of Ishmael's birth to the effect that he was fated to become an outlaw: "his hand will be against every man, and every man's hand against him" (Genesis 16:12). "I am an Ishmael by instinct as much as by accident of circumstances, but if I keep out of society I shall be less vulnerable than Ishmaels generally are" (Samuel Butler, *The Way of All Flesh*, 1903).

Ishtar (ishtahr) Personification of love or fertility. Ishtar was the goddess of love in Babylonian and Assyrian mythology, equivalent to the Roman

Venus. *In her sequined costume and veils she came down the stairs like Ishtar descending to earth.*

Isis *See* LIFT THE VEIL OF ISIS.

Islands of the Blest Heaven; paradise. The Greek epic poet Hesiod (eighth century B.C.) identified paradise by this name and placed the location of the islands in the far west, at the end of the known world. Elsewhere they were dubbed the *Fortunate Islands,* or *Isles,* or *Happy Islands.* Here chosen heroes could spend eternity relaxing in pleasant surroundings. *This part of the world is so beautiful and so peaceful it could be mistaken for an earthly paradise, and many call these isles the Islands of the Blest. See also* ELYSIAN FIELDS.

Isocrates (īsokrateez) Archetype of a great orator. Isocrates (436–338 B.C.) was a celebrated orator of ancient Athens and a famous teacher of the arts of eloquence. Among those to be likened to Isocrates was Esprit Fléchier (1632–1710), the bishop of Nîmes, who was well known for his funeral orations and dubbed the French Isocrates. *After his address to the Senate the young man was quickly recognized as a leading figure on the political stage, the Isocrates of his party.*

Israel (izreeăl, izrayăl) The name of the Jewish state established in Palestine in 1948. The name means "God fights" and, according to Genesis 32:28, was bestowed upon Jacob after he wrestled with an angel. Jacob was the father of 12 sons, each of whom became the founder of one of the 12 tribes of Israel. The word Israel thus came to be applied to the Hebrew nation and subsequently the Jews and their state. *He is revered today as one of the patriarchs of Israel.*

Is Saul also among the prophets? *See* SAUL.

it is better to give than to receive The act of giving is more noble and rewarding than that of receiving. The proverb is of biblical origin, appearing in Acts 20:35 in the form "It is more blessed to give than to receive." "'Tis better to Give than to Receive, but yet 'tis Madness to give so much Charity to Others, as to become the Subject of it our Selves." (Samuel

Palmer, *Moral Essays on some of the most Curious and Significant English, Scotch, and Foreign Proverbs,* 1710).

it is not for every man to go to Corinth *See* CORINTH, IT IS NOT FOR EVERY MAN TO GO TO.

ivory shoulder of Pelops (p<u>ee</u>lops) A person's distinguishing characteristic. The phrase alludes to the legend of Pelops, son of Tantalus, king of Lydia, who was killed by his father and served up as a meal to the gods in order to test the limits of their knowledge. The gods realized what Tantalus was offering them and restored Pelops to life. Unfortunately the goddess Demeter had already consumed the lad's shoulder, so a shoulder of ivory was fashioned to complete his restoration. Tantalus was consigned to hell for his presumption in challenging the wisdom of the gods, while in due course Pelops became the king of Elis. *This birthmark, as unique and striking as the ivory shoulder of Pelops, distinguished him from the mass of people around him.*

I was a stranger, and ye took me in An expression of gratitude for an act of kindness shown toward a person in need. The line comes from Matthew 25:35: "For I was an hungred, and ye gave me meat: I was thirsty, and ye gave me drink: I was a stranger, and ye took me in: Naked, and ye clothed me." *"I was a stranger and ye took me in," quoted their unexpected guest as he lifted his glass in jovial salute to his hosts.*

Ixionian wheel (iksee<u>o</u>neeăn) A source of endless torment. In Greek legend, Ixion was a king of Thessaly who murdered his father-in-law and sought to seduce Hera. Zeus fooled him by sending him a cloud in the form of Hera and then had him bound to a perpetually revolving wheel of fire as punishment. The cloud subsequently gave birth to the centaurs. "Round and round, then, and ever contracting towards the button-like black bubble at the axis of that slowly wheeling circle, like another Ixion I did revolve" (Herman Melville, *Moby-Dick,* 1851).

Jacob's ladder (jaykobz) A ladder of rope or cable used to board a ship; a variety of plant *(Polemonium caeruleum)* with leaves positioned in a ladder-like arrangement. The original Jacob's ladder was a ladder connecting earth with heaven, envisaged in a dream by Jacob recounted in Genesis 28:12. The ladder itself was said to have 15 rungs, representing the virtues. The stone that Jacob used as a pillow when he had his dream was traditionally identified as the Stone of Scone, used in Scottish coronations. *The boys had rigged a serviceable Jacob's ladder to climb up to their treehouse.*

Jael (jayl) A treacherous, deadly woman. According to the Bible (Judges 4–5), Jael, whose name means "wild goat," was the wife of Heber the Kenite and feigned hospitality when her husband's enemy, the Canaanite general Sisera, arrived, giving him milk to drink and a tent to sleep in. While Sisera slept, Jael took a tent peg and drove it into his head with a hammer. Because this murder was committed in defense of Israel, Jael acquired the status of an Old Testament heroine, and her name is some-times quoted as an archetype of feminine courage. "Bravo, Jael! The wife of Heber the Kenite was no braver woman than you!" (Dinah Craik, *John Halifax,* 1856).

January The first month of the year. January was named after Janus, the Roman god of doors, thresholds, bridges, and beginnings. Because he watched over doorways he was widely worshiped for his power to ward off evil influence. Like January itself, which marks the end of the old year and the beginning of the new, Janus was usually described as having two faces turned in opposite directions at the same time; thus, anyone today who is suspected of hypocrisy or double-dealing may be called ***Janus-faced*** or ***Janus-headed.*** The word ***janitor*** also originated with Janus, alluding to his role as a guardian or doorkeeper. *He gave her a look that was as chilly as January and strode down the steps and into the street without so much as a backward glance.*

Jason *See* ARGONAUT.

jawbone of an ass A weapon, especially a relatively humble one, that can nonetheless be used with great effectiveness. The reference is biblical, alluding to Samson's escape from the ropes binding him and his subsequent slaying of many of his Philistine enemies using the jawbone of an ass that he had snatched up: "With the jawbone of an ass, heaps upon heaps, with the jawbone of an ass have I slain a thousand men" (Judges 15:15). "Oh, the delicate mistiming of women! She has carefully / Snapped in half my jawbone of an ass" (Christopher Fry, *The Lady's Not for Burning,* 1949).

jealous God *See* SINS OF THE FATHERS.

Jehoshaphat *See* JUMPING JEHOSHAPHAT; VALLEY OF JEHOSHAPHAT.

Jehovah (jăhōvă) God or a godlike figure. Jehovah is the personal name of God whose meaning was revealed to Moses (Exodus 3:14–15; 6:2–5). The name was arrived at as a means of referring to the Almighty, whose name was otherwise deemed too sacred to be uttered by mortal lips. Jehovah is an anglicization of *YeHoWaH,* or *Yahweh,* from the letters *YHWH,* which constitute the tetragrammaton, representing the Hebrew words *Elohim* ("God") and *Adonai* ("My Lord"). "It [Yahweh] emphasizes that God is the one who is eternal, unique, unchangeable and always actively present with his people. It expresses God's role as Israel's Redeemer and covenant Lord" (*NIV Thematic References Bible,* p. 1,383). "We shudder as we read the grim words of the Jehovah of the ancient Hebrews; and yet not all the learning of modern times has availed to deliver us from the cruel decree, that the sins of the fathers shall be visited upon the children" (Upton Sinclair, *Damaged Goods,* 1913).

jehu (jēehyoo) A coachman or driver, especially one who drives in a furious or dangerous manner. The biblical Jehu was the son of Nimshi and a king of Israel, as recounted in 2 Kings 9:20, in which a watchman comments on the approach of his chariot: "The driving is like the driving of Jehu the son of Nimshi; for he driveth furiously." The reason Jehu was driving his chariot so furiously (as was his custom) on this occasion was that he was on his way to kill King Jehoram and overthrow the dynasty of Ahab and Jezebel, thus ending worship of the pagan Baal. "A drunken postilion . . . who frightened her by driving like Jehu the son of Nimshi, and shouting hilarious remarks at her" (George Eliot, *Adam Bede,* 1859).

Jephthah's daughter (jĕpthăz) A chaste woman; a virgin. According to the account given in Judges 11:29–40, Jephthah was a judge of Israel who vowed to sacrifice the first living thing he met on returning home should he be victorious in battle against the Ammonites. He won the battle but on returning home was aghast to be greeted by his own unmarried daughter. The girl was allowed two months in which to go into the mountains and lament the fact that she would die a virgin and was duly sacrificed at the end of that time. *It appeared she had vowed to retain her virginity to the end of her days, like some reincarnated Jephthah's daughter.*

jeremiad (jerămīăd) A lengthy lamentation about life or a gloom-laden prophecy of disaster. The word is derived via French from the name of the Old Testament prophet Jeremiah, who is remembered for his stern warnings to Judah of God's judgment against idolatry, immorality, and false prophets (as in chapters 10, 14, and 16). Jeremiah became very unpopular (being thrown into prison and into a cistern) and was known as the Prophet of Doom. "Jeremiah also spoke about a fresh hope. He promised a new and lasting covenant which God would write on his people's hearts, characterized by the inwardness of genuine faith. . . . He also spoke of the restoration of Jerusalem, which Jeremiah symbolized by buying a plot of land as the Babylonians besieged the city . . . and of a new king in David's line to replace the corrupt monarchy of his own day" (Selman and Manser, *Hearthside Bible Dictionary,* p. 122). Even today any person who complains at length about the state of the world or who voices gloomy predictions about the future may be labeled a *Jeremiah.* "Since the world began there have been two Jeremys. The one wrote a Jeremiah about usury, and was called Jeremy Bentham" (Edgar Allan Poe, *Diddling,* 1850).

Jericho *See* WALLS OF JERICHO.

jeroboam (jerăbōăm) A very large wine bottle, with a capacity of three liters. Jeroboam (c. 931–910 B.C.) was a king of Israel who in 1 Kings 11:28 is described as "a mighty man of valour," hence the humorous adoption of his name as that of a large bottle in the 19th century. He promoted idol worship and "did sin, and . . . made Israel to sin." *By the end of the night the tables were laden with jeroboams.*

Jerusalem *See* NEW JERUSALEM.

Jesus wept! (jeezăs) An exclamation of exasperation. This is the shortest verse in the Bible, appearing in John 11:35. *The chief of the engineers surveyed the chaotic scene below and wiped a grimy hand across his brow. "Jesus wept! We'll be here all night."*

jethroization (jethrōizayshăn) The practice of delegating authority and responsibility to others. The allusion is to the biblical Jethro, who became concerned about the health of his son-in-law Moses and advised him to delegate some of his less important duties as a judge to others (as recorded in Exodus 18:1–27). *The new manager seemed to believe so wholeheartedly in the practice of jethroization that by the end of his first week people were wondering what there was left for him to do.*

jezebel (jezăbel) A shameless, immoral woman. Jezebel was the daughter of Ethbaal, the king of Tyre and Sidon, and the wife of Ahab, king of Israel. Her evil deeds included the murder of the Lord's prophets and their replacement by the prophets of Baal and the attempted murder of Elijah. Elijah foretold a bad end for Jezebel with the words "The dogs shall eat Jezebel by the wall of Jezreel" (1 Kings 21:23), and she eventually met her death when she was hurled out of a palace window on the orders of King Jehu after she adorned herself with cosmetics and tried to seduce him: Her blood spattered the wall, as Elijah had predicted, and her body was torn apart by dogs (2 Kings 9:30–37). Any woman who is suspected of loose, immoral behavior may be dubbed a jezebel; if she wears heavy makeup she is likely to be condemned as a ***painted jezebel.*** "I have been a Jezebel, a London prostitute, and what not" (Samuel Richardson, *Pamela,* 1740).

Job, patience of *See* PATIENCE OF JOB.

Job's comforter (jōbz) A person whose attempts to give comfort to another in distress only serve to intensify the other's misery. The allusion is to the biblical Job, who is visited by three sympathetic friends, Eliphaz, Bildad, and Zophar (described as "miserable comforters" in Job 16:2), who tactlessly attribute his current misfortunes to his disobedience to God. *As soon as news of his disappointment got abroad his front doorbell did not stop ringing with Job's comforters come to trawl through the ashes of his dream.*

Job's wife (jōbz) A wicked woman; a woman who offers evil advice to others. In the biblical story of Job and his multifarious sufferings, his wife does little to alleviate his agony, merely advising him to "curse God, and die" (Job 2:9–10). In some medieval versions of the story she actually exacerbates Job's pain by tossing water on his boils or by whipping him. *This Job's wife waged an unceasing campaign to have all aid to the refugees cut off and redirected to causes more to her liking.*

Jocasta *See* OEDIPUS COMPLEX.

John the Baptist (jon, <u>bap</u>tist) A person who preaches or speaks out in defiance of hostile opinion, especially one who urges Christian repentance. John the Baptist was the prophet who foretold the coming of Christ and went on to baptize Jesus Christ in the Jordan River (Matthew 3:1–15; Mark 1:4–11; Luke 3:1–22). Jesus regarded him as the last and greatest prophet, fulfilling the promise of a second Elijah (Matthew 11:11–14). Despite a successful ministry, he was killed by Herod Antipas for criticizing Herod's marriage to his sister-in-law (Matthew 14:1–12). "He was a John the Baptist who took ennoblement rather than repentance for his text" (Thomas Hardy, *The Return of the Native,* 1880). *See also* VOICE CRYING IN THE WILDERNESS.

Jonah (jōnă) A person who brings bad luck wherever he or she goes. The biblical Jonah was a prophet who was blamed for the storm that lashed the ship in which he was fleeing from God's command to go and preach repentance to the people of Nineveh (Jonah 1:4–12). To appease the storm and save the ship, Jonah readily agrees to be cast into the water "for I know that for my sake this great tempest is upon you." On being tossed into the sea he is swallowed by a "great fish" (often presumed to be a whale), inside which he spends three days and nights before being disgorged safely on land and subsequently making his way to Nineveh as commanded. To Jonah someone means to throw them overboard. "I felt some sentiment that it must be a judgment on us also. The Jonah, in my mind, was Mr Earnshaw" (Emily Brontë, *Wuthering Heights,* 1847).

Jonathan *See* DAVID AND JONATHAN.

Jordan passed (jordăn) Death completed, heaven attained. The phrase refers to the Jordan River in the Holy Land and alludes to the miraculous dryfooted crossing of the river by the Israelites led by Joshua on their way to the Promised Land (located on the western side and often considered a metaphor for Heaven), as recounted in Joshua 3:7–17. *Her long struggle was over, Jordan passed and no more suffering to be borne. See also* CROSS OVER JORDAN.

jorum (jorăm) A large drinking bowl, especially one used to contain punch. The name may refer to the biblical king Joram of Hamath who offered "vessels of silver, and vessels of gold, and vessels of brass" (2 Samuel 8:10) as gifts to King David following the latter's victory over Hadadezer. "At the same table, with both her elbows upon it, was Mrs Jiniwin; no longer sipping other people's punch feloniously with teaspoons, but taking deep draughts from a jorum of her own" (Charles Dickens, *The Old Curiosity Shop,* 1840–41).

Joseph (jōzef) A person who remains immune even to the most alluring sexual temptations. The allusion is to the biblical story of Joseph and POTIPHAR'S WIFE (Genesis 39), in which Joseph, an overseer in Potiphar's house, steadfastly resists seduction by her, resulting eventually in her falsely accusing him of making improper advances and having him thrown into prison. *For months he had been a veritable Joseph in the face of the most tempting of prospects, but the sight of her exposed thigh was too much.*

jot or tittle A tiny amount. The phrase comes from Christ's Sermon on the Mount, in which he denies that he comes to destroy the law but rather to fulfill it: "For verily I say unto you, Till heaven and earth pass, one jot or one tittle shall in no wise pass from the law, till all be fulfilled" (Matthew

5:18; Luke 16:17). Here *jot* signifies the Greek letter iota *(i)*, the smallest letter in the Greek alphabet, while *tittle* is the slight extension of certain letters of the Hebrew alphabet that is used to distinguish one character from another. "Go ye back to London. We have nothing for you. By no jot or tittle do we abate our demands, nor will we until the whole of those demands are yielded" (John Galsworthy, *The Forsyte Saga,* 1922).

jovial *See* BY JOVE.

Jubal (joobăl) A musician or the muse of music and song. Jubal is identified in the Bible as the son of Lamech and Adah and described as the father of "all such as handle the harp and organ" (Genesis 4:21). *This Jubal played like a god, his fingers a blur upon the strings.*

jubilee A 50th anniversary and the festivities with which such an occasion may be celebrated. The word has biblical origins (Leviticus 25 and 27), harking back to the jubilees held after seven successive Sabbaths of years (49 years) to commemorate the deliverance of the Israelites from Egypt. Jubilee years, which were ushered in with the blowing of a *jobel* (Hebrew for a "ram's horn"), were marked by the fields being allowed to rest uncultivated, by the restoration of land to those to whom it originally belonged and by the release of Jewish slaves. "Wodger of the Purple Fawn and Mr Jaggers the cobbler, who also sold second-hand ordinary bicycles, were stretching a string of union-jacks and royal ensigns (which had originally celebrated the Jubilee) across the road" (H. G. Wells, *The Invisible Man,* 1897).

Judas (joodăs) A traitor; a hypocrite. The allusion is to Judas Iscariot, who at Gethsemane betrayed Christ to the Romans for THIRTY PIECES OF SILVER (Matthew 26:14). He identified Christ to his captors by kissing him (Matthew 26:47–49), hence a *Judas kiss* signifies an act of betrayal disguised as a demonstration of friendship. Another adoption of the name of Judas may be found in the *Judas slit* or *Judas hole,* the name of the small peephole in a cell door through which a prisoner may be watched or inspected by his or her captors. The elder tree is sometimes known as the *Judas tree* because it was from an elder that Judas is supposed to have hanged himself in remorse for his actions (Matthew 27:5). A *Judas goat,* meanwhile, is someone who deceitfully leads others into danger (as one goat may lead others to slaughter). "What could you do? You could be Judas to yo' own mother to save yo' wuthless hide! Would anybody b'lieve it?" (Mark Twain, *Pudd'nhead Wilson,* 1894).

judge not, that ye be not judged Do not be too hasty to condemn others, as you may invite unwelcome criticism of yourself. The sentiment comes originally from Christ's Sermon on the Mount (Matthew 7:1–5) and is usually quoted as a warning to keep one's unfavorable opinions of others to oneself. "It may seem strange that any men should fare to ask a just God's assistance in wringing their bread from the sweat of other men's faces; but let us judge not, that we be not judged" (Abraham Lincoln, "Gettysburg Address," 1863).

judgment day A day upon which something will be judged or decided once and for all. The biblical Day of Judgment, as described in the Book of Matthew (such as 11:22–24; 12:36; 13:49; 25:31–33), will come at the end of time. Following Christ's *Last Judgment* of all souls, from his throne on the *judgment seat* (Romans 14:10), the good will receive their eternal reward in heaven, while the ungodly will be punished in hell. "Davy at the first crash had howled, Anne, Anne, is it the Judgment Day? Anne, Anne, I never meant to be naughty, and then had buried his face in Anne's lap and kept it there, his little body quivering" (Lucy Maud Montgomery, *Anne of Avonlea,* 1909).

judgment of Paris (paris) A difficult case or argument to decide, especially one in which there is no solution that will satisfy all parties. The expression refers to an episode in Greek legend in which Paris, the handsome son of King Priam of Troy, was invited to decide which of the three goddesses Hera, Pallas Athene, and Aphrodite was the fairest. Faced with such a perilous decision, Paris awarded the prize to Aphrodite, who had bribed him with the promise of the most beautiful woman in the world. His decision made Hera and Pallas Athene his bitter enemies and led ultimately to the fall of Troy. "On the appointed afternoon, all Simla rode down to Annandale to witness the Judgment of Paris turned upside down" (Rudyard Kipling, *Cupid's Arrows,* 1888). *See also* APPLE OF DISCORD.

judgment of Solomon (<u>so</u>lămăn) Great wisdom, as required to solve a particularly difficult dispute or problem. The allusion is to a biblical dispute (1 Kings 3:16–28) brought before King Solomon, who was widely respected for his wisdom and sense of justice, by two prostitutes who were both claiming possession of the same child. Having heard their cases, Solomon calmly proposed cutting the child in half so that the women could have equal shares; the woman who showed anxiety about this proposal proved she was the real mother and was accordingly awarded custody of the infant. The biblical account records Solomon's prayer for wisdom (1 Kings 3:5–15) and the giving by God to him of "a wise and understanding heart" (verse 12). "'The devil take all halves and quarters!' said the Captain; 'were it in my option, I could no more consent to the halving of that dollar, than the woman in the Judgment of Solomon to the disseverment of the child of her bowels'" (Sir Walter Scott, *A Legend of Montrose,* 1819).

judgment seat *See* JUDGMENT DAY.

juggernaut (<u>ju</u>gernot) A large, heavy truck; any immense object, force, or concept with seemingly unstoppable momentum. The word comes from Hindu mythology, specifically from the name Jagganath, which was one of the many titles adopted by the god Vishnu. Idols of Jagannath are traditionally borne on massive wheeled vehicles pulled by thousands of pilgrims at an annual festival held in the city of Puri in eastern India in his honor. Popular belief has it that extreme devotees of Jagganath regularly make sacrifices of themselves by lying down in front of the huge wheels carrying his image and being crushed to death, although the reality may be that these are simply unfortunates who have lost their footing in the press of worshipers. "It's as if he were some horrible old Juggernaut and I had to see my children's own father throwing them under the wheels to keep him satisfied" (Booth Tarkington, *Alice Adams,* 1921).

Julian calendar (<u>joo</u>leeăn) The calendar that preceded the present Gregorian calendar. The system was named after the Roman emperor Julius Caesar (100–44 B.C.), who introduced the system in 46 because the existing system (based on the lunar month rather than the solar year) had led to the Roman year being a full three months ahead of where it should have been. The fact that Caesar's own calendar meant that each year was longer by 11 minutes than it should have been eventually persuaded Pope Gregory XIII to replace it in 1582 with the so-called Gregorian calendar, which was subsequently adopted by Britain and its colonies in 1752, when 11 days (September 2–14) were omitted to correct the long-standing inaccuracy of the former system. People who did not understand the rationale behind this latest updating feared they were being robbed of the time and protested vigorously under the slogan "give us back our 11 days." Ethiopia ranks among the few countries that still retain the Julian calendar. *Such ideas belong to a different time, to the era of the Julian calendar and gladiatorial combat.*

July The seventh month of the year. July was named after the Roman emperor Julius Caesar (100–44 B.C.) on the command of Mark Antony (c. 82–30 B.C.); it was originally known as Quintilis. *Her smile was as sunny as July.*

Jumping Jehoshaphat! (jăhŏshăfat) A mild oath. According to 1 Kings 22, Jehoshaphat, whose name means "Jehovah is judge," was one of the kings of Judah from 873 to 849 B.C. As king he promoted the religious education of his people and was renowned for his godly ways. The adjective *jumping* would appear have become attached purely for reasons of onomatopoeic appeal. *Jumping Jehoshaphat! The building's on fire!*

June The sixth month of the year. June was probably named after the moon goddess Juno, the wife and sister of Jupiter and the Roman equivalent of Hera in Greek mythology. Another theory suggests the month may have been named in honor of the Junius family of ancient Rome, from which came some of the murderers of Julius Caesar (100–44 B.C.). *In the conservatory it was as hot as June.*

Junoesque (joonōesk) Regally beautiful. The adjective alludes to Juno, the wife and sister of Jupiter, who was renowned for her great beauty and dignity. This stateliness was reflected in the adoption of her name as an epithet for the peacock, sometimes referred to as the **Junonian bird.** As Jupiter's queen she was identified as the guardian of mortal women and the protector of marriage. Juno was, however, also well known for her jealous anger at the faithless behavior of her husband, and many references to her name in literature relate to the ***anger of Juno.*** "She seldom ran—it did not suit her style, she thought, for being tall, the stately and Junoesque was more appropriate than the sportive or piquante" (Louisa May Alcott, *Little Women*, 1868–69). *See also* MONEY.

Jupiter (joopiter) The largest of the planets and the fifth from the Sun. In Roman mythology Jupiter was the king and ruler of the gods, equivalent of the Greek Zeus. His name literally means "bright heaven." *"By Jupiter!" exclaimed the colonel. "I see what you mean." See also* BY JOVE.

justified by works *See* FAITH WITHOUT WORKS.

kalends *See* CALENDS.

karma (<u>kah</u>rmă) The essence of a person's spiritual being. The concept of karma is a central idea in both Hindu and Buddhist thought, and it is the state of a person's karma at the end of his or her life that decides the nature of the individual's next incarnation. In modern usage the word is often taken to refer generally to fate or to a person's soul or sense of spiritual well-being. *She resolutely refused to allow her karma to be disrupted by the disturbing news coming at her on the television and radio and settled down to spend the evening with a good book.*

Kedar's tents (<u>kee</u>dahrz) The world of the human race. The expression is biblical in origin, alluding to Kedar, the son of Ishmael who is identified in Genesis 25:13 as the forbear of a tribe of nomadic Arabs. The phrase itself appears in Psalm 120:5: "Woe is me, that I sojourn in Mesech, that I dwell in the tents of Kedar!" *They found the old beggar's body the following day. Some time during the night he had made his escape from Kedar's tents.*

keep oneself unspotted from the world To keep oneself free of the corruptions of the world. The expression is biblical: "Pure religion and undefiled before God and the Father is this, To visit the fatherless and widows in their affliction, and to keep himself unspotted from the world" (James 1:27). "Then there was an interval and a scene with his people, who expected much from him. Next a year of living unspotted from the world in a third-rate depot battalion where all the juniors were children, and all the seniors old women; and lastly he came out to India, where he was cut off from the support of his parents, and had no one to fall back on in time of trouble except himself" (Rudyard Kipling, *Plain Tales from the Hills,* 1888).

keys of the kingdom The keys to heaven or more generally any means of access to authority or privilege. The phrase appears in Matthew 16:18–19, where Christ addresses Peter: "And I say also unto thee, That thou art Peter, and upon this rock I will build my church; and the gates of hell shall not prevail against it. And I will give unto thee the keys of the kingdom of heaven: and whatsoever thou shalt bind on earth shall be bound in heaven: and whatsoever thou shalt loose on earth shall be loosed in heaven." The symbol of crossed keys subsequently became an emblem of the papacy, and Peter is commonly depicted as the doorkeeper of heaven. *Winning a seat in the Senate seemed to him like being given the keys of the kingdom, but reality turned out to be very different.*

kick against the pricks To resist or protest against prevailing opinion or conditions. The expression comes from the biblical Book of Acts, in which Saul is struck by a bright light while on the road to Damascus and addressed by Christ himself: "And the Lord said, I am Jesus whom thou persecutest: it is hard for thee to kick against the pricks" (Acts 9:5). The phrase refers to the kicking of an ox or horse when goaded or spurred. "Paul was laid up with an attack of bronchitis. He did not mind much. What happened happened, and it was no good kicking against the pricks" (D. H. Lawrence, *Sons and Lovers,* 1913).

kill the fatted calf To offer a guest the finest food or other fare available; to arrange a lavish celebration. The phrase is biblical in origin, coming from the parable of the PRODIGAL SON in which the father welcomes his younger son home with a generous feast: "Bring hither the fatted calf, and kill it; and let us eat, and be merry" (Luke 15:23). "'Well, here I am. Kill the fatted calf, Warmson, let's have fizz'" (John Galsworthy, *The Forsyte Saga,* 1922).

kill the messenger To punish the bearer of bad news rather than tackle the source of it. The expression comes from the tragedy *Antigone* (c. 442 B.C.) by the Greek playwright Sophocles: "None love the messenger who brings bad tidings." Variants include ***shoot the messenger.*** *Political columnists agreed that the dismissal of the vice president's aide was a case of killing the messenger rather than going to the real source of the problem.*

King Log (log) A peace-loving ruler who rules with a gentle hand. The allusion is to a Greek fable about some frogs who petition Zeus for a king.

When the god provides them with a log as their monarch, the frogs complain, and Zeus sends them a stork instead, which immediately sets about eating them. "We have all heard of King Log; but, in these jostling times, one of that royal kindred will hardly win the race for an elective chief-magistracy" (Nathaniel Hawthorne, *The House of the Seven Gables,* 1851).

king of kings A supremely powerful king or other authority. The phrase comes from the Bible, in which it is one of the titles used to describe God (as in Ezekiel 26:7 and 1 Timothy 6:15) and Jesus Christ (as in Revelation 17:14). It has been borne formally by some Eastern monarchs over the centuries and was adopted as a title by several rulers of Ethiopia. *The managing director likes to remind other directors that he is the king of kings. Contrary opinions are not encouraged.*

kiss of Judas *See* JUDAS.

kiss the hem of his garment *See* HEM OF HIS GARMENT, TOUCH THE.

knock and it shall be opened *See* SEEK AND YE SHALL FIND.

know not what they do, they Said of those who act without realizing the significance of their actions or the consequences that may follow. The phrase is a quotation from Christ on the Cross, when he requests divine forgiveness for those who have put him to death: "Father, forgive them; for they know not what they do" (Luke 23:34). "'Yes, Mrs Reed, to you I owe some fearful pangs of mental suffering. But I ought to forgive you, for you knew not what you did . . .'" (Charlotte Brontë, *Jane Eyre,* 1847). *See also* FATHER, FORGIVE THEM.

know someone from Adam, not to To be entirely ignorant of someone's identity. The expression alludes to the biblical Adam (Genesis 2:19), who as the first man ever to live, should surely be familiar to everyone. *This grizzled old veteran claimed to know my grandfather, but Grandpa protested that he did not know him from Adam.*

know them by their fruits To make judgments about a person's character based on his or her behavior or actions. The phrase is biblical in origin, coming from Matthew 7:16–20, in which Christ warns against FALSE PROPHETs: "Ye shall know them by their fruits. Do men gather grapes of thorns, or figs of thistles? Even so every good tree bringeth forth good fruit; but a corrupt tree bringeth forth evil fruit . . . Wherefore by their fruits ye shall know them." *We'll see if his claims to be a reformed person are backed up by his actions. As the good book says, "You will know them by their fruits."*

Kronos *See* CRONOS.

laborer is worthy of his hire, the A person who does work for others deserves to be paid. The proverb comes from Luke 10:7, which quotes Christ as saying, "And in the same house remain, eating and drinking such things as they give: for the labourer is worthy of his hire." (See also 1 Timothy 5:18.) Variants include the Roman proverb *the dog must be bad indeed that is not worth a bone.* "Your service will not be altogether gratuitous, my old friend—the labourer is worthy of his hire" (Sir Walter Scott, *St Ronan's Well,* 1824).

labor of love Work undertaken voluntarily, for the love of doing it, rather than for payment. The phrase is biblical in origin, appearing at 1 Thessalonians 1:3: "Remembering without ceasing your work of faith, and labour of love, and patience of hope in our Lord Jesus Christ, in the sight of God and our Father." "Her willing feet were never tired of taking steps for those who had smoothed her way; her skilful hands were always busy in some labour of love for them" (Louisa May Alcott, *Eight Cousins,* 1874).

labor of Sisyphus *See* SISYPHEAN.

labors of Hercules (<u>her</u>kyooleez) A series of daunting, almost impossibly demanding tasks. The allusion is to the 12 challenges that were imposed on the Greek hero HERCULES by his cousin King Eurystheus of Tiryns. In order, they were killing the terrible Nemean lion; vanquishing the many-headed serpent called the Hydra; capturing the formidable Erymanthean boar; taking possession of the Sacred Hind of Arcadia; destroying the Stymphalian birds; cleaning out the Augean stables; capturing the human-eating mares of King Diomedes of Thrace; acquiring the girdle of Hippolyta, queen of the Amazons; capturing the Cretan bull; taking the oxen of Geryon; killing the dragon Ladon and bringing back the Golden Apples of the Hesperides; and, finally, taking the three-headed dog Cerberus from his station in Hades. Hercules successfully performed all of these tasks. *By the end of the week the team felt as if they had completed the labors of Hercules.*

labyrinth (labărinth, labrinth) A mazelike arrangement of paths, rooms, passages, concepts, etc., in which it is easy to get lost. In Greek mythology the original labyrinth was the system of tunnels and chambers constructed by Daedalus for King Minos of Crete to house the terrible Minotaur, described as half man and half bull. Each year, as punishment for the murder in Athens of Androgeos, the son of King Minos, the Athenians were obliged to give up 14 youths to be fed to the Minotaur as a sacrifice. This continued until THESEUS succeeded in killing the monster, armed with a sword given to him by the king's daughter Ariadne and with a ball of thread that he had unraveled in order to find his way out by retracing his steps. It has been suggested that the legend of the labyrinth of Crete may have been inspired by the complex ground plan of the huge royal palace at Knossos, built around 1700 B.C. and unearthed by Arthur John Evans, a British archaeologist, in A.D. 1900. By extension, anything that is considered complicated or convoluted may be described as *labyrinthine.* "Such an elaborately developed, perplexing, exciting dream was certainly never dreamed by a girl in Eustacia's situation before. It had as many ramifications as the Cretan labyrinth, as many fluctuations as the Northern Lights, as much colour as a parterre in June, and was as crowded with figures as a coronation" (Thomas Hardy, *The Return of the Native,* 1878).

Lachesis *See* FATES.

laconic (lăkonik) Terse; concise; pithy; using a minimum of words. The word alludes to Laconia, the Greek district of which Sparta was the capital in classical times. The inhabitants of Laconia pursued a spare, simple lifestyle and were renowned for their abruptness and terseness of speech, hence the modern meaning of the word. "Jude did not pause to remember that, in the laconic words of the historian, 'insulted Nature sometimes vindicated her rights' in such circumstances" (Thomas Hardy, *Jude the Obscure,* 1895).

Ladon *See* LABORS OF HERCULES.

Laelaps (laylaps) Personification of speed. In Greek mythology Laelaps was the name of a hound that could outrun any quarry. *The hound leapt like Laelaps from the shadows, straight for the duke's unprotected throat.*

Laestrygonians (līstrigōneeănz) Cannibals. The Laestrygonians, or **Lestrigons,** were a legendary tribe of cannibal giants who, according to Homer, came into contact with ODYSSEUS and his companions when they landed in Sicily in the course of their long journey home. *Local rumor had it that the missing tourists must have fallen prey to a tribe of old-fashioned Laestry-gonians high up in the mountains.*

Lais (layis) Archetype of a beautiful prostitute. Lais was born in Sicily in the fifth century B.C. and became one of the most famous of all Greek cour-tesans after being carried off to Corinth after an Athenian raid. Admired by Demosthenes, Xenocrates, and Diogenes, she moved to Thessally and even-tually met her end at the hands of a mob of jealous women, who pricked her to death with their bodkins. *This Lais of the Waterfront was a familiar sight among the dockyard bars, but no one had an unkind word to say about her.*

lake of fire and brimstone See FIRE AND BRIMSTONE.

Lamb of God Jesus Christ as a symbol of meekness and the perfect sacri-fice for sin. The epithet is applied to Christ in John 1:29: "The next day John seeth Jesus coming unto him, and saith, Behold the Lamb of God, which taketh away the sin of the world." *In his daily existence and dealings with others he strove manfully, but with little success, to imitate the example set by the Lamb of God.*

lamb to the slaughter A defenseless victim; someone who is apparently too naive or powerless to defend his or her interests, especially one who ventures into danger without complaining or protesting. The expression is biblical in origin, appearing in Isaiah 53:7 as "He was oppressed, and he was afflicted, yet he opened not his mouth: he is brought as a lamb to the slaughter, and as a sheep before her shearers is dumb, so he openeth not his mouth," and in similar form in Acts 8:32. In Isaiah the lamb is under-stood to be the suffering servant, identified in Acts as Jesus Christ. "Brother, brother: let them rage and kill: let us be brave and suffer. You must go: as a lamb to the slaughter" (George Bernard Shaw, *Androcles and the Lion,* 1912).

lame, the halt, the blind, the *See* MAIMED, THE HALT, AND THE BLIND, THE.

lamia (<u>lay</u>meeǎ) A female demon; a witch. According to Greek mythology, the Lamia was a hideous monster with the head and breasts of a woman and the body of a serpent. Originally a queen of Libya and a lover of Jupiter, she was transformed into a child-eating monster after her children were abducted by the jealous Juno. "Lamia is a serpent transformed by magic into a woman. The idea of both is mythological, and not in any sense physiological. Some women unquestionably suggest the image of serpents; men rarely or never" (Oliver Wendell Holmes, *Elsie Venner,* 1859–60).

lamp of Phoebus (<u>fee</u>bǎs) The sun. *The lamp of Phoebus had risen high in the sky, and there was barely a shadow in sight. See also* PHOEBUS.

land flowing with milk and honey A real or imaginary place where life is easy and all good things are readily available. The phrase appears in the Bible in a description of the PROMISED LAND to which the Israelites aspired: "I am come down to deliver them out of the hand of the Egyptians, and to bring them up out of that land unto a good land and a large, unto a land flowing with milk and honey; unto the place of Canaanites, and the Hittites, and the Amorites, and the Perizzites, and the Hivites, and the Jebusites" (Exodus 3:8). *Refugees continue to pour into the country, expecting to find it a land flowing with milk and honey.*

land of Beulah (<u>byoo</u>lǎ) A land of ease and plenty; the PROMISED LAND. In its original biblical context (Isaiah 62:4) Beulah, meaning "married," stands in contrast to "Desolate." In John Bunyan's *Pilgrim's Progress* (1678) it is depicted as a pleasant land where pilgrims pass their time until summoned to the Celestial City. *The preacher depicted California, with its orchards and vineyards, as a new land of Beulah, where all would live a life of contentment and harmony.*

land of giants *See* GIANTS IN THE EARTH.

land of Goshen (gōshăn) A place where inhabitants can enjoy conditions of peace and plenty. The original land of Goshen was the fertile territory in which the Israelites were allowed to settle in Egypt during their captivity (Genesis 47:6). While the rest of the country was ravaged by the plagues of Egypt, the land of Goshen remained unharmed (Exodus 8:22 and 9:26). *They were reluctant to leave the peaceful valleys where they had spent so many years in peace and safety, like the Israelites in the land of Goshen.*

land of Nod The realm of sleep or sleep itself. The land of Nod is identified in Genesis 4:16 as an area EAST OF EDEN to which Cain was exiled after murdering his brother Abel: "And Cain went out from the presence of the LORD, and dwelt in the land of Nod, on the east of Eden." In its original context Nod denoted "wandering" rather than "sleep." The term became a popular name for sleep after Jonathan Swift used it for such in *A Complete Collection of Genteel and Ingenious Conversation* (1731). It has been suggested that Nod has its origins in the nodding of the head when a person is drowsy. "At last I slid off into a light doze, and had pretty nearly made a good offing towards the land of Nod, when I heard a heavy footfall in the passage, and saw a glimmer of light come into the room from under the door" (Herman Melville, *Moby-Dick,* 1851).

land of promise *See* PROMISED LAND.

land of the living The realm of the living; alive. The expression appears several times in the Bible, for example in Isaiah 53:8: "He was taken from prison and from judgment: and who shall declare his generation? for he was cut off out of the land of the living: for the transgression of my people was he stricken." "He had spoken of it as yet to no one, and he thought that he was resolved not to do so while Sir Louis should yet be in the land of the living" (Anthony Trollope, *Doctor Thorne,* 1858).

Laocoön (layahkăwahn) Archetype of a prophet who suffers for telling the truth. In Greek legend Laocoön was a priest of Apollo who warned his fellow Trojans against bringing the TROJAN HORSE within the walls of Troy. As he prepared to sacrifice a bull to Poseidon, he and his two sons were set upon and killed by two sea serpents (an event memorably depicted by a huge statue by an unknown sculptor of classical times found in Rome in

1506 and today known simply as *The Laocoön*). "'I don't know what to do,' cried Scrooge, laughing and crying in the same breath; and making a perfect Laocoon of himself with his stockings. 'I am as light as a feather, I am as happy as an angel, I am as merry as a schoolboy'" (Charles Dickens, *A Christmas Carol,* 1843).

Laodamia (layōdaymeeǎ) Archetype of a loving, devoted wife. According to Greek legend Laodamia was the wife of King Protesilaus of Thessaly, who despite knowing from the oracle at Delphi that the first of the Greeks to set foot on the Trojan shore was doomed to death, became the first of the invading Greeks to land at the start of the Trojan War. Protesilaus was duly slain by Hector. The grieving Laodamia begged the gods to grant her an audience with her dead husband. The gods allowed Protesilaus to return to the mortal world for three hours, and when the time was up, Laodamia voluntarily accompanied him to Hades. The episode subsequently furnished the English poet William Wordsworth with the material for his celebrated poem "Laodamia" (1815). *Like Laodamia, she refused to leave her husband's side, even accompanying him to the guillotine.*

Laodicean (layōdiseeǎn) Lukewarm; timid; indecisive, especially with regard to religious matters. The allusion is to the early Christian inhabitants of "lukewarm" Laodicea, who are described as half hearted in their attitude toward religion in Revelation 3:15–16: "I know thy works, that thou art neither cold not hot; I would thou wert cold or hot. So then because thou art lukewarm, and neither cold not hot; I will spue thee out of my mouth." "He felt himself to occupy morally that vast middle space of Laodicean neutrality which lay between the Communion people of the parish and the drunken section" (Thomas Hardy, *Far from the Madding Crowd,* 1874).

lares and penates (lahreez, penayteez) Home or cherished domestic or personal possessions that are essential to a home. In ancient Roman society the Lares and Penates *(dii penates)* were the household gods who influenced domestic matters (although they were originally spirits who presided over crossroads). The *lar familiaris* was the protective spirit of the founder of the house. The Penates guarded the inner spaces and storerooms. Each family had its own guardian spirits, which were venerated at special shrines in the home that went with the family when it moved. The phrase in time came to represent domestic matters in general and ultimately cherished personal belongings or household effects. "He said a man was not to be dictated to. I said a man was. He said a man was not to be insulted, then. I said he was right there—never under my roof, where the Lares were sacred, and the laws of hospitality paramount" (Charles Dickens, *David Copperfield,* 1849–50).

lash of scorpions *See* SCOURGE OF SCORPIONS.

last Adam *See* ADAM.

last gasp, at the At the point of death; at the very last moment. The phrase appears in the apocryphal Book of 2 Maccabees 7:9. "None of them at all except such Roman Catholics as should have the luck to have a priest handy to sandpaper their souls at the last gasp, and here and there a presbyterian. No others savable. All the others damned" (Mark Twain, *Letters from the Earth,* 1909).

Last Judgment *See* JUDGMENT DAY.

last shall be first and the first last, the *See* FIRST SHALL BE LAST, THE.

Last Supper A last meal eaten before facing an ordeal of some kind or the unfolding of some event. The allusion is to the meal taken by Christ and his disciples the night before his Crucifixion and during which he instituted the *Eucharist.* The occasion, also referred to as the *Lord's Supper,* is described in the Bible in Matthew 26:26–28; Mark 14:22–25; Luke 22:17–20; and 1 Corinthians 11:23–26. "It was over a chicken vindaloo supper prepared by Ffion in their Yorkshire home that Mr Hague came to the grim realisation that it was all over. . . . Only two friends, who shared their 'last supper', had been informed in advance" (*Times,* June 9, 2001).

Last Trump The end of the world; JUDGMENT DAY. The signal for the end of the world will be a blast on Gabriel's trumpet, when the dead will rise for judgment: "We shall not all sleep, but we shall all be changed, in a moment, in the twinkling of an eye, at the last trump" (1 Corinthians

15:51–52). "'How like a first night at the Opera!' he thought, recognising all the same faces in the same boxes (no, pews), and wondering if, when the Last Trump sounded, Mrs. Selfridge Merry would be there with the same towering ostrich feathers in her bonnet, and Mrs. Beaufort with the same diamond earrings and the same smile" (Edith Wharton, *The Age of Innocence,* 1920).

laurels (lorăls) Honor; distinction; fame. The ancient Greeks crowned the champion at the Pythian Games with a wreath of laurels, the evergreen laurel having long held sacred status. Subsequently many athletic champions as well as prominent poets and military leaders of the ancient world were honored with laurel crowns, and since medieval times winners of certain accolades and high offices have been termed *laureates.* By extension to *rest on one's laurels* means to rely on past successes rather than trying to achieve new ones and to *look to one's laurels* means to need to make a new effort to maintain one's lead over others. "'I never heard your Grace / So much in the vein for preaching; let the Cardinal / Look to his laurels, sir'" (Oscar Wilde, *The Duchess of Padua,* 1891).

law of the Medes and Persians (meedz, perzhuns) A rule or practice that is followed with great strictness or rigidity and is to all appearances unalterable. The phrase appears in a passage in Daniel 6:8, in which a group of advisers suggests that King Darius issue a decree under the terms of which any person praying to anyone other than the king should be thrown into the lions' den: "Now, O King, establish the decree, and sign the writing, that it be not changed, according to the law of the Medes and Persians, which altereth not." The laws of the Medes and Persians had been merged since 550 B.C. when the Persian king Cyrus the Great gained control of Media. "'I am laying down good intentions, which I believe durable as flint. . . . and at this moment I pass a law, unalterable as that of the Medes and Persians'" (Charlotte Brontë, *Jane Eyre,* 1847).

law unto oneself, a Disregarding the wishes and conventions of others in favor of what one wants or believes. The phrase is biblical in origin, appearing in Romans 2:14: "For when the Gentiles, which have not the law, do by nature the things contained in the law, these, having not the law, are a law unto themselves." In the original context the meaning is that the moral nature of the Gentiles serves in place of the law of Moses to show God's demands. In this sense, the Gentiles are "a law unto themselves." "The wind, which had hauled round, rose at sundown and blew steadily. There was not enough sea, though, to disturb even a dory's tackle, but the Carrie Pitman was a law unto herself" (Rudyard Kipling, *Captains Courageous,* 1897).

lay hands on the ark *See* ARK OF THE COVENANT.

lay not up treasures upon earth It is futile devoting one's life to the hoarding of worldly riches. The sentiment is voiced by Christ in his Sermon on the Mount, as recounted in Matthew 6:19–20: "Lay not up for yourselves treasures upon earth, where moth and rust doth corrupt, and where thieves break through and steal: But lay up for yourselves treasures in heaven, where neither moth nor rust doth corrupt, and where thieves do not break through nor steal." *Walking through the huge house cluttered with paintings and valuable furniture while its owner lay dead in his bed reminded her forcibly of the old adage Lay not up treasures upon earth.*

lazaretto (lazăretō) A hospital where people with contagious diseases, especially leprosy, may be treated in quarantine. The term *lazaretto,* or *lazaret,* was arrived at through the combination of the names of the beggar Lazarus (see DIVES) and Nazaret (from Santa Maria di Nazaret), the name of a church in Venice that housed a hospital. Lepers have oftentimes been referred to as *lazars* in Lazarus's memory. "The Lieutenant-Governor had arranged that he should not be driven to the ordinary lazaretto, but to Fort Mannel, where apartments were ready for him and his party" (J. G. Lockhart, *The Life of Sir Walter Scott,* 1839).

Lazarus (lazărăs, lazrăs) A person who unexpectedly emerges revived after dying or renewed after apparently ceasing to have anything further to offer. The allusion is to the *raising of Lazarus* as described in the New Testament in John 11:1–44. Lazarus was raised from the dead by Christ upon the entreaties of his sisters Mary and Martha. Christ recited the words "I am the resurrection, and the life: he that believeth in me, though he were dead, yet shall he live, and whosoever liveth and believeth in me shall never die" (John 11:25–26), and when the stone that sealed the tomb of Lazarus was rolled away, the dead man rose and emerged at Christ's command. ". . . the former chancellor used his Lazarus-like return from a four-year exile on the back benches to appeal for tolerance and a search for the centre ground" (*Guardian,* July 18, 2001). *See also* DIVES; LAZARETTO.

lead us not into temptation A plea not to be tempted into doing something one should not. The phrase is a quotation from the Lord's Prayer, as given in Matthew 6:13. In modern usage it is usually voiced whenever a person is faced with some tempting, mildly illicit opportunity. "'Lead us not into temptation but deliver us from evil.' But what is temptation? What is evil? Is this evil—is this temptation?" (Anthony Trollope, *Barchester Towers,* 1857).

Leander *See* HERO AND LEANDER.

lean years *See* FAT YEARS AND LEAN YEARS.

leaven the lump To redeem something much larger by introducing a smaller element of good. The metaphor, which alludes to the small amount of yeast (leaven) that is required for a whole lump of dough to be raised for baking, comes from 1 Corinthians 5:6: "Your glorying is not good. Know ye not that a little leaven leaveneth the whole lump?" "Except for literary men and painters, present in small quantities to leaven the lump, Becket was, in fact, a rallying point for the advanced spirits of Land Reform" (John Galsworthy, *The Forsyte Saga,* 1922).

Leda (leedă) The 13th satellite of Jupiter, discovered in 1979. In Greek mythology Leda was the daughter of Thestius and the wife of Tyndareus, king of Sparta. She attracted the amorous attentions of Zeus, who seduced her in the form of a swan while she was bathing. As a consequence of this she laid eggs from which hatched HELEN OF TROY and the twins CASTOR AND POLLUX. *She took the goose everywhere with her, looking for all the world like Leda and the swan.*

left hand know what your right hand is doing, do not let your Do not make an ostentatious show of your good deeds. The expression comes from Matthew 6:3–4, in which Christ in his Sermon on the Mount advises that those who give alms should keep it as much as possible a secret, even, as it were, from themselves: "But when thou doest alms, let not thy left hand know what thy right hand doeth: That thine alms may be in secret: and thy Father which seeth in secret himself shall reward thee openly." In modern usage the phrase is more often a symbol of a failure in communication between two parts of the same organization. *This confusion seems to illustrate that as far as this administration is concerned, the left hand does not know what the right hand is doing.*

legion, my name is *See* MY NAME IS LEGION.

Lemnian actions (lemneeăn) Barbaric or inhuman behavior. The phrase alludes to Roman legend, specifically to the island of Lemnos, which was the scene of two infamous massacres. In the first of these the men of Lemnos killed the children of the Athenian women they had abducted. In the second massacre the men were slain by their outraged wives. Fortunately, the troubled and severely depopulated island was then visited by the Argonauts, whose couplings with the women of Lemnos resulted in a compensatory boost in the birthrate. *Such Lemnian actions are increasingly leading to the perpetrators making appearances before international courts of justice.*

Lenten (lentăn) Frugal; meager, especially in relation to food. The adjective comes from Lent, the period of fasting between Ash Wednesday and Easter in the Christian calendar. The tradition of Lent is itself a commemoration of the 40 days and 40 nights spent by Christ in the wilderness, as described in Matthew 4:1–2. "But none can say / That Lenten fare makes Lenten thought" (Alfred Tennyson, *Tiresias,* 1885).

Leonidas *See* THERMOPYLAE.

leopard cannot change its spots, a It is impossible for a person to change his or her essential character or nature. The proverb comes from the Bible, appearing in Jeremiah 13:23: "Can the Ethiopian change his skin, or the leopard his spots? then may ye also do good, that are accustomed to do evil." *His parents hoped he would mend his ways once he went to college, but a leopard cannot change its spots.*

lesbian (lesbeeăn) A female homosexual. The word (a late-19th-century coinage) has its origins ultimately in the island of Lesbos in the eastern Aegean, where the Greek poetess Sappho (fl. 580 B.C.) was born. Sappho's passionate verse celebrated love between women, hence lesbian, or *sapphic,* came to describe such relationships. Sappho was married to a wealthy man named Cercolas and according to one legend threw herself into the sea in despair over her unrequited love for the boatman Phaon. The belief that she was herself a lesbian is speculative, although the tone of her poetry does suggest at least an ardent attachment to her female friends. *All her friends knew she was a lesbian, but her parents had never suspected a thing.*

Lestrigons *See* LAESTRYGONIANS.

lethe (leethee) Forgetfulness; oblivion; death. In Greek mythology Lethe was the name of one of the rivers over which the dead crossed on their way to Hades. When they drank from its waters they immediately forgot all their deeds and actions in the mortal world. "Minds that have been unhinged from their old faith and love, have perhaps sought this Lethean influence of exile, in which the past becomes dreamy because its symbols have all vanished, and the present too is dreamy because it is linked with no memories" (George Eliot, *Silas Marner,* 1861).

let him who is without sin cast the first stone People should not criticize or punish others when they may be equally guilty of wrongdoing themselves. The proverb is of biblical origin, appearing in John 8:7, in which Christ admonishes the mob threatening to stone the woman taken in adultery: "He that is without sin among you, let him first cast a stone at her." "Thou knowest who said, 'Let him who is without sin among you cast the first stone at her!' There have been plenty to do that. Thou art not the man to cast the last stone, Stephen, when she is brought so low" (Charles Dickens, *Hard Times,* 1854). *See also* GO AND SIN NO MORE.

let my people go A plea for mercy, especially to one who imposes his or her will on others. The expression comes from the Bible, appearing in Exodus, when Moses and Aaron ask Pharaoh to release the Israelites from their captivity: "And afterward Moses and Aaron went in, and told Pharaoh, Thus saith the LORD God of Israel, Let my people go" (Exodus

5:1). In modern usage the phrase is sometimes used ironically. *When it became clear how late they would have to work, the foreman flung his arms up in mock horror with a cry of "Let my people go!"*

let not your left hand know *See* LEFT HAND KNOW WHAT YOUR RIGHT HAND IS DOING, DO NOT LET YOUR.

letter killeth, the *See* LETTER OF THE LAW, THE.

letter of Bellerophon (băle̲răfăn, băle̲răfon) A letter or other message that poses a threat to the person who delivers it. The allusion is to the Greek legend of Bellerophon, who was seduced by Proteus's wife, Antaea. Antaea then told her husband that she had been raped by Bellerophon. Proteus asked Bellerophon to carry a letter to her wife's father, Iobates, king of Lycia, in which (unbeknownst to Bellerophon) he repeated Antaea's accusation and requested that Bellerophon be put to death. Iobates was fond of Bellerophon and declined to kill him himself, instead dispatching him on a series of hazardous missions. When Bellerophon succeeded in all these tasks, Iobates relented and made him his heir. *The secretary carried the message to the head of the department, little realizing that it was a letter of Bellerophon and she was taking him instructions for her own dismissal.*

letter of the law, the Rigid adherence to the rules, especially when seen as negating the spirit behind them. The expression alludes to 2 Corinthians 3:5–6, in which Paul writes, "Not that we are sufficient of ourselves to think any thing as of ourselves; but our sufficiency is of God; Who also hath made us able ministers of the new testament; not of the letter, but of the spirit: for the letter killeth, but the spirit giveth life." "'I was going to explain that although I am aware you have infringed the letter of the law, and made yourself liable to proceedings which may, perhaps, be unpleasant—' 'I ain't liable to anything unpleasant at all, Mr Emilius'" (Anthony Trollope, *The Eustace Diamonds,* 1873).

letter of Uriah (yoorī̆ă) A treacherous letter, especially one in which the writer feigns friendship. The reference is to 2 Samuel 11:15, which relates how DAVID gave his lover Bathsheba's husband, Uriah, secret orders to carry to Joab. These orders instructed Joab to leave Uriah in the thick of the fighting so that he would be killed, leaving David free to pursue his relationship with Bathsheba and eventually marry her. *He delivered the message himself, unaware that, like the letter of Uriah, it contained instructions for his own downfall.*

let the day perish *See* CURSE THE DAY I WAS BORN.

let the dead bury the dead Do not grieve over people who are dead or things that are past but concentrate on the present. The expression is biblical in origin, appearing in Matthew 8:21–22: "And another of his disciples said unto him, Lord, suffer me first to go and bury my father. But Jesus said unto him, Follow me; and let the dead bury their dead." "March 21, night. Free. Soul free and fancy free. Let the dead bury the dead. Ay. And let the dead marry the dead" (James Joyce, *Portrait of the Artist as a Young Man,* 1914–15).

let there be light An exclamation upon a sudden revelation, a moment of comprehension, or any act shedding light upon a scene or matter. The phrase is a quotation from Genesis 1:3: "God said, Let there be light: and there was light." "Does like join itself to like; does the spirit of method stir in that confusion, so that its embroilment becomes order? Can the man say, Fiat lux, Let there be light; and out of chaos make a world?" (Thomas Carlyle, *On Heroes and Hero Worship and the Heroic in History,* 1841).

let thou thy servant depart in peace *See* NUNC DIMITTIS.

let us now praise famous men Let us give praise where it is due. The expression comes from the apocryphal book of Ecclesiasticus (Sirach) 44:1 and is often used in memorial services. *The two professors have always been very modest about their achievements, but with the presentation of this award the time has come for us to praise famous men.*

let us reason together *See* SINS BE AS SCARLET.

leviathan (lĕvīăthăn) A vast or immensely powerful force or thing, especially a massive organization, state bureaucracy, etc. The name comes from that of a monstrous beast mentioned at several points in the Bible, for example, "Canst thou draw out Leviathan with a hook?" (Job 41:1). Other examples are Psalm 74:14, Psalm 104:26, and Isaiah 27:1. The legend of Leviathan has its origins in a much older myth in which God overcomes a terrible sea monster (possibly inspired by a crocodile, whale, or python) representing chaos. "The fog seemed to break away as though split by a wedge, and the bow of a steamboat emerged, trailing fog-wreaths on either side like seaweed on the snout of Leviathan" (Jack London, *The Sea Wolf,* 1904). *See also* BEHEMOTH.

lift the veil of Isis (Īsis) To go to the heart of a great mystery. The allusion is to the inscription on a statue of Isis, the principal goddess of ancient Egypt, which read: "I am that which is, has been, and shall be. My veil no one has lifted. The fruit I bore was the Sun." *With this scientific breakthrough scientists in this field are just beginning to lift the veil of Isis as regards the cloning of humans.*

light of the world Jesus Christ. This appellation appears in John 8:12: "Then spake Jesus again unto them, saying, I am the light of the world: he that followeth me shall not walk in darkness, but shall have the light of life." *There are several celebrated paintings of Christ as the light of the world.*

light under a bushel *See* HIDE ONE'S LIGHT UNDER A BUSHEL.

like a lamb to the slaughter *See* LAMB TO THE SLAUGHTER.

like a thief in the night *See* THIEF IN THE NIGHT, LIKE A.

like a vestal virgin *See* VESTA.

like Caesar's wife *See* CAESAR'S WIFE MUST BE ABOVE SUSPICION.

like mother, like daughter A woman's character and behavior tend to reflect her mother's character and behavior. The sentiment comes from Ezekiel 16:44: "Behold, every one that useth proverbs shall use this proverb against thee, saying, As is the mother, so is her daughter." Related proverbs include *like father, like son. She was a pretty little girl but inherited an acerbic sense of humor. Like mother, like daughter, as they say.*

like people, like priest The way a spiritual leader's followers behave reveals that leader's true character. The proverb comes from the Bible, appearing in Hosea 4:9: "And there shall be, like people, like priest: and I will punish them for their ways, and reward them their doings." The saying is also encountered in the form *like priest, like people. The congregation—like people, like priest—showed considerable reluctance to voice their true feelings.*

like the walls of Jericho *See* WALLS OF JERICHO.

lilies of the field Spiritual matters, especially as considered superior to earthly things. The phrase comes from Matthew 6:28–29, in which Christ, in his Sermon on the Mount, chooses the lilies of the field as an emblem of the spirit: "And why take thee thought for raiment? Consider the lilies of the field, how they grow; they toil not, neither, do they spin; And yet I say unto you, That even Solomon in all his glory was not arrayed like one of these." Various attempts have been made to identify lilies of the field with a particular plant, suggestions including the white daisy *Anthemis palaestina,* the poppy anemone *Anemone coronaria,* and the crown marguerite *Chrysanthemum coronarium.* To **consider the lilies** means do not worry and do not strive to provide oneself with material benefits, but trust to providence for what is needed" *(Oxford Dictionary of Current Idiomatic English,* vol. 2 p. 115). "Solomon's court fool would have scoffed at the thought of the young Galilean who dared compare the lilies of the field to his august master" (Oliver Wendell Holmes, *Over the Tea-Cups,* 1891).

Lilith Archetype of a female demon or monstrous woman. Although she is not actually named in the Bible, Lilith features in Christian legend as the first wife of ADAM, who was exiled from Eden after making Adam's life a misery. By him she was supposed to have given birth to a swarm of devils. After her banishment she became a demon haunting various remote places at night and attacking women in childbirth. She is sometimes identified as the "screech-owl" mentioned in Isaiah 34:14. *Mad with rage, with her long hair tangled and matted, she hurtled through the ruined house, screaming like some demented Lilith.*

lily of the valleys *See* ROSE OF SHARON.

lion in the way A contrived excuse for not doing something one does not feel like doing. The expression comes from Proverbs 26:13: "The slothful man saith, There is a lion in the way; a lion in the streets." It may also be encountered in the variant forms *lion in the path* and *lion in the streets.* ". . . but it was three miles off, and there was a lion in the way: they must pass in sight of Squire Raby's house" (Charles Reade, *Put Yourself in His Place,* 1870).

lions' den *See* DANIEL IN THE LIONS' DEN.

lion shall lie down with the lamb Idyllic view of a future in which natural enemies will be reconciled and live in peace. The expression appears in Isaiah 11:6–7, which contains a prophecy of peace and safety in the future messianic age: "The wolf also shall dwell with the lamb and the leopard shall lie down with the kid; and the calf and the young lion and the fatling together; and a little child shall lead them. And the cow and the bear shall feed; their young ones shall lie down together: and the lion shall eat straw like the ox." ". . . the time is come when the past should be buried in oblivion; when my family should take Mr Micawber by the hand, and Mr Micawber should take my family by the hand; when the lion should lie down with the lamb, and my family be on terms with Mr Micawber" (Charles Dickens, *David Copperfield,* 1849–50).

little cloud no bigger than a man's hand *See* CLOUD NO BIGGER THAN A MAN'S HAND.

live by bread alone *See* MAN CANNOT LIVE BY BREAD ALONE.

live by the sword shall die by the sword, those who Those who employ violence to their own ends will eventually fall victim to violence themselves. The proverb is of biblical origin, appearing in Matthew 26:52: "Then said Jesus unto him, Put up again thy sword into his place: for all they that take the sword shall perish with the sword." "'Had He wished help,' he said, 'He could have summoned legions of archangels from heaven, so what need had He of your poor bow and arrow? Besides, bethink you of His own words—that those who live by the sword shall perish by the sword'" (Sir Arthur Conan Doyle, *The White Company,* 1891).

live dog is better than a dead lion, a *See* LIVING DOG IS BETTER THAN A DEAD LION, A.

live off the fat of the land *See* FAT OF THE LAND.

living dog is better than a dead lion, a It is better to compromise and thus survive than perish through one's refusal to adapt. The proverb is found in Ecclesiastes 9:4: "To him that is joined to all the living there is hope: for a living dog is better than a dead lion." It is also found in the form *a live dog is better than a dead lion.* "When the lion is shot, the dog gets the spoil. So he had come in for Katherine, Alan's lioness. A live dog is better than a dead lion" (D. H. Lawrence, *The Woman, Who Rode Away,* 1928).

loaves and fishes *See* FEEDING THE FIVE THOUSAND.

Locusta (lōkăstă) Archetype of a woman who murders someone she is supposed to be nursing. The allusion is to the imperial nurse who poisoned the emperor Claudius on the instructions of his wife, Agrippina, and his son Britannicus on the instructions of Agrippina's son Nero. She was rewarded by Nero but put to death by his successor, Galba. *The midwife has been arrested on suspicion of acting Locusta to her defenseless charges.*

locusts, plague of *See* PLAGUE OF LOCUSTS.

loins, gird up thy *See* GIRD UP THY LOINS.

Log *See* KING LOG.

Loki (lōkee) Personification of mischief and evil. In Norse mythology Loki was identified as the god of mischief and destruction. He was the sworn enemy of the good gods and caused the death of Odin's son Balder after tricking the blind god Hod into striking Balder with a bough of mistletoe, the one thing to which Balder was fatally vulnerable. As punishment he was chained to a rock, sentenced to remain there until the gods are overthrown. *The more the jury heard, the more the defendant began to seem a truly evil man, the equal of any Loki or Lucifer.*

look to one's laurels *See* LAURELS.

Lord giveth and the Lord taketh away, the Things provided by God can just as easily be taken away by him. The proverb is of biblical origin, appearing in Job 1:21 as "Naked came I out of my mother's womb, and naked shall I return thither: the Lord gave, and the Lord hath taken away." *The minister shook his head sadly over the child's body and murmured, "The Lord giveth and the Lord taketh away."*

Lord, how long? *See* HOW LONG, O LORD?

Lord is my shepherd, the *See* GREEN PASTURES.

lord of the flies *See* BEELZEBUB.

Lord's Supper *See* LAST SUPPER.

lost tribes of Israel Something that is irretrievably lost, leaving no trace. The biblical account of the flight from Egypt (in the books of Exodus through Joshua) describes how the Jewish people settled in the PROMISED LAND, where the sons and grandsons of JACOB founded the 12 tribes of Israel. Upon the death of Solomon (1 Kings 11:41) the tribes separated into two kingdoms, the southern kingdom which was called Judah (formed by the tribes of Judah, Simeon, and part of Benjamin) and the northern kingdom which was called Israel (formed by the tribes of Asher, part of Benjamin, Dan, Ephraim, Gad, Issachar, Manasseh, Naphtali, Reuben, and Zebulun). The northern kingdom was overrun by the Assyrians in 722 B.C. and was sent into exile, subsequently vanishing from history as an identifiable group. Over the centuries they became known as "the (10) lost tribes," and various communities around the world have claimed descent from them. *Trying to track the family down after all these years was like trying to trace one of the lost tribes of Israel.*

Lotophagi *See* LOTUS-EATER.

Lot's wife Archetype of an individual who brings about his or her own downfall through disobedience. The reference is to Genesis 19:26 and

the story of Lot and his wife and family who, on account of Lot's goodness, were forewarned by angels of the destruction of SODOM AND
GOMORRAH and given time to leave on condition that they did not look
back as the cities were laid waste with FIRE AND BRIMSTONE: "Escape for
thy life; look not behind thee, neither stay thou in the plain" (Genesis
19:17). Lot's wife disobeyed this command, perhaps regretting the loss
of the worldly pleasures Sodom and Gomorrah represented, and was
turned into a pillar of salt as punishment. (See also Luke 17:32.) In modern usage the tale is often evoked as a warning both to eschew worldly
things and never to look back. The area around the Dead Sea, where the
cities of Sodom and Gomorrah are said to have been located, is well
known for its unusual salt formations. "Very well; I hope you feel the
content you express: at any rate, your good sense will tell you that it is
too soon yet to yield to the vacillating fears of Lot's wife" (Charlotte
Brontë, *Jane Eyre,* 1847).

lotus-eater (lōtǎs) A daydreamer; a person who lives in a state of blissful
indolence and forgetfulness, especially one induced by drugs. The phrase
alludes to an episode in Homer's *Odyssey* (c. 700 B.C.), which described
how Odysseus and his men arrived at the land of the lotus-eaters, or
Lotophagi, in North Africa. When some of the heroes ate the honeyed
fruit of the lotus (also spelled *lotos*) they fell into such a state of dreamy
torpor that they lost all will to continue their journey home and had to be
carried back to the ships by their leader. The episode was rendered in verse
form by Alfred, Lord Tennyson as "The Lotos-Eaters" (1833). The lotus of
the original story has been tentatively identified as the date, the jujube, or
one of various other trees and plants. "Her presence brought memories of
such things as Bourbon roses, rubies, and tropical midnights; her moods
recalled lotus-eaters and the march in 'Athalie'; her motions, the ebb and
flow of the sea; her voice, the viola" (Thomas Hardy, *The Return of the
Native,* 1880).

love of money is the root of all evil, the *See* MONEY IS THE ROOT OF ALL EVIL.

love passing the love of women A friendship that is so intense it surpasses
any ordinary attraction between a man and a woman. The phrase appears
in David's lament for his companion Jonathan, as recorded in 2 Samuel

1:26: "I am distressed for thee, my brother Jonathan: very pleasant hast thou been unto me: thy love to me was wonderful, passing the love of women." In modern usage the term is usually used in reference to male friendship, sometimes as a circumlocution for homosexual love. "He was an older brother to Paul Riesling, swift to defend him, admiring him with a proud and credulous love passing the love of women" (Sinclair Lewis, *Babbitt,* 1922). *See also* DAVID AND JONATHAN.

love thy neighbor Treat others with charity, respect, and tolerance. The proverb is of biblical origin, appearing in Leviticus 19:18: "Thou shalt not avenge, nor bear any grudge against the children of thy people, but thou shalt love thy neighbour as thyself: I am the LORD." It is quoted by Jesus in Matthew 5:43, 19:19, 22:38 and Mark 12:31 and by Paul in Romans 13:9 and Galatians 5:15. It is also found in James 2:8. Contemporary extensions of the proverb include "Love your neighbor, but don't pull down the fence" and "Love your neighbor, but leave his wife alone." *The group of youngsters were discussing current events, and one of them pointed out that loving thy neighbor seemed to have gone out of style among world leaders.*

love your enemies Forgive your enemies rather than retaliate against them. The sentiment was expressed by Christ in the course of his Sermon on the Mount, as recorded in Matthew 5:44–45: "But I say unto you, Love your enemies, bless them that curse you, do good to them that hate you, and pray for them that despitefully use you, and persecute you; That ye may be the children of your Father which is in heaven: for he maketh his sun rise on the evil and on the good, and sendeth rain on the just and on the unjust." "That was love. 'Love your enemies as yourself!' was a divine word, entirely free from any church or creed" (Zane Grey, *Riders of the Purple Sage,* 1912).

Lucian (<u>loo</u>shăn) Personification of the follies and vices of a given age. Lucian is the central character in what is usually called *The Golden Ass,* a satirical romance of the second century A.D. written by Apuleius. Lucian is a young man who is accidentally turned into a donkey and in this guise has a series of adventures, in the course of which he is much abused before returning to his human form. *In Don Quixote, Cervantes provided his contemporaries with a Lucian for the age of chivalry.*

Lucifer (<u>loo</u>sifer) Personification of evil. Lucifer is identified in the Bible as the leader of the angels who rose in rebellion against God and consequently fell, as described in Isaiah 14:12: "How art thou fallen from heaven, O Lucifer, son of the morning!" Lucifer became the devil of Christian tradition, also going by the name SATAN. The name Lucifer means "light-bearer" in Latin and as a result was for a time adopted as a name for a friction match in the 19th century. "'O Rebecca, Rebecca, for shame!' cried Miss Sedley; for this was the greatest blasphemy Rebecca had as yet uttered; and in those days, in England, to say, 'Long live Bonaparte!' was as much as to say, 'Long live Lucifer!'" (William Makepeace Thackeray, *Vanity Fair,* 1847–48).

Lucullan (loo<u>kă</u>lăn) Lavish; luxurious; opulent. Lucius Licinius Lucullus (c. 110–56 B.C.) was a Roman general and consul who acquired great wealth as a result of his success on the battlefield in Asia against Mithridates VI, king of Pontus. Lucullus became famous for his lavish lifestyle, especially his fabulous banquets, after his retirement to Rome around 66. He spent enormous sums on entertaining his guests and was credited with being the first to introduce cherries to Italy. Any sumptuous feast or other display of opulence may now be dubbed a *Lucullan banquet.* The word is sometimes encountered in the forms *Lucullian* or *Lucullean.* When a person dines well alone it may be said on such an occasion that *Lucullus sups with Lucullus,* in reference to the reply that Lucullus gave when asked who his guests would be one evening when a particularly fine meal was being prepared. *Guests at the castle were treated to a Lucullan banquet, with the finest wines and choicest meats.*

lukewarm Laodicea *See* LAODICEAN.

lyceum (līsee̅ăm) A school; a public concert or lecture hall. The original Lyceum was the open-air school in a grove on the banks of the Ilissus River in Athens where Aristotle engaged his pupils in discussions of philosophy. "I did not see why the schoolmaster should be taxed to support the priest, and not the priest the schoolmaster; for I was not the State's schoolmaster, but I supported myself by voluntary subscription. I did not see why the lyceum should not present its tax bill, and have the State to back its demand, as well as the Church" (Henry David Thoreau, *Civil Disobedience,* 1849).

lyncean (lin<u>see</u>ăn) Having exceptionally keen eyesight. The allusion is to Lynceus, the Argonaut who was renowned for sharpsightedness. He was reputed to able to see right through the Earth and to be able to make things out many miles away. *You would need to have eyesight of truly lyncean brilliance to be able to read the words on that board from a mile away.*

Lysistrata (lī<u>sis</u>trătă) Archetype of a woman who uses her sexuality to get her own way. Lysistrata is the central character in a comedy of the same name by the Greek playwright Aristophanes, first produced in 411 B.C. When she suspects the men of Athens and Sparta of not working hard enough to end the long war between their countries, Lysistrata and the other wives of both sides agree to withdraw all sexual favors from their spouses until the latter come to some agreement. The men rapidly agree to a peace treaty and normal marital relations are resumed, to the relief of all. *The local womenfolk threatened to adopt Lysistrata-style tactics unless their demands were agreed to by the end of the day.*

$$m$$

Maecenas (mi̲s̲eenăs) A generous patron of the arts, especially literature. Gaius Cilnius Maecenas (c. 70–8 B.C.) was a wealthy Roman noble and a favorite of the emperor Augustus until he was obliged to go into seclusion later in life. He was celebrated as a patron of literature and included Horace and Virgil among the writers to whom he lent his support. *The literati were nothing if not sycophantic in their response to the great man's generosity, hailing him as a veritable Maecenas for the new century.*

maenads *See* BACCHANTE.

magdalen (ma̲gdălăn) A reformed prostitute; a house for reformed prostitutes. The name alludes to the biblical Mary Magdalene (or Magdalen), a woman from whom Christ had cast "seven devils" (Luke 8:2). She has traditionally been thought to be the unnamed woman of Luke 7:36–50, though the biblical narrative does not warrant this. The woman, who according to the biblical account was "a sinner" (possibly a prostitute) now reformed, wept with remorse over her past sins when Jesus came to the house of the Pharisee. She washed his feet with her tears, drying them with her hair. Mary Magdalene was the first person to see Christ after the Resurrection (Mark 16:9). In art Mary Magdalene is conventionally depicted as weeping. *With great reluctance she allowed herself to be persuaded into the local magdalen, where she was scrubbed, scolded, and entreated not to return to her old ways. See also* MAUDLIN.

magi (ma̲yjī) Astrologers. The original Magi are traditionally thought of as the three wise men from the East who, according to Matthew 2:1, came to Bethlehem with gifts of gold, frankincense, and myrrh to celebrate the birth of Christ. Later traditions presented the Magi as the kings *Caspar*,

Melchior, and *Balthazar*, but this suggestion is not supported by the Gospels. It is thought that the biblical Magi may have come from Persia or southern Arabia. *When the young woman had finished, the three professors nodded sagely, for all the world like three bearded and bespectacled magi.*

Magnificat (magnĭfikat) A hymn of praise and by extension any instance of praise. In its strictest sense the term refers to Mary's joy at the news that she was to bear Christ, as related in Luke 1:46–55. Her words "Magnificat anima mea Dominum" ("My soul doth magnify the Lord") form an important part of Roman Catholic vespers and also appear in the liturgy of the Anglican and Orthodox Churches. "There is the lesson of 'Cinderella,' which is the same as that of the Magnificat—exaltavit humiles. There is the great lesson of 'Beauty and the Beast'; that a thing must be loved before it is loveable" (G. K. Chesterton, *Orthodoxy,* 1909).

Magog *See* GOG AND MAGOG.

maimed, the halt, and the blind, the Those members of society who suffer from some physical disability. The phrase, used often in the context of charity giving, is a quotation from Luke 14:13, in which Christ advises the wealthy that they should invite the poor, the maimed, the lame, and the blind to their houses rather than other rich friends and neighbors. "Some of them did us no great honour by these claims of kindred; as we had the blind, the maimed, and the halt amongst the number" (Oliver Goldsmith, *The Vicar of Wakefield,* 1766).

mammon (mămăn) Money or the desire for material wealth. An Aramaic word meaning "riches," it appears in Matthew 6:24 and Luke 16:9–13 in the course of warnings that excessive interest in worldly riches is incompatible with devotion to God. "Ye cannot serve God and mammon." Several later writers, including Edmund Spenser (1552/53–99) and John Milton (1608–74), chose to personalize material greed in the form of an avaricious pagan god or devil called Mammon. Material wealth that has been acquired by dubious means may sometimes be referred to as *mammon of unrighteousness* (as in Luke 16:9). "Mr Crimsworth . . . frequented no place of worship, and owned no God but Mammon" (Charlotte Brontë, *The Professor,* 1857). *See also* NO MAN CAN SERVE TWO MASTERS.

man after his own heart, a A person who shares the same opinions, enthusiasms, or interests as another. The expression comes from 1 Samuel 13:14, in which Samuel rebukes Saul: "But now thy kingdom shall not continue: the LORD hath sought him a man after his own heart, and the LORD hath commanded him to be captain over his people, because thou hast not kept that which the LORD commanded thee." "As for Passepartout, he was a true Parisian of Paris. Since he had abandoned his own country for England, taking service as a valet, he had in vain searched for a master after his own heart" (Jules Verne, *80 Days Around the World,* 1873). *The leader of the community association spent several years grooming his successor, wanting a man after his own heart.*

man born of woman The human race, especially with regard to the short-lived nature of human existence. The phrase comes from Job 14:1–2, in which Job laments, "Man that is born of a woman is of few days, and full of trouble. He cometh forth like a flower, and is cut down: he fleeth also as a shadow, and continueth not." "Well-a-well, man that is born of woman is of few days and full of trouble, as the Scripture says, and I reckon it's so" (Mark Twain, *The Adventures of Tom Sawyer,* 1876).

man cannot live by bread alone It takes more than such basic necessities as food to constitute a full human life. The proverb comes from the Bible, appearing at Deuteronomy 8:3: "Man doth not live by bread only, but by every word that proceedeth out of the mouth of the LORD." It is quoted by Jesus Christ in his temptation (Matthew 4:4). "Man, we know, cannot live by bread alone but hang me if I don't believe that some women could live by love alone" (Joseph Conrad, *Chance,* 1913).

man cannot serve two masters *See* NO MAN CAN SERVE TWO MASTERS.

manes *See* APPEASE HIS MANES.

Manichaean (manăkeeăn) Holding a dualistic view of the universe based on the perceived primordial conflict between light and dark and good and evil. Manichaeism, which incorporated elements of several religious doctrines, among them Gnosticism, Buddhism, Christianity, and Zoroastrianism, was named after the Persian prophet Manes (or Mani or Manichaeus), who promulgated such a philosophy in the third century A.D. *The government's policy has a Manichaean quality, drawing a clear distinction between good practice and bad and making no allowance for anything in between.*

Manlius *See* GEESE THAT SAVED THE CAPITOL.

manna from heaven (<u>ma</u>nă) A welcome gift, discovery, or otherwise much-needed source of relief. The phrase appears in Exodus 16:14–15, in which "manna" miraculously raining down from heaven provides the Israelites with sustenance during their 40-year sojourn in the wilderness: "And when the dew that lay was gone up, behold, upon the face of the wilderness there lay a small round thing, as small as the hoar frost on the ground. And when the children of Israel saw it, they said to one another, It is manna: for they wist not what it was." It is described as looking like coriander seed and tasting like honey. Speculation about what form of food manna actually was has suggested that it may have come from the tamarisk tree. "Brian Sedgemore, the leftwing Labour MP, spoke for dozens in Blunkett's own party when he called the proposed legislation 'manna from heaven for any future or present home secretary who wants to establish a police state'" (*Guardian,* November 23, 2001).

man of lawlessness *See* ANTICHRIST.

man of sorrows Jesus Christ, especially an artistic depiction of Christ at the Crucifixion. The traditional image of the man of sorrows depicts Christ wearing his crown of thorns and with the wounds in his palms and side clearly visible. The title comes from Isaiah 53:3, in which it is prophesied that the Messiah would be "a man of sorrows, and acquainted with grief." "It seems to me as if you were stretching out your arms to me, and beckoning me to come and take my ease and live for my own delight, and Jesus, the Man of Sorrows, was standing looking towards me, and pointing to the sinful, and suffering, and afflicted" (George Eliot, *Adam Bede,* 1859).

mantle of Elijah (ălĭjă) Authority or leadership. In the Bible the phrase alludes to the mantle worn by the Hebrew prophet Elijah, known especially for his contest with the prophets of Baal on Mount Carmel (1 Kings 18:18–46). When Elijah was carried up to heaven by a whirlwind, his mantle was taken up by his chosen successor Elisha as a symbol of the authority he thus assumed (1 Kings 19:19; 2 Kings 2:13–14). Any person who succeeds to a position of authority or leadership is thereby said to *assume the mantle of Elijah.* "But like the prophet in the chariot disappearing in heaven and dropping his mantle to Elisha, the withdrawing night transferred its pale robe to the breaking day" (Herman Melville, *Billy Budd, Foretopman,* 1891).

many are called, but few are chosen Though many people may think themselves capable of doing something or be considered as candidates for something, only a few are actually likely to receive the opportunity to do so. The proverb first appears in the Bible in Matthew 20:16, in which Christ tells the parable of the laborers in the vineyard and emphasizes the challenge faced by all those who seek admission to heaven: "So the last shall be first, and the first last: for many be called, but few chosen." "There must also be the recollection which seeks to transform and transcend intelligence. Many are called, but few are chosen—because few even know in what salvation consists" (Aldous Huxley, *After Many A Summer,* 1939).

many mansions *See* HOUSE OF MANY MANSIONS.

many waters cannot quench love True love will not be extinguished by disappointment or setbacks. This proverbial observation comes from Song of Solomon 8:7, where it reads, "Many waters cannot quench love, neither can the floods drown it." The British novelist Thomas Hardy adopted the phrase in *Far From the Madding Crowd* (1874) to distinguish between profound love and more superficial attraction: "Where, however, happy circumstances permit its development, the compounded feeling proves itself to be the only love which is as strong as death—that love which many waters cannot quench, nor the floods drown, beside which the passion usually called by the name is evanescent as steam."

Marah (mahrah) A source or cause of bitterness. Marah, which means "bitterness" in Hebrew (see Ruth 1:20), was the name of an oasis some three days' journey from the Red Sea where the Israelites sought to slake their thirst. The waters proved bitter, however, and it was not until God had shown Moses a plant whose foliage would sweeten the water that

they were able to drink (Exodus 15:23–25). "In his petition for a blessing on the meal, the poor old man added to his supplication, a prayer that
the bread eaten in sadness of heart, and the bitter waters of Marah,
might be made as nourishing as those which had been poured forth from
a full cup and a plentiful basket and store" (Sir Walter Scott, *The Heart of
Midlothian,* 1818).

maranatha *See* ANATHEMA.

marathon A long-distance cross-country running race and by extension
any lengthy or arduous struggle or effort. Marathon was the name of a village northeast of Athens, and the plains nearby were the site of a climactic
battle between the Greeks and a much larger invading Persian army in 490
B.C. Defeat in the battle would have left the way open to Athens, but the
vastly outnumbered Greeks triumphed and the Persians were routed. In
order to prevent the Persians from launching a new attack on Athens from
a different direction, a runner was ordered to take the news and warning
to the citizens before the enemy could regroup. The messenger ran the 26
miles, 385 yards as fast as he could and successfully got word to the city in
time. His remarkable feat is still commemorated in the running of the
marathon over a similar distance to that covered by the original messenger
in the modern OLYMPIC GAMES. The ancient Greek runner is sometimes
identified by name as Pheidippides, although the latter actually ran from
Athens to Sparta to seek help before the battle. *After this marathon effort few
members of the task force had the physical or mental stamina to offer further resistance to the proposals.*

March The third month of the year. It was named after MARS, the Roman
god of war, and before the introduction of the JULIAN CALENDAR marked
the beginning (first month) of the year. It also marked the period of the
year when generals could launch new battle campaigns, hence the link
with the warlike Mars. *March is a time of signals and alarms and the true beginning of the year, as far as nature is concerned.*

mark of Cain (kayn) A brand or other distinguishing mark that bears witness to some past crime or misdeed. According to the biblical account of
Abel's murder at the hands of his brother Cain, Cain was branded by God

with a special mark so that those who met him would refrain from killing him out of vengeance: "And the LORD set a mark upon Cain, lest any finding him should kill him" (Genesis 4:15). Tradition has it that the mark took the form of a bloodstained brand on Cain's brow. In modern usage a mark of Cain, or **curse of Cain,** is generally understood to be a mark of punishment rather than protection. "The commitment is total and to opt out of the system is a mark of Cain" (*Guardian,* July 19, 1991). *See also* CAIN AND ABEL.

mark of the beast A physical mark or something else that indicates a person's association with evil. In the book of Revelation (13:16–17, 16:2, and 19:20) an angel punishes those who bear the mark of the beast, a brand on the right hand or forehead signifying those who, at the behest of a creature risen up from the earth, worship a seven-headed beast from the sea. Those who criticize a person or activity as evil are said to *set the mark of the beast* on the object of their condemnation. In the Royal Navy the lapel flashes of midshipmen are traditionally nicknamed marks of the beast. "Each of these creatures, despite its human form, its rag of clothing, and the rough humanity of its bodily form, had woven into it—into its movements, into the expression of its countenance, into its whole presence— some now irresistible suggestion of a hog, a swinish taint, the unmistakable mark of the beast" (H. G. Wells, *The Island of Doctor Moreau,* 1896).

marriage in Cana *See* WATER INTO WINE.

Mars (marz) The personification of war. Though generally identified as the god of war in Roman mythology, Mars began as a god of spring growth who was venerated for keeping livestock safe from threat. Later he became strongly associated with the warlike instinct, and the area in Rome where soldiers trained was dubbed the Field of Mars. He was also identified as the father of ROMULUS AND REMUS. *The king assumed the guise of Mars himself, personally ordering his battalions forward and ranging his magisterial eye over the entire field of battle. See also* MARCH.

Martha (mart̆hă) A woman who is constantly occupied with domestic chores. According to Luke 10:38–42, when Christ visited the home in Bethany of the sisters Martha and MARY, Martha carried on preparing a meal while Mary broke off to listen to Christ's words. When Martha complained that her sister was leaving her to do all the work, she was gently rebuked by Christ: "Martha, Martha, thou art careful and troubled about many things: But one thing is needful: and Mary hath chosen that good part, which shall not be taken away from her" (Luke 10:41–42). Martha is now honored as the patron saint of homemakers. "Her paradise was not a tranquil one, for the little woman fussed, was over-anxious to please, and bustled about like a true Martha, cumbered with many cares" (Louisa May Alcott, *Little Women,* 1868–69).

Mary (<u>mai</u>ree) A quiet, contemplative woman. According to Luke 10:38–42, Mary, the sister of MARTHA, listened attentively to Christ's words while her sister carried on with her domestic chores. *Unlike her sister, who busied herself in the connecting room, the other girl sat like Mary quietly in the corner mulling unhappily over her father's words. See also* VIRGIN MARY.

Mary Magdalene *See* MAGDALEN; MAUDLIN.

massacre of the innocents A complete rout or comprehensive annihilation of a defenseless enemy. The phrase refers to the systematic killing of all male children two years old and younger that according to Matthew 2:1–16 took place in Bethlehem on the orders of Herod the Great in an attempt to stop the prophecy from coming true that one of these boys was destined to become king of the Jews. In modern usage the phrase is not limited to acts of murderous slaughter but may also be applied to any seemingly merciless action against innocent or defenseless parties. "Herod reigns in France, and over all the earth, and begins each year his massacre of the innocents; and if it be not blasphemy against the sacredness of life, I say that the most happy are those who have disappeared" (Upton Sinclair, *Damaged Goods,* 1913).

maudlin Foolishly tearful, sentimental, or rambling. The word comes from the name of Mary Magdalene (or Magdalen), conventionally depicted in art as weeping. (See MAGDALEN.) "I hurried back to that door and glanced in. Alas, there was small room for hope—Backus's eyes were heavy and bloodshot, his sweaty face was crimson, his speech maudlin and thick, his body sawed drunkenly about with the weaving motion of the ship" (Mark Twain, *Life on the Mississippi,* 1883).

Maundy Thursday (<u>mahn</u>dee) The Thursday before Easter, commemorating the Last Supper. *Maundy* comes from the Old French *mandé* (meaning "commanded"), a translation of the Latin *mandatum* ("commandment"), which appears in a quotation of Christ's: "Mandatum novum do vobis," meaning "A new commandment I give unto you" (John 13:34). The commandment in question is "That ye love one another; as I have loved you." The day is marked by special services, and in Britain the monarch presents specially minted coins called *Maundy money* to a small number of elderly people (one for each year of the present reign). This custom recalls the former tradition of monarchs and bishops honoring Christ, who showed his humility by washing the feet of his disciples and of a few select poor people and by handing out food and clothes. *The Maundy Thursday service will be broadcast from the cathedral at an earlier hour this year.*

mausoleum (mahzōleĕăm) A tomb, especially one of imposing dimensions, or a place that is as lifeless or gloomy as a tomb. The term is an allusion to the magnificent tomb of Mausolus, king of Caria (d. 353 B.C.), which was constructed at Halicarnassus in the fourth century B.C. and was included among the seven wonders of the ancient world. Some 140 feet high and complete with huge statues of Mausolus and his wife, it is thought to have been destroyed by an earthquake in medieval times. "Of course, Aunt Myra could not be neglected, and, with secret despair, Rose went to the 'Mausoleum,' as the boys called her gloomy abode" (Louisa May Alcott, *Eight Cousins*, 1874).

May The fifth month of the year. It was named after Maia, the Roman goddess of spring and fertility. *She was in the May of her life, fresh and young and blooming.*

meander To follow a winding, twisting course; to ramble aimlessly. The word is an allusion to the Meander River in Phrygia, whose many windings are supposed to have inspired Daedalus to build the LABYRINTH. "She always returned, with greater emphasis and with an instinctive knowledge of the strength of her objection, 'Let us have no meandering.' Not to meander myself, at present, I will go back to my birth" (Charles Dickens, *David Copperfield*, 1849–50).

measure for measure A matching response, revenge, or other return; tit for tat. The expression is best known as the title of a tragicomedy by William Shakespeare (1604) but is actually biblical in origin, appearing in Matthew 7:2: "For with what judgment ye judge, ye shall be judged: and with what measure ye mete, it shall be measured to you again." "All things are double, one against another—Tit for tat; an eye for an eye; a tooth for a tooth; blood for blood; measure for measure; love for love" (Ralph Waldo Emerson, "Compensation," 1841).

meat that ye know not of A private source of solace, sustenance, or other support, especially of a spiritual nature. The expression comes from John 4:32 in which the disciples entreat Christ to eat something but receive the reply that "I have meat to eat that ye know not of." *When asked how he supported himself, the wizard cryptically replied to his followers, "I have meat you know not of."*

mecca (mĕkă) An ultimate goal or ambition, a place that attracts many visitors or tourists. The term comes from Mecca, a city in modern Saudi Arabia that has special significance in Islamic lore as the birthplace of MUHAMMAD and as a result is the destination for Muslims taking the hajj, or pilgrimage that all the faithful are supposed to take at least once in their lifetime. "East Grafton was the ancient habitat of the race, and Penhallow Grange, where "old" John Penhallow lived, was a Mecca to them" (Lucy Maud Montgomery, *Chronicles of Avonlea,* 1912).

Medea (mĕdeeă) A vengeful, jealous, and cruel woman, especially one believed to be a sorceress. In Greek legend Medea was the daughter of the king of Colchis, an enchantress who helped her lover Jason and the Argonauts in their quest for the GOLDEN FLEECE. The victims of her cruelty included her own brother Absyrtus (whom she cut into pieces to delay pursuit by her father), Jason's uncle Pelias, and ultimately the princess Glauce and her father King Creon of Corinth after Jason decided to abandon Medea and marry Glauce. She also killed the children she had borne Jason and, after seeking shelter at the court of King Aegeus, sought to poison the king's son Theseus. When this plot failed she fled to Colchis. *The rest of the family were jaundiced in their opinion of the old lady, generally agreeing she had behaved like a Medea over her husband's relatively innocuous lapse.*

Medes and Persians, law of the *See* LAW OF THE MEDES AND PERSIANS.

medusa (me<u>doo</u>să) Alternative name for a jellyfish. The creature received its name through a fancied resemblance between its tentacles and the snake hair of the fearsome Medusa, one of the GORGONS. According to legend, she acquired her loathsome appearance as punishment for offending the goddess Athena by consorting with Poseidon in the temple of Athena. Medusa was finally slain by Perseus when he cut off her head. *It rapidly emerged that the affair was more complicated than first imagined, with as many tentacles as a medusa.*

meek as Moses (<u>mō</u>ziz) Long suffering; uncomplaining; quietly accepting. In the Bible meekness is interpreted not as weakness but rather in terms of humility or gentleness of spirit. It is because of the devoutness and restraint of the biblical prophet Moses under the taunts of Aaron and Miriam that God actively defends him from his enemies and helps him to deliver his people from slavery (Numbers 12:3). By the same token, Christ is also described as "meek" (Matthew 11:29; 21:5). In modern usage meekness is more likely to be understood to signify an inclination to accept one's lot and may just as readily be interpreted as a sign of weakness as praiseworthy restraint. "He wasn't the able seaman you see now. He was meek as Moses" (Lucy Maud Montgomery, *Anne's House of Dreams,* 1915).

meek shall inherit the earth, the Those who are humble in heart will receive their just reward in the end. The proverb comes from the Bible, appearing in Matthew 5:5: "Blessed are the meek: for they shall inherit the earth." Modern variants on the theme have included J. Paul Getty's quip "The meek shall inherit the earth, but not its mineral rights." "Blessed are the meek, blessed are the failures, blessed are the stupid, for they, unknown to themselves, have a grace which is denied to the haughty, the successful, and the wise" (Arnold Bennett, *Anna of the Five Towns,* 1902). *See also* BEATITUDE.

Megaera *See* FURIES.

Melchior *See* MAGI.

Melchizedek (melki̯zădek) A person without parents; a priest whose service to God is without end. Melchizedek is identified in Genesis 14:18–20 and elsewhere as a high priest of Salem who was "without father, without mother, without descent, having neither beginning of days, nor end of life; but made like unto the Son of God; abiding a priest continually." Melchizedek, whose name means "king of righteousness," blessed Abraham and is depicted as an Old Testament precursor of Jesus Christ (Hebrews 7). "He would hold his secret knowledge and secret power, being as sinless as the innocent; and he would be a priest forever according to the order of Melchisedec" (James Joyce, *A Portrait of the Artist as a Young Man*, 1915).

Meleager *See* CALYDONIAN BOAR HUNT.

Melpomene *See* MUSES.

Menalcas (menalkas) A shepherd or other rural character. The allusion is to a minor character in Virgil's *Eclogues* (42–37 B.C.) and also in the *Idylls* of Theocritus (c. 310–250 B.C.). *The crew eventually found what they wanted in the local bar, a withered old Menalcas who knew everything about the hills and forests and, even better, all there was to know about the folklore of the region.*

mene, mene, tekel, upharsin *See* WRITING ON THE WALL.

Menechmians (menekmeeănz) People who resemble one another closely. The word originated in reference to the comedy *Menaechmi* by Plautus (c. 254–184 B.C.), the plot of which depends on the confusions of identity resulting from the striking similarity between the central characters. Centuries later it provided the basis for *The Comedy of Errors* (c. 1594) by William Shakespeare. *When they were dressed similarly, few people could tell these two Menechmians apart, and many were the confusions and embarrassments that ensued.*

mentor A wise and faithful adviser or teacher, especially one who gives advice to someone younger or less experienced. In Greek mythology, Mentor was identified by Homer as the trusted friend of ODYSSEUS and, in the absence of Odysseus during the Trojan War, the tutor of his son Telemachus. When Telemachus went in search of his father, the goddess

Athena took the guise of Mentor to accompany him. "He did not think it expedient to receive her alone. He consulted his mentor, Mr Dove, and his client, John Eustace, and the latter consented to be present" (Anthony Trollope, *The Eustace Diamonds,* 1873).

Mercury (<u>merk</u>yăree) Epithet for a messenger or, alternatively, a thief. In Roman mythology Mercury was the god of commerce, thieves, and traffic, equivalent to the Greek Hermes. He remains best known as the messenger of the gods and is conventionally depicted wearing the pair of winged sandals that gave him great speed. The adjective *mercurial* (meaning "lighthearted" or "volatile") was originally applied by astrologers to people born under the influence of the planet Mercury and were thereby supposed to have fanciful, changeable natures. *Like her mother, she had a mercurial character, melancholy one moment but laughing the next as if she didn't have a care in the world.*

mercy seat *See* THRONE OF GRACE.

Merops's son (<u>mer</u>opsiz) A person who mistakenly thinks he or she can put everything right. The reference is to the legendary PHAETON, reputedly the son of King Merops of Ethiopia, who thought he could steer the car of PHOEBUS (actually the Sun itself) safely through the sky and only narrowly avoided setting the Earth on fire. In modern usage the term is usually applied to agitators or demagogues. *The butler murmured darkly something about Merops's son but oozed out of the room before he could be questioned more closely, leaving us all wondering to whom he had been referring.*

Meshach *See* FIERY FURNACE.

Messalina (mesă<u>lee</u>nă) A lustful, sexually voracious woman. Valeria Messalina (c. A.D. 22–48) married the future emperor Claudius at the age of 15 and after he achieved power three years later, wielded immense influence through him, controlling imperial appointments and ordering the deaths of political opponents. Although faithful in the early years of her marriage in order to forestall any doubts about the paternity of her son Britannicus, she subsequently became notorious for her many sexual conquests, who included notable political and military figures.

She was eventually undone when rumors of a mock wedding she had gone through with the consul designate Gaius Silius reached Claudius, who had her executed for treason in her own garden. The name has been applied to several individuals since classical times, notably to Catherine the Great (1729–96), who was dubbed the Modern Messalina. *"My god,"* *cried the director, clutching his temple. "I asked for a Goldilocks, and they've sent* *me Messalina!"*

messiah (mă͟sīă) Someone who is hailed as a savior, especially one who has been long awaited. Derived from the Hebrew word *masiah,* meaning "anointed," it is one of the titles by which Jesus Christ is often referred to (for example, in Matthew 16:16 and 26:63 and in John 1:41). The name *Christ* is a translation into Greek of *Messiah.* The coming of a messiah was predicted by such Old Testament prophets as Isaiah, Jeremiah, and Ezekiel, and since biblical times the title has often been applied to leaders who are expected to restore the fortunes of a particular people or other group. "For a year Vida . . . was healthily vexed by Carol's assumption that she was a sociological messiah come to save Gopher Prairie" (Sinclair Lewis, *Main Street,* 1920).

mess of pottage *See* SELL ONE'S BIRTHRIGHT FOR A MESS OF POTTAGE.

Methuselah *See* AS OLD AS METHUSELAH.

Michaelmas (mĭkălmăs) September 29, marking the feast of St. Michael the Archangel. Michael is identified in the Bible as the prince of the angels, who protected the Jewish people (Daniel 12:1) and led the celestial army against Satan (Jude 9). Traditionally Michaelmas Day was one of the four quarter-days upon which various rents and other payments became due; some British universities still have a Michaelmas term in the autumn. *The Michaelmas term is relatively short this year.*

Midas touch (mīdăs) The ability to turn virtually any project into a success; a golden touch. The reference is to King Midas of Phrygia, who was granted his wish to be able to turn anything he touched to gold. His newfound talent backfired, however, when he found that his food and drink (and even his daughter, according to one version of the tale) turned to gold at his touch, and soon he was begging to be returned to his original condition. This was eventually achieved by his bathing in the waters of the Pactolus, from which time the river has always been edged by golden sand. "So twenty years, with their hopes and fears and smiles and tears and such, / Went by and left me long bereft of hope of the Midas touch" (Robert Service, *Ballads of a Cheechako,* 1909).

mighty fallen, how are the *See* HOW ARE THE MIGHTY FALLEN!

mighty hunter *See* NIMROD.

Milesian tales (mīleezheăn) Short stories of a characteristically obscene nature. The original collection of such stories was compiled by and named after the Greek writer Aristides of Miletus, who lived in the second century B.C. The tales, which have not survived to modern times, were ultimately the work of one Antonius Diogenes. *The group at the bar was swapping Milesian tales in subdued tones, broken every now and then by unsuppressible gusts of delighted laughter.*

milk and honey *See* LAND FLOWING WITH MILK AND HONEY.

millennium "A period of 1,000 years, often referring to the period before Satan's final overthrow" (Revelation 20) when Satan is bound and believers are resurrected and reign with Christ. It has been interpreted in different ways: "as a symbol of the present time between Christ's first and second comings (*amillennialism*), of a time when Christ will return and reign on earth before the final resurrection (*premillennialism*), and of a period of great success for the church and the gospel before Christ's second coming (*postmillennialism*)" (Selman and Manser, *Hearthside Bible Dictionary,* p. 162). The millennium was expected by some to begin in the year 1000, but when this did not happen various theories based on different readings of the biblical text were put forward as to the possible date. Similar expectations were raised, and disappointed, in 2000. "You hear talk, sometimes, 'd make you think the millennium had come—but right the next breath you'll hear somebody hollerin' about "the great unrest." You BET there's a 'great unrest'!" (Booth Tarkington, *The Turmoil,* 1915).

millstone around one's neck An inescapable and onerous obligation or duty that tends to handicap a person's efforts. The expression comes from Matthew 18:6, which delivers a warning against those who would lead a child astray: "But whoso shall offend one of these little ones which believe in me, it were better for him that a millstone were hanged about his neck, and that he were drowned in the depth of the sea." *His obligations to his family are a real millstone around his neck.*

Milo (mīlō) Personification of great physical strength. Milo was a famous Greek athlete who lived in Crotona toward the end of the sixth century B.C. Legend has it that he once carried a four-year-old heifer through the stadium at Olympia before eating the entire animal, and also that he met his death after attempting to pull apart a partially riven oak tree, becoming trapped by the hands and in this helpless condition being devoured by wolves. *This new Milo seemed not to know the limits of his strength and looked about him for a new way to impress the growing crowd with his prodigious muscle power.*

Minerva *See* ATHENA; INVITA MINERVA.

Minotaur *See* LABYRINTH.

mint A place where money is manufactured. The word comes from the Latin *moneta* (meaning "money"), which was in turn a reference to an alternative title (meaning "the admonisher") for the Roman goddess Juno. It was next to the temple of Juno in Rome that the city's money was coined. *All the new coins will have to be returned to the mint and replaced by a new issue.* *See also* MONEY.

Miriam (mireeăm) A person who sings, especially one who sings with joy. The allusion is to the biblical Miriam, a prophetess and the elder sister of Moses and Aaron, who urged the Israelites to sing with joy to celebrate their safe crossing of the Red Sea: "Sing ye to the LORD, for he hath triumphed gloriously" (Exodus 15:20–21). *The news she received on the telephone was evidently good, for she is now dancing with her handkerchief and singing like the biblical Miriam in a spirit of reckless gaiety.*

miserable comforters *See* JOB'S COMFORTER.

mite *See* WIDOW'S MITE.

Mithras (<u>mithr</u>ăs) The Sun or a personification of light. Mithras was a Persian god of light and truth and was also venerated by the Romans. The word itself means "friend." *"Mithras reveals all," whispered the archaeologist as the sun's rays entered the tomb, lighting the way ahead.*

mithridatism (<u>mith</u>ridaytizăm) Immunity to a poison acquired through the consumption of gradually increased doses of it over a long period. The term is a reference to Mithridates VI, king of Pontus (c. 132–63 B.C.), who became famous for his supposed immunity to poison acquired in this manner. Ultimately Mithridates tried to commit suicide after being defeated by Pompey the Great, only to find no poison would kill him. In the end he had to resort to ordering a soldier to put him to death with his sword. *The emperor's survival when all around him perished was a cause of much conjecture, and suggestions that the solution lay in mithridatism have never been fully discounted.*

Mnemosyne *See* MUSES.

Mohammed *See* MUHAMMAD.

Moirae *See* FATES.

Moloch (<u>mah</u>lăk, <u>mō</u>lok) A god or other power who demands the sacrifice of what a person holds most dear. According to Leviticus 18:21, Moloch (or Molech) was an Ammonite god to whom followers sacrificed their children in the Valley of Hinnom outside Jerusalem. Over the centuries the name has been applied to various dreadful rulers and instruments of death, including war and, during the French Revolution, the guillotine. "Artists are the high priests of the modern Moloch" (George Bernard Shaw, *An Unsocial Socialist,* 1887).

moly (<u>mō</u>lee) An herb with magical properties. This mysterious herb was allegedly given by Hermes to Odysseus to make him immune from spells cast by the sorceress Circe. It was described as having a black root and a milk-white flower. The name has since been associated with several plants, including wild garlic. *She could not describe the medicine the shaman had administered to her but concluded that it was some modern equivalent of the magical moly that Odysseus had used to protect himself from the witchcraft of Circe.*

Momus (mōmăs) A person who complains about everything. In Greek mythology Momus was the god of ridicule who was obliged to flee heaven after incurring the wrath of the other gods. Even Venus, renowned for the flawless perfection of her beauty, was mocked by Momus for the sound her feet made when she walked. "I do not think, I will tell you candidly, that Wickham is a person of very cheerful spirit, or what one would call a—' 'A daughter of Momus,' Miss Tox softly suggested" (Charles Dickens, *Dombey and Son,* 1848).

money Currency in the form of banknotes, coins, etc. The word has its origin in the Latin *moneta* (meaning "money"), which was in turn an alternative title, in this case (meaning "the admonisher"), for the Roman goddess Juno (see JUNOESQUE). It was beside the temple of Juno in Rome that the city's money was coined. *In these surroundings people tend to be judged by how much money they earn. See also* MINT.

money changers in the temple *See* CAST MONEY CHANGERS OUT OF THE TEMPLE.

money is the root of all evil The desire for material wealth will lead people to commit all manner of crimes and other misdeeds. The saying is a misquotation from 1 Timothy 6:10: "For the love of money is the root of all evil: which while some coveted after, they have erred from the faith, and pierced themselves through with many sorrows." "The urbane activity with which a man receives money is really marvelous, considering that we so earnestly believe money to be the root of all earthly ills. . . . Ah! how cheerfully we consign ourselves to perdition!" (Herman Melville, *Moby-Dick,* 1851).

Mordecai at your gate, a (mordăkī) An irritatingly persistent or nagging person. The biblical Mordecai is described in the book of Esther as a devout Jew who serves at the court of King Ahasuerus (Xerxes) of Persia. He warns the king of a plot to assassinate him, incurring the wrath of

Haman, who frames Mordecai and persuades Ahasuerus to order his hanging (see HANG AS HIGH AS HAMAN). Haman is denounced by Mordecai's cousin Esther, however, and is himself hanged in Mordecai's place, and Mordecai is rewarded by being made second only to the king in status. The phrase *a Mordecai at your gate* alludes to Mordecai's stubborn habit of going every day to the house where Esther had been kept as a concubine to demand news about her. *You might as well give in because I don't tend to let this drop: I will be a veritable Mordecai at your gate.*

morphine Alkaloid extracted from opium and used as an anesthetic and sedative in medicine. The name is an allusion to Morpheus, the god of dreams in Greek mythology and the son of the god of sleep, Somnus. *Soldiers routinely carried ampoules of morphine to provide immediate pain relief to casualties in the field.*

mosaic A decoration made up of small pieces of colored glass or stone. The word comes from the Greek *mouseios* (meaning "of the Muses") and is thus an allusion to the MUSES, who were believed to provide all manner of artistic inspiration as patrons of the arts and sciences. *The sun's rays pouring through the stained glass were split into a kind of mosaic.*

Moses (mōziz) The archetype of a wise old (and probably bearded) man. The biblical Moses was the prophet who with God's help led the Israelites out of captivity in Egypt; the accounts of his life are related in the books of Exodus, Leviticus, Numbers, and Deuteronomy. Outstanding leaders who have successfully led their people in times of trouble are sometimes compared to the biblical patriarch, although the name is also applied to any venerable old man. *The old man sat like Moses on a block of marble and waited patiently for the crowd to gather round him.* See also MOSES BASKET; MOSES' ROD.

Moses basket (mōziz) A portable basket for babies. The name alludes to the cradle made of papyrus in which, according to Exodus 2:3, the infant Moses was placed by his mother among the reeds of the Nile to conceal him from Pharaoh's soldiers, who had orders to kill all male children of Jewish parentage: "And when she could not longer hide him, she took for him an ark of bulrushes, and daubed it with slime and with pitch, and put the child therein; and she laid it in the flags by the river's brink." Moses was found by Pharaoh's daughter when she came down to the river to bathe and was entrusted to the safekeeping of her nurse. *In the end we bought them a Moses basket for their new baby.*

Moses' rod (mōziz) A divining rod. The name alludes to the rod with which, according to Exodus 7:9, Moses performed miracles before Pharaoh. It was also with this rod or one similar to it that Moses struck water from a rock, as related at Exodus 17:6. *He held the Moses' rod loosely in his outstretched hands and began to pace down the garden, watching it intently.* See also SMITE THE ROCK.

mote and beam An insignificant fault and a more major one. The origins of the phrase lie in Christ's Sermon on the Mount, in which he warns those who seek to tackle the minor faults of others to consider first their own failings: "Why beholdest thou the mote that is in thy brother's eye, but considerest not the beam that is in thine own eye?" (Matthew 7:3). *Mote* relates to a tiny particle of dust or a chip of wood, while *beam* signifies a more substantial piece of timber. References to *motes in thy brother's eye* are usually heard when a person is suspected of hypocrisy. *He was tackling things in entirely the wrong order, failing to deal with the mote in his own eye before wrestling with the beam in his brother's.*

moth and rust corrupt *See* LAY NOT UP TREASURES UPON EARTH.

Mount Olympus *See* OLYMPIAN.

Mount Parnassus *See* PARNASSIAN.

mount Pegasus *See* PEGASUS.

Mount Pisgah (pizgah) A place or point that affords optimism about or foresight into the future. According to Deuteronomy 34:1, Moses ascended Mount Pisgah in order to get a glimpse of the Promised Land in the distance just before he died. *His account of the view from Mount Pisgah left us all feeling very buoyant.*

Mount Sinai (sīnī) A place or situation where a person comes face to face with some revelation or challenge. In the Bible, Mount Sinai, or **Horeb,** is identified as the hill where Moses received the Ten Commandments from God (Exodus 20 and 31:18 and Deuteronomy 5). *Feeling like Moses on Mount Sinai he struggled to take in the import of this new revelation.*

mouths of babes and sucklings, out of the *See* OUT OF THE MOUTHS OF BABES AND SUCKLINGS.

much study is a weariness of the flesh *See* OF MAKING MANY BOOKS.

Muhammad (mōhahmed, măhahmed) The founder of Islam, whose teachings form the basis of modern Islamic faith. Muhammad (570–632), or **Mohammed**, was forced to leave MECCA because of his teachings in 610; he fled to Medina with his followers but returned as conqueror of Mecca in 630. He is venerated today as the prophet of God, whose beliefs are enshrined in the Qur'an, or Koran.

Muses Personifications of artistic and creative inspiration. In Greek mythology the Muses were nine in number, namely Clio (the muse of history), Euterpe (of lyric poetry), Thalia (of comedy), Melpomene (of tragedy), Terpsichore (of choral dance and song), Erato (of love songs), Polyhymnia (of songs to the gods), Urania (of astronomy), and Calliope (of epic poetry). They were identified as the daughters of Zeus and Mnemosyne (the goddess of memory) and had a temple on Mount HELICON in Boeotia. Related words include *music* and *museum. He tottered on the edge of the cliff, bottle in hand, lamenting loudly that the Muses had deserted him and there was nothing left to live for. See also* MOSAIC; TENTH MUSE.

music of the spheres A type of celestial music supposedly created by the movements of the spheres, which in the Ptolemaic system of cosmology carried the planets and stars around the Earth. The concept of the sublime harmony of the universe being expressed in the form of music was devised by the Greek philosopher and mathematician Pythagoras. "He said that, the people of their island had their ears adapted to hear 'the music of the spheres', which always played at certain periods, and the court was now

251

prepared to bear their part, in whatever instrument they most excelled" (Jonathan Swift, *Gulliver's Travels*, 1726).

mustard seed *See* GRAIN OF MUSTARD SEED.

my brother's keeper Someone who has responsibility for another person and should know where he or she is and what he or she is doing. The phrase alludes to the biblical story of CAIN AND ABEL and the former's indignant reply when asked by God where Abel is: "I know not: Am I my brother's keeper?" (Genesis 4:9). In fact, Cain has murdered Abel and is trying to deny any knowledge of the crime. "I am not my brother's keeper. I cannot bring myself to judge my fellows; I am content to observe them" (William Somerset Maugham, *The Summing Up*, 1938).

my cup runneth over Good things are coming in abundance. The expression comes from Psalm 23:5–6, in which the blessings of God are described: "Thou preparest a table before me in the presence of mine enemies: thy anointest my head with oil; my cup runneth over. Surely goodness and mercy shall follow me all the days of my life." In the translation in the *Book of Common Prayer*, the phrase is ***my cup shall be full***. *A new job, a new home, getting married all in one year . . . Louise felt that her cup was indeed running over.* "Her in-box runneth over with new mail" (*Guardian*, August 13, 2001).

My God, why hast thou forsaken me? A cry of desperation or despair at one's abandonment by God or others. According to Matthew 27:46 and Mark 15:34 these were the words of Christ at the time of the Crucifixion: "And about the ninth hour Jesus cried with a loud voice, saying Eli, Eli, lama sabachtani? That is to say, My God, my God, why hast thou forsaken me?" *That evening nothing went right for him at the casino, and by eleven o'clock he was reduced to glaring forlornly up at the fan on the ceiling and mentally intoning, My God, why hast thou forsaken me? See also* SEVEN LAST WORDS.

my name is legion We are many in number, usually referring to evil spirits or other undesirable persons or phenomena. The phrase comes from Mark 5:9, in which Christ encounters a man possessed by a host of demons, the first of which explains, "My name is Legion." Roman legions comprised between 4,000 and 6,000 soldiers. Christ expelled the demons and transferred them to a herd of swine, who promptly drowned themselves in deep water. "And there I found what appalled me; a zoo of lusts, a bedlam of ambitions, a nursery of fears, a harem of fondled hatreds. My name was legion" (C. S. Lewis, *Surprised by Joy,* 1955). *See also* GADARENE.

myrmidon (<u>mer</u>midon) A devoted follower or henchman; a servant or other person who follows orders without question or scruple. According to Greek mythology the original Myrmidons were a race of people from Thessaly who were created by Zeus from ants (***murmex*** in Greek means "ant") after the previous inhabitants of the country had been wiped out by plague. The Myrmidons were famed for their loyalty to Achilles during the Trojan War, although they were also notorious for their brutality. The term *myrmidon* is often quoted today in relation to gangs of ruffians or thugs but may on occasion also be applied to the forces of law and order, with the police sometimes being referred to as ***myrmidons of the law.*** "Within eight days she was to enter an appearance, or go through some preliminary ceremony, towards showing why she should not surrender her diamonds to the Lord Chancellor, or to one of those satraps of his, the Vice-Chancellors, or to some other terrible myrmidon" (Anthony Trollope, *The Eustace Diamonds,* 1873).

my yoke is easy I can bear my burden or responsibility with ease. The phrase appears in Matthew 11:28–30, in which Christ says to his followers, "Come unto me, all ye that labour and are heavy laden, and I will give you rest. Take my yoke upon you, and learn of me; for I am meek and lowly in heart: and ye shall find rest unto your souls. For my yoke is easy, and my burden is light." "It was easy to be good. God's yoke was sweet and light. It was better never to have sinned" (James Joyce, *Portrait of the Artist as a Young Man,* 1914–15).

𝑛

Naboth's vineyard (nayboths) Something of value that is coveted and obtained from its rightful owner by another, stronger person using dishonest or extreme means. The phrase alludes to the biblical tale of Naboth, whose vineyard neighboring the royal grounds in Jezreel attracted the avaricious attention of AHAB, king of Israel, and his wicked wife, Jezebel. According to 1 Kings 21, Naboth refused to sell his land and was subsequently made the target of trumped-up charges of blasphemy and was stoned to death, together with his children. The vineyard duly passed to Ahab. *The estate, like Naboth's vineyard, went to the relative with the most money and thus the greatest influence with the lawyers rather than to the relative with the strongest moral right to the inheritance.*

naiad *See* NYMPH.

naked and ye clothed me, I was *See* I WAS A STRANGER, AND YE TOOK ME IN.

name is legion, my *See* MY NAME IS LEGION.

name of God in vain, take the *See* TAKE THE NAME OF GOD IN VAIN.

naphtha (naftha, naptha) A bituminous distillation obtained by boiling coal tar (although it also occurs naturally in certain places). It appears in Greek legend in the story of Medea, in which it is identified as the magical substance smeared by a sorceress upon the wedding robe of Glauce, daughter of King Creon, causing her to be burned to death just before her marriage to Jason. "Masses of the slimy and sulphurous substance called naphtha, which floated idly on the sluggish and sullen waves, supplied those rolling clouds with new vapours, and afforded awful testimony to the truth of the Mosaic history" (Sir Walter Scott, *The Talisman,* 1825).

narcissism Obsessive interest in or love of oneself. The allusion is to the Greek legend of Narcissus, a beautiful young man who rejected all suitors and was punished by falling in love with his own reflection in a pool of water. Unable to fulfill his desire, he wasted away at the water's edge until the gods finally relented and turned him into a flower, known ever since as a *narcissus.* A variation of the story has Narcissus falling in love with his reflection and in trying to embrace it being drowned and then resurrected as the flower. "It was Narcissism in him to love the city so well; he saw his reflection in it; and, like it, he was grimy, big, careless, rich, strong, and unquenchably optimistic" (Booth Tarkington, *The Turmoil,* 1915). *See also* ECHO.

narrow way *See* STRAIGHT AND NARROW.

Nathan *See* EWE LAMB.

Nativity, the The birth of Jesus Christ (Matthew 1:18–2:12; Luke 2:1–40); commemorations of this event held during the Christmas period. The original Cave of the Nativity, where Christ is thought to have been born (although there is no definite suggestion in the Bible that the birth took place in a cave), is traditionally located under the chancel of the basilica of the Church of the Nativity in Bethlehem. "Attached to the bolster by a towel, under his father's bayonet and the oleograph depicting the Nativity, sat the baby" (John Galsworthy, *The Forsyte Saga,* 1922).

Nazarene (nazăreen) Someone who comes from the town of Nazareth in Israel. The term is usually reserved for Christ, who spent his childhood there (Matthew 2:23). "'Let not your heart be troubled, neither let it be afraid,' said the Nazarene. Clare chimed in cordially; but his heart was troubled all the same" (Thomas Hardy, *Tess of the D'Urbervilles,* 1891).

Nazareth, good thing come out of *See* GOOD THING COME OUT OF NAZARETH.

Nazirite (nazărīt) A person who is set apart from the rest of the population because of his or her religious beliefs. The Nazirites, or *Nazarites,* are described in the Bible (Numbers 6:2–6) as individuals who demonstrate their devotion to God by abstaining from wine, never cutting their hair, and avoiding contact with dead bodies. Samson and probably Samuel and John the Baptist were Nazirites. Today the term may be applied to those who attempt to keep themselves separate from the world for religious reasons, especially if they have an unkempt appearance or long, untrimmed hair. *The valley was a refuge for Nazirites and other outcasts whose presence would not be tolerated in the surrounding towns and villages.*

Neaera (nieeră) A female lover; a sweetheart. Neaera, a Greek nymph, appears in the writings of Horace, Tibullus, and Virgil. "Were it not better done as other use, / To sport with Amaryllis in the shade, / Or with the tangles of Neaera's hair?" (John Milton, *Lycidas,* 1637).

nebuchadnezzar (nebăkădnezer, nebyăkădnezer) A wine bottle with a capacity equivalent to that of 20 standard bottles (approximately 15 liters). Nebuchadnezzar II (605–562 B.C.) was the evil king of Babylon who took the Israelites into captivity in Babylon, as described in Daniel 1–4 and 2 Kings 24–25. He was punished for his wickedness by going insane and ended his days grazing in a field like an animal. The adoption of his name for the wine bottle, the huge size of which reflects his own inflated arrogance, seems to date from the early 20th century. *The old gentleman generously offered to host the occasion, making a note to himself to ask the wine merchants to provide a nebuchadnezzar of wine, if such a thing could still be had in this day and age.*

nectar A sugary fluid produced by flowers and, by extension, any exceptionally delicious drink. In Greek mythology nectar was identified as the drink of the gods on Olympus and was believed to confer immortality on those who tasted it. "He was back in a minute with a big dipperful of stale brown water which tasted like nectar, and loosed the jaws of Disko and Tom Platt" (Rudyard Kipling, *Captains Courageous,* 1897). *See also* AMBROSIA.

Nefertiti (neferteetee) An archetype of feminine beauty. Nefertiti was queen of Egypt in the 14th century B.C. and the wife of Akhenaton. Her beauty is preserved in a celebrated portrait bust. *Her profile was striking, imperious yet sensual, like some pale-skinned Nefertiti.*

Nemean lion *See* LABORS OF HERCULES.

nemesis (nemăsis) Retribution or an agent of it. In Greek mythology Nemesis was identified as the goddess of retribution, described by the poet Hesiod (c. 800 B.C.) as the daughter of Erebus (hell) and Nyx (night). Nemesis enacted the revenge of the gods upon mortals who had offended them through such sins as pride and insolence. In modern usage the term is usually taken to refer to a person's inescapable doom, especially to any stubborn rival or hindrance that seems fated to bring about his or her downfall or failure. "It was one of the most cynical political decisions in recent memory and, unsurprisingly, Nemesis has come back to haunt the railways" (*Guardian,* May 26, 2001).

nepenthe (nipenthee) A drug or other agent that induces sleep or serves to make a person forget his or her griefs or troubles. The word comes from the Greek *ne* ("not") and *penthos* ("grief"). It is mentioned in Homer's *Odyssey* (c. 700 B.C.) as a drug given to Helen by Polydamna to make her forget her cares. "'I know not Lethe nor Nepenthe,' remarked he; 'but I have learned many new secrets in the wilderness'" (Nathaniel Hawthorne, *The Scarlet Letter,* 1850).

Neptune (neptoon) A personification of the sea itself and nautical matters in general. In Roman mythology, Neptune was the god of the sea, the equivalent of the Greek POSEIDON. *They gave up trying to save the ship and threw themselves into the waves, putting their trust in Neptune to bring them to shore.*

nereid *See* NYMPH.

Nero (neerō) An archetype of despotic cruelty and depravity. Nero, originally Lucius Domitius Ahenobarbus (A.D. 37–68), was brought up under the protection of the emperor Claudius, but as emperor himself (54–68), Nero was infamous for his irrational behavior and cruelty. Contemporaries murdered on his orders included his mother, Agrippina; his first wife, Octavia; his second wife, Poppaea (whom he kicked to death while pregnant); and his rival Brittanicus, while those obliged to commit suicide for opposing him included the philosopher Seneca and the poet Lucan. *Power seems to have gone to his head: Colleagues who used to be his admirers have accused him publicly of behaving like Nero. See also* FIDDLE WHILE ROME BURNS.

Nessus, shirt of *See* SHIRT OF NESSUS.

nestor (ne͟ster) A wise old man; the most experienced and wise member of a particular group or company. Nestor was a legendary king of Pylos and the oldest of the Greek commanders in the Trojan War. Renowned for his eloquence, Nestor was widely respected for the wisdom of his counsel and did much to alleviate tensions between other Greek leaders when they fell out with each other. His contemporaries even considered him the equal of the gods as an adviser because of his prudence and experience. "The Nestor of the Hebrew camp, in him the words of the Psalmist were anticipated, that he bore fruit in old age, and to the last was fat and flourishing" (F. B. Meyer, *Joshua,* 1893).

new Adam *See* ADAM.

new Jerusalem (jǎroo͟sǎlǎm) Heaven, paradise, or some other kind of perfect community. The phrase comes from the Bible (Revelation 21:2): "And I John saw the holy city, new Jerusalem, coming down from God out of heaven, prepared as a bride adorned for her husband." In its biblical context the phrase refers specifically to heaven, but it has since been applied to many other kinds of utopia: "It may not have been a new Jerusalem, but the Lansbury estate in London's east end was designed to capture the post-war mood of optimism generated by the Festival of Britain" (*Guardian,* July 11, 2001).

new wine in old bottles New ideas, materials, etc., are wasted if not accompanied by new practices, methods, and so forth. The phrase comes from Christ, who advised his followers that his new teachings demanded new practices to go with them: "Neither do men put new wine into old bottles: else the bottles break, and the wine runneth out, and the bottles perish: but they put new wine into new bottles, and both are preserved" (Matthew 9:16–17). The image alludes to the fact that the tanned animal skins used as bottles in Christ's time tended to be much less elastic and therefore prone to splitting if used more than once. *Many experts felt that the tweaked version of the railroad-safety system was not sufficient—it was a case of new wine in old bottles.*

Nicodemused into nothing (nikădeemăst) Wrecked or ruined (as in one's prospects) through rumor and insinuation. The phrase alludes to the biblical Nicodemus, who attempted to defend Christ before the authorities on the grounds that he should not be tried in his absence (John 3 and 7:50–52). "How many Caesars and Pompeys . . . might have done . . . well in the world . . . had they not been Nicodemused into nothing" (Laurence Sterne, *The Life and Opinions of Tristram Shandy, Gentleman,* 1759–67).

Niflheim (nifălhīm) The underworld. This Norse version of the underworld was believed to be cold, dark, and misty and very different in character to VALHALLA, where chosen heroes feasted with Odin. It comprised nine worlds to which those who died of old age or disease were consigned after death. The word itself means "mist home." *When the mist rolls in from the sea the Danish marshes become menacing and are peopled with ghosts, taking on the character of some dread Niflheim.*

night cometh, when no man can work An injunction to undertake things while the opportunity is there, for it will soon pass. The sentiment is biblical in origin, appearing as a quotation of Christ: "I must work the works of him that sent me, while it is day: the night cometh, when no man can work" (John 9:4). "Repent—resolve, while yet there is time. Remember, we are bid to work while it is day—warned that 'the night cometh when no man shall work'" (Charlotte Brontë, *Jane Eyre,* 1847). "'Still there are works which, with God's permission, I would do before the night cometh.' Dr Arnold was thinking of his great work on Church and State" (Lytton Strachey, *Eminent Victorians,* 1918).

Nike (nīkee) The personification of victory. Nike was the goddess of victory in Greek mythology and was usually depicted with wings and carrying a palm or wreath. Her name is best known today as a trade name for a brand of sportswear. *The spirit of Nike hovers over the stadium as the victors come forward for the presentation.*

nil admirari (neel admi<u>rah</u>ree) Unimpressed; indifferent. The expression, which in Latin literally means "to admire nothing," comes from the *Epistles* of the Roman poet Horace (65–8 B.C.). "Very many men nowadays besides the archdeacon adopt or affect to adopt the nil admirari doctrine; but nevertheless, to judge from their appearance, they are just as subject to sudden emotions as their grandfathers and grandmothers were before them" (Anthony Trollope, *Barchester Towers,* 1857).

nil desperandum (neel despă<u>rahn</u>dăm) Never give in to despair. This nugget of proverbial advice comes from the writings of the Roman poet Horace (65–8 B.C.). "This hitch in the mainspring of the domestic machinery had a bad effect upon the whole concern, but Amy's motto was 'Nil desperandum', and having made up her mind what to do, she proceeded to do it in spite of all obstacles" (Louisa May Alcott, *Little Women,* 1868–69).

Nimrod (<u>nim</u>rod) A daring or skillful hunter of animals. Nimrod, the grandson of Ham, is identified in Genesis 10:9 as a "mighty hunter before the LORD." His kingdom included Babylon, Erech, and Akkad. According to legend, he acquired the link with hunting because he wore the animal skins that God had given to Adam for clothing, and it was through the divine influence of these that he could subdue any beast he encountered. Medieval tradition named Nimrod as the builder of the tower of Babel, and in former times his name was often applied to tyrants. The epithet is more often applied today to hunters of big game or to outstanding figures in sports. "You may think that Herr Doctor Kennicott is a Nimrod, but you ought to have seen me daring him to strip to his B. V. D.'s and go swimming in an icy mountain brook" (Sinclair Lewis, *Main Street,* 1920).

Nineveh and Tyre (<u>nin</u>ăvă, tīr) Great cities that face ruination through the evil ways of their inhabitants. According to Nahum 3:7 and Ezekiel 25–26, the wealthy cities of Nineveh and Tyre were both destroyed as a result of the indulgent lifestyles of their citizens, who had ignored warnings of the fate they risked. Nineveh was a capital of Assyria and now lies in ruins on the opposite bank of the Tigris to modern Mosul in Iraq; the site of Tyre, once an important port in Syria and later the capital of Phoenicia, is occupied by a small fishing village called Sur in southern Lebanon. Their names are usually invoked as a warning against the wicked or conceited: "Lo, all our pomp of yesterday / Is one with Nineveh and Tyre" (Rudyard Kipling, "Recessional," 1897). To John Masefield, in his poem "Cargoes" (1903), however, Nineveh represented not the threat of ruin but rather a distant exoticism: "Quinquireme of Nineveh from distant Ophir / Rowing home to haven in sunny Palestine."

ninth plague of Egypt (eejipt) Impenetrable darkness. According to the Old Testament book of Exodus, God sent 10 plagues to punish the Egyptians for oppressing the Israelites and failing to acknowledge God's power. The ninth of these took the form of "a thick darkness in all the land of Egypt three days" (Exodus 10:22). "By reason of the density of the interwoven foliage overhead, it was gloomy there at cloudless noontide, twilight in the evening, dark as midnight at dusk, and black as the ninth plague of Egypt at midnight" (Thomas Hardy, *Far from the Madding Crowd,* 1874). *See also* EGYPTIAN DARKNESS; PLAGUES OF EGYPT.

Niobe (nīōbee) The archetype of the inconsolable grieving mother. In Greek mythology Niobe was the daughter of Tantalus and wife of Amphion, king of Thebes, with whom she had 12 children. When she arrogantly boasted herself superior to the goddess Leto, who had only two children (Apollo and Diana), Leto's offspring punished her by killing all 12 of her children with arrows. The inconsolable Niobe was herself turned into a stone on Mount Sipylus in Lydia but even in this petrified form was said still to weep tears for her children. In canto iv of *Childe Harold* (1819) Lord Byron subsequently dubbed Rome after the fall of the empire the *Niobe of nations.* "Like Niobe, all tears" (William Shakespeare, *Hamlet,* 1601).

nirvana (nervahnǎ) A state of euphoric bliss or spiritual ecstasy. Nirvana is the aim of both the Buddhist and Hindu religions, a state achieved by transcending such ordinary human preoccupations as pain, passion, and anxiety and through this extinguishing any sense of personal identity. "And then gradually my mind drifted away into strange vague dreams, always with that black face and red tongue coming back into them, and so I lost myself in the nirvana of delirium, the blessed relief of those who are too sorely tried" (Sir Arthur Conan Doyle, *Tales of Terror and Mystery,* 1923).

Nisus and Euryalus (nīsăs, yooreeălăs) An archetype of perfect friendship. Nisus and Euryalus were two Trojans who journeyed to Italy with Aeneas and died during night attack on the camp of the Rutulians while the enemy was deep in drunken sleep. Unfortunately Euryalus lost his life in the fight, and when Nisus tried to avenge his friend, he too was killed. The friendship of Nisus and Euryalus has long since become proverbial. *The boys vowed to escape or die together in the attempt, faithful to the end like Nisus and Euryalus.*

Noah's ark *See* ARK.

Noah's wife (nōăz) A quarrelsome, obstreperous wife. Tradition has it that when Noah tried to usher his family into the Ark to escape the Flood (Genesis 7:13), his wife refused. The quarrel between Noah and his wife was one of the stock scenes of medieval mystery plays. *She was a regular Noah's wife, always shrieking abuse at her hapless mate, and few men relished the prospect of crossing her threshold.*

Nod, land of *See* LAND OF NOD.

noise of many waters *See* VOICE OF MANY WATERS.

no jot or tittle *See* JOT OR TITTLE.

noli me tangere (nōlee mee tanjăree) Latin for "touch me not." The phrase is spoken by Jesus Christ after the Resurrection, when he appears to Mary Magdalene as she is weeping at his empty tomb: "Touch me not; for I am not yet ascended to my Father" (John 20:17). "This precious aunt of yours is become insensibly a part of my constitution—Damn her! She's a *noli me tangere* in my flesh which I cannot bear to be touched or tampered with" (Tobias George Smollett, *The Expedition of Humphry Clinker,* 1771).

no man can serve two masters It is impossible to be faithful to two different causes, organizations, employers, etc., at the same time. This proverb has biblical origins, appearing in the form, "No man can serve two masters: for either he will hate the one, and love the other; or else he will hold to the one, and despise the other. Ye cannot serve God and mammon" (Matthew 6:24). "Not serve two masters?—Here's a youth will try it—Would fain serve God, yet give the devil his due" (Sir Walter Scott, *Kenilworth*, 1821). *See also* MAMMON.

no more spirit in her *See* QUEEN OF SHEBA.

no new thing under the sun *See* NOTHING NEW UNDER THE SUN.

noonday demon Indolence, vanity, or some other sin to which a person may be most susceptible when all is going well. The phrase is biblical in origin, appearing in Psalm 91:4–6, where it warns against dangers that can arise when least expected: "His truth shall be thy shield and buckler. Thou shalt not be afraid for the terror by night; Nor for the arrow that flieth by day; nor for the pestilence that walketh in darkness; nor for the destruction that wasteth at noonday." It is usually applied nowadays to threats that come in disguise or, specifically, to the temptations to laziness that come with middle age. *Financially secure and comfortable in his surroundings, he no longer resisted the lures of his noonday demons and began to spend his evenings slumped in front of the television, humming softly to himself.*

no other gods before me *See* THOU SHALT HAVE NO OTHER GODS BEFORE ME.

no peace for the wicked There is always some task to be done, considering the interruptions and disturbances of daily life. The phrase comes from Isaiah 57:21, where it implies that those who are given to evil can expect no respite from anxiety and fear: "There is no peace, saith my God, to the wicked." In modern parlance the expression is usually applied ironically, typically when a person feels obliged to cut short a rest in order to meet the demands of others or return to work that needs to be done. *But there is no peace for the wicked, and hardly had she sat down but there was a knock at the front door and she had to get up again.*

no respecter of persons The treatment of others without favor or prejudice, regardless of their status, wealth, etc. The phrase is biblical in origin, for example, "Then Peter opened his mouth, and said, Of a truth I perceive that God is no respecter of persons" (Acts 10:34). In Deuteronomy 1:17 Moses instructs those who are to sit as judges as follows: "Ye shall not respect persons in judgment; but ye shall hear the small as well as the great; ye shall not be afraid of the face of man; for the judgment is God's." "The law, gentlemen, is no respecter of persons in a free country" (James Fenimore Cooper, *The Pioneers,* 1823).

Norns (nornz) The fates. In Norse mythology, the Norns were three goddesses (Urd, Verdandi, and Skuld) who spun the threads of destiny and exercised supreme control over the fates of both mortals and gods. *The three controllers of the company were like the Fates, or the Norns of the Vikings, cutting the threads of life as they thought fit and thus closing down entire networks and departments without warning.*

no room at the inn No vacancy; no space available. The expression comes from the Bible, where it appears in Luke 2:7, which relates how Joseph and the pregnant Mary arrived at Bethlehem only to find the rooms in the local inn were all taken, obliging them to sleep in the stable: "No room for them in the inn." *We had hoped to stay at the hotel overlooking the town square, but the place was packed for the carnival and there was no room at the inn.*

not by bread alone *See* MAN CANNOT LIVE BY BREAD ALONE.

nothing new under the sun What appears to be new often turns out to be nothing more than a revival or reintroduction of an old idea. This familiar comment on the changeless nature of things is biblical in origin, appearing in Ecclesiastes 1:9: "The thing that hath been, it is that which shall be; and that which is done is that which shall be done: and there is no new thing under the sun." "'They're after something quite new—something that's never been heard of before.' 'My dear fellow! There is nothing new under the sun'" (George Orwell, *Coming Up for Air,* 1939).

not peace but a sword A threat of violence or other stern action, as opposed to a pacific approach. The phrase appears in Matthew and Luke, where it is attributed to Christ: "Think not that I am come to send peace on earth: I came not to send peace, but a sword. For I am come to set a man at variance against his father, and the daughter against her mother, and the daughter in law against her mother in law" (Matthew 10:34–35). Critics usually defend the militaristic tone of the passage by interpreting it as a metaphorical comment directed toward Christ's followers, warning them that their commitment to God might bring them on occasion into conflict with their own families. "He had brought not peace to the city, but a sword" (W. Somerset Maugham, *Catalina,* 1948).

not worth a bone, the dog must be bad indeed that is *See* LABORER IS WORTHY OF HIS HIRE, THE.

number of the beast The devil's number; 666. The mystical reputation of the number depends on its appearance in Revelation 13:18: "Let him that hath understanding count the number of the beast: for it is the number of a man; and his number is Six hundred threescore and six." Various explanations have been put forward for the origins of the number, most of them based on the numerical values given to the letters of certain names, such as that of the wicked Roman emperor Nero, among others. Over the centuries the number has been associated with many other figures accused by their enemies of being the Antichrist, including Martin Luther, Napoléon Bonaparte, and Kaiser Wilhelm II. *He noticed that his new telephone number ended with the number of the beast, but he quickly shrugged off the momentary unease that welled up in his mind.*

Nunc Dimittis (nunk di_mi_tis) A canticle granting permission to leave, especially to depart this life. The words appear in the opening line of the prayer of Simeon, which is sung in evensong in the Anglican Church: "Nunc dimittis servum tuum Domine" ("Lord, now lettest thou thy servant depart in peace"), taken from Luke 2:29–35. By extension, if people are said to *receive their Nunc Dimittis* they are understood to have permission to depart; if they *sing their Nunc Dimittis* they are understood to be happy to be going. "I shall finish my artist's life with your face; but I shall want a bit of those shoulders, too . . . If they aren't divine I will eat my hat. Yes, I will do your head and then—nunc dimittis" (Joseph Conrad, *The Arrow of Gold,* 1919).

nymph A young woman or girl, especially one with a lithe, youthful figure. The nymphs of Greek and Roman mythology were minor female deities of nature associated with specific locations, including rivers, trees, and mountains. They were said to remain perpetually young (though not actually immortal themselves) and to be very beautiful and generally friendly toward mortals. Several mortal heroes, including Achilles, had mothers who were nymphs. They could be subdivided into five broad types: the *dryads* and *hamadryads* lived in trees and groves; the *naiads,* in freshwater; the *Nereids* inhabited the waters of the Mediterranean; the *Oceanids* lived in the outer oceans; and the *oreads,* in grottoes and mountains. "When not engaged in reading Virgil, Homer, or Mistral, in parks, restaurants, streets, and suchlike public places, he indited sonnets (in French) to the eyes, ears, chin, hair, and other visible perfections of a nymph called Therese" (Joseph Conrad, *The Mirror of the Sea,* 1906).

O

obsidian (ob<u>s</u>ideeăn) Glassy volcanic rock formed by rapid solidification of lava. The name comes from the Latin *obsianus lapis* (meaning "stone of Obsius") and is thought to have acquired the *d* through an inaccurate rendering of Obsius, the name of the person who first discovered the rock in Ethiopia, according to Pliny the Elder (A.D. 23–79). "At my side hung one of the Indian weapons that serve them instead of swords, a club of wood set on both sides with spikes of obsidian, like the teeth in the bill of a swordfish" (H. Rider Haggard, *Montezuma's Daughter,* 1899).

Oceanid *See* NYMPH.

Oceanus (ōseeănăs) Alternative name for the Atlantic Ocean. In Greek mythology the Titan Oceanus was the god of the river that was supposed to flow around the Earth and was identified as the father of all the deities and nymphs of the world's waters. As the Greeks learned more about the world around them, Oceanus came to signify only the furthermost seas and oceans and the Atlantic in particular. *In her dreams she sailed with him upon the waters of Oceanus.*

O death, where is thy sting? *See* DEATH, WHERE IS THY STING?

Odin (ōdin) The king of the gods in Scandinavian mythology and a personification of wisdom. According to legend Odin (known elsewhere as **Woden, Wodin,** or **Wotan**) achieved his great wisdom by drinking from the giant Mimir's well, a privilege he obtained in exchange for one of his eyes. Also venerated as the god of war, poetry, and the dead, he became the husband of Frigga and the father of Thor and Balder. *Her grandfather presided* *over the family like some dreadful Odin, dispensing rewards and punishments according to his own unchallenged will.*

Odysseus (ōdĭseeăs) Archetype of the heroic adventurer. According to Greek legend Odysseus, also known as **Ulysses,** was the son of King Laertes of Ithaca and one of those who sought the hand of the beautiful Helen of Troy and swore to protect her. This oath led ultimately to the Trojan War, in which Odysseus played a prominent role. Having helped in the final victory over the Trojans as one of the warriors concealed in the wooden horse, he set off back home to be reunited with his wife, Penelope. However, having offended the gods, he was not allowed to complete his journey for a full 10 years (see ODYSSEY). On his return he slaughtered the various suitors who were trying to claim Penelope and was reunited with his son, Telemachus. It was not long, however, before he embarked on further wanderings. His name is now synonymous with the courageous adventurer, although the Greek poet Homer and others tended to emphasize his cunning and even depicted him as willy and scheming rather than simply brave. *If she was in trouble, he would be her Odysseus, negotiating all obstacles and traversing all chasms to rescue her from the dangers that pressed her on all sides.*

odyssey (ahdăsee) A lengthy journey or quest, typically one in which the person concerned has to overcome many obstacles. The word comes from Homer's epic poem the *Odyssey* (c. 700 B.C.), in which he relates the adventures of the Greek hero ODYSSEUS during the course of the perilous 10-year journey he undertook to return home after the fall of Troy. ". . . Nick could imagine how disconcerting his departure must be on the eve of their Grecian cruise which Mrs. Hicks would certainly call an Odyssey" (Edith Wharton, *Glimpses of the Moon,* 1922).

Oedipus complex (edăpăs) The unconscious sexual attraction of a boy for his mother and associated hostility toward his father (and more rarely the same attraction of a daughter for her father). The term, coined by the Austrian psychoanalyst Sigmund Freud (1856–1939), is an allusion to the Greek legend of Oedipus, the son of King Laius and Queen Jocasta of Thebes, who was brought up in ignorance of his parentage and ultimately killed his own father in a quarrel and married his own mother before realizing he was their son. When the truth came out, Oedipus put out his own eyes and went into exile, eventually dying at Colonus near Athens, while Jocasta committed suicide. Related words include the adjective *oedipal*. *The only motivation the detective could suggest to explain the crime was some kind of extra-twisted Oedipus complex.* See also ELECTRA COMPLEX.

offending Adam *See* WHIP THE OFFENDING ADAM.

of making many books The human appetite for books can never be satisfied and thus the business of making them will never come to an end. The sentiment was first voiced in the Bible in Ecclesiastes 12:12: "Of making many books there is no end; and much study is a weariness of the flesh." It is often delivered as also a warning against excessive intellectualism. "Solomon saith truly, 'Of making many books there is no end,' so insatiable is the thirst of men therein: as also endless is the desire of many in buying and reading them" (Thomas Fuller, *The Holy and the Profane State,* 1642).

of such is the kingdom of heaven *See* SUFFER THE LITTLE CHILDREN.

Og of Bashan *See* BULL OF BASHAN.

Oh, for the wings of a dove! *See* WINGS OF A DOVE.

old Adam *See* WHIP THE OFFENDING ADAM.

old as Methuselah *See* AS OLD AS METHUSELAH.

old men dream dreams Even the old may harbor dreams about the future. The expression comes from Joel 2:28, which looks forward to the messianic age when all, young and old, will share in the Spirit of God: "Your old men shall dream dreams, your young men shall see visions." Some later writers suggested that another reading may be that young men's visions are clearer—and hence more reliable—than old men's dreams. In modern usage the phrase is usually quoted in discussions of idealism and ambition. *Her grandfather grinned ruefully and noted, "Old men dream dreams, you know."*

Old Nick *See* SATAN.

Old Testament Sometimes used to describe stern, retributive justice or thinking. The Old Testament is that part of the Bible describing the history of Israel. It is divided into the five books of the Pentateuch (Genesis through Deuteronomy); the historical books of Joshua through Esther; the books of poetry and wisdom, Job through Song of Solomon, including Psalms; and the books of the prophets Isaiah to Malachi. In particular thinking the God of the Old Testament is sometimes seen as less forgiving than that of the New Testament, but closer reading of the Bible shows that both testaments describe God as holy, yet also kind and loving. *He was a believer in Old Testament justice—short, sharp, and entirely merciless.*

olive branch A peace offering or symbol of peace. The olive branch has had special significance as a peace symbol since classical times. A Greek myth relates how Poseidon and Athena both competed to be chosen patron of the city of Athens. Poseidon tried to bribe the citizens with the offer of a horse, which represented his strength and courage, while Athena presented them with an olive tree, representing peace and prosperity. Athena won and the new city was named in her honor. The olive branch also has significance in Christian and Jewish iconography as it was an olive leaf that the dove brought back to Noah as a sign that the waters of the Flood were finally receding (Genesis 8:11). "We are now not armed for war, but approach the reverend towers of the old cathedral with an olive branch in our hands." (Anthony Trollope, *Barchester Towers,* 1857).

Oliver *See* ROLAND.

Olympia; Olympiad *See* OLYMPIC GAMES.

Olympian (ălimpeeăn) Godlike; majestic; superior; aloof. According to Greek mythology the home of the gods (sometimes called the Twelve Olympians) was located on the snowy summit of ***Mount Olympus*** in northern Greece, hidden from human sight by clouds. Here the gods lived in wonderful palaces and held meetings in a great council chamber or were entertained by the Muses with the lyre and song. "I think I shall have a lofty throne for you, godmamma, or rather two, one on the lawn and another in the ballroom, that you may sit and look down upon us like an Olympian goddess" (George Eliot, *Adam Bede,* 1859). *See also* OLYMPIC GAMES.

Olympic Games (ălĭmpĭk) International athletics competition held every two years, alternating for summer sports and winter sports. The modern Olympic Games, first held in Athens in 1896, were modeled on the famous competitions held in ancient Greece, in which competitors from all over the Greek world participated in foot races, wrestling, boxing, and chariot racing, among other events. These contests took place on a plain on the west coast of the Peloponnesus, which included the sacred grove of Olympian Zeus, hence the region's name, *Olympia.* The victor was presented with a garland of wild olive branches taken from a sacred olive tree, and special privileges were confirmed upon the winners and their families. The four-year period between the ancient games was called an *Olympiad,* although this term is now taken to mean the whole festival of the games themselves. The modern games are now the most important event in the worldwide sporting calendar. Competitors and especially medalists are often referred to as *Olympians. Do you have to get up at five o'clock in the morning to train? After all, it's only a village fun run, not the Olympic Games! See also* MARATHON.

Olympus, Mount *See* OLYMPIAN.

omega *See* ALPHA AND OMEGA.

omphalos (omfălăs) A central point or source. The word means "navel" in Greek and in ancient times was the name of the oval stone in the temple of Apollo at Delphi that was supposed to mark the center of the earth. *As far as the professor was concerned his desk was the omphalos of his world, the place where his ideas became crystal, or, on bad days, burned to ashes.*

onanism (ōnănĭzăm) Coitus interruptus; masturbation. The word originated through reference to the biblical character Onan, who according to Genesis 38:1–10 found himself expected to take his brother's widow, Tamar, after the former died. This was in observance of the ruling that a man should support his brother's widow as a matter of duty if his brother had died without children. Reluctant to consummate the union out of respect for his brother, Onan "spilled his seed on the ground," hence the adoption of his name for the practice of coitus interruptus (and occasionally any other form of birth control) or masturbation. *The* *minister muttered something dark about the evils of onanism and excused himself hurriedly.*

on earth peace *See* GOODWILL TO ALL MEN.

one jot or tittle *See* JOT OR TITTLE.

one little ewe lamb *See* EWE LAMB.

only I am left *See* I ONLY AM LEFT.

on the horns of a dilemma *See* HORNS OF A DILEMMA.

on the shoulders of giants Profiting from the knowledge, discoveries, and insights of illustrious predecessors to make further progress, particularly in relation to scholarship. This expression comes from the epic poem *Pharsalia* by the Roman poet Lucan (A.D. 39–65): "Pygmies placed on the shoulders of giants see more than the giants themselves." Today the phrase is often associated with the English scientist Sir Isaac Newton (1642–1727), who quoted the line when praised for his achievements. *It must be remembered in this moment of triumph that this new young team has only gotten this far by climbing on the shoulders of giants.*

Ophir *See* GOLD OF OPHIR.

oracle A source of authoritative information, especially about the future. The concept of the oracle goes back to classical mythology and to the celebrated oracles at Delphi, Dodona, Oympia, and elsewhere. These shrines were consulted by pilgrims over the course of many centuries in the hope of receiving revelations from the gods about the future, usually delivered through the priestesses who attended these sites. The advice offered was typically obscure in content and capable of being interpreted in several different ways. Today the term *oracle* is variously applied to places, people, and branches of the media. Those who succeed against the odds in influencing the future in their favor, meanwhile, are people who **work the oracle.** *The man frowned and turned to consult the oracle, his wife. See also* DELPHIC.

order of Melchizedek *See* MELCHIZEDEK.

oread *See* NYMPH.

original sin A state of sin considered to be the innate condition of the whole human race since the FALL of Adam. In modern usage the phrase is sometimes used more loosely and may refer to a range of either fundamental or relatively trivial failings. "'Some people are naturally good, you know, and others are not. I'm one of the others. Mrs Lynde says I'm full of original sin.'" (Lucy Maud Montgomery, *Anne of Green Gables,* 1908).

Orion (ărīon) A constellation of stars near Canis Major. Supposedly resembling the figure of a giant with a belt of three stars representing a sword, a lion's skin, and a club, it takes its name from that of a Boeotian giant who was renowned as a hunter and according to Greek legend was raised to the stars after his death (in some accounts, slain by the goddess Artemis). *The alcohol had gone straight to her head, and she had to lie down in the grass, gazing up with bewilderment at distant Orion.*

Orpheus (orfeeăs) An archetype of a master musician. Orpheus, the son of Apollo and Calliope, was a Thracian lyre player who was instructed in music by the Muses and became so fine a musician he could enchant wild beasts and even rocks and trees with his playing. He sailed with the Argonauts but faced his sternest test when he attempted to retrieve his wife, *Eurydice,* from the underworld after she died from a snakebite. Having played his lyre to Hades, it was agreed that he could have Eurydice providing he did not look back to see her as they returned to the world above. Unfortunately Orpheus could not resist the temptation to see if this wife was following him, and Eurydice was promptly returned to the underworld. Grief at this loss left Orpheus embittered toward other women, and ultimately he met his own end when he was torn to pieces by the women of Thrace in a Bacchanalian frenzy after he offended them. His skill as a musician is still remembered, and the adjective *orphean* denotes anything melodious or enchanting. *After the concert the critics hailed him as a veritable Orpheus.*

ostracism The practice of deliberately excluding someone from a particular group, society, etc., after he or she has committed a perceived offense of some kind. The word has its origins in the customs of the ancient Greeks. In order to protect their democratic system from tyrants it was possible once a year for Greek citizens to name the one person they wished to see exiled from Athens for being too powerful or ambitious. The "ballots" were written on shards of broken pottery (in Greek, *ostrakon*) and then counted. The person with the most votes was obliged to go into exile for at least 10 years. The custom fell into disuse after 417 B.C., when two mistrusted politicians, Alcibiades and Nicias, combined to avoid being ostracized and instead secured the ostracism of their harshest critic, Hyperbolus. Persons thus exiled were not considered disgraced, but the word in its modern usage necessarily casts a pall of shame over the person concerned. "He said to himself that she was too light and childish, too uncultivated and unreasoning, too provincial, to have reflected upon her ostracism, or even to have perceived it" (Henry James, *Daisy Miller,* 1879).

our daily bread *See* DAILY BREAD.

Our Father *See* PATERNOSTER.

outer darkness The most distant darkness, as a judgment for those who reject the light of God's truth. The phrase is biblical in origin, appearing in Matthew 8:12 in the words of Christ himself: "But the children of the kingdom shall be cast into outer darkness." (See also Matthew 22:13 and 25:30.) ". . . and the Chief priest of Corporate Affairs demanded of the Lord High Editor that the poor scribe who inhabiteth the back page be cast into the outer darkness" (Alan Williams, *Modern Railways,* May 2001). *See also* WEEPING AND GNASHING OF TEETH.

out-Herod Herod (herud) To outmatch someone in something, especially in cruelty. The allusion is to Herod the Great (c. 37–4 B.C.), the ruler of Judaea who ordered all the male infants of Bethlehem put to death in an attempt to secure the death of the newly born Christ (Matthew 2:16–18). It was William Shakespeare, in his play *Hamlet* (c. 1601), who first employed the phrase: "I would have such a fellow whipped for o'erdoing Termagant: it out-herods Herod: pray you, avoid it." "James' wish to learn as many languages as possible may well have been fired by the desire to out-Leyden Leyden" (K. M. Elisabeth Murray, *Caught in the Web of Words,* 1979).

out of the ark *See* ARK.

out of the eater came forth meat *See* OUT OF THE STRONG CAME FORTH SWEETNESS.

out of the abundance of the heart the mouth speaks People cannot resist talking about the things that most preoccupy them. The proverb has biblical origins, appearing at Matthew 12:34: "O generation of vipers, how can ye, being evil, speak good things? for out of the abundance of the heart the mouth speaketh." Also encountered in the variant form.

out of the fullness of the heart the mouth speaks. *She guessed her mother had promised not to say anything, but out of the fullness of the heart the mouth speaks.*

out of the mouths of babes and sucklings Children often recognize—and voice—truths that older, more experienced people do not perceive. The proverb is biblical in origin, appearing at Psalm 8:2 as "Out of the mouth of babes and sucklings hath thou ordained strength" and at Matthew 21:16 as "Yea; have ye never read, Out of the mouth of babes and sucklings thou hast perfected praise?" The fuller version of the phrase is usually given as *out of the mouths of babes and sucklings come great truths.* A variant runs *from the mouths of babes come words of wisdom.* "There was something fantastic to him in this sudden philosophising by one whom he had watched grow up from a tiny thing. Out of the mouths of babes and sucklings—sometimes!" (John Galsworthy, *The Forsyte Saga,* 1922).

out of the strong came forth sweetness Sweet and gentle things can come from the unlikeliest sources. The allusion is to the riddle posed by Samson and related at Judges 14:5–10. Having killed a lion with his own hands and subsequently seeing a swarm of bees in the carcass, Samson challenged the Philistine guests at a wedding feast to solve the riddle implicit in the statement "Out of the eater came forth meat, and out of the strong came forth sweetness" (Judges 14:14). The solution (given to the Philistines by Samson's wife) lies in the eater being the lion and the sweetness being the honey produced by the bees. *It was a surprise when the author of this tender love poem turned out to be the grizzled old cowboy in the corner, but then out of the strong came forth sweetness.*

out-Timon Timon *See* TIMON.

oxen of Geryon *See* LABORS OF HERCULES.

O ye of little faith Expression of lamentation at another's lack of confidence in something, especially when his or her doubts have been proved groundless. The phrase is biblical in origin, appearing in Matthew 6:30, which reads: "Wherefore, if God so clothe the grass of the field, which to day is, and to morrow is cast into the oven, shall he not much more clothe you, O ye of little faith?" *You didn't think we would get here on time, did you, O ye of little faith.*

paean (<u>pee</u>ăn) A song or other expression of praise. The original paeans were composed in honor of the Greek god Apollo, whose alternative titles included Paian, a name denoting his status as physician to the gods. Other words from the same root include the flower name *peony,* the blooms of which were formerly prized for their medicinal properties. "This quickly took us out of range of Red-Eye, and the last we saw of him was far out on a point of land, where he was jumping up and down and chanting a paean of victory" (Jack London, *Before Adam,* 1907).

painted Jezebel *See* JEZEBEL.

palace guard *See* PRAETORIAN GUARD.

paladin (<u>pal</u>ădin) A defender or champion of a particular cause. The original paladins were the 12 legendary heroes who fought for the emperor CHARLEMAGNE (742–814), ruler of the Franks and Holy Roman Emperor. They represented the highest ideals of chivalry and were prepared to die in the struggle against wrong. "Edricson and Terlake rode behind him in little better case, while Ford, a careless and light-hearted youth, grinned at the melancholy of his companions, and flourished his lord's heavy spear, making a point to right and a point to left, as though he were a paladin contending against a host of assailants" (Sir Arthur Conan Doyle, *The White Company,* 1891). *See also* ROLAND.

Palamedes (pal<u>ă</u>meedeez) An ingenious person. According to Greek legend Palamedes was a Greek commander who persuaded the reluctant ODYSSEUS to join the campaign against Troy. Odysseus had feigned madness in order to excuse himself from going, demonstrating his insanity by yoking an ox and a horse to his plow and using them to plow the sand with salt. Palamedes cleverly tricked him into betraying his true state of mind by placing Odysseus's son, Telemachus, in the path of the plow, obliging Odysseus to change course and thus reveal his mastery of his senses. Odysseus eventually got his revenge by framing Palamedes for treachery and having him stoned to death. Other alleged proofs of the ingenuity of Palamedes included his invention of four letters of the Greek alphabet as well as of the lighthouse, scales, measures, discus, and dice. *Even as a research student he established a reputation of being quite a Palamedes.*

Palinurus (pali<u>noo</u>răs) A pilot, especially one who is careless or irresponsible. In Roman myth and Virgil's *Aeneid,* Palinurus served as helmsman under Aeneas but was washed overboard after he fell asleep and was murdered when he reached land three days later. *Like Palinurus, our pilot was more concerned with his own comfort than he seemed to be with the safety of the vessel.*

palladium (pă<u>lay</u>deeăm) A safeguard; something that gives protection. The original Palladium was a wooden statue of Pallas Athena supposedly thrown out of heaven by Zeus and retrieved by the Trojans. Tradition had it that the safety of Troy depended on the protection of this statue. It was eventually stolen by Odysseus and Diomedes, and the city fell to the Greeks. In modern usage the term is typically applied to freedom of speech or something else that is considered a guarantee of the safety of a country or constitution. *This measure will act to some degree as a palladium against further encroachments.*

Pan (pan) Personification of disorder and licentiousness. According to Greek mythology, Pan was a nature god who protected flocks and the shepherds who tended them but who also enjoyed tormenting wanderers in the forests and woods where he roamed (see PANIC). He was usually depicted with horns and goats' feet, attributes that were subsequently passed on to the devil of Christian lore. "Of the rushing couples there could barely be discerned more than the high lights—the indistinctness shaping them to satyrs clasping nymphs—a multiplicity of Pans whirling a multiplicity of Syrinxes" (Thomas Hardy, *Tess of the D'Urbervilles,* 1891). *See also* PANPIPES.

panacea (panăseeă) A universal remedy or cure. The word alludes to Panacea, the daughter of Aesculapius, the Greek god of medicine and healing. "This was a relief to Mrs. Peniston, who could give herself up to her own symptoms, and Lily was advised to go and lie down, her aunt's panacea for all physical and moral disorders" (Edith Wharton, *The House of Mirth,* 1905).

Pandora's box (pandorăz) A source of manifold unforeseen difficulties that once released are hard to bring back under control. The phrase alludes to Greek mythology and the legend of the beautiful Pandora, the first woman, and the box or jar she possessed containing all the problems that if unleashed would lead to the downfall of humanity. She was instructed to entrust this box to the man she married. One legend has it that Pandora (whose name means "all gifts") opened the box out of curiosity to see what was inside, while another has her eventual husband, Epimetheus, opening it against her advice. In either event the box was opened, and the human race has since been beset by a multiplicity of sorrows and problems. Only hope remained within. "We unlock the genetic code and open a Pandora's box of ethics" (Philip Yancey, *Reaching for the Invisible God,* 2000).

panem et circenses *See* BREAD AND CIRCUSES.

panic A feeling of terror, anxiety, and confusion. The word is Greek in origin, referring to the god PAN, the lecherous god of forests and shepherds who was notorious for playing tricks on travelers in valleys and mountains, typically by springing out on them unexpectedly or by making menacing noises in the undergrowth. Any sensation of fear welling up for no apparent reason came to be dubbed *panikos,* hence the modern word, which completed its journey to English via the French *panique* around the early 18th century. *Panic spread quickly through the crowd as news of the executions passed from one person to another.*

Panoptes *See* ARGUS.

panpipes A musical wind instrument consisting of various reeds of different lengths bound together. It was named after the Greek nature god Pan, who is supposed to have devised the instrument. The legend goes that Pan pursued the nymph Syrinx, but she escaped from him by hiding in the earth and being turned into reeds, from which the thwarted Pan made his set of pipes. Panpipes may also be known as *pipes of Pan* or as a *syrinx*. *He sat on the ground blowing softly into a set of panpipes and eyeing her quizzically.*

pantheon (pantheeon, pantheeăn) A group of distinguished or revered individuals. In ancient Greece and Rome the Pantheon (from the Greek meaning "all of the gods") was a temple dedicated to the gods collectively. The famous pantheon in Rome was built by the emperor Hadrian in the second century A.D., incorporating an older structure built by Agrippa in 27 B.C., and became a Christian church in 609. In due course the term came to be applied to all the gods collectively of any religion and thus to any group of outstanding individuals, especially to national heroes and memorials built in their honor. "How will the demi-gods in your Pantheon—I mean those legendary persons you call saints—intercede for you after this?" (Thomas Hardy, *Jude the Obscure,* 1895).

Paphian (payfeeăn) A prostitute. The word originally meant "relating to Venus" and came about as an allusion to the city of Paphos on Cyprus, where Venus, the Roman goddess of love, was worshiped. *A Paphian by trade, she became a popular figure in high society, though heartily disliked by other women.*

parable of the sower Story illustrating the point that there are various responses to God's word. The parable is related in Mark 4:3–9: "Hearken; Behold, there went out a sower to sow; And it came to pass, as he sowed, some fell by the way side, and the fowls of the air came and devoured it up. And some fell on stony ground, where it had not much earth; and immediately it sprang up, because it had no depth of earth: But when the sun was up, it was scorched; and because it had no root, it withered away. And some fell among thorns, and the thorns grew up, and choked it, and it yielded no fruit. And other fell on good ground, and did yield fruit that sprang up and increased; and brought forth, some thirty, and some sixty, and some an hundred. And he said unto them, He that hath ears to hear, let him hear." Jesus explains the parable in verses 13–20. Perhaps a better name would be the parable of the soils: The same seed is sown in different soils. Some seed *falls by the wayside,* analogous to the word immediately being taken away by Satan. Some seed falls on stony ground and so does not take root, like those who receive the word gladly but quickly fall away when times become difficult. Other seed falls among thorns, which choke the growth of the plants, much like those for whom "the cares of this world, and the deceitfulness of riches, and the lusts of other things" (verse 19) come in and kill off the growth. But in the final case seed falls on good ground where people hear and receive the word and are greatly fruitful and productive. *The story graphically illustrated the truth behind the biblical parable of the sower.* See also FALL BY THE WAYSIDE; FALL ON STONY GROUND.

parable of the talents Story emphasizing the belief that all people will be judged at the Last Judgment according to the life each has led. The parable is related by Christ in Matthew 25:14–30, which compares the behavior of three servants after their master entrusts to each a sum of money. (A talent was originally a measure of weight and later a unit of coinage.) Two of the men invest the money sensibly, earning a considerable amount of interest, while the third hides the money in the ground and returns no more than the sum that was entrusted to him in the first place. On his return the master congratulates the two who have used the money wisely and rebukes the third for doing nothing with it, the moral being that God-given opportunities and talents should be faithfully used. *Then began the usual secular imitation of the parable of the talents with each of the candidates being questioned in detail about their previous employment history.*

parable of the wheat and tares Story illustrating the point that God allows good and evil to coexist. The parable is related in Matthew 13:25–30 and 13:36–43, where workers are told not to remove tares, or weeds, sown by the enemy. Jesus explains that the field is the world and the wheat, or "good seeds," are the children of the kingdom. The enemy is the devil, and the weeds are the children of the evil one. This parable illustrates the point that God allows good and evil to coexist, although eventually justice will be done and evil will be destroyed. *"'I hope there will be more wheat and fewer tares every years,' said Amy softly"* (Louisa May Alcott, *Little Women,* 1868–69).

parable of the wise and foolish virgins Story illustrating the difference between those who are farsighted and prepared and those who are improvident and unprepared. This parable, recorded in the Bible in Matthew 25:1–13, describes the wedding custom of the day. The bridegroom went in the evening to the bride's home to collect her, followed by a procession to his home, lit by torch-bearing friends. In the story, the bridegroom was late and the torchbearers, all virgins, fell asleep. When the groom arrived, five foolish virgins did not have enough oil to relight their lamps and went to buy more, later being refused entry to the celebrations. Five wise virgins were prepared, however: They had brought extra oil. Jesus explained that people should be alert and ready for him when he returns at the end of the age. ". . . a little food, enough to keep us for three or four days if necessary, together with some matches and a good supply of oil, since, as Bastin put it, he was determined not to be caught like the foolish virgins in the parable" (H. Rider Haggard, *When the World Shook,* 1919).

paradise Heaven or any idyllic place or condition in which a person's desires or aspirations are fully realized. The word comes from the Greek *paradeisos,* meaning "garden" or "park," and appears in the Old Testament in descriptions of the GARDEN OF EDEN (Genesis 2:8) and in the New Testament as a synonym for the Christian heaven (Luke 23:43; 2 Corinthians 12:4; and Revelation 2:7). *The new mall is a paradise for shoppers.*

Parcae *See* FATES.

Paris (paris) Archetype of a beautiful young man. Paris, the second son of King Priam of Troy, played a pivotal role in bringing about the Trojan War by carrying off Helen, the wife of Menelaus, and thus causing the Greeks to lay siege to the city. When Troy finally fell, Paris was wounded by Philoctetes, who returned him to his wife, Oenone. She refused to heal Paris's grievous wound, so he returned to Troy, where he died before a repentant Oenone could reach him. Overcome with grief, Oenone hanged herself. *The general's son was as beautiful as Paris and as cantankerous as Donald Duck. See also* JUDGMENT OF PARIS.

Parnassian (pahrnaseeăn) Of or relating to literature, especially poetry. The term alludes to **Mount Parnassus,** the mountain in central Greece that was held sacred to Apollo and the MUSES, who inspired artistic and creative enterprise. The term came to be particularly associated with a school of French poets, headed by Charles-Marie-René Leconte de Lisle, that flourished toward the end of the 19th century. The phrase to *climb Parnassus* means to write poetry. "Such a concert of treble voices uttering accents like these had not been heard since the great Temperance Festival with the celebrated 'colation' in the open air under the trees of the Parnassian Grove,—as the place was christened by the young ladies of the Institute" (Oliver Wendell Holmes, *Elsie Venner,* 1861).

Parthian shot (p̲a̲h̲rheeăn) A parting shot; a final hostile remark, glance, or gesture made on departure. The expression alludes to the practice of Parthian archers, who carried on firing arrows behind them even as they retreated. The Parthians were a nomadic Persian race. They developed the tactic of avoiding a direct confrontation when outnumbered, instead relying on their skill as mounted archers to make an impression on their enemy. *As he left he could not resist firing one last Parthian shot at his rival in the form of a taunt about the latter's sense of humor.*

parting of the Red Sea *See* CROSSING OF THE RED SEA.

pass all understanding To be difficult to understand. The phrase is a quotation from Philippians 4:7: "And the peace of God, which passeth all understanding, shall keep your hearts and minds through Christ Jesus." *The professor's explanation of the theory of relativity passed all understanding, and we understood little more about the subject when he had finished than we did when we came in.*

pass by on the other side *See* GOOD SAMARITAN.

paternoster A set form of words recited as a prayer or charm. The word comes from the Latin *pater noster* (meaning "Our Father"), the opening words of the Lord's Prayer and an alternate name for the recitation, which appear in Matthew 6:9 and Luke 11:2. *She recited the rhyme every morning, a personal paternoster of her own invention.*

patience of Job (jōb) Endless patience in the face of great difficulty or suffering. Job's patience despite the manifold disasters that God inflicted

on him in order to test his faith (as related in the book of Job) is proverbial and is referred to in James 5:11. *These threads are so tangled that whoever
unravels them will need the patience of Job.*

patrician Aristocratic; fatherly. The word comes from the Latin *patres,*
meaning "fathers," a title reserved for the senators of Rome and their families to distinguish them from the more humble populace (see PLEBEIAN).
"Sir Leicester receives the gout as a troublesome demon, but still a demon
of the patrician order" (Charles Dickens, *Bleak House,* 1852–53).

Patroclus *See* ACHILLES AND PATROCLUS.

Paul *See* ROAD TO DAMASCUS.

pax (paks) Peace; truce. In Roman mythology Pax was the goddess of
peace, equivalent to the Greek IRENE. She was often depicted by the Romans
holding an olive branch, a symbol of peace or reconciliation still familiar
today. *The younger lad called out "Pax," and the fight came to an abrupt end.*

peace, goodwill toward men *See* GOODWILL TO ALL MEN.

peace for the wicked, no *See* NO PEACE FOR THE WICKED.

peacemakers, blessed are the *See* BEATITUDE.

peace of God which passeth all understanding *See* PASS ALL UNDERSTANDING.

pearl of great price Something of great value or importance. The phrase
is biblical in origin, appearing in Matthew 13:45–46 in one of Christ's
parables describing the value of spiritual riches: "Again, the kingdom of
heaven is like unto a merchant man, seeking goodly pearls: Who, when he
had found one pearl of great price, went and sold all that he had, and
bought it." *Government contracts are pearls of great price, and competition for
them is usually intense.*

pearls before swine Something good or valuable that is offered to or in the
possession of a person who cannot appreciate it. The expression comes

from Matthew 7:6: "Give not that which is holy unto the dogs, neither cast ye your pearls before swine, lest they trample them under their feet, and turn again and rend you." "Against establishment predictions—polite variants on the theme 'pearls before swine'—the project worked, and still flourishes" (*Guardian,* September 12, 2001).

pearly gates The entrance to heaven or, more loosely, heaven itself. The gates of the Christian heaven are described in Revelation 21:21: "And the twelve gates were twelve pearls; every several gate was of one pearl: and the street of the city was pure gold, as it were transparent glass." *She expressed the hope that by the time she came to appear before the pearly gates of heaven, she would be reconciled with her daughter.*

pedagogue (pĕdăgog) A teacher, especially one that is pedantic or dogmatic. In ancient Greece a *pedagogos* (meaning "boy leader") was a slave who was required to accompany the children of his master whenever they left their home. "Their children from earliest childhood / Grew up together as brother and sister; and Father Felician / Priest and pedagogue both in the village, had taught them their letters / Out of the selfsame book, with the hymns of the church and the plain-song" (Henry Longfellow, *Evangeline,* 1849).

Pegasus (pegăsăs) Archetypal flying horse; any speedy mount, animate or mechanized. In Greek mythology Pegasus was a winged horse that arose from the blood of MEDUSA when Perseus cut off her head. The Corinthian hero Bellerophon, with the aid of Athena, managed to catch Pegasus, mount him, and kill the CHIMERA, but when Bellerophon tried to fly on Pegasus to heaven, he fell off and was lamed. Pegasus carried on upward, however, and became a constellation. Another tradition has it that the spring of the Hippocrene on Mount Helicon poured forth where Pegasus had struck a hoof, and hence Pegasus has always been linked with the MUSES, who dwelled on Mount Helicon. Thus to **mount Pegasus** means to embark on creative or artistic work. *He bestrode the motorbike as if it was Pegasus and the front wheel reared up in the air as he twisted the throttle.*

Peleus *See* APPLE OF DISCORD.

Pelion *See* PILE PELION ON OSSA.

Pelops *See* IVORY SHOULDER OF PELOPS.

penalty of Adam *See* ADAM'S CURSE.

penates *See* LARES AND PENATES.

Penelope (penelăpee) Archetype of the dutiful, loyal wife and the personification of patience. In Greek mythology Penelope is the wife of ODYSSEUS, king of Ithaca, who waited patiently at home while he was absent fighting in the Trojan War. After 10 years of warfare Odysseus set off for home but was delayed by the gods, and it was another decade before husband and wife were reunited. In the meantime Penelope had to resist the advances of more than 100 suitors and their insistent demands that she marry one of them. In order to appease them she promised to marry one of them once she had finished weaving a shroud for her father-in-law. The suitors reluctantly agreed to this proposal, unaware of the fact that each night Penelope unwove the threads she had worked on during the day so that the shroud was no nearer being complete. A *web of Penelope* is therefore a metaphor for a task that has no end. Fortunately for Penelope, just as the patience of the 100 suitors was wearing out, Odysseus arrived home and slaughtered all rivals for his wife's hand. "Whatever I see you doing, you're not really there: you are waiting—like Penelope when she did her weaving" (D.H. Lawrence, *Sons and Lovers,* 1913).

Penthesilea (penthăsileeă) A strong, commanding woman. According to Greek mythology Penthesilea was the daughter of Ares and the queen of the AMAZONs, whom she led to the aid of the Trojans after the death of Hector. She died in combat with Achilles, who lamented over the death of such a good-looking, courageous woman. *She is the Penthesilea of the Democratic Party.*

peony *See* PAEAN.

peri (peeree) A beautiful girl. In Persian mythology a peri was a malevolent spirit who attacked crops and caused eclipses, among other disastrous acts. They were subsequently depicted in the Qur'an and elsewhere as gentle creatures resembling fairies. ". . . and then, how delightfully refreshing is the sight, when, perhaps, some ex-member, hurled from his paradise like a fallen peri, reveals the secret of that pure heaven" (Anthony Trollope, *Doctor Thorne,* 1858).

Periclean (periklĕeăn) Wise; eloquent; honest. The word refers to the respected Athenian statesman and soldier Pericles (c. 500–429 B.C.), who assumed the reins of power in 460 and oversaw a golden era in Athenian democracy and the arts. Important achievements under his leadership included the building of the Parthenon. Typical of the stories about his integrity, on his death it was reported that he had not enriched himself beyond what he had inherited by a single drachma. *His last speech to the Senate was typically Periclean.*

Persephone (persefănee) Personification of the cycle of the seasons. In Greek mythology Persephone (***Proserpina*** to the Romans) was identified as the daughter of Zeus and Demeter and was snatched away to the underworld to be the wife of Hades, the lord of the dead. Zeus eventually gave in to the distraught Demeter's requests for her return, but Persephone had disregarded the instruction not to eat anything while in the underworld (as this would bind her there forever) and eaten the seeds of a pomegranate. As a compromise it was agreed that Persephone would be allowed back to the living world for part of the year but would have to return to Hades for the remaining months. Her arrival in the upper world is heralded by the coming of spring, while her return to Hades marks the beginning of winter. *Persephone had scattered spring flowers through the meadow.*

Perseus (perseeăs) Archetype of the classical hero. In Greek mythology Perseus is the central character in a number of heroic episodes, including the killing and cutting off the head of MEDUSA and the rescue of ANDROMEDA, who became his wife. He was also a model ruler of Argos and Tiryns and was credited with the foundation of Mycenae. *He felt like Perseus facing Medusa, undaunted but unable to look directly at the danger that threatened him.*

phaeton (fayătăn) A light, four-wheeled horsedrawn carriage with two seats. In Greek mythology Phaëthon (or Phaëton) was identified as the son of the sun god Helios (or Apollo), although elsewhere he was also described as MEROPS'S SON (referring to King Merops of Ethiopia). Phaëthon decided to try his hand at steering his father's chariot—the sun—across the sky and very nearly set fire to the Earth by flying too close. As it was, Libya was reduced to a parched desert while the rest of Africa was similarly scorched. The earth was saved from further damage when Zeus killed Phaëthon with a thunderbolt. The swan is sometimes called **Phaeton's bird** in commemoration of Cycnus, son of Neptune, who was inconsolable after the death of his friend Phaëthon and was eventually transformed into a swan by Apollo and placed among the constellations. "From the drawing room they could distinguish nothing in the lane, and were indebted to Mr Collins for the knowledge of what carriages went along, and how often especially Miss De Bourgh drove by in her phaeton, which he never failed coming to inform them of, though it happened almost every day" (Jane Austen, *Pride and Prejudice,* 1813).

phalanx (faylanks) A closely ranked, unyielding mass of people; a body of people united in a common cause. The name was originally given to an ancient Greek and Macedonian battle formation in which spearsmen sheltered behind a wall of shields. "I feel that I can face an army with banners—or all the professors of Redmond in one fell phalanx—with a chum like Priscilla by my side" (Lucy Maud Montgomery, *Anne of the Island,* 1915).

Pharisee (fairăsee) A self-righteous or hypocritical person, especially one who insists on legalistically and slavishly observing rules, regardless of the intent behind them. The Pharisees (a name meaning "separated") were members of a Jewish sect that emerged in the second century B.C. "Despite their original emphasis on God's law, or Torah, their insistence on equal prominence for oral law and their emphasis on human behavior rather than God's work brought them into conflict with Jesus. Jesus accused some Pharisees of being hypocrites because their teaching was inconsistent with their actions" (Selman and Manser, *The Hearthside Bible Dictionary,* p. 184). Jesus denounced them in the "seven woes" (Matthew 23:1–36). "Woe unto you, scribes and Pharisees, hypocrites! For ye are like unto whited sepulchres, which indeed appear beautiful outward, but are within full of dead men's bones, and of all uncleanness. Even so you also outwardly appear righteous unto men, but within ye are full of hypocrisy and iniquity" (Matthew 23:27). "But he's got tongue enough to speak disrespectful about's neebors, for he said as I was a blind Pharisee—a-usin' the Bible i' that way to find nick-names for folks as are his elders an' betters!—and what's worse, he's been heard to say very unbecomin' words about Your Reverence" (George Eliot, *Adam Bede,* 1859).

pharos (faírus) A lighthouse or beacon. The name comes from that of the small island off the Egyptian coast where Ptolemy II (308–246 B.C.) built a lighthouse made of white marble, subsequently included among the seven wonders of the ancient world. The lighthouse was destroyed in an earthquake in 1375. *The fleet was guided by the light of a pharos marking the entrance to the bay.* See also EIGHTH WONDER OF THE WORLD.

pheasant A long-tailed bird of the family Phasianidae, the males of which have brightly colored plumage. The bird's name means "bird of the Phasis," the Phasis being the classical name for a river of Colchis, the present-day Rioni River, which flows into the Black Sea. Legend has it that pheasants originated from that area and were brought elsewhere by the Argonauts. *A white pheasant stalked imperiously back and forth in front of the house.*

Pheidippides *See* MARATHON.

Philemon and Baucis (fǎleemǎn, fíleemǎn; bahsis) Archetypes of the generous, welcoming host. According to Greek legend Philemon and Baucis were an aged and impoverished Phrygian couple who welcomed the disguised Zeus and Hermes into their home after other richer people had turned the gods away. In gratitude the two deities saved the couple from a flood, turned their home into a temple, and granted their desire that neither of them should outlive the other. When the couple died, the gods transformed Philemon into an oak and Baucis into a linden tree, and their branches entwined. *Like Philemon and Baucis, the couple threw their door open to the strangers, beckoning them to come inside without delay.*

philippic (fǎlipik) An impassioned denunciation of an enemy; a bitter tirade. The word refers to the three scathing speeches made by the celebrated Athenian orator Demosthenes (384–322 B.C.) to bolster resistance against the threats posed to Athenian democracy by Philip II of Macedon (hence the "Philippics"). Philip intended to absorb Athens into his kingdom and, despite the efforts of Demosthenes, eventually succeeded in this ambition after defeating the Greeks at the Battle of Chaeronea in 338. In 322 the Macedonian ruler Antipater planned to kidnap Demosthenes but was thwarted when his quarry escaped to the island of Calauria and committed suicide there before another attempt to capture him could be made. The word was subsequently applied to Cicero's attacks *(Philippics)* on Mark Antony in 44 and 43 B.C. and thereby entered into general usage. "The talk, as usual, had veered around to the Beauforts, and even Mr. van der Luyden and Mr. Selfridge Merry, installed in the honorary arm-chairs tacitly reserved for them, paused to listen to the younger man's philippic" (Edith Wharton, *The Age of Innocence,* 1920). *See also* APPEAL FROM PHILIP DRUNK TO PHILIP SOBER; DEMOSTHENIC.

philistine (filăstīn) An uncultured, ignorant person. The original Philistines were a warlike non-Semitic people who in biblical times inhabited ancient Philistia in close and often hostile proximity to the Hebrews. Individual Philistines to attract special criticism included the giant GOLIATH (1 Samuel 17) and the seductive DELILAH (Judges 16). The term was subsequently taken up as a reference to any enemy and ultimately to individuals or societies perceived as lacking any cultural sophistication or intellectual enthusiasm. It was first used in its modern sense by university students in 17th-century Germany, who applied it to townsfolk who lacked a similar education, calling them "Philisters." It was transmitted to English through the writings of Matthew Arnold (1822–88), who applied it specifically to bourgeois opponents of art and literature. Archaeological finds suggest, however, that ancient Philistine society was not as brutish and materialistic as Hebrew writings suggest, and Philistine pottery in particular has been much admired. They were also skilled architects and metalworkers and apparently had well-developed political and commercial structures. "But clearly Anthony was no diplomatist. His brother-in-law must have appeared to him, to use the language of shore people, a perfect philistine with a heart like a flint" (Joseph Conrad, *Chance,* 1913).

Phintias *See* DAMON AND PYTHIAS.

phobia (fŏbeĕ) An obsessive, often irrational fear of something. The word is Greek in origin and alludes to Phobos, a son of Ares and Aphrodite and the Greek god of dread and alarm. Somewhat ironically he was conventionally depicted with the head of a lion. *His sister developed a phobia of snakes and ever after refused to go anywhere near the reptile house at the zoo.*

Phoebe (feebee) Personification of the Moon. Phoebe was identified in Greek mythology as the goddess of the moon and as one of the Titans, by whom Zeus sired Apollo and Artemis. *She uttered a brief prayer to Phoebe before slipping down into the moonlit street.*

Phoebus (feebăs) Literary name for the Sun. In Greek mythology the sun god Apollo was sometimes referred to by the name Phoebus (meaning "bright" or "shining one"). "He must have passed Mr Rugg on his way out, for, a minute or two afterwards, that ruddy-headed gentleman shone in at the door, like an elderly Phoebus" (Charles Dickens, *Little Dorrit,* 1855–57).

phoenix (feeniks) Something that rises anew in the face of defeat or adversity. This legendary bird appears in the mythology of ancient Egypt, ancient Greece, and early Christianity and was widely considered a symbol of immortality and life after death. According to most traditions the phoenix resembled an eagle, with gold and scarlet feathers, and lived for about 500 years. When the time came for it to die, it lay down on a pyre and allowed itself to be burned in the flames. It then emerged renewed from the ashes, hence the expression a *phoenix rising from the ashes.* ". . . and there she is with her plumage unruffled, as glossy as ever, unable to get old:—a sort of Phoenix free from the slightest signs of ashes and dust, all complacent amongst those inanities as if there had been nothing else in the world" (Joseph Conrad, *The Arrow of Gold,* 1919).

Phrynean (frīneeăn) Of or relating to a prostitute. Phryne was a famous and very wealthy Greek courtesan who lived in the fourth century B.C. Her beauty was widely admired, and she is supposed to have been the model for many celebrated statues. It is said she made so much money that she offered to pay for the rebuilding of the walls of Thebes. "Her underclothes are positively Phrynean" (Aldous Huxley, *Point Counter Point,* 1928).

physician, heal thyself Do not criticize others when you are guilty of the same failings; refrain from tackling the problems of others before you have dealt with your own difficulties first. The proverb is of biblical origin and is spoken by Christ to the people in the synagogue in Nazareth: "Ye will surely say unto me this proverb, Physician, heal thyself: whatsoever we have heard done in Capernaum, do also here in thy country" (Luke 4:23). "How can a man . . . teach sobriety or cleanliness, if he be himself drunken or foul? 'Physician, heal thyself,' is the answer of his neighbours" (Samuel Smiles, *Thrift,* 1875).

Pierian spring (pīereeǎn) Inspiration or learning. According to Greek mythology the Pierian spring lay on the slopes of Mount Olympus and was sacred to the MUSES. It was said that anyone who drank from the spring would enjoy wisdom or inspiration. "A little learning is a dangerous thing; / Drink deep, or taste not the Pierian spring" (Alexander Pope, *Essay on Criticism,* 1711).

pigmy *See* PYGMY.

Pilate's wife (pīlǎtz) A person who claims to have learned something important from a dream. In the New Testament the wife of PONTIUS PILATE discussed with her husband a distressing dream she had just had, warning him that he should avoid any involvement with the trial of Christ, who was about to be brought before his court: "Have thou nothing to do with that just man: for I have suffered many things this day in a dream because of him" (Matthew 27:19). *Like Pilate's wife, she urged him not to take this journey. She had dreamed that he lay in a white coffin.*

Pilate washed his hands *See* PONTIUS PILATE; WASH ONE'S HANDS OF.

pile Pelion on Ossa (peeleeǎn, ahsǎ) To heap difficulty upon difficulty or embarrassment upon embarrassment. The expression has its roots in Greek mythology and the legend of the GIANTS who tried to climb up to heaven by piling the mountain Pelion on top of Mount Ossa, in eastern Thessaly. *Then, piling Pelion on Ossa, the news came through that the date for the completion of the project had been moved forward by two weeks.*

pillar of fire A revelatory sign that serves as a guide to show the way. The allusion is to the biblical story of the pillar of fire—a *pillar of cloud* by day—set up by God to guide the Israelites out of the wilderness on their flight from Egypt, as related in Exodus 13:21–22. "You are unjust to women in England. And till you count what is a shame in a woman to be an infamy in a man, you will always be unjust, and Right, that pillar of fire, and Wrong, that pillar of cloud, will be made dim to your eyes, or be not seen at all, or if seen, not regarded" (Oscar Wilde, *A Woman of No Importance,* 1893). *See also* CLOUD BY DAY, PILLAR OF FIRE BY NIGHT.

pillar of salt *See* LOT'S WIFE.

pillars of Hercules (herkyooleez) The limits of the known world. In classical times the rocks on opposite sides of the entrance to the Mediterranean were called the Pillars of Hercules in allusion to the legend that Hercules separated them in order to reach Gades (modern Cádiz, in Spain). *Those two constellations are our pillars of Hercules, marking the extremes of the known universe.*

Pindaric verse (pindarik) A form of irregular verse characterized by its high-flown style. Such poetry, written in a variety of meters, was popularized by the English poet Abraham Cowley in the 17th century. Cowley mistakenly believed he was re-creating a form of verse composed by the celebrated Theban lyric poet Pindar (c. 522–443 B.C.). *There are few writers today who excel in the field of Pindaric verse.*

pipes of Pan *See* PANPIPES.

Pisgah *See* MOUNT PISGAH.

Piso's justice (pīsōz) Strictly correct but not in the spirit of justice, especially in relation to legal decisions. The phrase alludes to a story related by the Roman philosopher Seneca the Younger (c. 4 B.C.–A.D. 65) about a judge called Piso. Piso had condemned a prisoner to death on a charge of murder and delivered the man to a centurion for execution; however, the murder victim then appeared, and the centurion returned the prisoner to Piso. Piso responded by sentencing all three men to death, the prisoner on the grounds that he had already been sentenced, the centurion on the grounds that he had disobeyed his orders, and the supposed murder victim for causing the death of two innocent men. *It was generally agreed that this decision was harsh in the extreme, a good example of Piso's justice.*

pitch defiles *See* TOUCH PITCH AND BE DEFILED.

pit of the dragon *See* BOTTOMLESS PIT.

place of skulls *See* CALVARY.

plague of locusts A mob of people who eat or strip everything in sight. The allusion is to the biblical plague of locusts (Exodus 10:4–19), which was the eighth plague inflicted by God upon the Pharaoh of Egypt and led ultimately to the Exodus of the Jews. The locusts consumed all the food they could find. *The children descended upon the meal like a plague of locusts, and soon there was not a crumb remaining. See also* PLAGUES OF EGYPT.

plagues of Egypt (eejipt) The 10 disasters by which God punished the Egyptians for oppressing the Israelites and failing to acknowledge God's power (Exodus 7–12): the plague of water turned to blood, the plague of frogs, the plague of gnats, the plague of flies, the plague on livestock, the plague of boils, the plague of hail, the PLAGUE OF LOCUSTS, the plague of darkness (see EGYPTIAN DARKNESS; NINTH PLAGUE OF EGYPT), and the plague of the death of the firstborn. After the last plague, Pharaoh released the Israelites from bondage.

platonic (plătonik) Of or relating to a close, nonsexual relationship or more generally to any perfect, idealized vision or idea. Such a relationship, in which spiritual communion between individuals is believed superior to physical union, was first described by and thus named after the Greek philosopher Plato (c. 427–c. 347 B.C.) in his *Symposium* when he discussed the ideal relationship that his teacher Socrates had with the young men who studied under him. "The intimacy between them had been kept so abstract, such a matter of the soul, all thought and weary struggle into consciousness, that he saw it only as a platonic friendship" (D. H. Lawrence, *Sons and Lovers,* 1913). *See also* PLATO'S CAVE.

Plato's cave (pla̱ytōz) An image of the limits of human knowledge and perception. The phrase alludes to an allegory employed by the Greek philosopher Plato (c. 427–c. 347 B.C.) to illustrate how far removed ordinary perception is from a vision of ultimate reality. Plato propounded the image of some men chained in a cave in front of a fire so that all they could see were the shadows cast against the firelight: Knowing no better, they assumed the shadows were real. *For her it was like emerging into the sunlight of reality after years of being trapped in Plato's cave.*

play Cupid *See* CUPID.

plebeian (plebee̱ăn) Of or relating to the common people, the masses. The term was first adopted in ancient Rome to describe ordinary citizens, as opposed to slaves and citizens who made up the aristocracy (see PATRICIAN). "I believe you know how very much I dislike what are called family affairs, which are only fit for plebeian Christmas days, and have no manner of business with people of our condition" (Charles Dickens, *Barnaby Rudge,* 1841).

pleiad (plee̱ăd) A group of seven distinguished persons. The word comes from Greek mythology, specifically from the seven daughters of ATLAS, who were known as the Pleiades. The sisters were transformed into stars to protect them from pursuit by Orion or (according to another version) after they killed themselves in grief over the demise of their half sisters, the Hyades. The cluster of stars in the constellation of Taurus known as the Pleiades may, however, have gotten its name from the Greek *plein,* meaning "to sail," as sea conditions were generally calmer when this constellation was visible. *This pleiad of scientists has become the dominant influence in the field and threatens to revolutionize both theory and practice.*

plowshares *See* BEAT SWORDS INTO PLOWSHARES.

Pluto *See* HADES.

Plutus (plo̱otăs) Personification of wealth. In Greek mythology Plutus was the son of Demeter and was usually depicted as blind, dispensing wealth indiscriminately. He was also described as being lame, to represent the fact that rewards are slow to come, and with wings, because his gifts rapidly vanished. *She had become accustomed to spending much of her time in the realms of Plutus, eating at the Savoy and being driven everywhere in a chauffeured Rolls-Royce.*

Pluvius policy (plooveeăs) An insurance policy that offers coverage against a holiday being spoiled by wet weather. Pluvius was a surname sometimes given to JUPITER, the ruler of the Gods in Roman mythology. Jupiter was routinely worshiped as the giver of rain, upon which life depended. *The weather was so bad they promised that before they went away again they would check to see whether they could take out a Pluvius policy to compensate them if it happened again.*

Pollux *See* CASTOR AND POLLUX.

Polyhymnia *See* MUSES.

Polyphemus (pahlifeemăs) Archetype of a dim-witted brute; a Cyclops. In Greek mythology Polyphemus was a Sicilian Cyclops (see CYCLOPEAN) who fell in love with the nymph Galatea and, when she rejected him, killed her lover, Acis. According to Homer's ODYSSEY (c. 700 B.C.) Polyphemus took Odysseus and his men prisoner when they landed on Sicily and kept them in his cave with his sheep. In order to escape Odysseus put out Polyphemus's one eye with a sharpened stake and dressed his men in sheepskins so the blinded monster could not recognize them by touch. *The story of Odysseus and Polyphemus is a classic parable of superior intelligence and cunning outwitting brute force and stupidity.*

Pontius Pilate (ponshăs pīlăt) A person who is indifferent to cruelty or injustice as long as his or her own interests remain untouched; a person who refuses to take responsibility for his or her own actions; a hypocrite. Pontius Pilate was the Roman governor of Judaea (A.D. 26–36) who remained unconvinced of Christ's guilt at his trial but ultimately allowed him to be crucified in order to avoid provoking a riot (Matthew 27, Mark 15, Luke 23, and John 18). The expression *Pilate washed his hands* alludes to the biblical account of Pilate washing his hands in public as an expression of the fact that he refused to accept any blame for Christ's death. Legend has it that after the Crucifixion Pilate was overcome with remorse and committed suicide. *The district attorney, like some latter-day Pontius Pilate, refused point blank to accept that he was to blame for this miscarriage of justice.* See also PILATE'S WIFE; WASH ONE'S HANDS OF.

poor are always with us, the There will always be those who live in poverty and in need of assistance. The expression appears in Matthew 26:11, Mark 14:7, and John 12:8, which recount an incident in which a woman used expensive ointment to anoint Christ. The disciples rebuke the woman for her extravagance, but Christ protests, "Why trouble ye the woman? for she hath wrought a good work upon me. For ye have the poor always with you; but me ye have not always" (Matthew 26:10–11). "Still, with [the almshouse's] gateway and wicket Meek, in the midst of splendour, its humble walls seem to echo Softly the words of the Lord:—'The poor ye always have with you'" (H. W. Longfellow, *Evangeline,* 1849).

Poseidon (păsīdăn) The god of the sea. In Greek mythology Poseidon was one of the 12 gods of Olympus and a brother of Zeus. As the ruler of the oceans he was usually depicted with a trident and usually described as being violent and ill tempered. He was also feared as the god of earthquakes. *As far as anyone knows, both men were lost in the realm of Poseidon when their ship foundered.* See also NEPTUNE.

postmillennialism *See* MILLENNIUM.

Potiphar's wife (potifarz) A woman who gets revenge on a man who has rejected her advances by falsely accusing him of rape. Potiphar is described in Genesis 37:36 as one of Pharaoh's officers who bought JOSEPH as a slave and made him overseer of his household. Potiphar's wife tried to seduce Joseph, but he refused her, so in a rage she snatched some of his clothing and went to her husband to complain that Joseph had raped her, offering his clothing as corroborating evidence. Potiphar believed his wife's accusations, and Joseph was thrown into prison (Genesis 39:7–20). "A good housewife is of necessity a humbug; and Cornelia's husband was hoodwinked, as Potiphar was—only in a different way" (William Makepeace Thackeray, *Vanity Fair,* 1847).

potter's field A burial ground for paupers and unclaimed bodies. The original Potter's Field was, according to Matthew 27:7, a patch of ground outside Jerusalem that was purchased by the priests of the Temple as a burial place for the poor. The area was bought with the THIRTY PIECES OF SILVER that a remorseful Judas Iscariot had received as payment for betraying Christ and had returned to the Temple shortly before taking his own life. The cemetery's name referred to the land's former use as a source of clay for local potters. Subsequently the name was borrowed for pauper burial grounds at many locations throughout the Christian world. Another version claims that Judas himself bought the field with the thirty pieces of silver and died there (see ACELDAMA). "She is whimsical, and may really like to have the truth. It's quite clear her heart is as insensible to eloquence and poetry, as a Potter's Field wall, and it might answer to try her with a little truth" (James Fenimore Cooper, *Autobiography of a Pocket-Handkerchief,* 1843).

pour out the vials of wrath *See* VIALS OF WRATH.

powers that be, the The government or those in authority; the establishment. The phrase comes from Romans 13:1: "Let every soul be subject unto the higher powers. For there is no power but of God: the powers that be are ordained of God." *The powers that be have ordered that there should be no review of department policy.*

praetorian guard (preetōreeăn) The protectors or closest confederates of an individual or government in power. In ancient Rome the Praetorian Guard, instituted during the reign of Augustus, around 27 B.C., served as the bodyguards of the emperor. The very first such guards were a small body of elite soldiers chosen to protect a commanding officer on campaign and took their name from that of a commanding officer's tent, his *praetorium.* Members of the imperial Praetorian Guard, which numbered some 9,000 men under Augustus, wielded considerable power in their own right and on many occasions played a prominent role in installing or deposing the emperor. It is thought that at least nine emperors were murdered by the Praetorian Guard between the years A.D. 41 and 282. The Praetorian Guard was finally disbanded in 312, having lost its role to the army generals, upon whom emperors had come to rely directly for support. The term, sometimes rendered in the form *palace guard,* is still used today to refer to the cohorts of aides and confidants who attach themselves to those in power. The adjective *praetorian* may also be applied to regimes of a strong military, authoritarian character. *In times of trouble it is the duty of aides to gather around the president as a form of praetorian guard, sheltering him from further hostile attentions.*

Praxitelean (praksiteleeăn) Of the highest standard in sculpture. Praxiteles was an Athenian sculptor who flourished in the fourth century B.C. and was regarded as the finest sculptor Greece had ever known. His few surviving works include a statue of Hermes carrying the infant Dionysus. "She had bared her plump neck, shoulders, and arms to the moonshine, under which they looked as luminous and beautiful as some Praxitelean creation" (Thomas Hardy, *Tess of the D'Urbervilles,* 1891).

premillennialism *See* MILLENNIUM.

priapic (prīapik) Of or relating to the sexual urge in males; phallic. The word alludes to Priapus, the son of Dionysus and Aphrodite and the god of gardens and vineyards and of male reproductive power. *He was not too old to feel the need to satisfy the odd priapic urge, although he rarely did anything about it.*

price of wisdom is above rubies, the Nothing is more valuable than wisdom. This proverb is of biblical origin, appearing in Job 28:18: "No mention shall be made of coral, or of pearls: for the price of wisdom is above rubies." (See also Proverbs 3:15 and 8:11.) "Who can find a virtuous woman? for her price is far above rubies" (Thomas Hardy, *Tess of the D'Urbervilles,* 1891).

pricks, kick against the *See* KICK AGAINST THE PRICKS.

pride goeth before a fall Overconfidence and arrogance often result in humiliation or disaster. The proverb is of biblical origin: "Pride goeth before destruction, and an haughty spirit before a fall" (Proverbs 16:18). It is also encountered in the form *pride comes before a fall.* "'I suppose he thinks he'd be mayor himself,' said the people of Blackstable. They pursed their lips. 'Pride goeth before a fall'" (W. Somerset Maugham, *Cakes and Ale,* 1930).

priests of Bacchus *See* BACCHUS.

Prince of Darkness *See* SATAN.

Priscian *See* BREAK PRISCIAN'S HEAD.

Procris *See* UNERRING AS THE DART OF PROCRIS.

procrustean (prăkrăsteeăn, prōkrăsteeăn) Achieving conformity through the arbitrary use of violent or ruthless means, regardless of individual rights or circumstances. In Greek mythology Procrustes was a cruel, villainous highwayman who forced his victims to lie on an iron bed, stretching their bodies or lopping off their limbs to make them fit it perfectly. His name literally means "the stretcher." His notorious career came to a premature end when he was killed by Theseus. A *bed of Procrustes* or *procrustean bed* denotes a system, scheme, or standard to which others are obliged to conform. "A certain set of highly ingenious resources are, with the Prefect, a sort of Procrustean bed, to which he forcibly adapts his designs" (Edgar Allan Poe, "The Purloined Letter," 1845).

prodigal son A person who returns after a lengthy absence, having squandered his money. The allusion is to Christ's parable of the prodigal son related in Luke 15:11–32, in which a young man returns home after recklessly frittering away his inheritance. Instead of rebuking him for his profligacy, and braving the protests of his other son, who had stayed at home, the father welcomes him back and holds a lavish celebration in honor of the event. By much the same token a *prodigal* is someone who squanders his or her money. "Then he looked at the highly-coloured scripture pieces on the walls, in little black frames like common shaving-glasses, and saw how the Wise Men (with a strong family likeness among them) worshipped in a pink manger; and how the Prodigal Son came home in red rags to a purple father, and already feasted his imagination on a sea-green calf" (Charles Dickens, *Martin Chuzzlewit,* 1843–44). *See also* KILL THE FATTED CALF.

Promethean (prămeetheeăn) Exceptionally creative, inventive, or original. The word alludes to the Greek demigod Prometheus (whose name means "forethought"), who was credited with making the first man from clay. He later stole fire from Olympus and presented it to the human race and also taught mortals many artistic, medical, and agricultural skills. Because of his defiance of the gods in stealing fire from Olympus, Zeus had Prometheus chained to a rock so that an eagle (or vulture) could feed on his liver, which was magically restored each day. He was eventually rescued from this agony by HERCULES. Inspiration, creativity, or life itself is sometimes referred to as *Promethean fire.* "Now, don't you suppose, my inexperienced girl, that I cannot rebel, in high Promethean fashion, against the gods and fate as well as you" (Thomas Hardy, *The Return of the Native,* 1878).

promised land A place or situation believed to offer great happiness, fulfillment, and security. In the Old Testament the land of Canaan was promised by God to Abraham and his descendants, and thus Canaan came to be referred to as the Promised Land: "And the LORD appeared unto Abram and said, Unto thy seed will I give this land" (Genesis 12:7). In other contexts the same title is sometimes applied to heaven: "I just want to do God's will. And He's allowed me to go up to the mountain. And I've looked over. And I've seen the promised land" (Martin Luther King, speech, April 3, 1968). *See also* LAND FLOWING WITH MILK AND HONEY.

prophet is not without honor, save in his own country, a A person who issues warnings or advice is often taken least seriously by those closest to him or her. The proverb comes from Matthew 13:57, which describes how Christ was ill received in his home town of Nazareth and quotes him as saying: "A prophet is not without honour, save in his own country, and in his own house." Also encountered in the form *a prophet is without honor in his own country.* "In Florence the signori thought him an amusing fellow and his letters often made them laugh, but they had no great confidence in his judgment and never followed his advice. 'A prophet is not without honor save in his own country,' he sighed" (W. Somerset Maugham, *Then and Now,* 1946).

Proserpina *See* PERSEPHONE.

protean (prōteeăn, prōteeăn) Versatile; variable; changeable. The word comes from the name of the Greek sea god, Proteus, who tended the flocks of Poseidon and could change his shape at will. "Donald appeared not to see her at all, and answered her wise little remarks with curtly indifferent monosyllables, his looks and faculties hanging on the woman who could boast of a more Protean variety in her phases, moods, opinions, and also principles, than could Elizabeth" (Thomas Hardy, *The Mayor of Casterbridge,* 1886).

psyche (sīkee) The human mind or soul. The word alludes to Greek mythology and the beautiful Psyche, a mortal who was loved by Eros, the god of love, and visited by him each night on the condition that she did not ask his name or look at his face. Eventually Psyche, tricked by her sisters into thinking her secret lover was a monster, succumbed to temptation and looked on Eros's face in the lamplight. Eros fled but Psyche sought him out, and after lengthy wandering and many adventures they were reunited. Psyche was granted immortality and became the personification of the soul. *Somewhere deep in his psyche was a niggling desire to make himself heard, but he suppressed it with a deliberate effort.*

Ptolemaic (tolămayik) Of or relating to the theories of the Greco-Egyptian astronomer and mathematician Claudius Ptolemaeus, who flourished in the second century A.D. His theory that the universe revolved around the Earth remained unchallenged until the 16th century, when it was discredited by Nicolaus Copernicus. Since then *Ptolemaic* has been variously applied to theories or attitudes based on an assumption that the universe revolves around the Earth and human affairs. "Geology has initiated us into the secularity of nature, and taught us to disuse our dame-school measures, and exchange our Mosaic and Ptolemaic schemes for her large style" (Ralph Waldo Emerson, *Nature,* 1836).

Punic faith (pyoonik) Dishonest, deceitful, treacherous behavior; faithlessness. The Latin word for a Carthaginian was *Punicus* (a reference to their Phoenician origins), and the concept of Punic faith alludes to the hostility that existed between Carthage and ancient Rome during the Punic Wars of the third and second centuries B.C. Conscious that the influence of Carthage represented a serious threat to their own republic, Romans accused their Carthaginian enemies of all manner of dishonest, treacherous behavior, and the statesman Cato the Elder spoke for many when he took to ending each speech he made in the Senate with "Carthage must be destroyed." This was finally achieved with victory in the Third Punic War in 146 B.C. *As a further demonstration of his Punic faith he gave the authorities full details of his former employer's bank accounts.* See also CARTHAGINIAN PEACE.

pure all things are pure, to the   *See* UNTO THE PURE ALL THINGS ARE PURE.

purgatory (pergătoree) A state or place of suffering or torment. In Catholic tradition purgatory is the temporary abode of those spirits who are obliged to spend a period of time being purged of their sins before they can enter heaven. Scriptures that are alluded to in support of this teaching include 2 Maccabees 12:44–45 of the Apocrypha, Matthew 12:32, John 14:2, and 1 Corinthians 3:11–15. The name itself comes from the Latin *purgatorium* ("place of cleansing"). "From the surface of the water rose a dense cloud of steam. Alphonse groaned out that we were already in purgatory, which indeed we were, though not in the sense that he meant it" (H. Rider Haggard, *Allan Quatermain,* 1887).

Pygmalion (pigmaylyăn, pigmayleeăn) A person who creates or re-creates another individual and then becomes obsessed with the creation. In Greek mythology Pygmalion was a sculptor who, repelled by the flaws of mortal women, fashioned a statue of the perfect woman, calling her GALATEA. This act angered Aphrodite, the goddess of love, who punished Pygmalion by making him fall in love with his creation. Driven to distraction by the fact that he could not consummate his love, Pygmalion begged the gods to breath life into the figure. Eventually Aphrodite agreed to his request, and Galatea became a real, living woman. The central theme of the myth, a warning to those who obsessively pursue an artistic ideal, provided the basis for George Bernard Shaw's play *Pygmalion* (1913), in which a linguist sets himself the intellectual challenge of passing off a common flower vendor as an aristocrat lady and in the process neglects his own emotional attachment toward her until it is too late. The play was subsequently turned into the musical *My Fair Lady* (1956), which in turn became a movie (1964). *As her manager he assumed the role of her Pygmalion, transforming her from a talented hopeful into a fully rounded professional.*

pygmy Something or someone very small or insignificant. Pygmies, or *pigmies,* were featured in classical lore as a legendary race of dwarfs living in central Asia and were first recorded in the writings of Homer (c. eighth century B.C.). The word itself comes from the Greek *pygme,* a measure of length equivalent to the distance from a person's elbow to the knuckles. When HERCULES went into battle with the pygmies he overcame them by rolling them up in his lion skin. The name was subsequently applied to certain peoples of equatorial Africa characterized by their small stature, although they are considerably larger than the pygmies of classical legend, who used miniature hatchets to cut individual ears of corn and had to wage war annually against the cranes that fed on them. *Although a significant player in the home market, the company is a pygmy on the international stage.*

Pylades and Orestes (pīlaydeez, oresteez) Archetypes of devoted friendship. Pylades and Orestes appear in the writings of Homer (c. eighth century B.C.) as a model of perfect friendship. Orestes was the son of Agamemnon, while Pylades was Agamemnon's nephew. *Like Pylades and Orestes, they would have done anything for each other.*

pylon A steel structure supporting high-tension electrical cables or other equipment. The original pylons were the monumental gateways that were a chief feature of ancient Egyptian temples. *Most electrical companies today try to put their cables underground rather than hoist them up in the air on long chains of pylons running across the countryside.*

Pyramids *See* EIGHTH WONDER OF THE WORLD.

Pyramus and Thisbe (pirămăs, thizbee) Archetypal tragic lovers of classical legend. Pyramus and Thisbe were two lovers who defied their parents' opposition to their match and arranged to meet in a remote place where Thisbe, arriving first, was attacked by a lion. Thisbe fled, and when Pyramus arrived, all he found was her bloody scarf. Assuming she was dead, he killed himself, only for Thisbe to find his body and commit suicide in turn. *When she found his apparently lifeless body, the young woman swooned on the spot, a virtual modern reenactment of Pyramus and Thisbe.*

Pyrrhic victory (pi̱rik) A hollow victory; a victory so costly that its bene-fits are relatively insignificant. Pyrrhus (312–272 B.C.) was a king of Epirus, in western Greece, who waged a lengthy campaign against Rome. Following the battle of Asculum (279), which he won narrowly and only at the cost of many of his men, he is said to have exclaimed, "One more such victory and we are undone!" By the time he returned to Epirus he had lost two-thirds of his army. Such a victory may also be called a *Cadmean victory* in allusion to the Greek legend of Prince Cadmus, who fought and killed a dragon, but a host of armed men subsequently sprang up from the dragon's teeth, which Cadmus had planted in the ground. Cadmus threw a stone into their midst and all but five died in the ensuing mayhem (hence the phrase). *Pleased though they were to secure the house after such a long strug-gle, it was a Pyrrhic victory, for there would be very little left in the kitty after they had met the dramatically inflated purchase price.* See also SOW DRAGON'S TEETH.

Pythagorean theorem (păthagăree̱ăn) Mathematical rule that the square of the length of the hypotenuse is equal to the sum of the squares of the lengths of the other two sides of a right triangle. Pythagoras (c. 580–c. 500 B.C.) was a Greek philosopher and mathematician. It seems that this theo-rem was familiar to ancient Egyptian surveyors and the Babylonians at least 100 years before Pythagoras. *Children are expected to have mastered the basic laws of mathematics, such as the Pythagorean theorem, by the time they take their first major set of examinations.*

Pythias *See* DAMON AND PYTHIAS.

python A family of large, nonvenomous snakes native to Africa, southern Asia, and Australia that kill their prey by constriction. They are named after a monstrous snake of Greek mythology called the Python. Legend had it that this serpent arose from the mud following the flood sent by Zeus that drowned everyone except Deucalion and his wife, Pyrrha. The Python became the guardian of Delphi until killed by Apollo, who set up his oracle there and established the *Pythian Games* to celebrate his vic-tory. *The feather boa curled like a python round her generous figure.*

Queen of Heaven Title traditionally bestowed upon the VIRGIN MARY in the Catholic and Orthodox liturgies. Mary was crowned Queen of Heaven on her Assumption, and a Feast of Mary the Queen was subsequently instituted by Pope Pius XII (1876–1958). Her other titles include *Queen of Angels, Queen of Apostles, Queen of Confessors, Queen of Patriarchs, Queen of Peace, Queen of Prophets, Queen of Saints,* and *Queen of Virgins.* "But he believed in his mother and sisters as though they were heaven-born; and he was one who could believe in his wife as though she were the queen of heaven" (Anthony Trollope, *The Eustace Diamonds,* 1873). *See also* ASHTORETH.

Queen of Sheba (<u>shee</u>bă) Legendary queen whose name is sometimes applied pejoratively to woman who is suspected of dressing or otherwise behaving in an inappropriately grand manner. The biblical Queen of Sheba, described in 1 Kings 10:1–13, 2 Chronicles 9:1–9 and 12, and elsewhere, is a shadowy figure, supposedly the proud ruler of an area equating to modern Ethiopia and Yemen. She visited Solomon in Jerusalem in order to confirm for herself the tales she had heard of both his wisdom and of the magnificence of his palaces. She was greatly humbled when these tales were proved accurate, and "there was no more spirit in her" (1 Kings 10:4–5). According to some accounts she and Solomon became lovers. Her name is usually invoked as a criticism of women who are guilty of pretensions of grandeur or haughty behavior, but it may also sometimes symbolize vanquished pride, as in Thomas Hardy's *Tess of the D'Urbervilles* (1891), in which Tess laments, "I'm like the poor Queen of Sheba who lives in the Bible. There is no more spirit in me." "'You ought'—'Ought what, sir?' demanded the lady, gazing at her husband with the air of a Queen of Sheba" (Honoré de Balzac, *Cousin Pons,* 1847).

quick and the dead, the The living and the dead. The phrase appears in the Apostles' Creed (in the *Book of Common Prayer*), in which Christ is identified as the judge of the living and the dead: "From thence he shall come to judge the quick and the dead." It appears in the Bible in similar form in Acts 10:42, 2 Timothy 4:1, and 1 Peter 4:5. In modern usage it is usually quoted with parodic intent. *Local tradition insisted that the old churchyard was a place of macabre happenings, where the quick and the dead came face to face.*

Quis custodiet ipsos custodes? (kwis kăstōdeeăt ipsos kăstōdayz) Who will guard the guards themselves? This proverbial word of warning emphasizing the need for those in authority to be themselves accountable to others comes from the writings of the Roman satirist Juvenal (c. A.D. 55–c. 140), specifically Satire VI. Juvenal addressed it originally to nervous husbands who hired others to guard the chastity of their wives. The line continues to be quoted today whenever doubt is cast about the trustworthiness of people occupying posts of considerable power, authority, or opportunity. "The bad measures or bad appointments of a minister may be checked by Parliament; and the interest of ministers in defending, and of rival partisans in attacking, secures a tolerably equal discussion: but quis custodiet custodes? who shall check the Parliament?" (John Stuart Mill, *Considerations on Representative Government,* 1861).

Quo vadis? (kwō vahdis) Whither goest thou? This formal challenge comes directly from the Vulgate version of John 13:36, in which the words are addressed by Peter to Christ at the Last Supper. (See also John 16:5.) According to one legend, a variant origin of the phrase is when Christ appears in a vision during Peter's flight from Rome to escape martyrdom. When Christ replies "To Rome to be crucified again," a chastened Peter turns back to the capital to face his own execution. The quotation was subsequently used as a title for several major religious paintings depicting the episode. A novel of the same title (1895) by the Polish writer Henryk Sienkiewicz, who depicted Rome during the reign of Nero, has been staged and filmed several times. *The sentry leveled his rifle and uttered the time-honored quo vadis as instructed by his sergeant.*

race is not to the swift nor the battle to the strong, the It is not always the stronger or faster side that wins the contest. This proverbial observation has biblical origins: "The race is not to the swift, nor the battle to the strong, neither yet bread to the wise, nor yet riches to men of understanding, nor yet favour to men of skill; but time and chance happeneth to them all" (Ecclesiastes 9:11). "Poor child! she lay . . . trying to work out . . . why the race is not to the swift, nor the battle to the strong" (Charlotte Mary Yonge, *Pillars of House,* 1873).

Rachel weeping for her children A woman in the throes of grief, especially one mourning her dead child. According to Genesis 29–35, Rachel was the second wife of Jacob and the mother of Joseph and Benjamin. She died giving birth to Benjamin but subsequently is described as weeping over the fate of her descendants when they were about to be carried off into captivity in Babylon: "Rachel weeping for her children refused to be comforted for her children, because they were not" (Jeremiah 31:15). (See also Matthew 2:17–18.) "But by her halting course and winding, woeful way, you plainly saw that this ship that so wept with spray, still remained without comfort. She was Rachel, weeping for her children, because they were not" (Herman Melville, *Moby-Dick,* 1851).

Ragnarok (ragnărok) A cataclysmic struggle resulting in universal disaster. In Norse mythology the world will end in a climactic battle between the good and evil gods. *The impact of the two armies was so titanic it seemed for a moment he was witnessing the fighting of some Ragnarok in which all creation would be destroyed. See also* GÖTTERDÄMMERUNG.

rain falls on the just and the unjust, the Some things affect the good and the bad regardless of their virtues or lack of them. The phrase comes from

Christ's Sermon on the Mount: "That ye may be the children of your Father which is in heaven: for he maketh his sun to rise on the evil and on the good, and sendeth rain on the just and on the unjust" (Matthew 5:45). The passage is sometimes quoted as a reminder to leave retribution against one's enemies to God. *The rain falls on the just and on the unjust fella, but chiefly on the just because the unjust has stolen his umbrella.*

raise Cain (kayn) To stir up a fuss; to cause a noisy disturbance. The phrase alludes to the story of CAIN AND ABEL, specifically to Cain's violent temper, which was the underlying cause of his murdering his brother (Genesis 4:5). In centuries past Cain's name was adopted as a euphemism for the devil, as most people hesitated to mention the latter's name for fear of summoning him. "And look at Charles Second, and Louis Fourteen, and Louis Fifteen, and James Second, and Edward Second, and Richard Third, and forty more; besides all them Saxon heptarchies that used to rip around so in old times and raise Cain" (Mark Twain, *The Adventures of Huckleberry Finn*, 1884).

raising of Lazarus *See* LAZARUS.

rape of the Sabine women (saybīn) Archetype of a mass abduction of women. The allusion is to a legendary episode of early Roman history, according to which the first Romans, under the leadership of Romulus, finding themselves short of females, invited their male Sabine neighbors to a festival and meanwhile invaded Sabine territory and carried off their womenfolk by force. War subsequently broke out between the two sides, but they were eventually reconciled. *It was like the rape of the Sabine women, terrified girls seeking to elude the clutches of their grinning partners.*

reap the whirlwind *See* SOW THE WIND AND REAP THE WHIRLWIND.

reap what you sow The benefit you receive depends on what you have put in. The phrase comes from Paul's letter to the Galatians: "God is not mocked: for whatsoever a man soweth, that shall he also reap" (Galatians 6:7). (See also 2 Corinthians 9:6.) The same image of reaping and sowing is evoked at Matthew 25:24, where it appears in the parable of the talents: "Lord, I knew thee that thou art an hard man, reaping where thou hast not sown, and gathering where thou hast not strawed." *As children they had been brought up with the maxim that you reaped what you sowed, so the qualities of respect, honesty, and hard work stood them in good stead throughout their lives.*

receive one's Nunc Dimittis *See* NUNC DIMITTIS.

Rechabite (rekăbīt) A teetotaler, especially one who is a member of the Independent Order of Rechabites (founded 1835) or another similar temperance society. Rechab was a biblical character who encouraged his family and his descendants to abstain from alcoholic drink and live strict, moderate lives (Jeremiah 35:1–19). *His uncle was a Rechabite who would not allow alcohol of any kind in the house.*

redeem the time Do not waste time. The origins of the phrase are biblical, being a quotation from Paul's letter to the Ephesians: "See then that ye walk circumspectly, not as fools, but as wise. Redeeming the time, because the days are evil" (Ephesians 5:15–16). "'Therefore,' urged the good man, his voice trembling with emotion, 'redeem the time, my unhappy brethren, which is yet left'" (Sir Walter Scott, *The Heart of Midlothian,* 1818).

Red Sea *See* CROSSING OF THE RED SEA.

rehoboam (reeăbōăm) A large wine bottle, equivalent to six standard-sized bottles. It takes its name from Rehoboam (10th century B.C.), a son of Solomon, the last king of the united Israel, and the first king of Judah (1 Kings 11:43). His name means "expansion of the people." *It has been many years since anyone ordered a rehoboam of claret at this particular restaurant.*

remnant *See* SAVING REMNANT.

Remus *See* ROMULUS AND REMUS.

render unto Caesar (seezer) Surrender to your masters the things that they are entitled to demand. The phrase appears in the Bible in Matthew 22:21 and Luke 20:25, where it is given as Christ's reply to the Pharisees' question as to whether it was lawful to pay tribute to Caesar (hoping to trick Jesus into a confession of open disloyalty to the emperor): "Then saith he unto them, Render therefore unto Caesar the things which are Caesar's; and unto God the things that are God's." The implication in Christ's reply is that there are some things that Caesar is not entitled to ask for and that his authority is limited. *When it comes to taxes, there is little alternative but to bite the bullet and render unto Caesar what is Caesar's.*

respecter of persons, no *See* NO RESPECTER OF PERSONS.

rest on one's laurels *See* LAURELS.

rhadamanthine (radămanthin, radămanthīn) Stern and incorruptible in judgment. In Greek mythology Rhadamanthus was the son of Zeus and Europa and brother of King Minos of Crete. Having established his reputation as a wise and incorruptible judge in life, he became one of the judges of the dead in the underworld, alongside Minos and Aeacus. "He accordingly addressed a carefully considered epistle to Sue, and, knowing her emotional temperament, threw a Rhadamanthine strictness into the lines here and there, carefully hiding his heterodox feelings, not to frighten her" (Thomas Hardy, *Jude the Obscure,* 1896).

rhesus factor (reesăs) Protein found in the red blood cells of most people. The rhesus factor, or *Rh factor,* was named after the rhesus monkey, a macaque from southern Asia that is widely used in medical research and in whose blood this protein was first discovered. The monkey in turn was named after Rhesus, king of Thrace and an ally of Troy, who according to Greek myth was killed by Odysseus and Diomedes as they stole his horses. Legend had it that if the horses fed on the grass of the Trojan plain and drank from the Xanthus River, Troy would never fall. *The presence of the rhesus factor in a person's blood is not normally a problem but can cause a hemolytic reaction, especially during pregnancy or following a blood transfusion that lacks this agglutinogen.*

rich man enter heaven *See* CAMEL: GO THROUGH AN EYE OF A NEEDLE.

riddle of the Sphinx (sfinks) The legendary riddle posed by the Sphinx or any particularly challenging riddle, puzzle, or problem. According to Greek mythology the Sphinx prevented anyone from entering the city of

Thebes unless they could solve the riddle What creature goes on four legs in the morning, two legs at noon, and three in the evening? Those who got the answer wrong suffered instant death, but if someone answered correctly, the Sphinx's power would be destroyed. Oedipus correctly identified the answer as "man," because he crawls as a child, walks as an adult, and proceeds with the aid of a staff in old age. Oedipus thus saved the city and won the hand of Queen Jocasta, at the time ignorant of the fact that she was his mother (see OEDIPUS COMPLEX). "The Interviewer had attempted the riddle of the Sphinx, and had failed to get the first hint of its solution" (Oliver Wendell Holmes, *A Moral Antipathy,* 1885).

right hand offend thee See IF THY RIGHT EYE OFFEND THEE.

rise, take up thy bed, and walk Get out about your business (usually said after the removal of some impediment). The phrase is a quotation from John 5:1–9, which relates the story of the crippled man at the Pool of Bethesda who was cured and "made whole" by Jesus with these same words. (See also Mark 2:9.) *The doctor took one look at the malingerer, snorted and ordered him to rise, take up his bed, and walk.*

rise from the ashes See PHOENIX.

rivers of Babylon See BY THE RIVERS OF BABYLON.

roads lead to Rome, all See ALL ROADS LEAD TO ROME.

road to Damascus (dămaskăs) A process of revelation resulting in a fundamental change of viewpoint or opinion (typically the result of a sudden, even miraculous insight). The allusion is to the episode in the New Testament (recounted in Acts 9:1–19, 22:1–21, and 26:1–23), in which Saul of Tarsus has a vision of the risen Christ while on his way to Damascus to persecute Christians there. Saul immediately declares himself a Christian and, as Paul, in due course becomes one of the apostles and a great Christian missionary. A *road-to-Damascus experience* is a sudden, dramatic revelation resulting in a fundamental change of view or way of life. "You don't reach Downing Street by pretending you've travelled the road to Damascus when you haven't even left home" (*Guardian,* October 14, 1989).

roar like a bull of Bashan *See* BULL OF BASHAN.

Roland (rōlănd) A hero of exemplary virtue and courage. Roland and Oliver were two of the 12 paladins who served at the court of the emperor CHARLEMAGNE. Roland was Charlemagne's nephew and became Oliver's inseparable friend after the two fought an evenly matched duel that lasted for five consecutive days with each matching the other's blow, hence the saying *a Roland for an Oliver* for "tit for tat" or "a blow for a blow." The names of *Roland and Oliver* as a combination are still sometimes evoked as archetypes of perfect friends. Both knights died celebrated deaths in battle after being betrayed to the Saracens at Roncesvalles in Spain in 778, a last stand immortalized in the 11th-century French epic poem *La chanson de Roland.* Although faced with vastly superior odds, Roland, who was also known as "the Christian Theseus" and "the Achilles of the West," stoutly refused to blow his horn Olivant to summon help from Charlemagne until it was almost too late. When he did finally blow the horn, Ganelon persuaded Charlemagne that Roland was merely hunting deer, and the warriors' fate was sealed. A variation of the legend claims that Roland survived the battle but died some time later of starvation or thirst while trying to cross the Pyrenees; hence, if a person is doomed to *die like Roland,* he or she faces a similar end. *His chivalrous behavior on this occasion earned him the reputation of a latter-day Roland, although those who knew him better were inclined to scoff at this. See also* ROUNCEVAL.

Roman holiday A public performance that features extravagant acts of barbarity and debauchery. The entertainments that took place in the arenas of ancient Rome were notorious for their cruelty, which included gladiatorial combats to the death and the throwing of captives to wild animals. Such bloodthirsty extravaganzas were prohibited by Emperor Constantine I in A.D. 325 but soon revived and carried on until 405. "For I have written about the Coliseum, and the gladiators, the martyrs, and the lions, and yet have never once used the phrase 'butchered to make a Roman holiday.' I am the only free white man of mature age, who has accomplished this since Byron originated the expression" (Mark Twain, *The Innocents Abroad,* 1869).

Rome *See* ALL ROADS LEAD TO ROME; FIDDLE WHILE ROME BURNS; ROMULUS AND REMUS; WHEN IN ROME, DO AS THE ROMANS DO.

Romulus and Remus (<u>rom</u>yălăs, <u>ree</u>măs) The legendary founders of Rome, whose names are still frequently invoked in references to the city. Romulus and Remus were variously identified as the twin sons of Mars and Rhea Silvia or of Aeneas' daughter Ilia. Because Rhea Silvia was a vestal virgin, obliged to maintain her virginity on pain of death, the twins seemed doomed but were saved by the gods and suckled by a she-wolf. Romulus killed Remus during an argument over where they should site their city and in due course became the first king of Rome. *The company the two brothers built around their initial idea has become one of the biggest conglomerates in the world, and they are still honored as the Romulus and Remus upon whom this huge empire was constructed.*

room at the inn, no *See* NO ROOM AT THE INN.

root of all evil *See* MONEY IS THE ROOT OF ALL EVIL.

Roscius (<u>rosh</u>ăs) An outstanding actor. This epithet alludes to Quintus Roscius Gallus (c. 126–62 B.C.), who was a celebrated comic actor on the Roman stage and a friend of Cicero. Likewise, the adjective *Roscian* describes a theatrical performance of great skill. Among later performers compared with Roscius were Shakespeare's contemporary Richard Burbage (c. 1567–1619), who was described as "another Roscius"; Thomas Betterton (1635–1710), who was known as the "British Roscius"; and William Betty (1791–1874), who was called the "Young Roscius." "The celebrated provincial amateur of Roscian renown" (Charles Dickens, *Great Expectations,* 1860).

rose of Sharon (<u>shar</u>ăn) An unidentified flower whose beauty is variously taken to represent love or loveliness, especially as a description of Jesus Christ. The image of the rose of Sharon occurs in the biblical Song of Solomon 2:1–2, in which it is put into the mouth of the bride: "I am the rose of Sharon, and the lily of the valleys." The flower in question has been tentatively identified as the autumn crocus, asphodel, or narcissus, which flourished on the plain of Sharon, a fertile area on the coast of ancient Palestine. "'The Rose of Sharon and the Lily of the Valley,'—answered the Prior, in a sort of snuffling tone; 'but your Grace must remember she is still but a Jewess'" (Sir Walter Scott, *Ivanhoe,* 1819).

Rose Without a Thorn An epithet of the Virgin Mary. The name alludes to the fact that according to Catholic tradition Mary is deemed to be without the taint of original sin, just as the rose lacked thorns when it first grew in Paradise; it acquired its thorns (sins) when planted on earth after the expulsion of Adam and Eve from the Garden of Eden, thus coming to represent the moral imperfections of the human race. *To the other villagers she was a perfect example of innocence and virtue, a Rose Without a Thorn.*

rounceval (rownsival) Very large or strong. Also spelled *rouncival,* the word is probably an anglicization of Roncesvalles, in Spain, where ROLAND and his colleagues fell in their final battle. Years later various large bones found at the site were rumored to belong to these great heroes. Large marrowfat peas are sometimes called *rounceval peas,* and substantially built women may sometimes be dubbed *rouncevals. The abbess was of such imposing proportions that Rouncival, nay, Gargantuan, would not have been misplaced.*

Rubicon *See* CROSS THE RUBICON.

rule, golden *See* GOLDEN RULE.

rule with a rod of iron To rule harshly; to exercise authority with severity. The expression comes from the Bible, occurring in Revelation 2:27, 12:5, and 19:15 and in Psalm 2:9. "Emmeline took after her father; she was big and dark and homely, and she was the most domineering creature that ever stepped on shoe leather. She simply ruled poor Prissy with a rod of iron" (Lucy Maud Montgomery, *Chronicles of Avonlea,* 1912).

Ruth (rooth) The archetype of a devoted, loyal woman. A Moabite widow, Ruth promised never to desert her mother-in-law: "Intreat me not to leave thee, or to return from following after thee: for whither thou goest, I will go; and where thou lodgest, I will lodge: thy people shall be my people, and thy God my God" (Ruth 1:16). Her kindness to her mother-in-law impressed the wealthy Boaz, and in due course he and Ruth were married and Ruth subsequently appeared in the genealogy of Matthew 1:5 as the great-grandmother of King David. "Perhaps the selfsame song that found a path / Through the sad heart of Ruth, when, sick for home, / She stood in tears amid the alien corn" (John Keats, "Ode to a Nightingale," 1819). *See also* WHITHER THOU GOEST, I WILL GO.

Sabbath A period of rest. The allusion is to the Jewish Sabbath, which is traditionally reserved for religious worship rather than work (Exodus 20:8–11 and Deuteronomy 5:12–15). According to the book of Genesis (2:2), God rested from creating the earth on the seventh day, dictating that it become a day of rest and worship for the faithful. The word comes from the Hebrew *shabbath* (meaning "rest"). A *Sabbath day's journey* (Acts 1:12) is a short and easy journey, an allusion to the Law of Moses, which forbade Jews to travel any further than the distance between the Ark of the Covenant and the edge of their camp (about two-thirds of a mile). "Not even Lizzie Eustace, on behalf of her cousin Frank, would have dared to disturb Mr Gowran with considerations respecting a pony on the Sabbath" (Anthony Trollope, *The Eustace Diamonds,* 1873).

Sabine women *See* RAPE OF THE SABINE WOMEN.

sackcloth and ashes A public display of grief or remorse. The tradition of donning clothing made of sackcloth and scattering ashes over one's head as a sign of mourning or repentance dates back at least to biblical times, as described in the book of Esther: "And in every province, whithersoever the king's commandment and his decree came, there was great mourning among the Jews, and fasting, and weeping, and wailing; and many lay in sackcloth and ashes" (Esther 4:3). (See also Esther 4:1, Jonah 3:6, Matthew 11:21, and Luke 11:13.) "She felt that she might yet recover her lost ground, that she might yet hurl Mr Slope down to the dust from which she had picked him and force her sinning lord to sue for pardon in sackcloth and ashes" (Anthony Trollope, *Barchester Towers,* 1857).

sacrificial lamb Someone or something sacrificed to appease an enemy and thus avert a greater disaster. The allusion is to the Old Testament practice of sacrificing lambs and other animals at the altar in order to give thanks to God, obtain atonement and forgiveness, and restore a right relationship between the people and God (see, for example, Genesis 8:20, Exodus 29:38–41, and Leviticus 4:1–3). "A dreadful performance could see Mr Byers offered up as a sacrificial lamb" (*Guardian,* February 20, 2002).

Sadducee (sajăsee, sadyăsee) A person who stubbornly refuses to believe a commonly accepted truth. The allusion is to the Sadducee sect of the time of Christ who accepted the authority only of the written Law and rejected a belief in the Resurrection and angels and demons. Supposedly named after the high priest Sadoq, who was reputed to have founded the sect, they, like the Pharisees, were hostile toward Jesus Christ and his teachings (Matthew 22:23–33, Mark 12:18–27, and Luke 20:27–38). They lost influence after the fall of Jerusalem in A.D. 70. "I was quite drawn out to speak to him; I hardly know how, for I had always thought of him as a worldly Sadducee. But his countenance is as pleasant as the morning sunshine" (George Eliot, *Adam Bede,* 1859).

Saint Stephen's loaves Rocks. The reference is to the stoning to death of Saint Stephen, the first Christian martyr, who died c. A.D. 35 after being accused of blasphemy (as described in Acts 6:1–8:2). By the same token to be *fed with Saint Stephen's bread* is a euphemism for being stoned to death. *At this unwelcome news she feared the mob would start to toss Saint Stephen's loaves at her, in time-honored fashion.*

Salamis (salămis) Archetype of a great naval victory. The Battle of Salamis took place between the Greek and Persian fleets in 480 B.C. in the waters of the Saronic Gulf, between the island of Salamis and the Greek mainland. The Greeks achieved a famous victory over their Persian enemies, the whole battle being witnessed by the Persian leader Xerxes from Mount Aegaleos. *The staff had planned this Salamis for months, hoping to lure the enemy's chief vessels away from the relative safety of the coastal waters.*

salary (salăree) A set payment received for employment. The word comes ultimately from the Latin *sal* (meaning "salt") and alludes to the ancient practice of paying Roman soldiers stationed inland (away from the sea, the usual source of salt in the ancient world) a *salarium* with which to purchase salt, at that time a valuable commodity. The connection with salt had been forgotten by medieval times, but the word remained current. Related phrases include ***worth one's salt*** (meaning "worth the salary one is paid"). "Her husband was a retired tradesman, who had realized a very comfortable fortune; but could not be prevailed upon to give a greater salary than twenty-five pounds to the instructress of his children" (Anne Brontë, *Agnes Grey,* 1845).

salmanazar (salmănazăr) A large wine bottle, equivalent to 12 standard bottles. It is named after eighth-century B.C. Assyrian king Shalmaneser V, who appears in the Bible (2 Kings 17:3). *The company stopped providing salmanazars for the hotels of New York several decades ago.*

Salome (sălōmee, salōmay) A seductive, deceitful temptress. The allusion is to the biblical Salome, the stepdaughter of Herod Antipas, who (at the prompting of her mother) demanded the head of JOHN THE BAPTIST; she had been promised whatever she wanted in payment for her dancing before her stepfather (Matthew 14:1–12 and Mark 6:16–29). *This Salome, in a figure-hugging red gown and long black gloves, advanced slowly toward their table with a predatory look in her half-closed eyes.*

salt of the earth A person or group of people admired for their sterling qualities. The phrase comes from Christ's Sermon on the Mount, as related in Matthew 5:13: "Ye are the salt of the earth: but if the salt have lost its savour, wherewith shall it be salted? It is thenceforth good for nothing, but to be cast out, and to be trodden under foot of men." The reference is to the use of salt as a preservative, preventing food from going rotten. "Retired sea-captains, in easy circumstances, who talked of farming as sea-captains are wont; an erect, respectable, and trustworthy looking man, in his wrapper, some of the salt of the earth, who had formerly been the salt of the sea" (Henry David Thoreau, *Cape Cod,* 1865).

Samaritan *See* GOOD SAMARITAN.

Samian letter (saymeeăn) The letter *y.* The allusion is to Pythagoras, who was born on Samos in the sixth century B.C. and who used the Greek upsilon (equivalent to the modern *y*) as a symbol of the divergence between vice and virtue. Pythagoras himself is sometimes referred to as the *Samian sage*. "When reason doubtful like the Samian letter, / Points him two ways, the narrower the better" (Alexander Pope, *The Dunciad*, 1728).

Samson (sămsăn) A person of exceptional physical strength. The allusion is to the biblical Samson, a judge of Israel, who was renowned for his great strength. His feats included tearing a lion apart with his bare hands, catching 300 foxes, and knocking down 1,000 men with the jawbone of a donkey (as related in Judges 13–16). He was brought low, however, by the wiles of DELILAH, who cut off the long hair on which his strength depended and had his eyes gouged out. Once his hair grew back, however, his strength returned. When his Philistine enemies amassed in the temple of Dagon, Samson gripped the two central pillars of the temple and pushed them down, causing the whole building to collapse, killing everyone inside (Judges 16:30). "He passed the remainder of the afternoon in a curious high-strung condition, unable to do much but think of the approaching meeting with her, and sadly satirize himself for his emotions thereon, as a Samson shorn" (Thomas Hardy, *The Mayor of Casterbridge*, 1886). *See also* EYELESS IN GAZA; SAMSON, BLIND, GRINDS IN PRISON.

Samson, blind, grinds in prison (sămsăn) Reference to a worker who is obliged to work long and hard under terrible conditions. The allusion is to the fate of the biblical SAMSON, who was betrayed by Delilah, subsequently blinded, then forced to work in the mills of the Philistines (Judges 16:21). *A cursory examination of the maquiladora reminded the inspector forcibly of Samson, blind, grinds in prison. See also* EYELESS IN GAZA.

Samuel (sămyăwăl, sămyăl) Archetype of a prophet whose prophecies always come true. The allusion is to the biblical Samuel, the prophet and judge who anointed Saul and David (as related in 1 Samuel 9–10 and 16). *By this time the old man had acquired a reputation as the party's Samuel, divining long before any others which way the political wind was likely to blow.*

sanctum sanctorum *See* HOLY OF HOLIES.

sandals of Theramenes *See* WEAR THE SANDALS OF THERAMENES.

sapphic *See* LESBIAN.

Sapphira *See* ANANIAS CLUB.

Sarah (<u>sair</u>ă) Archetype of an older mother. The allusion is to Sarah, the elderly but childless wife of ABRAHAM, who in Genesis 17:15–22 prayed to God for a child and later gave birth to Isaac. *Like the biblical Sarah, she bore her first child at an age when most women are nearly grandmothers.*

Sardanapalus (sahrdănapălăs) Archetype of an extravagant, luxury-loving tyrant, especially one given to effeminate pleasures. Sardanapalus was probably a fictional character resulting from the combination of three kings of ancient Assyria—Ashurbanipal, Shamash-shum-ukin, and Sin-shar-ishkun—who reigned around the seventh century B.C. Sardanapalus whiled away much of his time wearing women's clothing and enjoying such activities as spinning and making clothes. He gave up his self-indulgent ways, however, when threatened by invasion and inflicted several heavy defeats on his enemies until after a long siege at Nineveh, he set fire to everything he owned, including his concubines and himself, on a funeral pyre. "Pleasure shall preside at my last moments, as it has presided at my whole life! I will die like Sardanapalus, with my loves and my treasures around me; and the last of my guests who remains proof against our festivity shall set fire to my palace, as the kingly Assyrian set fire to his!" (Wilkie Collins, *Antonina,* 1850).

sardonic (sahr<u>d</u>onik) Scornful; mocking; derisive. The word derives ultimately from Greek legend about a poisonous herb that was supposed to grow on the island of Sardinia. Tradition had it that those who ate some of this acrid herb found themselves subject to uncontrollable spasms, their face being contorted into a rigid, unnatural smile. "I had started, on entering the room, at the skeleton, and I started once more at the dog. The old servant noticed me each time with a sardonic grin" (Wilkie Collins, *After Dark,* 1856).

Satan (<u>say</u>tăn) The devil. The word is a Hebrew term that actually means "the enemy" or "the accuser" (Job 1:6). In the New Testament Satan is described as a tempter (Matthew 4:1–11, Mark 1:11–13, and Luke

4:4–13), "the prince of this world" (John 12:31), and "the prince of the power of the air" (Ephesians 2:2). He seeks to undermine the kingdom of God, and he opposes and tests believers. The New Testament also presents the death of Jesus Christ on the cross as the decisive moment of Satan's defeat (John 12:31), which will be confirmed when Jesus Christ returns and Satan is punished and his work destroyed (Revelation 20:10). In the works of John Milton, he is identified as the fallen angel who challenges the rule of God in heaven and is exiled to hell as punishment for the rebellion he leads. His many other titles include **Prince of Darkness** and **Old Nick**. *He sat on top of the company like Satan presiding over hell. See also* BEELZEBUB; LUCIFER.

Saturday The seventh day of the week. It was named after Saturn, the Roman god of agriculture. *Tradition has it that weddings take place on Saturday.*

Saturn (<u>sa</u>tern) The sixth planet from the Sun. It was named after the Roman god of agriculture and vegetation, equivalent to the Greek Cronos and thus also representing time. According to legend Saturn was once a king of Italy who presided over a golden age of peace and plenty. "Thus, in reviewing the horoscope which your Lordship subjected to my skill, you will observe that Saturn, being in the sixth House in opposition to Mars, retrograde in the House of Life, cannot but denote long and dangerous sickness, the issue whereof is in the will of Heaven, though death may probably be inferred" (Sir Walter Scott, *Kenilworth*, 1821). *See also* SATUR-DAY; SATURNALIAN; SATURNINE.

saturnalian (sater<u>nay</u>leeăn) Of or relating to wild, unrestrained revelry. The allusion is to the Roman festival of Saturnalia, during which the harvest was celebrated—reputedly an occasion of much licentiousness and debauchery. All the schools and law courts were closed, and slaves were temporarily released from the strict rules that governed their lives to enjoy feasts at which they dressed up in the clothes of their masters. The festival was named after Saturn, the god of agriculture. "Altogether this time of trouble was rather a Saturnalian time to Kezia; she could scold her betters with unreproved freedom" (George Eliot, *The Mill on the Floss*, 1860).

saturnine (<u>sa</u>ternīn) Having a gloomy, taciturn temperament. The word is an allusion to the planet SATURN, which was traditionally supposed to exert a depressive influence. "He stands for a moment, saturnine in the ruddy light, to see who is present, looking in a singular and rather deadly way at Sir Howard; then with some surprise and uneasiness at Lady Cicely" (George Bernard Shaw, *Captain Brassbound's Conversion,* 1900).

satyr (<u>say</u>ter) A lecher; a man who exhibits abnormally strong sexual desire. According to Greek mythology satyrs were minor deities of the forest, depicted as having the bodies of unusually hairy men, the legs and feet of goats and short horns on their head. Representing the raw power of nature, they attended upon the god Dionysus and were notorious for their lustful ways. "'This is the face of a satyr.' 'It is the face of my soul'" (Oscar Wilde, *The Picture of Dorian Gray,* 1891).

Saul (sahl) Archetype of a troubled, melancholy ruler. Saul is identified in the Old Testament as the first king of Israel (1 Samuel 11:15), who led the Israelites to victory against the Philistines but clashed with the high priest Samuel and ultimately went mad and took his own life, upon which he was succeeded by David. The expression of surprise *Is Saul also among the prophets?* was uttered by those who knew Saul's character and then saw him prophesying (1 Samuel 10:11–12). Saul was also the name of the apostle Paul prior to his revelatory experience on the ROAD TO DAMASCUS and his subsequent conversion to Christianity (Acts 9:1–22). "'Many learned and great men have thought otherwise,' said Varney; 'and, not to flatter your lordship, my own opinion leans that way.' 'Ay, Saul among the prophets?' said Leicester. 'I thought thou wert sceptical in all such matters as thou couldst neither see, hear, smell, taste, or touch, and that thy belief was limited by thy senses'" (Sir Walter Scott, *Kenilworth,* 1821).

saving remnant A small group of survivors of a larger assembly who serve to redeem the whole. The phrase comes from Isaiah 10:20–23, in which Isaiah describes how the remaining Israelites would be brought back to the Promised Land after being defeated and exiled by the Assyrians. The Old Testament idea of a "remnant" is about people who have been saved or delivered from disaster rather than those who bring about the salvation of a larger group. The saving remnant is the group with which God can begin again and whose members will preserve the existence of Israel. "The remnant shall return, even the remnant of Jacob, unto the mighty God. For though thy people Israel be as the sand of the sea, yet a remnant of them shall return: the consumption decreed shall overflow with righteousness" (Isaiah 10:21–22). *The team will have to rely on a saving remnant of established stars if they are to remain at this level next season.*

say the word To give the go-ahead for something to be done. The expression derives from Matthew 8:8, when Christ is speaking to the Roman centurion whose servant lay paralyzed and suffering at home: "The centurion answered and said, Lord, I am not worthy that thou shouldest come under my roof: but speak the word only, and my servant shall be healed." The incident is also reported in Luke 7:1–10. "'I'll have it done, I will, by heavens! if you'll only say the word,' protested Sir Roger. But the doctor did not say the word, and so the idea was passed off" (Anthony Trollope, *Doctor Thorne,* 1858).

Scaevola (skeevălă) Archetype of a person who endures suffering without complaint. According to Roman legend Scaevola (meaning "left handed") was the nickname bestowed on one Gaius Mucius, who entered the camp of the invading Etruscan leader Lars Porsena with the intention of assassinating him during his siege of Rome. Unfortunately Gaius Mucius killed the king's secretary by mistake and was apprehended. Having been sentenced to death by burning, Gaius Mucius voluntarily held his right hand in the flames to show his indifference to his fate, keeping it there without flinching until it was quite burned away. Duly impressed, the Etruscans allowed him to go free and agreed to peace with the Romans. *Like Scaevola under torture, he endured the most severe physical abuse without a murmur.*

scales fell from his eyes This expression is used to describe a person who has been stripped of a former illusion and now recognizes the real truth of something. The expression comes from Acts 9:18, which describes the conversion of Paul on the ROAD TO DAMASCUS: "And immediately there fell from his eyes as it had been scales: and he received sight forthwith, and arose, and was baptized." "Then the scales fell from the eyes of the Seven, and one said, Alas, that we drank of the curious liquors. They have made us weary, and in dreamless sleep these two long centuries have we lain" (Mark Twain, *The Innocents Abroad,* 1869).

scapegoat A person who is made to take the blame for others. According to Leviticus 16, the Day of Atonement included a ceremony in which two goats were brought to the altar of the Tabernacle and lots were drawn to decide which would be sacrificed. The second goat was then symbolically laden with the sins of the Israelites and led into the wilderness and allowed to escape. The term *scapegoat* may be derived from the Hebrew *azazel* (which may have been the name of a demon believed to haunt desolate regions). "Madame Merle defended the luckless lady with a great deal of zeal and wit. She couldn't see why Mrs. Touchett should make a scapegoat of a woman who had really done no harm, who had only done good in the wrong way" (Henry James, *Portrait of a Lady,* 1881).

Scarlet Whore of Babylon *See* WHORE OF BABYLON.

scarlet woman A woman with a reputation for sexual promiscuity; a prostitute. The allusion is to the WHORE OF BABYLON, a sinful woman described as wearing scarlet in Revelation 17. "Nay, we might have judged that such a child's mother must needs be a scarlet woman, and a worthy type of her of Babylon!" (Nathaniel Hawthorne, *The Scarlet Letter,* 1850).

Scipio *See* CONTINENCE OF A SCIPIO.

Sciron (sīrăn) Archetype of a vicious robber. According to Greek legend Sciron waylaid travelers on the Scironian rock in Megara and made them wash his feet before he kicked them into the sea, where they were devoured by a sea monster. Sciron met his death at the hands of THESEUS. *He showed his enemies the mercy of a Sciron, taking pleasure in humiliating his victims before putting them out of their misery on a permanent basis.*

scourge of scorpions A particularly severe punishment. The phrase, also encountered as *lash of scorpions,* alludes to 1 Kings 12:11: "My father hath chastised you with whips, but I will chastise you with scorpions." *The rebels have threatened to unleash a scourge of scorpions, and the government is more nervous today than it has been for years.*

scrip and staff Wallet and stick, as symbols of earthly possessions, usually in the context of relinquishing them. The phrase appears in Mark 6:7–10,

Luke 9:3, and Matthew 10:10, in which Christ urges his disciples to forsake all possessions when embarking on their travels: "Take nothing for your journey, neither staves, nor scrip, neither brand, neither money; neither have two coats apiece." In medieval times the faithful often carried a staff as a sign that they were on pilgrimage, and somewhat perversely, a purse and staff became recognized emblems of pilgrimage. ". . . from that moment until the closing of the curtain it was music, just music—music to make one drunk with pleasure, music to make one take scrip and staff and beg his way round the globe to hear it" (Mark Twain, *What Is Man and Other Essays,* 1906).

Scylla and Charybdis *See* BETWEEN SCYLLA AND CHARYBDIS.

Scythian defiance (sitheeăn) A threat or gesture of resistance, especially one tersely delivered. The allusion is to the message the nomadic peoples of Scythia sent to Darius I, when he approached with an invading Persian army in 512 B.C. The Scythian ambassador arrived at the king's tent and without a word produced a bird, a frog, a mouse, and five arrows. It was explained to the king that the Scythians were warning him to fly away like a bird, hide in a hole like a mouse, or swim across the river like a frog or else suffer death by Scythian arrows five days later. The attempted Persian conquest failed. *This gesture of Scythian defiance did nothing in the long run to alter the inevitability of defeat.*

season, to every thing there is a; season for all things *See* TIME AND PLACE FOR EVERYTHING.

second Adam *See* ADAM.

second coming A triumphant return from obscurity. The reference is to the Second Coming, or *Second Advent,* of Jesus Christ, when he will visibly return at the end of history to judge the world, destroy evil, and consummate his kingdom (Matthew 16:27 and 24:30, Acts 1:11, 2 Thessalonians 1:3–10, and Revelation 1:7). *The star's return to the silver screen in this movie was greeted as a second coming, although he had never really been away.*

second mile *See* GO THE EXTRA/SECOND MILE.

seek and ye shall find Those who make some effort to get what they want are more likely to succeed. The proverb is of biblical origin, coming from Matthew 7:7–8, which commends the power of prayer: "Ask, and it shall be given you; seek, and ye shall find; knock, and it shall be opened unto you: For every one that asketh receiveth; and he that seeketh findeth; and to him that knocketh it shall be opened." It can also be found in Luke 11:9–13. *Finding the solution to this puzzle will not be easy, but seek and ye shall find.*

see the light To experience a significant revelation; to realize the truth. The allusion is to the revelation undergone by Saul on the ROAD TO DAMASCUS when he was suddenly bathed in a light from heaven and converted to a follower of Jesus Christ (Acts 9:1–22). *He claimed he saw the light at college: Before this he was a hardened atheist, but afterwards he was a devout Christian.* "Stonehenge solstice revellers see the light" (*Guardian,* June 22, 2001).

see through a glass darkly To glimpse the truth despite limitations of the senses. The quotation is from 1 Corinthians 13:12: "Now we see through a glass, darkly; but then face to face." In its original biblical context the phrase refers to the imperfect human understanding of God's purpose. *One day all knowledge will be complete, but for now we see through a glass darkly.* "Britain seen through a glass darkly" (*Guardian,* June 6, 2001).

Seian horse (see̱ăn) A possession that brings its owner bad luck. The allusion is to a fine horse that belonged to the Roman nobleman Cneius Seius. Seius was put to death on the orders of Mark Antony, and the horse's next owner, Cornelius Dolabella, similarly met a premature end, dying in battle in Syria. The horse then passed to Caius Cassius, who died a violent death after the battle of Philippi (42 B.C.), and it ultimately became the property of Mark Antony himself, who committed suicide in 30 B.C. after defeat at Actium. *Like the Seian horse, the jewel seemed to bring its owners nothing but bad luck and in some cases even death itself.*

seize the day *See* CARPE DIEM.

Selene (să̱le̱enee) Personification of the Moon. Selene, the daughter of the Titans Hyperion and Theia and the sister of Helios and Eos, was identified as the moon goddess in Greek mythology. When she fell in love with Endymion, a handsome shepherd boy, Endymion was cast into an eternal sleep so that Selene would always be able to visit him in his dreams. *Selene cast an eerie glow over the scene, bathing the dead and the living alike in her cool light.*

sell one's birthright for a mess of pottage To give up one's rights in something for a paltry sum or other reward. According to Genesis 25:29–34 ESAU foolishly sold his birthright to his treacherous twin brother, Jacob, in exchange for a bowl of soup or stew. "And Jacob sod pottage: and Esau came from the field, and he was faint: And Esau said to Jacob, Feed me, I pray thee, with that same red pottage; for I am faint: therefore was his name called Edom. And Jacob said, Sell me this day thy birthright. And Esau said, Behold, I am at the point to die: and what profit shall this birthright do to me? And Jacob said, Swear to me this day; and he sware unto him: and he sold his birthright unto Jacob. Then Jacob gave Esau bread and pottage of lentils; and he did eat and drink, and rose up, and went his way: thus Esau despised his birthright." "But he who sold his birthright for a mess of pottage existed, and Judas Iscariot existed, and Castlereagh existed, and this man exists!" (Charles Dickens, *Hard Times,* 1854).

Semiramis (săm̲ir̲ămis) Archetype of a powerful female ruler. Semiramis was the legendary founder of Babylon, a mortal Assyrian sometimes described as the daughter of the goddess Derceto. She married King Ninus of Assyria and persuaded him to hand over the crown to her, upon which she had him put to death. An immensely capable queen, she was herself murdered by her son Ninyas. Various queens and empresses have since aspired to her name, including Catherine II of Russia, who was dubbed the "Semiramis of the North." "'Have you completed all the necessary preparations incident to Miss Sedley's departure, Miss Jemima?' asked Miss Pinkerton herself, that majestic lady; the Semiramis of Hammersmith, the friend of Doctor Johnson, the correspondent of Mrs Chapone herself" (William Makepeace Thackeray, *Vanity Fair,* 1847–48).

Semite; Semitic *See* SHEM.

send a sow to Minerva (min̲erv̲ă) To attempt to teach something to a person who is already thoroughly familiar with the subject. The source of the image is a Latin proverb, which likens such behavior to a pig attempting to educate Minerva, the goddess of wisdom. *Lecturing a banker in ways in which to fleece customers is rather like sending a sow to Minerva.*

separate the sheep from the goats To cull the good or useful from the bad or useless. The expression originated from Matthew 25:31–33: "The Son of Man . . . shall separate them one from another, as a shepherd divideth his sheep from the goats: And he shall set the sheep on his right hand, but the goats on the left." It is also encountered in the form ***divide the sheep from the goats.*** "The political feelings of the country are, as a rule, so well marked that it is easy, as to almost every question, to separate the sheep from the goats" (Anthony Trollope, *Phineas Redux,* 1869). *See also* SEPARATE THE WHEAT FROM THE CHAFF.

separate the wheat from the chaff To divide what is valuable from what is worthless. The expression comes from Matthew 3:12, in which John the Baptist describes how Christ will judge the good and the bad on JUDGMENT DAY. *Chaff* describes the husks and other outer material of seed, which is separated from the good grain, in this case wheat, during threshing or winnowing. "Everything is most carefully gone into; we endeavour to sift the wheat from the chaff" (John Galsworthy, *The Forsyte Saga,* 1922). *See also* SEPARATE THE SHEEP FROM THE GOATS.

seraphic (săraˈfik) Serene; rapt. The word alludes to the seraphim, or seraphs, the highest of the nine orders of angels. According to the account in Isaiah 6:1–7 the seraphim are God's fiery six-winged attendants, who sing his praises around his throne. The word comes from *saraph* (meaning "to burn" in Hebrew). "There was a beggar in the street, when I went down; and as I turned my head towards the window, thinking of her calm seraphic eyes, he made me start by muttering, as if he were an echo of the morning: 'Blind! Blind! Blind!'" (Charles Dickens, *David Copperfield,* 1849–50).

Serbonian bog (serbōˈneeăn) A situation from which it is impossible to extricate oneself. The allusion is to a vast area of marshland of the same name that stretched from the isthmus of Suez to the Nile delta in ancient times and in which many armies were said to have been lost. It is now covered in sand. "The lingering twilight served to show them through this Serbonian bog, but deserted them almost totally at the bottom of a steep and very stony hill, which it was the traveller's next toilsome task to ascend" (Sir Walter Scott, *Waverley,* 1814).

Sermon on the Mount A lengthy and authoritative statement of principle, policy, etc. The allusion is to the Sermon on the Mount given by Jesus Christ to his disciples, as described in Matthew 5–7. The passage begins with the BEATITUDES and contains the Lord's Prayer. "This was the first of a series of moral lectures or Sermons on the Mount, which were to be delivered from the same place every Sunday afternoon as long as the fine weather lasted" (Thomas Hardy, *The Return of the Native,* 1880). *See also* CITY ON A HILL; DELIVER US FROM EVIL; ENTER INTO ONE'S CLOSET; GO THE EXTRA/SECOND MILE; HIDE ONE'S LIGHT UNDER A BUSHEL; IF THY RIGHT EYE OFFEND THEE; JOT OR TITTLE; JUDGE NOT, THAT YE BE NOT JUDGED; LAY NOT UP TREASURES UPON EARTH; LEAD US NOT INTO TEMPTATION; LEFT HAND KNOW WHAT YOUR RIGHT HAND IS DOING, DO NOT LET YOUR; LILIES OF THE FIELD; LOVE YOUR ENEMIES; MOTE AND BEAM; RAIN FALLS ON THE JUST AND THE UNJUST, THE; SALT OF THE EARTH; SUFFICIENT UNTO THE DAY IS THE EVIL THEREOF; TOMORROW WILL TAKE CARE OF ITSELF; TURN THE OTHER CHEEK; WOLF IN SHEEP'S CLOTHING.

serpent A source of trouble; an evil influence. The allusion is to the Serpent in the GARDEN OF EDEN, which is described as "more subtil than any beast of the field which the LORD God had made" (Genesis 3:1) and which tempts Eve into tasting the FORBIDDEN FRUIT of the Tree of Knowledge of Good and Evil, telling her that "in the day ye eat thereof, then your eyes shall be opened, and ye shall be as gods, knowing good and evil" (Genesis 3:5). The identification of the Serpent with the devil is based on Revelation 20:2: "And he laid hold on the dragon, that old serpent, which is the Devil, and Satan, and bound him a thousand years." *The serpent of international terrorism has reared its head, and suddenly no one is safe.*

serve God and mammon *See* NO MAN CAN SERVE TWO MASTERS.

serve two masters *See* NO MAN CAN SERVE TWO MASTERS.

Set (set) Incarnation of evil. Set, or **Seth,** featured in ancient Egyptian mythology as the god of fertility, warfare, and storms. He was usually depicted in the form of a dog and was described as the implacable foe of his brothers Horus and Osiris. *The sorcerer called upon Set to help him in his unearthly quest for revenge.*

set the mark of the beast *See* MARK OF THE BEAST.

seven last words The seven last sentences of Christ on the cross. They are as follows: "Eli, Eli, lama sabachthani? . . . My God, my God, why hast thou forsaken me?" (Matthew 27:46; see MY GOD, WHY HAST THOU FORSAKEN ME?), "Father, forgive them; for they know not what they do" (Luke 23:34; see FATHER, FORGIVE THEM; KNOW NOT WHAT THEY DO, THEY), "Today shalt thou be with me in paradise" (Luke 23:43), "Father, into thy hands I commend my spirit" (Luke 23:46), "Woman, behold thy son! . . . Behold thy mother!" (John 19:26–27), "I thirst" (John 19:28), and "It is finished" (John 19:30).

seven pillars of wisdom The fundamental truths upon which life depends. The phrase appears in Proverbs 9:1: "Wisdom hath builded her house, she hath hewn out her seven pillars." Various authorities have identified the seven pillars with the seven patriarchs—Adam, Enoch, Noah, Abraham, Isaac, Jacob, and Moses—while Augustine linked them to the seven churches that united to form the one true church. *These beliefs constitute the seven pillars of wisdom upon which the city has burgeoned over the last 20 years.*

seventy times seven Many times; ad infinitum. The phrase alludes to Matthew 18:21–22, in which Peter asks Christ, "Lord, how oft shall my brother sin against me, and I forgive him? till seven times? Jesus saith unto him, I say not unto thee, Until seven times: but, Until seventy times seven." "'Sir,' I exclaimed, 'sitting here, within these four walls, at one stretch, I have endured and forgiven the four hundred and ninety heads of your discourse. Seventy times seven times have I plucked up my hat and been about to depart—Seventy times seven times have you preposterously forced me to resume my seat" (Emily Brontë, *Wuthering Heights,* 1847).

seven wonders of the world *See* EIGHTH WONDER OF THE WORLD.

seven years of plenty A period of prosperity, especially one that is likely to be followed by a corresponding period of want. The phrase comes from the biblical episode of Pharaoh's dream of "seven well favoured kine and fatfleshed" being devoured by seven "ill favoured and leanfleshed kine" and seven withered ears of corn being consumed by seven good ears (Genesis 41:1–7). Joseph interpreted Pharaoh's dream as a prophecy of seven years of plenty being followed by seven years of famine (Genesis 41:25–32). *The market confidently expects at least seven years of plenty without having to worry about foreign debt.*

shadow of death *See* VALLEY OF THE SHADOW OF DEATH.

Shadrach, Meshach, and Abednego *See* FIERY FURNACE.

shake off the dust from/on one's feet To leave somewhere or disassociate oneself from someone as a result of the treatment one has received. The expression comes from Matthew 10:14, in which Christ advises his disciples what to do when they find themselves in places where their preaching receives a hostile reception: "And whosoever shall not receive you, nor hear your words, when ye depart out of that house or city, shake off the dust of your feet." "The message had been delivered, and Captain Batsby with a frown of anger on his brow was about to shake the dust off from his feet on the uncourteous threshold when there came another message, saying that Captain Batsby could go in and see Sir Thomas if he wished it" (Anthony Trollope, *Ayala's Angel,* 1881).

Sharon, rose of *See* ROSE OF SHARON.

Sheba, Queen of *See* QUEEN OF SHEBA.

sheep from goats *See* SEPARATE THE SHEEP FROM THE GOATS.

sheep to the slaughter *See* LAMB TO THE SLAUGHTER.

Shem (shem) Archetype of a homeless wanderer or vagrant. The allusion is to the biblical Shem, the eldest son of Noah, who according to the Book of Genesis received Noah's blessing after he and his brother

Japheth showed respect to their father when he was drunk. Noah promised his son that God "shall dwell in the tents of Shem" (Genesis 9:24–27), hence his association with wandering peoples and vagrants and his identification as the ancestor of the Hebrews. His name has also given rise to the words **Semite** and **Semitic**. *Like a latter-day Shem he spent years wandering with his family.*

shibboleth (shĭbăleth) A watchword or a generally accepted rule or fundamental precept; a phrase that is difficult to pronounce or a peculiarity of behavior, dress, etc., that is difficult to master and thus may be used to test whether a person belongs to a particular class, profession, or other group. In its original biblical context (Judges 12:1–16) the word (meaning "stream in flood" in Hebrew) was used by Jephthah to tell the Gileadites from their enemies the Ephraimites, who pronounced the word *sibboleth* and thus betrayed their identity and were summarily put to death. "If it works, then some of the old shibboleths about Saturday night being family entertainment night will be buried alongside Noel's House Party" (*Guardian,* July 2, 2001).

Shiloah (shīlōă) A place of heavenly peace and rest. The allusion is to Isaiah 8:6–7, in which Isaiah refers to the "waters of Shiloah that go softly," and also to John 9:1–11, in which Christ heals a blind man by sending him to wash his eyes in the pool of Shiloah, or **Siloam,** just outside Jerusalem. (*Shiloah* comes from the Hebrew word *shalah,* "to send"; *Siloam* is the Greek form used in the Book of John.) *After a lifetime of trouble and misfortune he found himself able to enjoy a brief respite beside the softly flowing waters of Shiloah.*

shining light A person who is recognized as one of the foremost figures in a particular field; a person who shows the way forward. The phrase comes from John 5:35, which describes John the Baptist: "He was a burning and a shining light: and ye were willing for a season to rejoice in his light." It also appears in Proverbs 4:18: "But the path of the just is as the shining light, that shineth more and more unto the perfect day." "She's a capital girl, and she ought to marry a missionary, or one of your reformer fellows, and be a shining light of some sort" (Louisa May Alcott, *An Old Fashioned Girl,* 1870).

shirt of Nessus (ne̱săs) A misfortune from which it is impossible to escape. The allusion is to the death of HERCULES, which came about after he put on a shirt soaked in the poisonous blood of the centaur Nessus, offered to him by his own wife, Deianeira. According to the legend Deianeira had become jealous after the dying Nessus told her Hercules had fallen in love with the beautiful Iole. Nessus also told her that by making her husband wear a shirt soaked in the centaur's blood her husband would be restored to her, so Deianeira dipped the shirt in Nessus's blood and sent it to her husband. The pain inflicted by the centaur's blood was so agonizing that ultimately Hercules sought relief from it by throwing himself onto a funeral pyre. "The words stuck to him like the shirt of Nessus, lacerating his very spirit" (Anthony Trollope, *Doctor Wortle's School,* 1881).

shoot the messenger *See* KILL THE MESSENGER.

shoulders of giants *See* ON THE SHOULDERS OF GIANTS.

show the cloven hoof *See* CLOVEN HOOF.

Shulamite (shoo̱lămīt) A remarkably beautiful woman. According to the Song of Solomon 6:13, the Shulamite is the beloved. The word could be a variant form of *Shunammite,* which means "a girl from Shunem," or a feminine form of *Solomon,* in which instance the word would signify "Solomon's girl." "Love her, Esther! She was to me more than the Shulamite to the singing king, fairer, more spotless; a fountain of gardens, a well of living waters, and streams from Lebanon" (Lew Wallace, *Ben Hur,* 1880).

shut up the bowels of compassion *See* BOWELS OF COMPASSION.

sibyl (si̱băl) A witch, sorceress, or fortune-teller. The word was originally applied in ancient Greece and Rome to the prophetesses (between four and 10 in number) who attended the oracles of the ancient world and delivered messages from the gods. The most famous of them was the sibyl of Cumae, who advised Aeneas on his journey to the underworld and was the supposed fount of the *sibylline books,* a set of prophetic sayings offering guidance in matters of policy and religion. These were kept in the temple of Jupiter on Capitoline Hill in Rome until they were lost in a fire in 83 B.C. "Poor Jotham, whose life paid the forfeiture of his folly, acknowledged, before he died, that his reasons for believing in a mine were extracted from the lips of a sibyl, who, by looking in a magic glass, was enabled to discover the hidden treasures of the earth" (James Fenimore Cooper, *The Pioneers,* 1823).

sign of the times Something that is viewed as symptomatic of present attitudes, fortunes, etc. The phrase comes from Matthew 16:3: "And in the morning, It will be foul weather to day: for the sky is red and lowring. O ye hypocrites, ye can discern the face of the sky; but can ye not discern the signs of the times?" There follows a list of signs of the times that will herald the Second Coming of Christ, such as the appearance of false prophets, wars and rumors of wars, nation rising against nation, famines, pestilences, and earthquakes. ". . . a special financial article in a hostile tone beginning with the words 'We have always feared' and a guarded, half-column leader, opening with the phrase: 'It is a deplorable sign of the times' what was, in effect, an austere, general rebuke to the absurd infatuations of the investing public" (Joseph Conrad, *Chance,* 1913).

Silenus (sīleenăs) Personification of a jovial, pleasure-loving man. Silenus was identified in Greek mythology as the foster father and teacher of Dionysus and considered the god of springs and running water. He shared many of the same characteristics as the SATYRs and was commonly depicted as a fat man riding drunkenly on a donkey or astride a wineskin, wearing a crown of flowers. "I will invite my friends to a last feast; a saturnalia in a city of famine; a banquet of death, spread by the jovial labors of Silenus and his fauns!" (Wilkie Collins, *Antonina,* 1850).

Siloam *See* SHILOAH.

Silvanus (silvaynăs) Personification of the countryside. Silvanus was identified in Roman mythology as the god of woodlands, fields, and flocks, the equivalent of the Greek god Pan. He was reputed to keep wolves away from livestock. *They spent the rest of the afternoon enjoying all the pleasures that Silvanus offered to visitors in that delightful glade.*

silver age A period of history considered inferior to a GOLDEN AGE. According to Hesiod (fl. c. 800 B.C.) and other poets of the classical era, the original silver age was the second of the ages of the world, when humans abandoned themselves to voluptuous and godless ways. *Commercialism has entirely replaced the artistic impulse in what has been termed a second silver age.*

silver cord *See* GOLDEN BOWL.

simony (sīmănee) The practice of buying and selling spiritual or church benefits such as pardons, relics, and ecclesiastical offices. The word comes from the name of Simon Magus, a sorcerer who lived in the first century A.D. and who, having converted to Christianity, sought to buy spiritual power from the apostles until rebuked by Peter (as related in Acts 8): "And when Simon saw that through laying on of the apostles' hands the Holy Spirit was given, he offered them money, saying, Give me also this power" (Acts 8:18–19). The word has also produced the verb *simonize* to describe such activity. *Some modern people could be accused of simony. They think they can buy their way into the kingdom of God.*

Sinai *See* MOUNT SINAI.

sing one's Nunc Dimittis *See* NUNC DIMITTIS.

sinister Ominous; threatening evil or harm. The word comes from the Latin *sinister* (meaning "left handed") and alludes to the ancient notion that in divination, portents that appeared toward the west (on the left of the augur, who traditionally faced north) were negative, while those that appeared toward the east (on the augur's right) were positive. "The hand he gave me was the hand I had bitten. I could not restrain my eye from resting for an instant on a red spot upon it; but it was not so red as I turned, when I met that sinister expression in his face" (Charles Dickens, *David Copperfield,* 1849–50).

Sinon (sīnon) Personification of a person who betrays others by deceit. Sinon was the Greek who convinced the Trojans that there was no danger in dragging the TROJAN HORSE, and the Greek warriors hidden inside it, within the city's walls. *He agreed to act as Sinon, volunteering to go to the meeting and tell anyone who would listen that management was now ready to negotiate.*

sins be as scarlet Even those who are guiltiest of the worst crimes may be forgiven. The phrase comes from Isaiah 1:18, in which sinners are reassured of the possibility of divine forgiveness: "Come now, and let us reason together, saith the LORD: Though your sins be as scarlet, they shall be as white as snow; though they be red like crimson, they shall be as wool." "What if this cursed hand / Were thicker than itself with brother's blood / Is there not rain enough in the sweet heavens / To wash it white as snow?" (William Shakespeare, *Hamlet,* 1603).

sins of the fathers The misdeeds of one generation may have to be atoned for by the generations that follow. The phrase comes from the second of the Ten Commandments, as rendered in Exodus 20:5, which warns that those who offend God may find their descendants must pay for their offenses: "Thou shalt not bow down thyself to them, nor serve them: for I the LORD thy God am a jealous God, visiting the iniquity of the fathers upon the children unto the third and fourth generation of them that hate me." "Do you believe in the sins of the father being revisited on the son?" (*Times,* January 8, 2002).

sin will find you out Crimes and other misdeeds invariably reveal themselves in time. The phrase comes from Numbers 32:23, in which Moses commands the reluctant Reubenites and the Gadites to cross the Jordan, warning them that if they refuse to do so they will have committed a crime against God: "But if ye will not do so, behold, ye have sinned against the LORD: and be sure your sin will find you out." "It sounds horrible and wicked enough, but he cannot be blamed too much, and be sure his sin will find him out" (H. Rider Haggard, *She,* 1887).

Sion *See* ZION.

siren (sīrăn) A seductive or beguiling woman; a temptress. According to Homer's *Odyssey* (c. 700 B.C.) the Sirens were sea nymphs (part women, part bird) who lured sailors and their ships to destruction with their enchanting singing; hence, a *siren song* signifies an extremely attractive and tempting but highly dangerous offer or invitation. Odysseus was curious to hear the song of the sirens and had himself tied to the mast of his ship while the rest of his crew plugged their ears with wax. When the Argonauts sailed past the Sirens, they kept themselves safe by listening instead to the superior singing of Orpheus, upon which the Sirens threw themselves into the sea and were turned into rocks. "Of course such a marriage was only what Newland was entitled to; but young men are so foolish and incalculable—and some women so ensnaring and unscrupulous—that it was nothing short of a miracle to see one's only son safe past the Siren Isle and in the haven of a blameless domesticity" (Edith Wharton, *The Age of Innocence,* 1920).

Sirius (sīreeăs) The brightest star in the sky, situated in the constellation of Canis Major. Also called the dog star, it was named Sirius by the Romans, who believed that dogs were most likely to go mad when the star was at its height (the so-called DOG DAYS of mid-summer). The word itself comes from the Greek *seirios* (meaning "scorching"). "The sky was still thick, but looking straight up he saw a single star, and tried vaguely to reckon whether it were Sirius, or—or—The effort tired him too much, and he closed his heavy lids and thought that he would sleep" (Edith Wharton, *Ethan Frome,* 1911).

Sisera *See* STARS IN THEIR COURSES.

Sisyphean (sisăfeeăn) Of or relating to a seemingly endless or futile effort. The allusion is to the punishment that was imposed by Tartarus upon Sisyphus, king of Corinth, for various misdemeanors. Sisyphus was condemned for eternity to push a large rock up a hill, only to find that when he reached the summit the rock tumbled all the way back to the bottom, so he had to begin all over again. By the same token any fruitless or never-ending task may be called a *burden* or *labor of Sisyphus. For years he had engaged in an apparently Sisyphean effort to persuade the government to change its mind.*

sit at the feet of Gamaliel *See* GAMALIEL.

skeleton at the feast A somber or melancholy note in otherwise joyous surroundings. This colorful image is of ancient origin, its earliest mention being in the *Moralia* of the Greek historian Plutarch (A.D. 46–120). According to Plutarch, who had traveled widely, the Egyptians were in the habit of placing a mummy among the diners at their feasts and celebrations as a reminder of their own mortality. In modern usage the term is often applied to a person who remains depressed and gloomy while those around him or her are throwing themselves into the festivities. "Blunt noticed this and remarked that I seemed to be attracted by the Empress. 'It's disagreeable,' I said. 'It seems to lurk there like a shy skeleton at the feast. But why do you give the name of Empress to that dummy?'" (Joseph Conrad, *The Arrow of Gold,* 1919).

skeptic A person who refuses to accept what he or she is told. The word comes from the Greek *skeptesthai* (meaning "to examine") and was adopted in the fourth century B.C. by the followers of Pyrrho as a name to describe their philosophical movement, otherwise known as Pyrrhonism. Essential to their beliefs were the notions that nothing could be proved beyond doubt and that only the reality of the sensations could be trusted. "'Am I a liar in your eyes?' he asked passionately. 'Little sceptic, you shall be convinced'" (Charlotte Brontë, *Jane Eyre,* 1847).

skin of one's teeth, by the By the narrowest of margins. The expression comes from Job 19:20: "My bone cleaveth to my skin and to my flesh, and I am escaped with the skin of my teeth." *He escaped serious injury only by the skin of his teeth.*

slaughter of the innocents *See* MASSACRE OF THE INNOCENTS.

Sleipnir (<u>sleep</u>neer) Archetype of a fast horse or other animal or vessel. Sleipnir was identified in Norse mythology as the eight-legged horse belonging to Odin. It was reputed to be able to outstrip the wind while running on land or water or in the air. *He patted his mount lovingly, as though convinced it would prove a new Sleipnir in the right conditions.*

smite them hip and thigh To beat someone thoroughly. The phrase comes from Judges 15:8, which describes how Samson exacted his revenge on the Philistines after they burned his wife and father-in-law, smiting them "hip and thigh with a great slaughter." ". . . the old Jew could for some time only answer by invoking the protection of all the patriarchs of the Old Testament successively against the sons of Ishmael, who were coming to smite them, hip and thigh, with the edge of the sword" (Sir Walter Scott, *Ivanhoe,* 1819).

smite the rock To perform a miraculous act. The reference is to Exodus 17:6 and Numbers 20:11, which relate how God instructed Moses to provide water for his people journeying in the wilderness: "Behold, I will stand before thee there upon the rock in Horeb; and thou shalt smite the rock, and there shall come water out of it, that the people may drink." When Moses struck the rock water poured forth. *This time there were no resources left to save them; the rock had been smitten one too many times.* See also MOSES' ROD.

sock A symbol of comic drama. The sock (in Latin *soccus*) was a low loose-fitting slipper commonly worn about the house in the ancient world and also worn on stage by comic actors. "Then to the well-trod stage anon / If Jonson's learned sock be on, / Or sweetest Shakespeare, fancy's child, / Warble his native wood-notes wild" (John Milton, *L'Allegro,* 1631). *See also* BUSKIN.

Socratic (sǎkratik) Of or relating to the philosophical approach of the Greek philosopher Socrates (c. 470–399 B.C.) or more generally to anyone who adopts unconventional philosophical ideas. Transmitted through his pupils Plato and Xenophon, as Socrates left no written account of his thinking, the ***Socratic method*** recommends the use of questions and answers to reach the truth. By employing ***Socratic irony*** (feigning ignorance in an argument) the interrogator may quickly reveal the greater ignorance of an opponent in a philosophical debate or encourage students to develop their own ideas about something. Socrates' own use of such tactics made him many enemies in Athens, and ultimately he was forced to commit suicide by drinking hemlock. "Mr Craig paused a moment with an emphatic stare after this triumphant specimen of Socratic argument" (George Eliot, *Adam Bede,* 1859).

Sodom and Gomorrah (sahdǎm, gǎmorǎ) A place that is notorious for depravity and vice, especially of a sexual nature. Sodom and Gomorrah are described in the book of Genesis as cities of corruption, and for this reason they are both destroyed by FIRE AND BRIMSTONE sent by God: "Then the LORD rained upon Sodom and upon Gomorrah brimstone and fire from the LORD out of heaven; And he overthrew those cities, and all the plain, and all the inhabitants of the cities, and that which grew upon the ground" (Genesis 19:24–25). The term *sodomy,* for anal intercourse, comes from the name of Sodom, whose inhabitants were infamous for such practices (Genesis 19:5). *The preacher warned his congregation in the strongest possible terms against following the sexual sins of Sodom and Gomorrah.*

soft answer turns away wrath, a A gentle response to an insult or other provocation will reduce tension and soothe the anger of others. This advice comes from Proverbs 15:1: "A soft answer turneth away wrath: but grievous words stir up anger." *The situation could easily have gotten out of hand, but the teacher, clearly knowing that a soft answer turns away wrath, calmed down both parties with a quiet word.*

Sol (sahl) Personification of the Sun. Sol was identified in Roman mythology as the sun god, equivalent to the Greek Helios. In Norse mythology Sol was identified as the maiden who steered the chariot of the Sun. *The beach was crowded with scantily clad tourists making their annual obeisance to the great god Sol.*

sold his birthright for a mess of pottage *See* SELL ONE'S BIRTHRIGHT FOR A MESS OF POTTAGE.

solecism (sahlăsizăm) A grammatical mistake; a violation of etiquette or good manners. The word, from the Greek *soiloikos* (meaning "speaking incorrectly"), alludes to the ancient Athenian colony of Soli (or Soloi) on the coast of Cilicia in Asia Minor, whose inhabitants spoke a form of Greek considered degenerate in comparison to Greek as spoken in Athens. "It often is so felt, but we are inclined to say that it never produces half the discomfort or half the feeling of implied inferiority that is shown by a great man who desires his visitor to be seated while he himself speaks from his legs. Such a solecism in good breeding, when construed into English, means this: 'The accepted rules of courtesy in the world require that I should offer you a seat; if I did not do so, you would bring a charge against me in the world of being arrogant and ill-mannered; I will obey the world, but, nevertheless, I will not put myself on an equality with you'" (Anthony Trollope, *Barchester Towers,* 1857).

Solomon   *See* JUDGEMENT OF SOLOMON; SOLOMON'S SEAL; SOLOMON'S TEMPLE.

Solomon's seal   (sŏlămănz)   A flowering plant of the genus *Polygonatum* and a member of the lily family. The plant owes its name to the shape of the prominent leaf scars on its stem that supposedly resemble seals. Another suggestion has it that it is so called because its roots may be used medicinally to seal wounds. The STAR OF DAVID emblem has always been closely associated with Solomon himself and is sometimes referred to as Solomon's seal. *Celandine and Solomon's seal were growing by the side of the road.*

Solomon's temple   (sŏlămănz)   A lavish building or other structure notable for its extravagance. The allusion is to the great Temple in Jerusalem built on the command of King Solomon. The Temple, as described in 1 Kings 5–8 and 2 Chronicles 3–7, was remarkable for the magnificence of its decoration, which included rich cedar wood panels and gold ornamentation. "In this process the chamber and its furniture grew more and more dignified and luxurious; the shawl hanging at the window took upon itself the richness of tapestry; the brass handles of the chest of drawers were as golden knockers; and the carved bed-posts seemed to have some kinship with the magnificent pillars of Solomon's temple" (Thomas Hardy, *Tess of the D'Urbervilles,* 1891).

solon   (sōlăn)   A wise lawgiver; any member of a legislative body. The allusion is to the Athenian statesman Solon, who in the sixth century B.C. repealed most of the unfeasibly severe laws imposed by the DRACONIAN code. His reforms did much to give power back to the Athenian people and helped to lay the foundation for Athenian democracy. "I saw thee once give a penny to a man with a long beard, who, from the dignity of his exterior, might have represented Solon" (Sir Walter Scott, *Redgauntlet,* 1824).

Somnus   (somnăs)   Personification of sleep. Somnus was the god of sleep in Roman mythology, equivalent to the Greek Hypnos. He was said to be a son of Night and a brother of Death. *The call of Somnus was almost irresistible, but he knew he must stay awake until the relief arrived at dawn.*

sons of Adam *See* ADAM.

sons of Bacchus *See* BACCHUS.

sons of Belial *See* BELIAL.

sons of thunder *See* BOANERGES.

sophistry (sahfistree) The use of subtle reasoning to deceive. The word alludes to the Sophists, wandering teachers and philosophers throughout ancient Greece in the fifth and fourth centuries B.C. The word means "wise man," although the widely variant skills and motives of these teachers meant that in time it came to refer to those who cynically used their cunning to mislead or dupe others. "He looked at her imploringly, as if he would willingly have taken a lie from her lips, knowing it to be one, and have made of it, by some sort of sophistry, a valid denial" (Thomas Hardy, *Tess of the D'Urbervilles,* 1891).

Sophoclean (sahfăkleeăn) Direct, simple, clear, and reasonable. The Greek playwright Sophocles (c. 496–406 B.C.) is considered perhaps the finest classical writer of tragic drama, seven examples of which survive out of a total of some 130. He is admired for his economy and simplicity of style and for his relatively straightforward approach to character and plot in such plays as *Oedipus Rex, Antigone,* and *Electra. No one present could have failed to be impressed by the Sophoclean explanation he gave of the company's actions.*

sop to Cerberus (serbărăs) A bribe or gift designed to neutralize a potential threat. In Greek mythology, Cerberus was the terrifying three-headed dog that guarded the entrance to the underworld. When a person died it was customary in classical times to place with the body a cake or some other choice offering with which to pacify Cerberus and thus gain entry to Hades unmolested. When Aeneas ventured into the underworld he went past Cerberus by feeding him a cake of honey and poppy that put him to sleep. *This offer of financial compensation is nothing more than a sop to Cerberus, a bribe to prevent the complainants from going to court.*

345

sounding brass or a tinkling cymbal A meaningless noise. The phrase comes from 1 Corinthians 13:1: "Though I speak with the tongues of men and of angels, and have not charity, I am become as sounding brass, or a tinkling cymbal." "I hearkened and hearkened the ministers, and read an' read at my prayer-book; but it was all like sounding brass and a tinkling cymbal: the sermons I couldn't understand, an' th' prayer-book only served to show me how wicked I was, that I could read such good words an' never be no better" (Anne Brontë, *Agnes Grey*, 1847).

sound of many waters *See* VOICE OF MANY WATERS.

sour grapes Resentment or bitter feelings, usually against something that one cannot enjoy oneself. The allusion is to Aesop's fable about a fox that on finding itself unable to reach a delicious bunch of grapes consoled itself with deciding that they were sour anyway. *He said that the book I wrote is not worth reading, but that is sour grapes because he would like to write one himself.*

sow dragon's teeth To plant the seeds of future conflict. The allusion is to Greek mythology, specifically to the story of Cadmus, who killed a dragon and was instructed to give half the dragon's teeth to the goddess Athena and to plant the other half in the ground. The latter sprouted into warriors who fought one another until only five were left. These survivors then accompanied Cadmus on his mission to found the city of Thebes. Athena gave her part of the teeth to the king of Colchis, who passed them on to Jason, leader of the Argonauts. Among other challenges Jason had to plant the teeth and kill the warriors who sprang up from them before he could secure the Golden Fleece (in which task he was eventually successful). *Few people realized at the time that those who agreed the compromises necessary to facilitate the state's foundation were actually sowing dragon's teeth that would lead to the loss of thousands of lives in the decades to come.* See also PYRRHIC VICTORY.

sow the wind and reap the whirlwind Those who behave irresponsibly or carelessly will find that they have to face disastrous consequences of their misdeeds later on. The expression is of biblical origin, appearing at Hosea 8:7: "For they have sown the wind, and they shall reap the whirlwind: it hath no stalk: the bud shall yield no meal: if so be it yield, the strangers shall swallow it up." In its original biblical context, it referred specifically to the idolatry of the Israelites, which proved a precursor to the Assyrian invasion. *People who behave so irresponsibly in the future will find that they sow the wind and reap the whirlwind.* See also REAP WHAT YOU SOW.

spare the rod and spoil the child Children who are overindulged and never disciplined will grow up to be unruly, maladjusted individuals. This advice, often quoted in defense of corporal punishment and other forms of firm discipline, comes from Proverbs 13:24: "He that spareth his rod hateth his son: but he that loveth him chasteneth him betimes." Further support for such chastisement may be found in Proverbs 23:13–14: "Withhold not correction from the child: for if thou beatest him with the rod, he shall not die. Thou shalt beat him with the rod, and shalt deliver his soul from hell." "'I ain't doing my duty by that boy, and that's the Lord's truth, goodness knows. Spare the rod and spile the child, as the Good Book says. I'm a laying up sin and suffering for us both, I know'" (Mark Twain, *The Adventures of Tom Sawyer,* 1876).

sparrow's fall *See* FALL OF A SPARROW.

Spartacus (spartăkăs) Archetype of a slave who rises up in revolt against his masters. Spartacus was a Thracian slave who was forcibly recruited to the gladiator school at Capua in Italy. He managed to escape and raised an army of slaves, who achieved a series of memorable victories in battle against the legions of ancient Rome. Ultimately he was killed when his army was defeated by Crassus in 71 B.C. The story of Spartacus has inspired a novel by J. Leslie Mitchell (1951), a ballet (1954), and a film (1960). *This lowly cleric long championed the rights of the dispossessed but like some latter-day Spartacus was doomed to defeat in the end.*

Spartan (spartăn) Austere; frugal; very strict, especially in relation to a person's lifestyle or upbringing. The people of Sparta, the capital city of Laconia, were renowned for their rejection of comfort and sophistication (which they were much given to early in their history) in favor of a much more rigorous, self-denying existence—adopted, it was said, at the prompting of the poet Tyrtaeus (fl. c. 650 B.C.). Great emphasis was put on physical endurance and self-discipline. Newborn babies were commonly left exposed on bare mountainsides so that the weak would die and only the strong would live to maturity. Children began military training at the age of seven, and the only respectable career was that of a soldier; mourning of those who fell in battle was discouraged. As a result the Spartans were widely respected in the ancient world as fighters, although the primitive state of their cultural life was decried by their more sophisticated neighbors, and their reluctance to accept new thinking led ultimately to defeat on the battlefield at the hands of the more sophisticated Macedonians. "But although she wondered, she could not help loving him the better for his odd combination of Spartan self-control and what appeared to her romantic and childish folly" (Virginia Woolf, *Night and Day,* 1919). *See also* LACONIC.

spears into pruninghooks *See* BEAT SWORDS INTO PLOWSHARES.

spheres, music of the *See* MUSIC OF THE SPHERES.

sphinx (sfinks) An inscrutable or enigmatic person. The allusion is to the Sphinx of Greek mythology, a monster with the body of a lion and the breasts and face of a woman that attacked Thebes and challenged its victims, on pain of death, to solve the seemingly insoluble RIDDLE OF THE SPHINX. Today the sphinx is best known through the surviving statue at Giza in Egypt, although the Egyptian version is male and lacks the wings that the Greek Sphinx was supposed to have. The word itself means "the strangler." "The distinction of Phipps is his impassivity. He has been termed by enthusiasts the ideal Butler. The Sphinx is not so incommunicable. He is a mask with a manner" (Oscar Wilde, *An Ideal Husband,* 1895).

spirit giveth life *See* LETTER OF THE LAW, THE.

spirit is willing, but the flesh is weak, the It is not always possible for a person to achieve or live up to the standards he or she espouses. In modern usage the line is usually quoted in circumstances where the speaker is apologizing for some moral lapse. The saying comes from Matthew 26:41, in which Christ warned his disciples to remain alert: "Watch and pray, that ye enter not into temptation: the spirit indeed is willing, but the flesh is weak." "Since then I have written many books; and though ceasing my methodical study of the old masters (for though the spirit is willing, the flesh is weak), I have continued with increasing assiduity to try to write better" (W. Somerset Maugham, *The Summing Up,* 1938). *See also* FLESH IS WEAK, THE.

spoil the Egyptians To plunder an enemy, especially through deception or subterfuge. According to Exodus 12:36 the Israelite women were told to take whatever they could from their Egyptian captors before the flight from Egypt: "And the LORD gave the people favour in the sight of the Egyptians, so that they lent unto them such things as they required. And they spoiled the Egyptians." *When the workers realized their dismissal was inevitable they elected to spoil the Egyptians by stealing every tool they could lay their hands on.*

spread one's net To prepare to capture or ensnare someone or something. The expression is of biblical origin, appearing at Proverbs 29:5: "A man that flattereth his neighbour spreadeth a net for his feet." *The government will have to spread its net very wide if it is to make any significant impact on tax evasion.*

spread the gospel To spread news of some kind; to support a particular belief, outlook, etc. The allusion is to the spreading of the Christian message, as undertaken originally by Christ's disciples (Mark 16:15). "Fifa is taking a risk in spreading the World Cup gospel" (*Guardian,* January 2, 2002).

stadium (staydeeăm) A sports arena with tiered seating for spectators. The word comes from the Greek *stadion,* which denoted a length of around 606 feet. This was the distance run by competitors on the sports track at Olympia, and in time the word came to be applied to the arena itself. Legend has it that Hercules himself set the length of the track at Olympia. *The competitors entered the stadium to a deafening roar.*

staff of Aesculapius (eskălaypeeăs) Emblem of the medical profession, including the American Medical Association and the Royal Medical Corps, consisting of a staff with a serpent entwined around. Aesculapius was the god of medicine or healing in Roman mythology, equivalent to the Greek Asclepius, who was reputed to have learned his skills from the centaur

Chiron and become the first physician prior to being slain by Zeus for compromising the god's power over living things. *Doctors with the organization wear badges bearing the staff of Aesculapius to denote their role as healers. See also* CADUCEUS.

star of David A symbol consisting of two superimposed equilateral triangles arranged in the form of a star. The origins of the symbol are uncertain but appear to go back to biblical times, although it is not mentioned specifically in the Bible or the Talmud. It was adopted by the first Zionist Conference in 1897 and in due course became the symbol on the flag of independent Israel. During the Nazi era, authorities implemented, beginning in 1939, the obligatory wearing of the star of David by Jews on their clothing as a "badge" displaying their racial origins. *The Jewish nation has united under the star of David and will stand together until the crisis is past. See also* SOLOMON'S SEAL.

stars in their courses Fate; destiny. The phrase is a quotation from Judges 5:20, which describes how "the stars in their courses fought against Sisera." *Sisera* was a Canaanite general who was doomed to defeat by Deborah and Barak and to his own murder at the hands of Jael, the wife of Heber (Judges 4:17–22). He has since become an archetype of a person who struggles futilely against his fate. "Thus the stars in their courses, fought for Darwin" (George Bernard Shaw, *Back to Methuselah,* 1921).

stations of the cross A series of landmark events. The original Stations of the Cross recorded 14 incidents that occurred during Christ's journey from the judgment hall in Jerusalem to his death by crucifixion at Calvary: 1) Christ is condemned to death, 2) Christ receives the cross, 3) Christ's first fall en route to Calvary, 4) Christ meets his mother, 5) Simon of Cyrene is made to carry the cross, 6) Christ's face is wiped by Veronica (a woman of Jerusalem), 7) Christ's second fall, 8) Christ comforts the women of Jerusalem, 9) Christ's third fall, 10) Christ is stripped of his garments, 11) Christ is nailed to the cross, 12) Christ dies on the cross, 13) Christ's body is taken down from the cross, and 14) Christ's body is laid in the tomb. Representations of these incidents are often arranged around the interior of a church and visited in sequence for prayer and meditation, especially during Lent. *Her divorce marked the last and most important of the* *personal stations of the cross she would have to endure on the road to artistic self-knowledge. See also* VIA DOLOROSA.

stentorian (sten<u>tor</u>eeăn) Very loud, especially as regards speaking, or forcefully expressed. The word alludes to a Greek herald called Stentor, whose voice (according to Homer) was so loud it was equivalent to those of 50 other men. He died after losing a shouting contest with Hermes, the herald of the gods. The word itself means "voice of bronze." "The stentorian tones of the auctioneer, calling out to clear the way, now announced that the sale was about to commence" (Harriet Beecher Stowe, *Uncle Tom's Cabin,* 1852).

Stephen *See* SAINT STEPHEN'S LOAVES.

stigmata (stig<u>mah</u>tă) The brands or other prominent marks or scars on a person's body, especially those associated with suffering or disgrace of some kind. The reference is ultimately to the Greek and Roman practice of branding slaves and criminals with a mark known as the *stigma,* but the word has particular relevance for Christians, who associate it with the wounds Christ sustained to his hands, feet, and side at the Crucifixion (John 19:16–36). Many saints and other holy people over the centuries have reportedly (and apparently miraculously) displayed similar bleeding wounds resembling those inflicted on Christ. "We know too well the child of syphilitic parents; the type is classical; the doctors can pick it out anywhere. Those little old creatures who have the appearance of having already lived, and who have kept the stigmata of all out infirmities, of all our decay" (Upton Sinclair, *Damaged Goods,* 1913).

still small voice An inner sense of right and wrong; the voice of one's conscience. In 1 Kings 19:11–13, God speaks to Elijah on Mount Horeb: "And he said, Go forth, and stand upon the mount before the LORD. And behold, the LORD passed by, and a great and strong wind rent the mountains, and brake in pieces the rocks before the LORD; but the LORD was not in the wind: and after the wind an earthquake; but the LORD was not in the earthquake: And after the earthquake a fire; but the LORD was not in the fire; and after the fire a still small voice . . . and said, What doest thou here, Elijah?" ". . . no louder, no softer; not thrusting itself on people's notice a bit the more for having been outdone by louder sounds—tink, tink, tink, tink. tink. It was a perfect embodiment of the still small voice, free from all cold, hoarseness, huskiness, or unhealthiness of any kind" (Charles Dickens, *Barnaby Rudge,* 1841).

stoic (st<u>o</u>ik) Accepting one's fate without showing emotion. The word alludes to the Stoics, members of a philosophical school founded in ancient Greece in the fourth century B.C. influenced by the teachings of Zeno of Citium, they recommended the repression of emotion and advocated the supremacy of a cool-headed, rational approach. They came to be called the Stoics because they held meetings at the Painted Portico, or *Stoa Poikile,* in Athens. "At the pronounced words and the spontaneous echo that voluminously rebounded them, Captain Vere, either thro' stoic self-control or a sort of momentary paralysis induced by emotional shock, stood erectly rigid as a musket in the ship-armourer's rack" (Herman Melville, *Billy Budd,* 1924).

stolen waters are sweet pleasures acquired illegally or through otherwise dubious means are all the more enjoyable. The sentiment comes from Proverbs 9:17: "Stolen waters are sweet, and bread eaten in secret is pleasant." ". . . his eyes dancing with all the glee of a forbidden revel; and his features, which have at all times a mischievous archness of expression, confessing the full sweetness of stolen waters, and bread eaten in secret" (Sir Walter Scott, *Redgauntlet,* 1824). *See also* FORBIDDEN FRUIT.

straight and narrow The honest or moral path. The phrase is biblical in origin, from Matthew 7:13–14, which warns that it is much easier to follow the path to eternal condemnation than it is to take the path that leads to salvation: "Enter ye in at the strait gate: for wide is the gate, and broad is the way, that leadeth to destruction, and many there be which go in thereat: Because strait is the gate, and narrow is the way, which leadeth unto life, and few there be that find it." (*Strait* in this context means "narrow.") "You can walk the straight and narrow, but with a little bit of luck you'll run amuck" (Alan Jay Lerner, "With a Little Bit of Luck," 1956).

strain at a gnat and swallow a camel To make much fuss over a relatively insignificant detail yet ignore what is important. The expression comes from Matthew 23:24, in which Christ compares the superficial attitude of the Pharisees to those who worry about the tiny insect that has fallen into their drink, while drinking down one of the largest of animals that has also fallen in: "Ye blind guides, which strain at a gnat, and swallow a camel." "Go where you may, you will attract attention; you will make an enemy of every ugly woman who looks at you. Strain at a gnat, Catherine, and swallow a camel. It's only a question of time" (Wilkie Collins, *The Evil Genius,* 1886).

strait and narrow *See* STRAIGHT AND NARROW.

stranger and ye took me in *See* I WAS A STRANGER, AND YE TOOK ME IN.

stranger in a strange land A person who is unfamiliar with his or her surroundings and the people near him or her. The origin of this phrase is Exodus 2:22: "And she, bare him a son, and he called his name Gershom: for he said, I have been a stranger in a strange land." The name Gershom sounds like the Hebrew for "an alien there." "After thirteen years of romantic mystery, the brethren who had wronged Joseph, came, strangers in a strange land, hungry and humble, to buy 'a little food'; and being summoned to a palace, charged with crime, they beheld in its owner their wronged brother" (Mark Twain, *The Innocents Abroad,* 1869).

streets of gold A place where there are plentiful opportunities to make an easy fortune. The expression comes from Revelation 21:21, in which John describes his vision of NEW JERUSALEM (the celestial city of heaven) in terms of streets paved with gold: "And the twelve gates were twelve pearls; every several gate was of one pearl: and the street of the city was pure gold, as it were transparent glass." "Oh, London is a fine town, A very famous city, Where all the streets are paved with gold" (George Colman the Younger, *The Heir-at-Law,* 1797).

strong, out of the *See* OUT OF THE STRONG CAME FORTH SWEETNESS.

strong meat Something that arouses repulsion, fear, or anger among people of a sensitive disposition. The phrase comes from Hebrew 5:12: "For when for the time ye ought to be teachers, ye have need that one teach you again which be the first principles of the oracles of God; and are become such as have need of milk, and not of strong meat." In this original biblical context the "strong meat" refers to more advanced teachings of God that the faithful are deemed not yet capable of absorbing. *The fascinating but scandalous subject of the professor's lecture was rather strong meat for some of the more impressionable members of his audience, who begged to be excused and left in some haste.*

stumbling block An obstacle that hinders progress. The phrase occurs several times in the Bible, as in Romans 14:13: "Let us not therefore judge one another any more: but judge this rather; that no man put a stumbling-block or an occasion to fall in his brother's way." "We've studied hard and Miss Stacy has drilled us thoroughly, but we mayn't get through for all that. We've each got a stumbling block. Mine is geometry of course, and Jane's is Latin, and Ruby and Charlie's is algebra, and Josie's is arithmetic" (Lucy Maud Montgomery, *Anne of Green Gables,* 1908).

Stygian (<u>stij</u>ăn) Dreadful; very gloomy; impenetrably dark. The word comes from the name of the *Styx,* the river that according to Greek mythology encircled Hades. The dead were carried across its waters by Charon the boatman. "A beam from the setting sun pierced the Stygian gloom" (H. Rider Haggard, *She,* 1887).

Stymphalian birds *See* LABORS OF HERCULES.

Styx *See* STYGIAN.

sub rosa (săb <u>rō</u>ză) Secretly; confidentially. The rose was a great favorite of the ancient Romans and among other qualities was understood to represent secrecy, an association it acquired either through its earlier identification with the Egyptian god Horus, who listed secrecy among his virtues, or through the legend that Eros bribed Harpocrates with a rose so that he would not tell Venus of their intimacies. Consequently a rose was sometimes suspended over council tables as a reminder that any conversations that took place happened "under the rose," that is, in confidence. Similarly a bouquet of roses over a doorway was supposed to be a sign that anything said inside would be kept confidential and thus all present could speak freely. The phrase had acquired a legal connotation by the 19th century, referring to the confidentiality that exists between lawyer and client. *By mutual agreement these meetings always took place sub rosa, and no records were made of what was said.*

such a time as this *See* FOR SUCH A TIME AS THIS.

suffer fools gladly To tolerate foolish people with patience. The expression comes from 2 Corinthians 11:19: "For ye suffer fools gladly, seeing ye yourselves are wise." In the original biblical reference Paul commends the Corinthians for their forbearance, underlining that it is a proof of wisdom to tolerate those who lack it. "A clever woman and thoroughly coached, thought I. Well, zikali was never one to suffer fools, and doubtless she is another of the pawns whom he uses on his board of policy" (H. Rider Haggard, *Finished,* 1917).

suffer the little children To show greater forbearance to children and other innocents. The phrase comes from Matthew 19:14, in which Christ tells his disciples that he welcomes children to come to him for his blessing: "Suffer little children to come unto me, and forbid them not: for of such is the kingdom of heaven." *Suffer* here means "let" or "allow." (See also Luke 18:15.) *The priest frowned as the boys raced about the vestry and reflected that it was not always easy to "suffer the little children," as he so often instructed his parishioners.*

sufficient unto the day is the evil thereof It is enough to worry about one's present troubles without concerning oneself with possible future problems as well. The expression comes from the account of Christ's Sermon on the Mount at Matthew 6:33–34: "Seek ye first the kingdom of God, and his righteousness; and all these things shall be added unto you. Take therefore no thought for the morrow: for the morrow shall take thought for the things of itself. Sufficient unto the day is the evil thereof." *There's no point in getting anxious about tomorrow—sufficient into the day is the evil thereof.* See also TOMORROW WILL TAKE CARE OF ITSELF.

sulk in one's tent To retreat into moody seclusion while nursing a private grievance. The reference is to the behavior of Achilles after he lost his prize of the beautiful slave girl Briseis to his rival Agamemnon, king of Mycenae, during the Trojan War. According to Homer's *Iliad* (c. 700 B.C.), Achilles retreated to his tent and only consented to come out again after the death of his close friend Patroclus. In his absence the Greeks sustained several serious reverses on the battlefield. Variants of the phrase include to *sulk like Achilles* and to *sulk like Achilles in his tent*. *After this initial reverse the party's candidate refused to take part in any more television showdowns and instead retired to sulk in his tent.*

sun go down on one's anger, don't let the Never end the day unreconciled with those with whom one has quarreled. This proverbial advice comes from Ephesians 4:26: "Be ye angry, and sin not: let not the sun go down upon your wrath." Variants include *don't go to bed angry*. *Her husband recalled the saying about not letting the sun go down on one's anger and resolved to go around to their neighbors' house to apologize before dinnertime.*

Susanna and the Elders *See* DANIEL COME TO JUDGMENT, A.

sweat of thy face *See* ADAM'S CURSE.

sword of Damocles (<u>dam</u>ăkleez) A looming threat; an impending danger. According to Greek legend Damocles was a nobleman who sought to ingratiate himself with Dionysus the Elder (405–367 B.C.) by remarking enviously upon the great happiness that Dionysus must enjoy as ruler of Syracuse. In response Dionysus invited Damocles to dine with him. Only after Dionysus had sat down to eat did Damocles realize that there was a sword suspended over his head by a single hair. Thus threatened, Damocles did not enjoy his meal and came to appreciate how Dionysus himself had to live with the perpetual fear of assassination or deposition by jealous enemies. "True, in old age we live under the shadow of Death, which, like a sword of Damocles, may descend at any moment" (Samuel Butler, *The Way of All Flesh*, 1903).

swords into plowshares *See* BEAT SWORDS INTO PLOWSHARES.

sybaritic (sibă<u>ri</u>tik) Pleasure-loving; luxurious; self-indulgent. The inhabitants of the town of Sybaris in ancient Lucania (southern Italy) were notorious for their pleasure-loving ways and their indulgence in all manner of comforts and luxuries. By the same token, any person who shows a fondness for the good things in life may be dubbed a **sybarite.** *The sybaritic ways of the urban young were never likely to win much approval among their elders.*

sycophant (sĭkōfănt, sīkōfănt) A person who flatters to win favor; a parasite; a toady. The word comes from the Greek *sykon* (meaning "fig") and *phainein* (meaning "to show"). It is supposed to allude to informants who told the ancient Greek authorities about neighbors who were illegally exporting figs or helping themselves to the fruit of sacred fig trees. Another derivation suggests a link with a class of Athenian lawyers called *sycophants,* who were known to blackmail their clients with the threat of revealing their guilt, thereby "shaking the fig tree" to obtain money or other favors. *Once in power the young king disposed of the aged counselors who had advised his mother and surrounded himself with sycophants.*

Symplegades (simplegădeez) Rocks or other obstacles that may prove treacherous to passing vessels. The Symplegades (meaning "clashing ones") were two moving rocks located at the entrance to the Black Sea. According to legend, these rocks would press together when a ship came between them, crushing it to pieces. The Argonauts successfully negotiated this obstacle by the ruse of sending a bird through the gap and then slipping through as the rocks opened again, sustaining only minor damage to the stern of the ship as they went through. Ever since then the Symplegades, sometimes called the **Cyanean rocks,** have been fused as one. "I saw fastened to a shed near the light-house a long new sign with the words 'Anglo Saxon' on it in large gilt letters, as if it were a useless part which the ship could afford to lose, or which the sailors had discharged at the same time with the pilot. But it interested somewhat as if it had been a part of the Argo, clipped off in passing through the Symplegades" (Henry David Thoreau, *Cape God,* 1865).

syrinx *See* PANPIPES.

tabernacle (tabernakăl) A shrine or other place of worship or by extension any building, cupboard, etc., in which something precious is preserved. The allusion is to the Tabernacle of the Old Testament, a portable sanctuary in which God was worshiped from the time of Moses to Solomon. It is described in Exodus 25–31 as a large tent (the Latin word *tabernaculum* meaning "tent") divided by a veil creating the HOLY OF HOLIES (an inner chamber), and an outer area called the Holy Place; the whole structure was surrounded by an enclosure. "Not a soul attended; one of the most anxious afternoons that he had ever known was spent by Richard in a vain discussion with Mrs Hollister, who strongly contended that the Methodist (her own) church was the best entitled to and most deserving of, the possession of the new tabernacle" (James Fenimore Cooper, *The Pioneers,* 1823).

table of Pythagoras (păthagorăs) The multiplication table as represented by a square divided into 100 squares. The multiplication table is traditionally credited to the Greek mathematician and philosopher Pythagoras (c. 580–c. 500 B.C.). *The table of Pythagoras is still in common use in classrooms around the world.*

Taenarum (taynahrăm) A gloomy, ominous place. Greek legend identified a cave at Taenarum, the southernmost tip of the Peloponnesus, as one of the entrances to the underworld. *He shuddered at the thought of being consigned to this melancholy hole in the ground, gaping like Taenarum, the portal to Hades.*

Tabitha *See* DORCAS SOCIETY.

take a little wine Drink a small amount of wine to settle the digestion. This proverbial piece of advice comes from 1 Timothy 5:23, in which Paul advised Timothy, "Drink no longer water, but use a little wine for thy stomach's sake and thine often infirmities." *"Take a little wine," said the general, offering to fill her glass. "It will do you a world of good."*

take in vain *See* TAKE THE NAME OF GOD IN VAIN.

take one's cross *See* BEAR / CARRY / TAKE ONE'S CROSS.

take the name of God in vain To show disrespect toward God; to blaspheme. The phrase comes from the third of the Ten Commandments, as given in Exodus 20:7: "Thou shalt not take the name of the LORD thy God in vain; for the LORD will not hold him guiltless that taketh his name in vain." In modern usage the phrase is used more widely, and any act of disrespect toward another person may be described in terms of taking that person's name in vain. *His mother dropped the vase in horror. She had never heard her son take the name of God in vain before.*

take the sword, perish with the sword *See* LIVE BY THE SWORD SHALL DIE BY THE SWORD, THOSE WHO.

take the wings of the morning *See* WINGS OF THE MORNING.

take time by the forelock *See* CARPE DIEM.

take up thy bed and walk *See* RISE, TAKE UP THY BED, AND WALK.

talents *See* PARABLE OF THE TALENTS.

tale that is told Life as a transient phenomenon with no more substance or importance than a story. The phrase comes from Psalm 90:8–9, which depicts God as a refuge for the human race: "Thou hast set our iniquities before thee, our secret sins in the light of thy countenance. For all thy days are passed away in thy wrath: we spend our years as a tale that is told." In 1605 William Shakespeare wrote in *Macbeth*, "Life's but a walking shadow, a poor player, / That struts and frets his hour upon the stage, / And then is heard no more; it is a tale / Told by an idiot, full of sound and fury, / Signifying nothing." "Thus man passes away; his name perishes from record and recollection; his history is as a tale that is told, and his very monument becomes a ruin" (Washington Irving, "Westminster Abbey," 1820).

tall poppy   A prominent member of society; a leader. The phrase alludes to the reply of Tarquinius Superbus, the seventh and last legendary king of Rome, when his son Sextus asked him how to subdue the inhabitants of the city of Gabii. Instead of answering in words, Tarquinius simply strode about his garden striking the heads off the tallest poppies with his stick. By this Sextus understood that if he executed all the most prominent people in the city the rest of the populace would fall in line. *Several tall poppies are expected to be scythed down as a result of official investigations into the industry.*

talmudic   (tal<u>moo</u>dik)   Of or relating to the Talmud, a body of Jewish ethical sources. The name derives from a Hebrew root word for "study." The Talmud is a record of wide-ranging discussions of ethical matters in the early centuries of the common era (A.D.) held both in the land of Israel and in Babylonia. All such discussions followed a formula: They began with a practical question or problem to which rabbis offered a response or solution, supported by reasoned argument, biblical references, and established principles and practices of an ethical or legal nature. Consensus was sought but not always achieved, and minority opinions were recorded and credited. By the year 200 the assembled material was edited for duplication and was structured logically for ease of reference. Six major orders (topics) were delineated, and each order was further subdivided. This editing process resulted in a work known as the Mishnah (from a word meaning "repeat" or "teach"), which in turn became the focus of discussion and was further extended and embellished. The resulting work was the Gemara (from a root meaning "complete"). The Mishnah and the Gemara, as well as subsequent contributions, were dovetailed into it. By 500 there were two versions of the Talmud: the Talmud Yerushalmi (Jerusalemite) and the more substantial Talmud Bavli (Babylonian), which is thought more authoritative and is referred to more frequently. Traditional observant Jews believe the Talmud to be the "oral Torah," mirroring the written Torah. The Talmud contains some legend and folklore, but most of this material is found in the Midrash. An archaic usage of *talmudic* denoted "cryptic" or "esoteric"—a usage that was offensive to Jews. *The precepts were traced to their talmudic source.*

tantalize To tease or torment someone with something desirable while at the same time preventing him or her from obtaining or enjoying it. The word alludes to the legend of Tantalus, mythical king of Phrygia and a son of Zeus. Tantalus was consigned to Hades after stealing his father's favorite dog, stealing ambrosia nectar and giving it to men, and killing his own son and serving him up as food for the gods. He was punished by being made to stand in water that retreated whenever he tried to drink it and under a bough bearing delicious fruit that remained just beyond his grasp. "To surround his interior with a sort of invidious sanctity, to tantalize society with a sense of exclusion, to make people believe his house was different from every other, to impart to the face that he presented to the world a cold originality—this was the ingenious effort of the personage to whom Isabel had attributed a superior morality" (Henry James, *Portrait of a Lady*, 1881).

Tarpeian rock (tahrpeeăn) A height from which a condemned person may be hurled to destruction. The reference is to Tarpeian Rock on the Capitoline from which criminals guilty of treason were thrown to their death in ancient Rome. Legend had it that it was named after Tarpeia, the daughter of the general who held the fortress on the hill against the Sabines. When the Sabines attempted to storm it, Tarpeia treacherously opened a gate to the invaders in the expectation of being rewarded with the gold bracelets they wore on their left arms but was instead crushed to death by the soldiers' shields, which they also carried on the left arms. *When the market crashed the towering stock exchange building became a Tarpeian rock from which stricken executives hurled themselves to oblivion.*

tartar (tahrter) A fearsome or formidable person, especially one with a shrewish character. The origins of the word lie in the Tartar, or *Tatar,* warriors who swept through postmedieval Asia and eastern Europe, spreading terror wherever they went. They were so called in reference to *Tartarus,* the Latin name for the lowest region of hell, because they seemed like demons from the underworld. According to Greek legend the region of Tartarus was reserved for the Titans and those criminals deserving of the most severe punishments. "At last Mr Guppy came back, looking something the worse for the conference. 'My eye, miss,' he said in a low voice, 'he's a Tartar!'" (Charles Dickens, *Bleak House*, 1852–53).

tears, vale of *See* VALE OF TEARS.

tears of Eos (<u>ee</u>os) The morning dew. The allusion is to the tears that were supposedly wept every morning by the Greek goddess Eos in mourning for her son Memnon, who was slain by Achilles during the Trojan War. *The lawns sparkled with the "tears of Eos" as the old romantic liked to say.*

teeth set on edge *See* SOUR GRAPES.

Teiresias *See* TIRESIAS.

telamon (<u>tel</u>ămăn) An architectural column in the shape of a male figure. The allusion is to Telamon, a mythological king of Salamis who participated in the CALYDONIAN BOAR HUNT and was one of the Argonauts. He is also identified as the father of Ajax and Teucer. *The temple portico was supported by a dozen telamons in the Greek style. See also* CARYATID.

Telemachus *See* ODYSSEUS.

tell it not in Gath (gath) Do not allow your enemies to make capital out of your misfortunes; be careful to whom you reveal your weaknesses. Gath is identified in 2 Samuel 1:17–20 as the city of the Philistines: "And David lamented with this lamentation over Saul and over Jonathan his son . . . the beauty of Israel is slain upon thy high places: how are the mighty fallen! Tell it not in Gath, publish it not in the streets of Askelon; lest the daughters of the Philistines rejoice, lest the daughters of the uncircumcised triumph." "Tell this not in Gath, lest the Scots rejoice that they have at length found a parallel instance among their neighbours, to that barbarous deed which demolished Arthur's Oven" (Sir Walter Scott, *Ivanhoe*, 1819).

Tellus (<u>tel</u>ăs) Personification of the Earth. Tellus was identified in Roman mythology as the goddess of the Earth, equivalent to the Greek GAEA. "On the following morning it was known that Lord De Terrier was with the Queen at Buckingham Palace, and at about twelve a list of the new ministry was published, which must have been in the highest degree satisfactory to the whole brood of giants. Every son of Tellus was included in it, as were also very many of the daughters" (Anthony Trollope, *Framley Parsonage,* 1861).

Tempe, vale of (<u>tempee</u>) A beautiful valley. The picturesque wooded valley of Tempe in Thessaly, situated between Mount Olympus and Mount Ossa, was considered sacred to Apollo and it was here that he pursued Daphne until she forever escaped his clutches by being transformed into a laurel tree. "Indeed, it is a question if the exclusive reign of this orthodox beauty is not approaching its last quarter. The new Vale of Tempe may be a gaunt waste in Thule; human souls may find themselves in closer and closer harmony with external things wearing a sombreness distasteful to our race when it was young" (Thomas Hardy, *The Return of the Native,* 1878).

ten commandments A set of rules that must not, under any circumstances, be broken. The original Ten Commandments were the laws revealed by God to Moses on the top of Mount Sinai for the guidance of the Israelites (as related in Exodus 20:3–17 and Deuteronomy 5:6–21). The first four describe the responsibilities of the Israelites to God; the last six describe their responsibilities to one another. Moses carried the Ten Commandments, inscribed by the finger of God on two stone tablets, down the mountain but later smashed them to pieces in disgust when he found that in his absence his people had begun to worship an idol called the Golden Calf. Subsequently Moses returned to Mount Sinai and was presented with two new stone tablets, which were placed in the Ark of the Covenant. "The business world needs the 10 commandments of email" (*The Guardian,* November 5, 2001). *See also* THOU SHALT HAVE NO OTHER GODS BEFORE ME; THOU SHALT NOT STEAL.

Tenth Muse Poetical inspiration, sometimes used in reference to a female poet or a literary woman; an inspiring or influential nontraditional art form. The allusion is to Sappho (c. 650–c. 580 B.C.), the poetess of Lesbos who was sometimes referred to as the Tenth Muse. "'You were right in telling me she would do me no good. But you were wrong in thinking I should wish to be like her.' 'Wouldn't you really like to be a tenth Muse, then, Maggie?' said Philip, looking up in her face as we look at a first parting in the clouds, that promises us a bright heaven once more" (George Eliot, *The Mill on the Floss,* 1860). *See also* MUSES.

terpsichorean (terpsikă<u>ree</u>ăn, terpsă<u>kor</u>eeăn) Of or relating to dancing. The allusion is to Terpsichore, identified in Greek mythology as the muse of choral dance and song (see MUSES) and conventionally depicted holding a lyre. "The old-fashioned fronts of these houses, which had older than old-fashioned backs, rose sheer from the pavement, into which the bow windows protruded like bastions, necessitating a pleasing chassez-dechassez movement to the time-pressed pedestrian at every few yards. He was bound also to evolve other Terpsichorean figures in respect of door-steps, scrapers, cellar-hatches, church buttresses, and the overhanging angles of walls which, originally unobtrusive, had become bow-legged and knock-kneed" (Thomas Hardy, *The Mayor of Casterbridge,* 1886).

tertium quid (<u>ter</u>sheeăm kwid, <u>ter</u>teeăm kwid) An unknown, unclassifiable, or nameless thing that has the features of two other things. The phrase is credited to the Greek philosopher and mathematician Pythagoras (c. 580–c. 500 B.C.), who once offered the following definition of a biped: "A man is a biped, so is a bird, and a third thing." According to Iamblichus (c. A.D. 250–c. 330), another Greek philosopher, the "third thing" Pythagoras had in mind was himself. "And there is another mode of dress open to him, which I can assure my readers is not an unknown costume, a tertium quid, by which semi-decorum and comfort are combined. The hunting breeches are put on first, and the black trowsers are drawn over them" (Anthony Trollope, *Hunting Sketches,* 1865).

Tethys (<u>tee</u>this) The sea; the third satellite of the planet Saturn. Tethys was one of the Titans of Greek mythology, a sea goddess who was the daughter of Uranus and the wife of Oceanus and by him became the mother of the sea nymphs called the Oceanids. *He slipped soundlessly over the side of the boat and into the welcoming arms of Tethys, goddess of the sea.*

Teucer (<u>tyoo</u>ser) Archetype of a skilled archer. According to Greek legend Teucer was the son of Telamon and Hesione and became famous for his skills in archery with the Greek army during the Trojan War. On his return from Troy he was sent into exile by his father for having failed to avenge the death of his brother, AJAX, at the hands of Odysseus. "'But,' thought he, 'I may, like a second Teucer, discharge my shafts from behind the shield of my ally; and, admit that he should not prove to be a first-rate poet, I am in no shape answerable for his deficiencies, and the good notes may very probably help off an indifferent text'" (Sir Walter Scott, *The Antiquary*, 1816).

Thais (<u>thay</u>ăs) A woman who uses her beauty to influence her lover. The original Thais was an Athenian courtesan of the fourth century B.C. who became the mistress of Alexander the Great. She exercised her influence over him to persuade him to order the burning of the palace of Persepolis. ""The lovely Thais sits beside you. Take the goods the gods provide you." I often say that to my wife, till the children have got calling her Thais. The children have it pretty much their own way with us, Mr Crawley'" (Anthony Trollope, *The Last Chronicle of Barset*, 1867).

Thalatta! (thă<u>la</u>ta) A cry of joy or triumph. Greek soldiers retreating from their Persian enemies were reputed to have exclaimed, "Thalatta! Thalatta!" (meaning "the sea! the sea!") on catching sight of the waters of the Black Sea. *Like the Greeks at the sight of their deliverance, he felt like shouting out "Thalatta! Thalatta!" at this first glimpse of his rescuers.*

Thalia (thă<u>li</u>ă) A source of poetical or comic inspiration. Thalia was one of the MUSES of Greek mythology, identified as the muse of comedy and pastoral poetry. The word comes from the Greek *thaleia* (meaning "blooming"). *Thalia herself would appear to have sat at his elbow, guiding his pen as a young man, but in his latter years she seems to have deserted him for other rivals.* See also THREE GRACES.

Thanatos (<u>tha</u>nătos) The personification of death. According to Greek mythology Thanatos was the son of Nyx, the goddess of night, and was identified as the god of death. In the first half of the 20th century Sigmund Freud selected *Thanatos* as a name for the universal death instinct. *This urge for self-destruction, the magnetic pull of Thanatos, is hard for some people to resist at such moments.*

Themis (<u>thee</u>mis) Personification of justice. Themis was identified in Greek mythology as the daughter of Uranus and Gaea and respected as the goddess of law and order, alongside her husband Jupiter. She is perhaps best known today through her visual representation, conventionally holding a cornucopia and a pair of scales. "By next day's post, the solicitor sent the case to London, a chef-d'oeuvre of its kind; and in which, my informant assured me, it was not necessary on revisal to correct five words. I am not, therefore, conscious of having overstepped accuracy in describing the manner in which Scottish lawyers of the old time occasionally united the worship of Bacchus with that of Themis" (Sir Walter Scott, *Guy Mannering,* 1815).

Theon's tooth (<u>thee</u>onz) A sharp or penetrating criticism. The allusion is to the ancient Roman poet Theon, who was noted for his biting satires. *It was clear that both actors were suffering acutely from the poisonous imprint of Theon's tooth in that morning's reviews of the performance.*

Theramenes, sandals of *See* WEAR THE SANDALS OF THERAMENES.

there is a time and a place for everything *See* TIME AND PLACE FOR EVERYTHING.

there is no peace for the wicked *See* NO PEACE FOR THE WICKED.

there is nothing new under the sun *See* NOTHING NEW UNDER THE SUN.

there was no more spirit in her *See* QUEEN OF SHEBA.

there were brave men before Agamemnon *See* BRAVE MEN BEFORE AGAMEMNON, THERE WERE.

Thermopylae (ther<u>mop</u>ălee) A decisive battle or moment, especially when facing overwhelming odds. It was at the narrow pass of Thermopylae in Thessaly (the only route connecting north and south Greece) that Leonidas and 300 Spartans heroically held off a much larger invading Persian army in 480 B.C., fighting to the death after being betrayed by a Greek traitor. Their courage became a symbol of Spartan indomitability. The word itself means "hot gates." "He would much prefer not to die. He would abandon a hero's or a martyr's end gladly. He did not want to make a Thermopylae, not be Horatius at any bridge, nor be the Dutch boy with his finger in that dyke" (Ernest Hemingway, *For Whom the Bell Tolls,* 1941).

Thersites (thersīteez) Archetype of an impudent, foul-tongued critic, especially one who criticizes everyone and everything. Thersites was a trouble-making deformed Greek warrior who was killed by a blow from Achilles during the Trojan War after daring to mock him for his grief over the death of his friend Penthesilea. "And first, it may be said, there is a pelting kind of thersitical satire, as black as the very ink 'tis wrote with . . ." (Laurence Sterne, *Tristram Shandy*, 1759).

Theseus (theeseeăs) Archetype of a mythological hero and adventurer. Theseus was the son of Aegeus, the king of Athens, and the central figure in a series of legendary encounters. These episodes included the slaying of the Minotaur, the conquest of the Amazons, taking part in the Calydonian hunt, and seeking the Golden Fleece. "'I will tell you what, Mistress Mary—it will be rather harder work to learn surveying and drawing plans than it would have been to write sermons,' he had said, wishing her to appreciate what he went through for her sake; 'and as to Hercules and Theseus, they were nothing to me. They had sport, and never learned to write a bookkeeping hand'" (George Eliot, *Middlemarch*, 1871–72).

thespian (thespeeăn) An actor. The word was originally coined in tribute to the Greek poet Thespis, who is traditionally credited with having been the founder of Greek tragic drama in the late sixth century B.C. With great success Thespis introduced the actor in the guise of a figure from history or legend as an alternative to the convention of the chorus narrating the action. As an adjective *thespian* is applied to anything of or relating to the theater as a whole. "Vergil Gunch thundered, 'When we manage to grab this celebrated Thespian off his lovely aggregation of beautiful actresses— and I got to admit I butted right into his dressing-room and told him how the Boosters appreciated the high-class artistic performance he's giving us.'" (Sinclair Lewis, *Babbitt*, 1922).

Thestylis (thestilis) A rustic maiden. The allusion is to the young female slave called Thestylis who appears in the *Idylls* of the Greek pastoral poet Theocritus (c. 310–250 B.C.). *He was immediately captivated by this Thestylis and her beautiful voice and within a month had written a dozen magnificent poems in her honor.*

Thetis's hair stone (<u>thee</u>tis) Rock crystal containing hairlike filaments. It is also called *Venus's hair stone.* The allusion is to Thetis, the leader of the sea nymphs known as the Nereids in Greek mythology and remembered as the mother of Achilles. *Instead of leaving, the little girl reached into her bag and handed him a crystal lump of the type some people call Thetis's hair stone.*

they know not what they do *See* FATHER, FORGIVE THEM.

they that sow the wind shall reap the whirlwind *See* SOW THE WIND AND REAP THE WHIRL WIND.

they toil not, neither do they spin *See* LILIES OF THE FIELD.

thief in the night, like a Suddenly; unexpectedly; surreptitiously. The phrase is biblical in origin, appearing in 1 Thessalonians 5:1–3, where it describes how Jesus Christ will return: "But of the times and the seasons, brethren, ye have no need that I write unto you. For yourselves know perfectly that the day of the Lord so cometh as a thief in the night. For when they shall say, Peace and safety; then sudden destruction cometh upon them, as travail upon a woman with child; and they shall not escape." "For the Son of Man cometh as a thief in the night, and there is not one of us can tell but what this day his soul may be required of him" (Samuel Butler, *The Way of All Flesh,* 1903).

thieves break through and steal *See* LAY NOT UP TREASURES UPON EARTH.

things in common, all *See* ALL THINGS IN COMMON.

things to all men, all *See* ALL THINGS TO ALL MEN.

thirty pieces of silver The price of an act of betrayal. The allusion is to the 30 shekels of silver that was paid by chief priests to JUDAS in exchange for information about Christ's whereabouts (Matthew 26:14–16), thus setting in motion the trail of events that led to the Crucifixion. According to Matthew 27:3–5 Judas soon repented of his deed and "cast down the pieces of silver in the temple, and departed, and went and hanged himself." Thirty shekels of silver was also the compensation laid down under the law of Moses for the loss of an ox. *Rumor has it that any executive who is prepared to give evidence against the company will be offered thirty pieces of silver in the form of an official pardon.* See also ACELDAMA; POTTER'S FIELD.

Thisbe *See* PYRAMUS AND THISBE.

Thomas, doubting *See* DOUBTING THOMAS.

Thor (thor) A man of enormous strength. Thor is identified in Norse mythology as the son of Odin and Frigga and the god of thunder and war. He was renowned for his great strength, which was redoubled by the belt he wore, and was conventionally depicted wearing iron gloves and carrying a great hammer (the Mjollnir). "Thaw with his gentle persuasion is more powerful than Thor with his hammer. The one melts, the other but breaks in pieces" (Henry David Thoreau, *Walden, or Life in the Woods,* 1854).

thorn in the flesh A persistent irritation or annoyance, especially one that cannot be easily escaped. The phrase comes from 2 Corinthians 12:7, in which Paul complains about his own troubles: "And lest I should be exalted above measure through the abundance of the revelations, there was given to me a thorn in the flesh, the messenger of Satan to buffet me, lest I should be exalted above measure." The precise nature of Paul's "thorn in the flesh" has been much debated and various chronic illnesses ranging from blindness to malaria have been proposed as the cause of his discomfort. There was, perhaps significantly, a sect of Pharisees whose practice was to insert thorns into their clothing to prick their legs as they walked and make them bleed. The phrase is also encountered as **thorn in the (one's) side.** "Sadly, it was a road accident . . . which finally took the wind from his quixotic career as byelection candidate, champion of lost causes, and thorn in the flesh of authority" (*Guardian,* April 7, 1986).

thorns, crown of *See* CROWN OF THORNS.

thou art the man You are the guilty person, or the person for the job in question. The quotation is biblical in origin, appearing in 2 Samuel 12:7 in the account of the adultery of DAVID AND BATHSHEBA. After Nathan told David the parable of the rich man who stole the ewe lamb belonging to his poor neighbor, David exclaimed that the rich man deserved to die, upon which Nathan replied, "Thou art the man." Nathan here was referring to David's "theft" of Bathsheba from her husband. The child who resulted from their union died a week after birth. *The girls would not listen to his denials of any involvement in the matter: It was clearly a case of "thou art the man."*

though he slay me, yet will I trust in him An expression of loyalty and faithfulness to someone, even though such loyalty may not be reciprocated. The expression comes from Job 13:15, in which Job resisted suggestions that, after all his troubles, he owed no duty of loyalty to God: "Though he slay me, yet will I trust in him: but I will maintain mine own ways before him." *The corporal gestured ruefully after the departing emperor and refused to voice any complaint at the harsh treatment he had received on the latter's orders. "Though he slay me, yet will I trust in him" was his only comment.*

thou shalt have no other gods before me Demand for unswerving loyalty (sometimes used ironically). This is the first of the TEN COMMANDMENTS, listed in Exodus 20 and Deuteronomy 5. *The men quickly realized that with the unyielding, yet generally just commander it was a case of "thou shalt have no other gods before me."*

thou shalt not steal Do not steal from others. This appears as the eighth of the TEN COMMANDMENTS (Exodus 20:15 and Deuteronomy 5:19). *"Thou shalt not steal," said the old woman severely as she retrieved the necklace from the little girl.*

thrasonical (thraysahnikăl, thrăsahnikăl) Boastful; arrogant; vain. The word alludes to Thraso, a soldier in the comedy *Eunuchus* by Terence (c. 185–c. 159 B.C.), who brags of his own achievements. "Novi hominem tanquam te: his humour is lofty, his discourse peremptory, his tongue filed, his eye ambitious, his gait majestical, and his general behavior vain, ridiculous, and thrasonical" (William Shakespeare, *Love's Labour's Lost,* 1594–95).

thread of destiny *See* FATES.

Three Graces Personifications of beauty and charm. The Three Graces were beautiful goddesses identified in Greek mythology as the sisters

Aglaia, Thalia, and Euphrosyne. "As for the graces of expression, a great thought is never found in a mean dress; but though it proceed from the lips of the Woloffs, the nine Muses and the three Graces will have conspired to clothe it in fit phrase" (Henry David Thoreau, *Week on the Concord and Merrimack Rivers,* 1849).

threescore years and ten The age of 70. Once considered the average length of time that a person might expect to live, the phrase comes from Psalm 90:10: "The days of our years are threescore years and ten; and if by reason of strength they be fourscore years, yet is their strength labour and sorrow; for it is soon cut off, and we fly away." "By and by we are called in to see an old baby, threescore years and ten or more old" (Oliver Wendell Holmes, *Elsie Venner,* 1861).

three wise men *See* MAGI.

throne of grace The throne of God and, by extension, heaven. The phrase appears in the letter to the Hebrews 4:16: "Let us therefore come boldly unto the throne of grace, that we may obtain mercy, and find grace to help in time of need." The term is sometimes associated with depictions of the Trinity, with God holding the body of Christ on his knees while the Holy Spirit, in the form of a dove, hovers overhead. Other names for the throne of grace include the *mercy seat.* "Ah, Mr Cassilis, my sin has found me out, you see! I am very low, very low; but I hope equally penitent. We must all come to the throne of grace at last, Mr Cassilis" (Robert Louis Stevenson, *New Arabian Nights,* 1882).

through a glass darkly *See* SEE THROUGH A GLASS DARKLY.

throw the apple of discord *See* APPLE OF DISCORD.

throw the first stone *See* LET HIM WHO IS WITHOUT SIN CAST THE FIRST STONE.

throw to the lions To expose someone to an unpleasant fate. The phrase harks back to ancient Rome, where army deserters, common criminals, and Christians were often put to death by being sent into the arena to face wild animals. The practice reached a peak during the reign of the emperor

Nero in the wake of the destruction of Rome in the fire of A.D. 64, for which the city's Christians had been blamed. *It seems the leadership has decided to cut its losses and throw the spokesman to the lions.*

Thule *See* ULTIMA THULE.

thumbs-up An indication of approval or encouragement, in which the thumb is pointed up and the other fingers are closed in a fist. This gesture is popularly supposed to have its origins in the gladiatorial arenas of ancient Rome. When a gladiator was defeated, the crowd was invited to decide his fate by showing a collective thumbs-up, in which case the gladiator was allowed to live, or a *thumbs-down,* in which case he was put to death. In reality no one is sure exactly what sign the crowd made with their thumbs to indicate their decision, as suggested by John Dryden's description of such a moment in his translation of the *Third Satire of Juvenal* (1693): "Influenced by the rabble's bloody will, / With thumbs bent back they popularly kill." The use of thumbs-up or thumbs-down as understood today may date back only as far as early Hollywood film reenactments of such gladiatorial contests. *The chairman has just given his thumbs-up to the new project, providing certain conditions are met in advance.*

Thursday The fifth day of the week. The day was named after THOR, the Norse god of thunder. *In Britain elections generally takes place on a Thursday. In the United States Thanksgiving is always the last Thursday in November.*

Thyestean feast (thīesteeăn) A feast at which human flesh is served. The reference is to Thyestes, a Greek who committed adultery with the wife of his brother Atreus. In revenge Atreus murdered the children of Thyestes and fed them to him at a banquet. Thyestes realized what he was being offered and fled the feast, laying a curse on his brother's household. *No one ever found the body, but few dared voice the suspicion that many shared, that the unlucky parents had unwittingly taken part in a Thyestean feast.*

thy will be done An expression of acquiescence to another's wishes. The phrase comes from the Lord's Prayer, as rendered in Matthew 6:9–10: "Our Father which art in heaven, Hallowed be thy name. Thy kingdom come. Thy will be done in earth, as it is in heaven." (See also Luke 22:42.)

"Thy will be done," replied the managing director's secretary with heavy irony as she gathered together the documents he had left on the desk for her.

tidings of great joy *See* GOOD TIDINGS OF GREAT JOY.

time and place for everything There is an appropriate time for all things and, therefore, times when certain things should not be said or done. The proverb has its origins in Ecclesiastes 3:1–8: "To everything there is a season, and a time to every purpose under the heaven: a time to be born, and a time to die; a time to plant, and a time to pluck up that which is planted; a time to kill, and a time to heal; a time to break down, and a time to build up; a time to weep, and a time to laugh; a time to mourn, and a time to dance . . . a time to get, and a time to lose; a time to keep, and a time to cast away; a time to rend, and a time to sew; a time to keep silence, and a time to speak; a time to love, and a time to hate; a time of war, and a time of peace." The saying is also encountered in the forms *time for all things, season for all things,* and *to every thing there is a season.* "'There is a time for everything, a time to embrace, and a time to refrain from embracing; the first is now going to be mine'" (Thomas Hardy, *Tess of the D'Urbervilles,* 1891). *See also* WORD IN SEASON.

time as this, for such a *See* FOR SUCH A TIME AS THIS.

time for all things *See* TIME AND PLACE FOR EVERYTHING.

timeo Danaos et dona ferentes *See* BEWARE OF GREEKS BEARING GIFTS.

time to be born, and a time to die *See* TIME AND PLACE FOR EVERYTHING.

Timon (tīmăn) Archetypal misanthrope. Timon was a rich Athenian citizen who spent his entire fortune on lavish entertainments for his friends. When his money was all gone, Timon found himself deserted by his erstwhile companions and became a recluse, living in a remote cave and bitterly avoiding all human contact, with the single exception of the exile Alcibiades. He was represented on stage in William Shakespeare's play *Timon of Athens* (1605). In modern usage his name appears most frequently in the phrase to *out-Timon Timon,* meaning to be even more misanthropic than Timon. *A sour and embittered Timon, he lurked on the fringes of society for years, savaging anybody who ventured near him.*

tinkling cymbal *See* SOUNDING BRASS OR A TINKLING CYMBAL.

Tiphys (tīfis) A pilot. According to Greek mythology Tiphys was the pilot for the Argonauts during their epic voyage of adventure. *Descended from many generations of pilots, he himself served as Tiphys to many major passenger liners plying the treacherous waters in that part of the world.*

Tiresias (tīreeseeas) Archetype of a wise old prophet. Tiresias, or *Teiresias,* was famed in Thebes for his prophetic gifts but was blinded by the gods for having seen Athena bathing in the fountain Hippocrene. Another version of the legend relates how Tiresias became involved in an argument between Zeus and Hera, who when Tiresias spent seven years transformed into a woman consulted him over the question of whether men or women experience more pleasure from sex. Tiresias declared that women found sex nine times more enjoyable than men and thus incurred the wrath of Hera, who blinded him in her rage. Zeus then granted Tiresias prophetic powers in compensation for the loss of his sight. It was Tiresias who revealed to Oedipus the awful truth that the latter had unwittingly murdered his father and married his mother. He was also reputed to understand the language of the birds and continued to dispense wisdom until a very advanced age. *The old man, like some venerable Tiresias, dispensed wisdom from his throne on the stoop for all the world.*

Tisiphone *See* FURIES.

titanic Immensely huge or powerful. The word makes reference to the Titans of Greek myth, the 12 primeval gods and goddesses identified as the sons and daughters of Uranus (the sky) and Gaea (the Earth). Legend had it that they ruled the earth in a golden age until the youngest of them, Cronus, overthrew Uranus and was subsequently himself overthrown by his son Zeus. He and the other Titans were consigned to Tartarus. By the same token a person or thing that is immensely huge or powerful may be called a *titan.* "On the Promenade des Anglais, where Ned Silverton hung on him for the half hour before dinner, he received a deeper impression of the general insecurity. Silverton was in a mood of Titanic pessimism" (Edith Wharton, *The House of Mirth,* 1905).

tithe of mint, anise, and cumin A relatively trivial obligation, duty, or other matter, usually in comparison with a much more significant matter that has been neglected. The phrase comes from Matthew 23:23, in which Christ criticized the Pharisees for busying themselves with trivialities while neglecting more important matters: "For ye pay tithe of mint and anise and cummin, and have omitted the weightier matters of the law, judgment, mercy and faith: these ought ye to have done, and not to leave the other undone." *This pitiful offering reminded her of the tithe of mint, anise, and cumin paid by the Pharisees, a very inadequate replacement for the total amount owed.*

Tithonus (tĭthōnăs) Archetype of a very old, decrepit person. According to Greek mythology Tithonus was the brother of King Priam of Troy and much admired by Eos, the goddess of the dawn, for his great beauty. When he prayed for the gift of immortality, Eos persuaded Zeus to grant him his wish, but as she had forgotten also to ask for the gift of eternal youth on his behalf, Tithonus became wizened and feeble as he aged. Unable to die, he was eventually transformed by Eos into a grasshopper. "And did you ever imagine that you and Nick, of all people, were going to escape the common doom, and survive like Mr. and Mrs. Tithonus, while all about you the eternal passions were crumbling to pieces, and your native Divorce-states piling up their revenues?" (Edith Wharton, *Glimpses of the Moon,* 1922).

tittle *See* JOT OR TITTLE.

Tityrus (tĭtīrăs) Poetical name for a shepherd. Shepherds appear with this name in the works of early Greek poets and of the Roman poet Virgil (70–19 B.C.). It was subsequently adopted for similar characters by such English poets as Geoffrey Chaucer (c. 1342–1400) and Edmund Spenser (1552–99). "Heroes and their feats / Fatigue me, never weary of the pipe / Of Tityrus, assembling as he sang / The rustic throng beneath his favourite beech" (William Cowper, *The Task,* 1785).

Tityus (tĭtyăs) Archetypal sufferer of great torment. According to Greek mythology Tityus was a giant who tried to rape Leto, the mother of Apollo and Artemis. As punishment he was consigned to the underworld, where a vulture perpetually tore out his liver. When he lay down on the ground his body covered nine acres. *Suddenly he envisioned the dreadful fate that could be in store for him, doomed to suffer eternal agony like some modern-day Tityus.*

Tiw *See* TYR.

to everything there is a season *See* TIME AND PLACE FOR EVERYTHING.

to him that hath *See* WHOSOEVER HATH, TO HIM SHALL BE GIVEN.

toil in the groves of Academe *See* ACADEMIA; GROVES OF ACADEME.

toil not, neither do they spin *See* LILIES OF THE FIELD.

tomorrow will take care of itself Do not worry about the future until it comes. The proverb comes from Christ's Sermon on the Mount: "Take therefore no thought for the morrow: for the morrow shall take thought for the things of itself" (Matthew 6:34). *His grandmother was notorious for her procrastination in such matters. She was a great believer in the philosophy tomorrow will take care of itself.* See also SUFFICIENT UNTO THE DAY IS THE EVIL THEREOF.

tongues, gift of *See* GIFT OF TONGUES.

tooth for a tooth *See* EYE FOR AN EYE.

Tophet *See* GEHENNA.

tortoise *See* HARE AND THE TORTOISE.

to the pure all things are pure *See* UNTO THE PURE ALL THINGS ARE PURE.

touch me not *See* NOLI ME TANGERE.

touch pitch and be defiled It is inevitable that if a person has dealings with wickedness he or she will be tainted with it. The proverb is from the apocryphal book of Ecclesiasticus (Sirach) 13:1: "He that toucheth pitch, shall be defiled therewith, and he that hath fellowship with a proud man, shall be like unto him." A concise variant may be found in the form *pitch defiles.* "Not in electioneering, Mr Romer, any more than in any other pursuits, can a man touch pitch and not be defiled; as thou, innocent as thou art, wilt soon learn to thy terrible cost" (Anthony Trollope, *Doctor Thorne,* 1858).

touch the hem of his garment *See* HEM OF HIS GARMENT, TOUCH THE.

Tower of Babel (baybăl, babăl) A scene of general confusion and noise. The allusion is to the biblical Tower of Babel, which according to Genesis 11:4–9 was built with the intention of reaching heaven. The Tower of Babel may have been a type of Babylonian temple called a ziggurat. Ziggurats were pyramid shaped, and some may have reached more than 325 feet (100 meters) high. God thwarted the efforts of the builders by making them speak in different languages so that no one could make him- or herself understood to another. The word *Babel* itself means "gate of God." *At the international airport, he stood still for a moment and listened to the many languages being spoken all around him. It was a veritable Tower of Babel.*

treasure in heaven *See* LAY NOT UP TREASURES UPON EARTH.

treasures upon earth, lay not up *See* LAY NOT UP TREASURES UPON EARTH.

tree is known by its fruit, the People should be judged not by their appearances but by how they act and by what they produce (for example, with reference to their offspring). The proverb is biblical in origin, coming from Matthew 12:33: "Either make the tree good, and his fruit good; or else make the tree corrupt, and his fruit corrupt: for the tree is known by his fruit." "If then the tree may be known by the fruit, as the fruit by the tree, then, peremptorily I speak it, there is virtue in that Falstaff" (William Shakespeare, *Henry IV Part 1,* 1597–98).

tree of knowledge A source of knowledge or wisdom. The phrase appears in biblical descriptions of the GARDEN OF EDEN, in which it is identified as the Tree of Knowledge of Good and Evil (Genesis 2:9). It is the disobedience of ADAM AND EVE in disregarding God's command not to eat of the fruit of this tree that leads to their expulsion from Paradise. Today the tree is sometimes interpreted as a symbol of the truth that the gaining of knowledge necessarily requires the loss of innocence, hence the expression *eat from the tree of knowledge* meaning to learn such knowledge. "And so the poor child, with her soul's hunger and her illusions of self-flattery, began to nibble at this thick-rinded fruit of the tree of knowledge, filling her vacant hours with Latin, geometry, and the forms of the syllogism" (George Eliot, *The Mill on the Floss,* 1860). *See also* FORBIDDEN FRUIT.

tree of life Life or the fount of life. The tree is described in Genesis 2:9 (and elsewhere) as a central feature of the GARDEN OF EDEN: "And out of the ground made the LORD God to grow every tree that is pleasant to the sight, and good for food; the tree of life also in the midst of the garden." The tree of life is generally interpreted as a symbol of God's gift of life. (See also Proverbs 3:18 and 11:30 and Revelation 2:7 and 22:1–19.) "But we have not to do with the wars of the Mulberry Hills and the Dry Docks. We must to Rooney's, where, on the most blighted dead branch of the tree of life, a little pale orchid shall bloom" (O. Henry, *Strictly Business,* 1910).

tribes of Israel *See* LOST TRIBES OF ISRAEL.

tribune of the people A democratic leader, specifically one who acts as a champion of public rights. In ancient Rome the senior rank of tribune denoted a chief magistrate, who wielded great influence in the city. During the revolt of 494 B.C. two tribunes were elected by the plebeians to prevent the patricians from taking revenge on the rebels (the number was subsequently increased to 10). Tribunes were immune from prosecution and had various powers of veto at their command. "The man on the little stool behind the President, is the Capo Lazzarone, a kind of tribune of the people, appointed on their behalf to see that all is fairly conducted: attended by a few personal friends" (Charles Dickens, *Pictures of Italy,* 1845).

tried and found wanting *See* WRITING ON THE WALL.

Triton (trītăn) A mythological sea creature; the larger of Neptune's two satellites. The Greek sea god Triton was the son of Poseidon and

Amphitrite and was said to have the upper half of a human fixed to a fish's tail. He is often depicted in art and literature blowing a horn formed from a conch shell in order to calm the sea at Poseidon's approach. His name is sometimes encountered in the form *a Triton among the minnows,* signifying a great person among inferiors. ". . . on the right of the stage is the public fountain, with a triton in green bronze blowing from a conch; around the fountain is a stone seat; the bell of the Cathedral is ringing, and the citizens, men, women and children, are passing into the Cathedral" (Oscar Wilde, *The Duchess of Padua,* 1891).

triumvirate (trīa̱mvirăt) Three people acting as one body. The original triumvirates were the groups of three magistrates who were appointed to fulfill various official functions in ancient Rome. The most famous triumvirate of all was the political alliance of Julius Caesar, Marcus Licinius Crassus, and Pompey the Great that wielded power from 60 B.C. "He showed her a letter which he was about to dispatch to Robespierre himself, vindicating his suspected patriotism, and indignantly demanding to be allowed to prove it by filling some office, no matter how small, under the redoubtable triumvirate which then governed, or more properly terrified, France" (Wilkie Collins, *After Dark,* 1856).

Troilus and Cressida (troylăs, kresidă) Archetypal tragic lovers. According to Homer's *Iliad* (c. 700 B.C.), Troilus was the youngest son of King Priam and Queen Hecuba of Troy and died in the course of the Trojan War. His romance with Cressida was a later invention of around the fourth or fifth century A.D. subsequently elaborated by medieval writers. "'Troilus loved and he was fooled,' said the more manly chaplain. 'A man may love and yet not be a Troilus. All women are not Cressids'" (Anthony Trollope, *Barchester Towers,* 1857).

Trojan (trōjăn) A hard-working, determined, or otherwise reliable person. The Trojans were much respected for their courage in battle, as evidenced in the course of the lengthy Trojan War against the Greeks, as related in Homer's *Iliad* (c. 700 B.C.) and Virgil's *Aeneid* (30–19 B.C.). The word, occasionally has other connotations: In William Shakespeare's day it could be used as a synonym for a robber or dissolute rogue. *He worked like a Trojan until dawn broke and the danger had passed.*

Trojan horse (<u>trō</u>jăn) A deception designed to undermine an enemy from within. The allusion is to the *wooden horse* with which the Greeks achieved the final overthrow of Troy at the conclusion of the Trojan War. According to Homer (in the *Iliad*, c. 700 B.C.) and Virgil (in the *Aeneid*, 30–19 B.C.), the Greeks built a large, hollow wooden horse and filled it with warriors before making a pretense of leaving their camps around Troy and sailing away. The Trojans, fooled into thinking the horse was an offering to the goddess Athena, dragged it within their walls. After dark the Greek warriors poured out of the horse and sacked the city. In modern usage a Trojan horse usually refers to an apparently harmless gift through which an enemy may be defeated or disrupted. The term has particular relevance in computer circles, where it can refer to an apparently innocent program or system that subsequently releases a damaging computer virus. "A 'Trojan horse' cancer treatment that slips inside tumour cells and destroys them with radiation has been successfully tested in the US" (*Times*, November 16, 2001). *See also* BEWARE OF GREEKS BEARING GIFTS.

Trophonius *See* CAVE OF TROPHONIUS.

Trump, Last *See* LAST TRUMP.

truth?, What is *See* WHAT IS TRUTH?

truth shall make you free, the Knowledge of the truth is the key to salvation. The sentiment is biblical in origin, appearing in John 8:31–32, in which Christ promised the Jews that if they obeyed his word, they would be his true disciples. Such knowledge—God's revelation of his truth—would set them free from sin: "If ye continue in my word, then are ye my disciples indeed; And ye shall know the truth, and the truth shall make you free." "'Well, if you won't accept Tennyson as an authority, perhaps you will believe the words of a Greater than he,' said Gilbert seriously. "'Ye shall know the truth and the truth shall make you free." I believe that, Anne, with all my heart. It's the greatest and grandest verse in the Bible—or in any literature'" (Lucy Maud Montgomery, *Anne's House of Dreams*, 1917).

Tuesday The third day of the week. It is named after Tiw (TYR), the Anglo-Saxon god of war and the sky. *Shrove Tuesday is the day before Lent begins, on Ash Wednesday.*

turn the other cheek To accept a personal insult or injury passively and without retaliating. The expression is biblical in origin, being quoted by Christ in the course of his Sermon on the Mount, as related in Matthew 5:38–39: "Ye have heard that it hath been said, An eye for an eye, and a tooth for a tooth: But I say unto you, That ye resist not evil: but whosoever shall smite thee on thy right cheek, turn to him the other also." "It is well, I think, that violent offences, when committed, should be met by instant rebuke. To turn the other cheek instantly to the smiter can hardly be suitable in these days, when the hands of so many are raised to strike" (Anthony Trollope, *The Last Chronicle of Barset,* 1867). *See also* EYE FOR AN EYE.

Tuscan Belonging to a relatively plain and unornamented order of classical architecture derived from the DORIC style. *The architects chose a grand but somewhat restrained Tuscan style for the portico of the bank's new headquarters in the center of the city. See also* CORINTHIAN; IONIC.

twilight of the gods *See* GÖTTERDÄMMERUNG.

twinkling of an eye, in the Instantaneously; very quickly; in the briefest time. The phrase comes from 1 Corinthians 15:51–52, in which Paul writes about the resurrection of the dead on the return of Christ: "Behold, I shew you a mystery; We shall not all sleep, but we shall all be changed, In a moment, in the twinkling of an eye, at the last trump: for the trumpet shall sound, and the dead shall be raised incorruptible, and we shall be changed." "I don't understand these matters very well, but from Fyne's narrative it seemed as if the creditors or the depositors, or the competent authorities, had got hold in the twinkling of an eye of everything de Barral possessed in the world" (Joseph Conrad, *Chance,* 1913).

two-edged sword Referring to something that is open to two different interpretations, such as an argument or policy that has an effect against both parties involved. The phrase comes from the Bible. Hebrews 4:12 reads: "For the word of God is quick, and powerful, and sharper than any two-edged sword, piercing even to the dividing asunder of soul and spirit, and of the joints and marrow, and is a discerner of the thoughts and intents of the heart." According to Revelation 1:16: "And he had in his right hand seven stars: and out of his mouth went a sharp two-edged sword: and his countenance was as the sun shineth in his strength.' (See also Revelation 2:12 and the apocryphal book of Ecclesiasticus (Sirach) 21:3.) "The honest soldier was confused. The lawyer's eloquence overpowered him. He felt guilty. Josephine saw his simplicity, and made a cut with a woman's two-edged sword. 'Sir,' said she coolly, 'do you not see it is an affair of money?'" (Charles Reade, *White Lies,* 1857).

two or three gathered together *See* WHERE TWO OR THREE ARE GATHERED TOGETHER.

Tyr (tir) Personification of war. Tyr, or *Tyrr* or *Tiw,* was identified in Norse mythology as the son of Odin and was revered as the god of war. *Valhalla must be bursting at the seams with young warriors recently slain at the call of Tyr.*

Tyre *See* NINEVEH AND TYRE.

_U_

Ubi sunt? (<u>oo</u>bee sănt) Where are they now? This lament in Latin on the transitory nature of earthly greatness has biblical origins, the words arising from a medieval reworking of David's lament for Saul and Jonathan: "The beauty of Israel is slain upon thy high places: how are the mighty fallen!" (2 Samuel 1:19). The _ubi sunt_ motif became a popular theme of medieval poetry, designating "a mood or theme in literature of lament for the mutability of things" _(Oxford English Dictionary). They were among the most celebrated players of their generation, but as is so often the case in the world of sport, once they retired, their names rarely cropped up outside the usual Ubi sunt? inquiries._

ultima Thule (ăltimă <u>thoo</u>lee, ăltimă <u>thy</u>oolee) A far-distant place; a remote destination; the ends of the earth or the very limit of what is attainable. Latin for "farthest Thule," ultima Thule in Roman times was the northernmost limit of the known world. Thule was identified by the Greek explorer Pytheas (flourished 300 B.C.) as being located six days' sailing beyond the north of Britain (possibly Norway, Iceland, or the Shetland Islands). Pliny the Elder described Thule in _Historia Naturalis_ (A.D. 77) as "an island in the Northern Ocean discovered by Pytheas, after sailing six days from the Orcades." The phrase appears in the first book of Virgil's _Georgics_ (c. 36 B.C.): "Tibi serviat Ultima Thule." "My cognizance of the pit had become known to the inquisitorial agents—the pit whose horrors had been destined for so bold a recusant as myself—the pit, typical of hell, and regarded by rumor as the Ultima Thule of all their punishments" (Edgar Allan Poe, "The Pit and the Pendulum," 1843).

Ulysses _See_ ODYSSEUS.

Ulysses' bow (<u>yoo</u>liseez) Something extremely difficult to handle or that only one person is able to use effectively. Legend has it that the great bow belonging to the Greek adventurer Ulysses (ODYSSEUS) could only be drawn by the celebrated hero himself. It was through his ability to draw his bow and his skill as an archer, specifically in shooting an arrow through 12 rings, that Ulysses was recognized by his wife, Penelope, when he returned home after 20 years away. The bow, which was also reputed to have prophetic powers, was at one time the property of Eurytus of Oechalia. *So many adventurers had come to grief trying to pull off this modern Ulysses' bow that it was soon believed that no one would ever succeed in the feat.*

understanding heart *See* JUDGMENT OF SOLOMON.

under the aegis of *See* AEGIS.

under the sun *See* NOTHING NEW UNDER THE SUN.

unequally yoked Improperly or unsuitably linked in a very close partnership (usually by marriage). The phrase is biblical in origin, being a quotation from 2 Corinthians 6:14 in which Paul warns the Corinthians, "Be ye not unequally yoked together with unbelievers." The phrase has been variously applied to marriages between Christians and non-Christians and more generally to any pair of partners deemed ill matched. *The two nations entered a coalition against their common enemy, but it quickly became apparent that they were unequally yoked.*

unerring as the dart of Procris (<u>pro</u>kris) Undeviating; deadly accurate. According to Greek legend the jealous Procris deserted her husband, Cephalus, and was presented by the sympathetic Diana with a dog that always caught its prey and a dart that always hit its target and then returned to its owner's hand. Unfortunately when Procris hid in some bushes to spy on her husband and any lover he might be with, she made too much noise, and thinking he was being stalked by a wild beast, Cephalus hurled his javelin into the bushes, killing her. Upon discovering his mistake Cephalus killed himself out of grief. *This last shaft was as unerring as the dart of Procris and left its victim stunned.*

unforgivable sin *See* UNPARDONABLE SIN.

unicorn A fabulous animal resembling a white horse with a single horn in the middle of its forehead, most familiar today as an emblem in heraldic devices. Its name derives from the Latin *unus cornus* ("one horn"). The unicorn made its first appearance in literature in the writings of Ctesias around 400 B.C. and was subsequently mentioned in many medieval bestiaries. Originally described as having a lion's tail, a stag's legs, and a horse's head and body, the unicorn was believed to be very fierce but also fatally attracted by chastity, allowing it to be tricked into laying its head in the lap of a young virgin and thus captured. Allusions to the unicorn in modern iconography usually invoke the creature's identification with chastity, although Christian tradition sometimes also depicts Christ as a unicorn. *He came to think of her as some elusive unicorn, uncatchable and remote from the ordinary world of men.*

unknown God An unidentified god or other object of veneration. The phrase alludes to the biblical story of Paul, who was on the way to speak to a group of skeptical Greek philosophers in Athens when he noted an altar inscribed with "TO THE UNKNOWN GOD" (Acts 17:23). On meeting his audience he asserted that all he aimed to do was to identify the god whom they already worshiped. It is thought that such altars were originally erected by Greeks as votive offerings when they were unsure which god they should thank. The phrase has been used in many contexts, including the title of John Steinbeck's novel *To a God Unknown* (1933). *This benefaction of an unknown God prompted many of the workers to offer silent prayers of thanks.*

unpardonable sin An offense (sometimes relatively trivial) that is considered certain to attract the condemnation of others. Although the phrase, sometimes rendered in the form ***unforgivable sin,*** does not actually appear in the Bible, it is the conventional way of describing the sin of blasphemy against the Holy Spirit (see Matthew 12:31–32 and Luke 12:10). The *NIV Thematic Reference Bible* defines the unforgivable sin as "The willful, outwardly expressed and impenitent slander against the Holy Spirit, when Jesus Christ's mighty works, clearly performed by the power of the Holy Spirit, are attributed to Satan, thus subjecting Christ to public disgrace" (p. 2,074). In general modern usage the phrase is sometimes employed in a parodic sense in reference to some minor social transgression or overstepping of accepted boundaries. "After all, for a seaman, to scrape the bottom of the thing that's supposed to float all the time under his care is the unpardonable sin" (Joseph Conrad, "Heart of Darkness," 1902).

unto dust shalt thou return You will not live forever. The phrase is biblical in origin, appearing in various forms at Genesis 2:7 and 3:19, Job 10:9 and 33:6, and Isaiah 64:8. It appears in Genesis 3:19 in the fuller form "dust thou art, and unto dust shalt thou return." In biblical usage dust and clay are symbols of mortality. Job subsequently echoes the phrase in protest at God's actions toward him: "Remember, I beseech thee, that thou hast made me as the clay; and wilt thou bring me into dust again?" (Job 10:9). Henry Wadsworth Longfellow, in "A Psalm of Life," wrote: "Dust thou art, to dust returnest." Today the term is most familiar in the form *ashes to ashes, dust to dust,* a phrase frequently spoken in the course of burial services. "Life is real! Life is earnest! / And the grave is not its goal; / Dust thou art, to dust returnest, / Was not spoken of the soul" (H. W. Longfellow, "A Psalm of Life," 1839).

unto the pure all things are pure How a person sees something and the influence that he or she exerts on it depend largely on the nature of his or her own moral character. The saying comes from the letter of Paul to Titus: "Unto the pure all things are pure: but unto them that are defiled and unbelieving is nothing pure; but even their mind and conscience is defiled" (Titus 1:15). The line is sometimes quoted in defense of an individual's right to read whatever he or she chooses to read or in other defenses of freedom of choice. *The priest refused to believe that what he was being told could be true, but then unto the pure all things are pure.*

Urania *See* MUSES.

Uranus (yoorănăs, yooraynas) A planet in the solar system, seventh in distance from the Sun. In Greek mythology Uranus was a personification of the sky, a god who ruled the universe and who by his own mother, Gaea (the Earth), fathered the Titans and Cyclopes. He was subsequently overthrown by his son Cronus, who thus separated heaven from earth. *The old lady warned him that his life would never be easy because of the baleful influence of Uranus in his birth chart.*

Uriah *See* LETTER OF URIAH.

use a little wine *See* TAKE A LITTLE WINE.

V

vale of tears Life as a series of misfortunes and sadnesses. The image of life as a vale of tears is believed to have biblical origins, being derived originally from the Valley of Baca (the Hebrew *bakah* meaning "weeping") mentioned in Psalm 84:5–6. Baca trees are balsams that exude gum in tearlike drops. "I excused myself and dropped to the rear of the procession, sad at heart, willing to go hence from this troubled life, this vale of tears, this brief day of broken rest, of cloud and storm, of weary struggle and monotonous defeat" (Mark Twain, *A Connecticut Yankee in King Arthur's Court,* 1889).

vale of Tempe *See* TEMPE, VALE OF.

Valhalla (valhalǎ) The afterworld, where the souls of the brave go after death. According to Norse mythology, Valhalla is situated in Asgard and is connected to Earth by a rainbow bridge. It consists of a vast banqueting hall with walls of gold and a roof made of warriors' shields. Here the souls of heroes slain in battle spend eternity engaging in mock battles, feasting with Odin and recounting their exploits. The wounds they sustain in combat are magically healed each day. In modern usage Valhalla may denote any place (real or otherwise) to which only the bravest or most distinguished of persons may be admitted in recognition of their achievements. "At first it looked like a vast blue fort or Valhalla; but when they began to tuck the coarse meadow hay into the crevices, and this became covered with rime and icicles, it looked like a venerable moss-grown and hoary ruin" (Henry David Thoreau, *Walden, or Life in the Woods,* 1854).

Valkyrie (valkiree, valkǎree) A formidable woman, especially one of statuesque proportions and Nordic appearance. In Norse mythology the Valkyries were the 12 beautiful blond handmaidens of Odin who roamed

391

battlefields on flying horses picking out the bravest of the slain and carrying them to VALHALLA where they might spend eternity in the company of other great heroes. The word *Valkyrie* literally means "chooser of the slain." In modern usage the Valkyries are most familiar from Wagnerian opera, in which they are conventionally depicted in horned Viking helmets and armor. "The lawn-mower was sincerely intended to pass longitudinally over the body of Mr. Collins from heel to head; and it was the time for a death-song. Black Valkyrie hovered in the shrieking air" (Booth Tarkington, *Penrod*, 1914).

valley of dry bones A situation in which life seems impossible; the abode of death. The phrase is a reference to Ezekiel 37, in which God puts Ezekiel "down in the midst of the valley which was full of bones . . . and, lo, they were very dry. And he said unto me, Son of man, can these bones live?" (Ezekiel 37:1–3). On God's command through the prophet, the bones rise up and live again. (The episode is usually considered an allegory of the restoration of Israel.) The valley of dry bones symbolizes a situation in which hope is completely gone because of the irreversibility of death. "As the dry bones shook and came together in that dreadful valley of Ezekiel's, so now a philosophical theorem, cerebrally entertained, began to stir and heave and throw off its gravecloths, and stood upright and became a living presence" (C. S. Lewis, *Surprised by Joy,* 1955).

valley of Jehoshaphat (jăhōshăfat) A location for the final judgment of the nations; any place where a final reckoning shall be held. The valley of Jehoshaphat is referred to in Joel 3:2, but since the name Jehoshaphat is a play on words for "Jehovah is judge," and the prophets were more concerned with the certainty and reality of future judgment than in its exact location, the language is probably metaphorical and its precise location is not known. ". . . nothing was to be found but dry, sapless, mouldering, and disjointed bones, such as those which filled the valley of Jehoshaphat" (Sir Walter Scott, *Ivanhoe,* 1820). *See also* JUDGMENT DAY.

valley of the shadow of death A situation in which death is close by or imminent. The phrase comes from Psalm 23:4: "Yea, though I walk through the valley of the shadow of death, I will fear no evil: for thou art with me; thy rod and thy staff they comfort me." John Bunyan, in the second part of

Pilgrim's Progress (1679), gives a fuller description of the valley: "The Valley it self . . . is as dark as pitch: we also saw there Hobgoblins, Satyrs, and Dragons of the Pit: We heard also in that Valley a continual howling and yelling, as of a People under unutterable misery; who there sat bound in affliction and Irons: and over that Valley hangs the discouraging cloud of confusion, death also doth always spread his wings over it: in a word, it is every wit dreadful, being utterly without Order." Other writers have generally accepted the gloomy nature of the valley. "One would have thought Inverary had been the Valley of the Shadow of Death, the inferior Chiefs showed such reluctance to approach it" (Sir Walter Scott, *A Legend of Montrose,* 1819).

vandal A person who deliberately defaces or otherwise spoils property. The original Vandals were a nomadic Teutonic people from central Europe (originally of Scandinavian origin) whose warlike behavior contributed to the final destruction of the Roman Empire in the fourth and fifth centuries A.D. They overran Gaul, Spain, and North Africa and sacked Rome in 455, causing widespread destruction to great works of art and buildings. The Vandals were especially notorious for looting and laying waste the lands that fell into their hands. "Though she did think that Uncle Tom had been worse than any vandal in that matter of selling her lover's magnificent works, still she was ready to tell of his generosity" (Anthony Trollope, *Ayala's Angel,* 1881).

vanity of vanities An act or belief that is considered entirely futile. The word *vanity* today generally signifies personal pride or conceit, but in its original biblical context the word suggested rather the notions of meaninglessness, emptiness, futility, or idolatry. The word appears many times in the Bible, notably in Ecclesiastes 1:2: "Vanity of vanities, saith the Preacher, vanity of vanities; all is vanity." The phrase is sometimes rendered in Latin as *vanitas vanitatum* or in another quotation from the same verse as *all is vanity.* "Oh how vain it is, the vanity of vanities, to live in men's thoughts instead of God's!" (Lytton Strachey, *Eminent Victorians,* 1918).

veil of Isis *See* LIFT THE VEIL OF ISIS.

veil of the temple rent A revelation or a moment of revelation. The image of a torn veil as a symbol of revelation is biblical in origin, referring to the moment of Christ's death on the cross, when "behold, the veil of the temple was rent in twain from the top to the bottom" (Matthew 27:51). (See also Mark 15:38, Luke 23:45, and Hebrews 6:19–20, 9:6–9, and 10:19–20.) The veil in question was the curtain in the Temple at Jerusalem that separated the Holy Place from the HOLY OF HOLIES (the innermost room of the tabernacle) (see Exodus 26:31). "The fact that the curtain prevented ordinary worshipers from entering the 'Most Holy Place' came to be seen as pointing to the much deeper separation between God and sinful humanity. The curtain thus came to be a symbol of the barrier placed between God and humanity by human sinfulness. At the time of the crucifixion of Jesus Christ, the curtain of the temple was torn. This dramatic event, noted in the Gospels, is seen as a symbol of one of the chief benefits brought about by the death of Jesus Christ: the barrier between God and humanity caused by sin has been torn down, so that there is now free access for believers to God on account of Christ's death" (*NIV Thematic Reference Bible,* p. 1,099). Legend has it that the veil was spun by the VIRGIN MARY herself. The image of the torn veil was variously taken up, for example, at the time of the Reformation (when it represented the abolition of the official priesthood), by Romantic poets (who used it as an image of the search for personal truth or liberty), and by many other writers as a simple image of spiritual, sexual, or other revelation. *This last thunderous communication brought him understanding. At last the veil of the temple was rent, and he comprehended for the first time how he had been betrayed.*

venereal *See* VENUS.

vengeance is mine My revenge over my enemy is complete. Generally quoted today by those who are gloating over some victory against their rivals, the phrase comes from the Bible, although it was originally meant to convey the desirability of leaving matters of retribution to divine providence. It appears in its original context in the form of a quotation of Paul writing to the Romans: "Dearly beloved, avenge not yourselves, but rather give place unto wrath: for it is written, Vengeance is mine; I will repay, saith the Lord" (Romans 12:19, quoting Deuteronomy 32:35). "'Thank God, that kept thine hand from blood-guiltiness, rash young man!' answered the curate. 'Vengeance is mine, saith the Lord, and I will repay it'" (Sir Walter Scott, *Kenilworth,* 1821).

veni, vidi, vici *See* I CAME, I SAW, I CONQUERED.

Venus (<u>vee</u>năs) The archetype of a feminine beauty. Venus was the Roman goddess of fertility and love and the equivalent of the Greek Aphrodite. According to mythology she emerged from the sea, variously from the foam of the waves or out of a seashell. She was herself the mother of Eros. In modern usage any woman described as a Venus is considered exceptionally beautiful. Other derivatives of the name of Venus include the adjective *venereal,* which variously refers to the genitalia and related sexual matters, especially to sexually transmitted diseases. "The sleeping Faun that lay in the alcove by the doorway had its twin brother that slumbered, and the silver Venus that stood in the sunlight held out her arms to a Venus as lovely as herself" (Oscar Wilde, *A House of Pomegranates,* 1891).

Venus's hair stone *See* THETIS'S HAIR STONE.

vesta (<u>vest</u>ă) A type of short match, found commonly in the home since its introduction early in the 20th century. The name is an allusion to Vesta, the Roman goddess of the hearth and the equivalent of the Greek Hestia, who was widely worshiped throughout the Roman Empire. Her sacred fire at the Temple of Vesta in the Forum at Rome was kept burning by specially chosen maidens known as the *vestal virgins.* These attendants were trained from the age of 10 and were expected to keep themselves pure; if they were found to have been unfaithful they faced death or severe punishment. In modern usage any woman who is deemed to place undue (or hypocritical) importance on her own chastity is likely to be accused of acting *like a vestal virgin. The young man struck a vesta against the rough wall and by its feeble light strained to see further into the room.*

via Dolorosa (<u>vee</u>ă dŏlă<u>rō</u>să, <u>vee</u>ă dō<u>lă</u><u>rō</u>sa) A painful or sorrowful experience; a period of suffering; any unfortunate series of events leading to a melancholy conclusion. Literally translated from Latin as "sad road," the original via Dolorosa was the route taken by Christ through Jerusalem on his way to the Crucifixion after his condemnation by Pontius Pilate (Matthew 27:31–33, Mark 15:20–22, Luke 23:26–33, and John 19:16–17). Although the site of Pilate's judgment hall is not known and the modern city plan bears little relation to that of 2,000 years ago, tradition identifies a particular route as that taken by Christ on his way to Golgotha, complete with 14 STATIONS OF THE CROSS marking the locations of certain events that took place in the course of the procession. "She was well aware that directly Mrs Neale received her money she went round the corner to drink ardent spirits in a mean and musty public-house—the unavoidable station on the Via Dolorosa of her life" (Joseph Conrad, *The Secret Agent,* 1907).

vials of wrath Vengeance, especially on the wicked. The allusion is biblical, referring, in the vision of John in Revelation 15:7, to the vials (bowls) "full of the wrath of God" that the seven angels will pour on the earth. With the emptying of the vials will come seven terrible plagues or other terrible afflictions (part of the Last Judgment). The image usually appears nowadays in the phrase *empty the vials of one's wrath* (signifying to discharge one's anger), although the phrase has made many appearances in literature, including in Joseph Conrad's *Typhoon* (1902), in which an approaching storm is described as "something formidable and swift, like the sudden smashing of a vial of wrath."

Virgin Mary Archetype of a virtuous, innocent woman. As the virginal mother of Christ (see Matthew 1:16–25 and Luke 1–2), Mary has special significance for Christians, especially within the Roman Catholic tradition. *She stared back at them unblinking, the Virgin Mary herself, and it was almost impossible to believe she could be guilty of the charges being laid at her feet. See also* QUEEN OF HEAVEN; ROSE WITHOUT A THORN.

visit the cave of Trophonius *See* CAVE OF TROPHONIUS.

voice crying in the wilderness A lone voice of protest raised against prevailing opinion, typically one expressing views that meet with an indifferent or openly hostile reception. The original voice in the wilderness was that of JOHN THE BAPTIST, who preached about the coming of Christ: "In those days came John the Baptist, preaching in the wilderness of Judaea, and saying, Repent ye: for the kingdom of heaven is at hand. For this is he that was spoken of by the prophet Esaias [Isaiah], saying, The voice of one crying in the wilderness, Prepare ye the way of the Lord, make his paths straight" (Matthew 3:1–3). (See also Mark 1:3, Luke 3:4, and John 1:23.) The phrase is typically applied to prophets whose words of warnings or advice are generally ignored. *She did her best to stop the committee from voting against the proposal, but hers was a voice crying in the wilderness, and the suggestion was thrown out.*

voice from the whirlwind Through the workings of nature God communicates to human beings. In Job 38:1 it is Job himself who hears the voice of God in a whirlwind, rebuking him for his complaints about the sufferings he has experienced and subsequently offering him comfort. In modern usage the phrase may refer to any message or moral that emerges out of a desperate situation. *Like a voice from the whirlwind, just when it seemed all hope was lost came the realization that if the submerged car was full of water it should become much easier to open the door and escape.*

voice in the wilderness *See* VOICE CRYING IN THE WILDERNESS.

voice of many waters A tremendous noise, specifically one considered equal to the crashing sound of the sea. The phrase comes from Psalm 93:4, which reads: "The LORD on high is mightier than the noise of many waters, yea, than the mighty waves of the sea." It is also encountered as the *noise of many waters* and as the *sound of many waters.* "I saw the mighty walls rushing asunder—there was a long tumultuous shouting sound like the voice of a thousand waters—and the deep and dank tarn at my feet closed suddenly and silently over the fragments of the House of Usher" (Edgar Allan Poe, "The Fall of the House of Usher," 1839).

voice of the turtle is heard in the land, the A call to love; the coming of spring. The phrase comes from the biblical Song of Solomon 2:11–12, in which it refers to the call of the turtledove heralding the coming of spring: "For, lo, the winter is past, the rain is over and gone; The flowers appear on the earth; the time of the singing of birds is come, and the voice of the turtle is heard in our land." "But he did; he told us at prayers in the Pilgrims' tent, last night, and he seemed as if he was reading it out of the Bible, too, about this country flowing with milk and honey, and about the voice of the turtle being heard in the land" (Mark Twain, *The Innocents Abroad,* 1869).

volcano A mountain or other opening in the Earth's crust from which fire and molten matter issue periodically; any potentially explosive situation.

The word has its roots in the name of Vulcan, the Roman god of fire and metalworking and the equivalent of the Greek Hephaestus. Although made lame by an injury resulting from his being thrown from heaven by his father, Jupiter, for taking his mother Juno's side in a quarrel, and described as very ugly in appearance, Vulcan became the husband of the beautiful but faithless Venus. Working at his forge, Vulcan created the thunderbolts hurled by Zeus and the suit of armor worn by Achilles. He also modeled the first mortal woman, Pandora, from clay. Other words that come from the name include *vulcanist,* a person who studies volcanoes, and *vulcanize,* to improve the natural properties of rubber by treating it with chemicals. "'Pray be serious,' remonstrated Neelie. 'We are both sitting on a volcano'" (Wilkie Collins, *Armadale,* 1866).

wages of sin Suffering of some kind as a punishment for the sins that a person may have committed. The phrase comes from Romans 6:23, in which Paul writes, "The wages of sin is death; but the gift of God is eternal life through Jesus Christ our Lord." In modern usage the suffering or punishment under consideration may be no more than a slight sense of guilt. "'The wages of sin, Watson—the wages of sin!' said he. 'Sooner or later it will always come. God knows, there was sin enough,' he added, taking up a brown volume from the table" (Sir Arthur Conan Doyle, *A Study in Scarlet,* 1887).

wailing wall A place where people gather to lament their woes. The allusion is to the Wailing Wall (also called the *Western Wall*) in Jerusalem, supposedly the only part of Herod's Temple left intact after the building was destroyed by the Romans in A.D. 70 and thus the focus for lamentations over the fall of Israel. This holy site is revered by Jews, who flock to pray there and to slip pieces of paper bearing prayers and requests between the stones. *The paper has an agony column that acts as a sort of wailing wall for those people working in the industry who feel they have been short-changed by their employers.*

walk on water To achieve the apparently impossible and emerge unscathed. The allusion is to the biblical episode (related in Mark 6:45–56 and Matthew 14:22–33) describing how Christ rescued his disciples during a storm by walking to their boat over the water of the Sea of Galilee. *Over the years his performances on the soccer field won him countless fans, many of whom believed he could walk on water if he chose to.*

walk with God *See* ENOCH.

walls of Jericho (jeriko) A seemingly invincible obstacle that is miraculously overcome without a blow being struck. The reference is to the biblical episode of the fall of the city of Jericho before the Israelites. Joshua 6:1–20 describes how Joshua and his forces, bearing the Ark of the Covenant, surrounded Jericho for six days. On the seventh day they awaited a signal from their leader "when the people heard the sound of the trumpet, and the people shouted with a great shout, that the wall fell down flat, so that the people went up into the city, every man straight before him, and they took the city." *Like the walls of Jericho, the board's objections against the proposal collapsed as soon as promises of substantial compensation were received.*

wander in the wilderness To languish as an outcast while out of office, in exile, or otherwise out of favor. The phrase, typically used in the context of party politics, is biblical in origin. It appears several times but is best known in reference to the period the Israelites spent wandering in the wilderness after their flight from Egypt under the leadership of Moses. Moses is quoted in Numbers 14:33 warning his people that it will be many years before their exile comes to an end: "Your children shall wander in the wilderness forty years." *After his expulsion from the party he spent nearly a decade wandering in the wilderness, quite unable to reclaim his position in the political limelight.*

war in heaven Conflict or disagreement at the highest level of an organization, company, or other institution or group. The allusion is to Revelation 12:7–9, which describes John's vision of a battle fought between the angels and Satan: "And there was war in heaven: Michael and his angels fought against the dragon; and the dragon fought and his angels, And prevailed not; neither was their place found any more in heaven." *Shortly after, rumors began to spread that those controlling the project had had a falling-out and war had broken out in heaven.*

washed in the blood of the lamb Redeemed by faith or otherwise purified. The phrase comes from Revelation 7:14, which describes a host of people in white robes before the throne of God: ". . . they which came out of great tribulation, and have washed their robes, and made them white in the blood of the Lamb." "Make them clean, oh God; wash away their offences in the blood of the Lamb; and when their spirits pass, oh receive Thou them into the heaven of the just" (H. Rider Haggard, *Allan Quatermain,* 1887).

wash one's hands of To refuse to accept guilt for some misdeed or to involve oneself further in a dubious or apparently ill-fated enterprise. The expression alludes to the episode in Matthew in which PONTIUS PILATE washes his hands to emphasize his refusal to accept any responsibility for crucifying Christ after the mob has rejected his offer of a pardon in favor of Barabbas: "When Pilate saw that he could prevail nothing, but that rather a tumult was made, he took water, and washed his hands before the multitude, saying, I am innocent of the blood of this just person: see ye to it" (Matthew 27: 24). *Following his dismissal as manager of the team he washed his hands of them and refused to accept any responsibility for any further disappointments in the competition.*

watch and pray Be alert and put your trust in God. The expression is biblical in origin, occurring in Matthew 26:41 and Mark 14:38 (where Christ is speaking to his disciples at Gethsemane). "I shall expect your clear decision when I return this day fortnight. Meantime, watch and pray that you enter not into temptation: the spirit, I trust, is willing, but the flesh, I see, is weak. I shall pray for you hourly" (Charlotte Brontë, *Jane Eyre,* 1847).

water into wine The miraculous transformation of something ordinary into something much more valuable. The allusion is to the biblical episode describing the *marriage in Cana,* during which Christ turned water into wine for the guests at a marriage feast (John 2:1–11). *The play went down well enough, but the critics were generally agreed that you can't turn water into wine.*

waters of Babylon *See* BY THE RIVERS OR BABYLON.

way of all flesh *See* GO THE WAY OF ALL FLESH.

way of a man with a maid, the The mysterious nature of relationships between the sexes. This reference to the mystery of sexual attraction is of biblical origin, appearing at Proverbs 30:18–19: "There be three things which are too wonderful for me, yea, four which I know not: The way of an eagle in the air; the way of a serpent upon a rock; the way of a ship in the midst of the sea; and the way of a man with a maid." *What on earth she saw in him I shall never know, but I suppose that's the mystery of the way of a man with a maid.*

way of transgressors, the The troubled, difficult lives of those who refuse to live by the law. The expression comes from Proverbs 13:15: "Good understanding giveth favour: but the way of transgressors is hard.""It is not enough to tell me that you worked hard to get your gold. So does the Devil work hard. The way of transgressors may be hard in many respects" (Henry David Thoreau, *Life Without Principle,* 1863).

weaker vessel Womankind; "a person less able to withstand physical or mental strain, temptation or exploitation, than others" (*Oxford Dictionary of Current Idiomatic English,* vol. 2, p. 579). The phrase comes from 1 Peter 3:7: "Likewise, ye husbands, dwell with them according to knowledge, giving honour unto the wife, as unto the weaker vessel, and as being heirs together of the grace of life; that your prayers be not hindered."The phrase is sometimes applied to people of either sex who are considered less capable than others but is generally avoided in contemporary usage as misogynistic and offensive to women. "'I'll give up smoking to please you, if you will give up something to please me,' said Prince, seeing a good chance to lord it over the weaker vessel at small cost to himself" (Louisa May Alcott, *Eight Cousins,* 1875).

wealth makes many friends The rich are never short of friends attracted by their wealth. The proverb is of biblical origin, appearing at Proverbs 19:4 in the form "Wealth maketh many friends; but the poor is separated from his neighbour." *She was a great believer in the old saw that wealth makes many friends and had no doubt that as soon as her son had snared a rich wife, they would be surrounded permanently by admirers.*

weariness of flesh *See* OF MAKING MANY BOOKS.

wear the sandals of Theramenes (the<u>ram</u>ăneez) To change one's views according to the prevailing fashion. Theramenes (died c. 404 B.C.) was a

Greek aristocrat who was notorious for his vacillating opinions and loyalties. *The vice president was accused of wearing the sandals of Theramenes, altering his standpoint for electoral gain.*

weaver's shuttle Something that goes very quickly, especially life. The phrase comes from Job's consideration of his own death: "My flesh is clothed with worms and clods of dust; my skin is broken, and become loathsome. My days are swifter than a weaver's shuttle, and are spent without hope" (Job 7:5–6). "She slid the length of the room; her tender shoulders swayed; her feet were deft as a weaver's shuttle; she laughed, and enticed Babbitt to dance with her" (Sinclair Lewis, *Babbitt,* 1922).

web of Penelope *See* PENELOPE.

wedding in Cana *See* WATER INTO WINE.

Wednesday The fourth day of the week. It was originally called Woden's Day, Woden being the Old English rendering of ODIN, the ruler of the gods and the god of wisdom, war, and culture in Norse mythology. *Ash Wednesday marks the beginning of Lent.*

weeping and gnashing of teeth The expression of extreme frustration, grief, or regret. The phrase comes from the biblical episode in which Christ foresees the Day of Judgment and describes the severe punishment of those who reject him: ". . . but the children of the kingdom shall be cast out into outer darkness: there shall be weeping and gnashing of teeth." (Matthew 8:12). (See also Matthew 22:13, 24:51, and 25:30 and Luke 13:28.) "There was weeping and wailing and gnashing of teeth in the camp of the outsiders now" (Mark Twain, *Life on the Mississippi,* 1883).

weighed in the balances and found wanting *See* WRITING ON THE WALL.

well done, good and faithful servant A compliment to someone on a job well done (sometimes intended ironically). The phrase is a quotation from Matthew 25:14–30, in which Christ relates the PARABLE OF THE TALENTS. *The general made an attempt to wipe the soup off his sleeve, then gazed wearily at the waiter as if to say "well done, good and faithful servant."*

What hath God wrought! What great things God has done! The sentiment comes from Numbers 23:23 and is remembered today chiefly through its being chosen as the first message to be transmitted by telegraphy on May 28, 1844. *A suggestion that trips to the Grand Canyon should be publicized under the slogan "What hath God wrought!" was not taken seriously by most present at the meeting.*

What is a man profited, if he shall gain the whole world? Material wealth and power is ultimately of no consequence. The sentiment was voiced by Christ in Matthew 16:26 and Mark 8:36, in which he compares transient earthly riches with a person's immortal soul: "For what is a man profited, if he shall gain the whole world, and lose his own soul? or what shall a man give in exchange for his soul?" "Only last Sunday dear Mr Scoles had been so witty in his sermon, so sarcastic: 'For what,' he had said, 'shall it profit a man if he gain his own soul, but lose all his property?'" (John Galsworthy, *The Forsyte Saga,* 1922).

What is man? A reminder that human beings are but one element in the order of things. According to Psalm 8:4–5 human beings rank below God and a little lower than the angels but above the beasts: "What is man, that thou art mindful of him? and the son of man, that thou visitest him? For thou hast made him a little lower than the angels, and hast crowned him with glory and honour." "What is man but a mass of thawing clay? The ball of the human finger is but a drop congealed" (Henry David Thoreau, *Walden,* 1854).

What is truth? What value does the truth have? This cynical observation is recorded in John 18:37–38 as Pontius Pilate's reply to the following assertion by Christ: "To this end was I born, and for this cause came I into the world, that I should bear witness unto the truth. Every one that is of the truth heareth my voice. Pilate saith unto him, What is truth?" "'The whole truth?' Miss Bart laughed. 'What is truth? Where a woman is concerned, it's the story that's easiest to believe'" (Edith Wharton, *The House of Mirth,* 1905).

whatsoever a man soweth, that shall he also reap *See* REAP WHAT YOU SOW.

whatsoever thy hand findeth to do One should dedicate oneself fully to the task in hand or to one's work in general. The expression comes from

Ecclesiastes 9:10: "Whatsoever thy hand findeth to do, do it with thy might, for there is no work, nor device, nor knowledge, nor wisdom, in the grave, whither thou goest." *The old cleric rolled up his sleeves and beamed at them both. "Whatsoever thy hand findeth to do," he said, with a shrug.*

wheat and tares *See* PARABLE OF THE WHEAT AND TARES.

wheel of fortune Fortune; fate. FORTUNA was the Roman goddess of fortune, who was variously prayed to, thanked, or blamed for the fickle workings of fate. She was conventionally depicted with a wheel in her hand, a symbol of inconstancy. Humans were often represented bound to the wheel and rising or falling as Fortune turned it. "Fortune good night; / Smile once more; turn thy wheel" (William Shakespeare, *King Lear,* 1607).

wheels within wheels A complicated and interconnected arrangement of forces or circumstances that typically exerts an obscure or surreptitious influence upon events. The allusion is to Ezekiel 1:16, in which Ezekiel describes his vision: "The appearance of the wheels and their work was like unto the colour of a beryl: and they four had one likeness: and their appearance and their work was as it were a wheel in the middle of a wheel." "Gertrude, truth is a very complex thing, and politics is a very complex business. There are wheels within wheels. One may be under certain obligations to people that one must pay" (Oscar Wilde, *An Ideal Husband,* 1895).

when in Rome, do as the Romans do One should conform to the manners, customs, and way of life practiced in one's surroundings. This piece of proverbial advice is generally credited to Saint Ambrose and appears in the text of his *Advice to Saint Augustine,* written in A.D. 387. The legend goes that this was the reply Ambrose gave when approached by Augustine (in correspondence from Milan) on the question of whether he should fast on Saturday, as they did in Rome, or ignore this custom, as they did in Milan. This sage saying is often clipped to ***when in Rome.*** Equivalents in other cultures include the advice "Never wear a brown hat in Friesland." *I don't like kissing total strangers, but in this country it's considered impolite not to, and when in Rome we must do as the Romans do.*

where neither moth nor rust doth corrupt *See* LAY NOT UP TREASURES UPON EARTH.

where the carcass is, there will the eagles be gathered People tend to gather where they see an opportunity to obtain some benefit for themselves. The proverb comes from Matthew 24:28: "For wheresoever the carcase is, there will the eagles be gathered together." Sometimes the phrase is encountered with *vultures* instead of *eagles*. *The press had already learned the news and descended upon the house, confirming that "where the carcass is, there will the eagles be gathered."*

where there's no vision, the people perish People cannot exist without having hopes and dreams to aim for. This is a quotation from Proverbs 29:18: "Where there is no vision, the people perish: but he that keepeth the law, happy is he." *Now that their last hope of rescue had disappeared, many gave up the struggle to go on, for where there's no vision, the people perish.*

where two or three are gathered together Wherever people meet in small groups. The phrase is biblical in origin, coming from Matthew 18:20, in which Christ reassures his followers that wherever they meet, he himself will be with them: "For where two or three are gathered together in my name, there am I in the midst of them." The expression is particularly associated with religious gatherings but is sometimes used in a more general sense for small gatherings of any kind. "Very singular to look into it: how a kind of order rises up in all conditions of human existence; and wherever two or three are gathered together, there are formed modes of existing together, habitudes, observances, nay gracefulnesses, joys!" (Thomas Carlyle, *History of the French Revolution*, 1837).

whip the offending Adam To punish someone for his or her sins in order to improve the future character. The reference is to Adam as the first man to disobey God and to fall into sin (Genesis 3). The use of Adam's name as a synonym for sin is also encountered in the expression *the old Adam,* describing sin in general terms. "Consideration, like an angel, came / And whipped the offending Adam out of him" (William Shakespeare, *Henry V,* 1599).

white as snow *See* SINS BE AS SCARLET.

whited sepulchre (<u>sep</u>ălker) Someone or something that appears dignified and perfect from the outside but is actually corrupt within. The image
is biblical in origin, coming from Matthew 23:27, in which Christ likens
the Pharisees to the whitewashed tombs (made of stone or otherwise set
in caves) of the dead: "Woe unto you, scribes and Pharisees, hypocrites! for
ye are like unto whited sepulchres, which indeed appear beautiful outward, but are within full of dead men's bones, and of all uncleanness." In
the time of Christ, Jewish tombs were usually painted white in order to
discourage the living from accidentally touching and thus defiling them.
"Surely it is high time that the whited sepulchre of the BBC is acquainted
with the reality that licence fees can be withheld" (*Daily Telegraph,* September 17, 2001).

whither thou goest, I will go Expression of complete devotion by a committed follower. The saying is of biblical origin, spoken by RUTH when
promising to accompany her mother-in-law, Naomi, to Bethlehem:
"Intreat me not to leave thee, or to return from following after thee: for
whither thou goest, I will go; and where thou lodgest, I will lodge: thy
people shall be my people, and thy God my God. Where thou diest, will I
die, and there will I be buried" (Ruth 1:16–17). "'I fear, my lord,' the girl
answered timidly. 'Then give me the basket.' 'Nay, my lord, whither thou
goest there I go also'" (H. Rider Haggard, *King Solomon's Mines,* 1886).

whole duty of man Religious faith or something else considered as a person's essential duty in life. The phrase comes from Ecclesiastes 12:13: "Let
us hear the conclusion of the whole matter: Fear God, and keep his commandments: for this is the whole duty of man." ". . . to buy it for as little
as he could possibly give, and sell it for as much as he could possibly get;
it having been clearly ascertained by philosophers that in this is comprised
the whole duty of man—not a part of man's duty, but the whole" (Charles
Dickens, *Hard Times,* 1854).

whom God hath joined together let no man put asunder No one should
come between husband and wife. This now-formulaic phrase from the
marriage service ("The Form of Solemnization of Matrimony" of the *Book
of Common Prayer*) warns third parties not to separate a married couple. The
phrase is a quotation from Matthew 19:6 and Mark 10:9, appearing as

Christ's response to questions put to him about divorce. It is sometimes quoted (often facetiously) in other contexts when separation threatens two people or things that should not be parted. "'The Church don't recognize divorce in her dogma, strictly speaking,' he says: 'and bear in mind the words of the service in your goings out and your comings in: What God hath joined together let no man put asunder'" (Thomas Hardy, *Jude the Obscure,* 1895).

Whore of Babylon (b̲abilon) A personification of corruption and sexual depravity. The allusion is to Revelation 17:1–7, which describes a whore mounted upon a scarlet beast with seven heads and 10 horns and with the words "Mystery, Babylon the Great, the Mother of Harlots and Abominations of the Earth" written on her forehead: "The woman was arrayed in purple and scarlet colour, and decked with gold and precious stones and pearls, having a golden cup in her hand full of abominations and filthiness of her fornication." In its biblical context the Whore of Babylon was a metaphor for Rome, pictured as the embodiment of corrupt earthly power. The Puritans later adopted the name as an insulting epithet for the Roman Catholic Church, and eventually it came to be used more generally. It also appears as the *Scarlet Whore of Babylon.* "I'd marry the W—— of Babylon rather than do anything dishonourable!" (Thomas Hardy, *Jude the Obscure,* 1895).

whoring after other gods Abandoning one's previous loyalties in favor of a new master. The expression comes from Judges 2:17, which refers to the lapse of the Israelites when they abandon God to worship pagan Canaanite gods (whose worship includes ritual prostitution). *For some years the senator's loyalty had been suspect, but this was the first time he had been openly accused of whoring after other gods.*

whosoever hath, to him shall be given Those who already have something are sometimes rewarded with more before those who have nothing. This saying of Christ is recorded in Matthew 13:11–12 when explaining why he used parables: "Because it is given unto you to know the mysteries of the kingdom of heaven, but to them it is not given. For whosoever hath, to him shall be given, and he shall have more abundance: but whosoever hath not, from him shall be taken away even that he hath" (Matthew 13:11–12). (See also Matthew 25:29, Mark 4:25, and Luke 8:18 and

19:26.) *The tax cuts for the wealthy is a straightforward case of "whosoever hath, to him shall be given."*

whosoever will save his life shall lose it Those who are preoccupied only with their own interests will in the long run be disappointed. The expression appears in Matthew 16:24–25, as well as in Mark 8:35 and Luke 9:24 and 17:33, where Christ tells his disciples: "If any man will come after me, let him deny himself, and take up his cross and follow me. For whosoever will save his life shall lose it: and whosoever will lose his life for my sake shall find it." *Their action could be judged foolhardy in the extreme, but then again, whosoever will save his life shall lose it.*

widow's cruse (krooz) A small but apparently never-ending supply of something. The allusion is to a biblical episode describing how Elijah sought help from a widow of Zarephath during a time of drought and famine. Elijah had been relying on the water of the brook Cherith and on food brought to him night and morning by ravens as sources of sustenance. But when the brook dried up God instructed him to seek out the widow, even though she had only "an handful of meal in a barrel and a little oil in a cruse" to offer him. In reward for this generosity, Elijah promised her that "The barrel of meal shall not waste, neither shall the cruse of oil fail, until the day that the Lord sendeth rain upon the earth" (1 Kings 17:12–14). *Like the widow's cruse of biblical fame, it seemed that the young hoodlum's supply of feeble jokes knew no end.*

widow's mite A small offering from someone who can ill-afford it. The allusion is to an episode described in Mark 12 and Luke 21, in which Christ favorably compares the tiny amount of money paid into the treasury by a poor widow with the larger amounts given by those who are better off: ". . . this poor widow hath cast more in, than all they which have cast into the treasury: for all they did cast in of their abundance; but she of her want did cast in all that she had, even all her living" (Mark 12:43–44). A *mite* was the lowest denomination in ancient Jewish coinage. "'Twas the boy's 'mite,' and, / like the 'widow's,' may / Perhaps be weigh'd / hereafter, if not now" (Byron, *Don Juan,* 1819–24).

wife, Lot's *See* LOT'S WIFE.

wife, Potiphar's *See* POTIPHAR'S WIFE.

wilderness, voice crying in the *See* VOICE CRYING IN THE WILDERNESS; WANDER IN THE WILDERNESS.

wind bloweth where it listeth, the The spirit, or the mind, moves wherever it chooses. The expression comes from John 3:6–8, in which Christ explains to Nicodemus the Pharisee what it means to be BORN-AGAIN: "That which is born of the flesh is flesh; and that which is born of the Spirit is spirit. Marvel not that I said unto thee, Ye must be born again. The wind bloweth where it listeth, and thou hearest the sound thereof, but canst not tell whence it cometh, and whither it goeth: so is every one that is born of the Spirit." "You are a happy man, Frank—you go and come, as the wind bloweth where it listeth" (Sir Walter Scott, *Rob Roy,* 1817).

wind of doctrine A changeable belief, especially one subject to a sudden whim or enthusiasm. The expression comes from Ephesians 4:14, in which Paul advises the Ephesians that there were many false teachings that would all too readily turn immature believers away from the right path: "Henceforth be no more children, tossed to and fro, and carried with every wind of doctrine." *She drifted from one school of thought to another, seemingly incapable of resisting being blown along by every wind of doctrine that wafted in her direction.*

wings of a dove The power of flight, especially from oppression of some kind. In Psalm 55:6 the narrator yearns for the wings of a dove in order to escape the hostilities of his enemies: "And I said, Oh that I had wings like a dove! for then would I fly away, and be at rest." This biblical exclamation is usually quoted as *Oh, for the wings of a dove!* "Pray don't suppose I write in anger; I am only sorry and disheartened. My state of mind resembles David's. If I had the wings of a dove, I would flee away and be at rest" (Wilkie Collins, *Armadale,* 1866).

wings of the morning A swift passage. The phrase comes from Psalm 139:9–10: "If I take the wings of the morning, and dwell in the uttermost parts of the sea; Even there shall thy hand lead me, and thy right hand shall hold me." Thus to *take the wings of the morning* means to make swift progress from somewhere. "'Fast enough,' said the Antiquary; 'the gentleman wished to take the wings of the morning, and bolt in the what d'ye call it,—the coach and four there'" (Sir Walter Scott, *The Antiquary,* 1816).

wisdom crieth in the streets Sensible advice is made known widely, but sometimes also meaning that such wisdom is ignored. The expression comes from Proverbs 1:20: "Wisdom crieth without; she uttereth her voice in the streets." *In times like these all reason flies out of the window, and wisdom crieth in the streets.*

wisdom is better than rubies It is preferable to be wise than rich. This is a quotation from Proverbs 8:11: "For wisdom is better than rubies; and all the things that may be desired are not to be compared to it." The sentiment is also encountered in the form *wisdom is better than wealth. She was very beautiful and very rich, it is true, but she was not very bright, and wisdom, they say, is better than rubies.*

wisdom of Solomon *See* JUDGMENT OF SOLOMON.

wise as serpents and harmless as doves Shrewd but innocent. The expression comes from Matthew 10:16, in which Christ instructs his 12 apostles: "Behold, I send you forth as sheep in the midst of wolves: be ye therefore wise as serpents, and harmless as doves." ". . . with little or no sharpness of faculty or any trace of wisdom of the serpent, nor yet quite a dove, he possessed that kind and degree of intelligence which goes along with the unconventional rectitude of a sound human creature" (Herman Melville, *Billy Budd, Foretopman,* 1924).

wise as Solomon *See* JUDGMENT OF SOLOMON.

Wise Men *See* MAGI.

wise virgins *See* PARABLE OF THE WISE AND FOOLISH VIRGINS.

Witch of Endor (<u>en</u>dor) Archetypal witch or medium with supernatural powers. The reference is to the sorceress of Endor, who (according to 1 Samuel 28:3–25) on the command of King Saul summoned up the spirit of the prophet Samuel; the spirit warned the king of his imminent defeat and death in battle against the Philistines. "I merely lit that fire because I was dull, and thought I would get a little excitement by calling you up and triumphing over you as the Witch of Endor called up Samuel. I determined you should come; and you have come! I have shown my power" (Thomas Hardy, *The Return of the Native,* 1880).

Woden; Wodin *See* ODIN.

woe is me Expression of self-pity at one's own plight. The expression appears several times in the Bible, for example, in Isaiah 6:5, when the prophet sees the Lord in his holiness and is then utterly dismayed at his own sin: "Then said I, Woe is me! for I am undone; because I am a man of unclean lips, and I dwell in the midst of a people of unclean lips: for mine eyes have seen the King, the LORD of hosts." The phrase is particularly associated with Jeremiah in the following lament: "Woe is me, my mother, that thou hast borne me a man of strife and a man of contention to the whole earth!" (Jeremiah 15:10). "Woe is me when all men praise me!" (George Bernard Shaw, *Saint Joan,* 1924).

woe to them that are at ease in Zion *See* AT EASE IN ZION.

wolf in sheep's clothing A person or thing that appears to be harmless but is masking its real, harmful nature. The allusion is to Matthew 7:15, in the Sermon on the Mount, in which Christ condemns FALSE PROPHETs who claim to be genuine; in reality they maliciously destroy the faithful: "Beware of false prophets, which come to you in sheep's clothing, but inwardly they are ravening wolves." The expression also evokes Aesop's fable about the wolf that disguises itself in a sheep's skin in order to evade detection by its intended prey. *The stranger gave the impression of being the friendliest and most trustworthy of men, but as things turned out he was a wolf in sheep's clothing.*

wolf shall dwell with the lamb *See* LION SHALL LIE DOWN WITH THE LAMB.

woman taken in adultery *See* GO AND SIN NO MORE; LET HIM WHO IS WITHOUT SIN CAST THE FIRST STONE.

wonders of the world *See* EIGHTH WONDER OF THE WORLD.

wooden horse *See* TROJAN HORSE.

Word, the The word of God; Jesus Christ, the second person of the Trinity, representing the communication of God to people. A translation of the Greek *logos,* the term appears in John 1:1: "In the beginning was the Word, and the Word was with God, and the Word was God." "The use of *logos* bonds not only the being of the God-man Jesus into one fused personality, but also bonds the natural and supernatural aspects of the written *logos.* Jesus the living Word, like the written Word, becomes the place of meeting, where God's hidden glory is unveiled and the Father becomes known" (Lawrence O. Richards, *Expository Dictionary of Bible Words,* 1985).

word and deed, in As one says and does. The expression is found in Romans 15:18, "to make the Gentiles obedient, by word and deed," and is alluded to in 2 Corinthians 10:11, "Let such an one think this, that, such as we are in word by letter when we are absent, such will we be also in deed when we are present," and in 1 John 3:18, "My little children, let us not love in word, neither in tongue; but in deed and in truth." ". . . she believed them still so very much attached to each other, that they could not be too sedulously divided in word and deed on every occasion" (Jane Austen, *Sense and Sensibility,* 1797–98).

word in season A timely warning or piece of advice. The phrase is biblical in origin, appearing in Isaiah 50:4 in the course of one of the Servant Songs: "The Lord GOD hath given me the tongue of the learned, that I should know how to speak a word in season to him that is weary: he wakeneth morning by morning, he wakeneth mine ear to hear as the learned." (See also 2 Timothy 4:2.) "'Or if there should be any little hitch between 'em,' thought the Captain, meaning between Walter and Mr Dombey, 'it only wants a word in season from a friend of both parties, to set it right and smooth, and make all taut again'" (Charles Dickens, *Dombey and Son,* 1848). *See also* TIME AND PLACE FOR EVERYTHING.

Word made flesh The embodiment of an idea or truth. The phrase comes from the Bible, appearing in John 1:14, which refers to the Word of God as Jesus Christ, hence God as a human being: "And the Word was made flesh, and dwelt among us, (and we beheld his glory, the glory as of the only begotten of the Father,) full of grace and truth." *Their leader was a magnificent figure, tall, handsome and courageous—heroism made flesh.*

Word of God *See* WORD, THE.

work the oracle *See* ORACLE.

worm that dieth not The conscience or something else that continues to exert a troubling influence. The phrase comes from Mark 9:43–44, which quotes Christ as saying, ". . . it is better for thee to enter into life maimed, than having two hands to go into hell, into the fire that never shall be quenched: Where their worm dieth not, and the fire is not quenched." ". . . his lord felt, amid all the pomp and magnificence we have described, the gnawing of the worm that dieth not" (Sir Walter Scott, *Kenilworth,* 1821).

wormwood and gall *See* GALL AND WORMWOOD.

worship the golden calf *See* GOLDEN CALF.

worth one's salt *See* SALARY.

wrath of Agamemnon (agămemnon) Extreme anger. According to Greek mythology when Agamemnon, king of Mycenae, was told that in order to appease the god Apollo he must return his prize, a Trojan girl named Chryseis, to her father, his anger knew no bounds. Unable to defy Apollo, he returned the girl but then demanded Achilles' prize, a girl named Briseis, provoking a violent quarrel between them. "The frogs and the mice would be nothing to them, nor the angers of Agamemnon and Achilles" (Anthony Trollope, *Barchester Towers,* 1857). *See also* BRAVE MEN BEFORE AGAMEMNON, THERE WERE.

wrath to come A future punishment or revenge. The phrase is biblical in origin, appearing in Matthew 3:7, Luke 3:7, and 1 Thessalonians 1:10, referring each time to the wrath of God for sinners at JUDGMENT DAY.

"Must I beg to him then? Must I kneel to him? Must I ask him to save me from the wrath to come?" (Anthony Trollope, *Lady Anna,* 1874).

writing on the wall A warning of imminent catastrophe or failure. The allusion is to the biblical story of BELSHAZZAR'S FEAST, which relates how King Belshazzar entertained a thousand nobles at a magnificent banquet at the royal palace, the food served on golden vessels looted from the Temple at Jerusalem (Daniel 5:1–28). The occasion ended in consternation when a spectral hand appeared and wrote the enigmatic words *"mene, mene, tekel, upharsin"* on the palace wall. Belshazzar was seized with fear (see BELSHAZZAR'S PALSY) and offered a share of his kingdom to any astrologer who could interpret the message. He was subsequently informed by Daniel that the words meant "MENE; God hath numbered thy kingdom, and finished it. TEKEL; Thou art weighed in the balances, and art found wanting. PERES; Thy kingdom is divided, and given to the Medes and Persians" (Daniel 5:26–28). That very night the Median and Persian armies swept into Babylon, conquering it and slaying Belshazzar. The phrase is also encountered as *handwriting on the wall.* "As the government announces plans to regulate its special advisers, is the writing on the wall for these little Machiavellis?" (*Guardian,* June 25, 2001).

X, Y

Xanthippe (zan<u>thi</u>pee, zan<u>ti</u>pee) An ill-tempered, peevish, shrewish woman; a nag. The original fifth-century B.C. Xanthippe, or *Xantippe,* was the wife of the Greek philosopher Socrates, who acquired a notorious reputation for her scolding of her husband, variously attributed to her impatience at her husband's neglect of her in favor of philosophical discussion and to his lack of interest in practical matters, specifically the business of making a living. Another school of thought has it that Socrates deliberately held his celebrated discussions in the open air primarily to escape his wife's censorious attentions. William Shakespeare subsequently referred to Xanthippe in her role as the archetypal nag in *The Taming of the Shrew* (c. 1593): "Be she as foul as was Florentius' love, / As old as Sibyl, and as curst and shrewd / As Socrates' Xanthippe, or a worse, / She moves me not." She reappears in a similar role in many other works, including the novel *Tom Jones* (1748) by Henry Fielding: "'By this Xanthippe' (so was the wife of Socrates called, said Partridge)—'by this Xanthippe he had two sons, of which I was the younger.'"

xanthous (<u>zan</u>thăs) Yellowish or reddish-yellow; having yellowish hair and a light complexion. The word is descended from the name of the Xanthus River (meaning yellow river), the ancient Greek name for the river Scamander and hence the name also of the city that sprang up on its banks. Legend has it that the river was named by the poet Homer, who noted how the fleeces of local sheep were stained golden red by its silt-laden waters. Another derivation, though, suggests a link with a Greek hero of the same name who reputedly routed a force of Trojans on the banks of the river. *They watched as a xanthous stain spread through the sluggish water.*

xenocratic (zenōkratik) Chaste; continent; unimpressed by wealth. Xenocrates (396–314 B.C.) was a Greek philosopher who combined the ideas of Pythagoras with those of his own teacher, Plato. Xenocrates' sense of personal virtue was so strong that he was immune even to the temptations proffered by the renowned courtesan Laïs, as alluded to by the Italian poet Ludovico Ariosto: "Warmed by such youthful beauty, the severe / Xenocrates would not have more been chaste" (*Orlando Furioso*, 1532). *She behaved with xenocractic indifference to all the fine things that were paraded before her by her wealthy admirers.*

Xerxes (zerkseez) A powerful leader. The original Xerxes I (c. 519–465 B.C.), king of Persia, attacked Greece at the head of a vast army of more than $2\frac{1}{2}$ million men, defeating his enemies at Thermopylae (480) but subsequently having to retreat after his fleet was scattered at the Battle of Salamis the same year and his army overcome at Plataea in 479. He was eventually murdered by Artabanus, the commander of his own bodyguards. The name *Xerxes* is usually associated with military and political leaders but may occasionally be applied more widely, as in Herman Melville's *Moby-Dick* (1851), in which it was applied to a stallion: "He was the elected Xerxes of vast herds of wild horses, whose pastures in those days were only fenced by the Rocky Mountains and the Alleghanies." *See also* ESTHER.

Yahweh *See* JEHOVAH.

Zeboiim *See* ADMAH AND ZEBOIIM.

zephyr (<u>ze</u>fer) A gentle breeze; a soft wind. The allusion is to Zephyrus, the god of the west wind in Greek mythology, identified as the son of Astraeus and Aurora and the father of Xanthus and Balius (the two immortal horses of Achilles) by the Harpy Podarge. The west wind itself was sometimes referred to by the name Zephyrus, which might itself have come ultimately from the Greek *zophos* (meaning "darkness" or "west"). "He felt a zephyr curling about his cheek, and turned. It was Bathsheba's breath—she had followed him, and was looking into the same chink" (Thomas Hardy, *Far from the Madding Crowd,* 1874).

Zeus (zoos) The king of the gods in Greek mythology and thus, by association, any person who makes decisions or dispenses advice from a position of apparently unquestionable authority. The son of Cronus and Rhea, he was reputed to rule heaven and earth from his seat on Mount Olympus in Thessaly and to be the father of many gods, demigods, and mortals. He is conventionally depicted with the lightning bolts that he could aim at will at those who displeased him. The name is thought to have come originally from the Greek for "bright." His equivalent in Roman mythology was the supreme god JUPITER. *For a short time the president was credited with having the insight and all-encompassing authority of a Zeus. See also* EIGHTH WONDER OF THE WORLD.

Zeuxis (<u>zook</u>sis) An artist noted for the realism of his or her work. The original Zeuxis, a fifth-century B.C. Greek painter famed for the verisimilitude of his painting, was a native of Heraclea in southern Italy. He is remembered chiefly for the contest in which and he and his younger rival,

Parrhasius, attempted to outdo each other with the realism of their still lifes. Zeuxis painted a bunch of grapes so realistic that birds tried to eat the fruit, but he subsequently admitted defeat when Parrhasius invited him to pull aside the curtain concealing his painting, only to find when he tried to grip the cloth that the curtain itself was painted. *Alone among the new generation of artists she has donned the mantle of Zeuxis through the lifelike character of her work.*

Zion (z̄ion) The name of the hill on which the city of Jerusalem was first built and sometimes called David's City. In biblical times, the city of Jerusalem grew significantly, and Mount Zion is now in the southeast of the old city of Jerusalem. In poetic and prophetic writing of biblical times, *Zion* referred to Jerusalem as a whole (for example, Isaiah 2:3 and 33:14) and even for the land and people of Judah as a whole (for example, Isaiah 10:24; 51:11, 16; and 59:20). The phrase **Daughter(s) of Zion** meant Jerusalem and its inhabitants, both male and female (see Isaiah 1:8 and Song of Solomon 1:5). Sometimes, confusingly, other parts of Jerusalem were also referred to as Zion, as is the case in Joel 3:17 and 21, which is actually indicating the Temple Mount. Zion has significance for Christians and Jews. For Christians, it signifies the church of God or the kingdom of heaven (as in Isaiah 4:2–6, Hebrews 12:22, and Revelation 14:1). For Jews, as early as the destruction of the first Temple and the exile of the Jews to Babylonia (586 B.C.), it expressed the yearning of the Jewish people for their homeland. Most famously this use of Zion appears in Psalm 137: ". . . we wept when we remembered Zion." This longing to return also found expression in Jewish prayer, which sometimes reflects the belief that God's presence has also been exiled from Zion. For example, one of the prayers said three (or more) times a day has, "Let our eyes behold Your return in mercy to Zion." The term *Zionism* first appeared in the 19th century. It encapsulated the idea of building up the land and the people and mostly referred to the movement to enable Jews in the diaspora to return to the land of Israel. Here, again, *Zion* represented Israel. The Zionist movement has taken many forms, and the term *Zionist* is shared by organizations with varying emphases in their political philosophies. Labor Zionists, for example, focus on Jewish self-determination and self-development. Religious Zionists focus on the land of Israel as a gift from God and the responsibility of Jews to fulfill God's commandments in the land of

Israel, including the commandment to inhabit the land. Since the creation of the state of Israel, Zionism has concentrated on the defense and development of Israel and continues as a movement for the upbuilding of the land and people. "Glorious things of thee are spoken, / Zion, city of our God! . . . / Blest inhabitants of Zion, / Washed in the Redeemer's blood — . . . / Saviour, if of Zion's city / I through grace a member am, . . . / Solid joys and lasting treasure / None but Zion's children know" (John Newton, "Glorious things of thee are spoken," Olney Hymns, 1779).

Zoilus (zoylăs) A spiteful critic. The allusion is to a Greek rhetorician of the name who lived in the fourth century B.C. and became notorious for his witty, biting remarks about the works of Isocrates, Plato, and Homer, among others, earning him the nickname "the Thracian Dog." It was specifically for his attacks on Homer's epics that he earned yet another moniker: "Homeromastix" (Homer's scourge). His most outrageous remarks concerning the writings of Homer included his dismissive description of the companions of Ulysses on the island of Circe as "weeping porkers." "The duty of the critic is to act as judge, not as enemy, of the writer whom he reviews; a distinction of which the Zoilus of the Messenger seems not to be aware" (Edgar Allan Poe, *Criticism,* 1850).

Bibliography

Cowie, A. P., R. Mackin, and I. R. McCraig. *Oxford Dictionary of Current Idiomatic English.* Vol. 2. Oxford, U.K.: Oxford University Press, 1983.

Fulghum, Walter, B., Jr. *A Dictionary of Biblical Allusions in English Literature.* Austin, Tex.: Holt, Rinehart and Winston, 1965.

Jeffrey, David Lyle, ed. *A Dictionary of Biblical Tradition in English Literature.* Grand Rapids, Mich.: William B. Eerdmans, 1992.

Lass, Abraham H., David Kiremidjian, and Ruth M. Goldstein. *The Facts On File Dictionary of Classical, Biblical, and Literary Allusions.* New York: Facts On File, 1987.

Manser, Martin H. *King James Bible Word Book.* Nashville, Tenn.: Thomas Nelson, 2002.

McGrath, Alister E., ed. *NIV Thematic Reference Bible.* Grand Rapids, Mich.: Zondervan, 1999.

NIV Study Bible. Grand Rapids, Mich.: Zondervan, 1995.

Oxford English Dictionary. 2d ed. Oxford, U.K.: Oxford University Press, 1989.

Selman, Martin J., and Martin H. Manser. *The Hearthside Bible Dictionary.* Nashville, Tenn.: Cumberland House, 1998.

Index

wash one's hands of 401

watch and pray 401

water into wine 401

waters of Babylon 54

way of all flesh 155

way of a man with a maid, the 401–402

way of transgressors, the 402

weaker vessel 402

wealth makes many friends 402

weariness of flesh 271

wear the sandals of Theramenes 402–403

weaver's shuttle 403

web of Penelope 288

wedding in Cana 401

Wednesday 403

weeping and gnashing of teeth 403

weighed in the balances and found wanting 415

well done, good and faithful servant 403

What hath God wrought! 404

What is a man profited, if he shall gain the whole world? 404

What is man? 404

What is truth? 404

whatsoever a man soweth, that shall he also reap 312–313

whatsoever thy hand findeth to do 404–405

wheat and tares 283

wheel of fortune 405

wheels within wheels 405

when in Rome, do as the Romans do 405

where neither moth nor rust doth corrupt 215

where the carcass is, there will the eagles be gathered 406

where there's no vision, the people perish 406

where two or three are gathered together 406

whip the offending Adam 406

white as snow 339

whited sepulchre 407

whither thou goest, I will go 407

whole duty of man 407

whom God hath joined together let no man put asunder 407–408

Whore of Babylon 408

whoring after other gods 408

whosoever hath, to him shall be given 408–409

whosoever will save his life shall lose it 409

widow's cruse 409

widow's mite 409

wife, Lot's 225–226

wife, Potiphar's 299

wilderness, voice crying in the 396–397, 400

wind bloweth where it listeth, the 410

wind of doctrine 410

wings of a dove 410

wings of the morning 410–411

wisdom crieth in the streets 411

wisdom is better than rubies 411

wisdom of Solomon 199

wise as serpents and harmless as doves 411

wise as Solomon 199

Wise Men 231–232

wise virgins 283–284

Witch of Endor 411–412

Woden; Wodin 269–270

woe is me 412

woe to them that are at ease in Zion 30–31

wolf in sheep's clothing 412